Table of Contents

Foreword

By Rob Kerr, Sportsnet FAN 960 Calgary

The easiest thing to fear is the unknown. What we don't understand or can't quite comprehend is simple to dismiss or run away from. I know this because I've done exactly that. Many of you are probably guilty of having done that as well.

But I'm getting ahead of myself. What I really want to talk about is how I met Rob Vollman. I was hosting a charity event and was circulating through the crowd when a pleasant fellow stopped me to say hello. The stranger said he knew me from *Sportsnet* TV and radio and then proceeded to tell me he was an author. When I asked him what he had written, I was surprised when he promptly produced a copy of his most recent effort. It wasn't a paperback novel, but *Hockey Abstract*.

My first thoughts were "whoa, don't say anything stupid" and "who carries around copies of his books at a fundraiser?" I immediately realized I was talking to someone from the analytics community. Far from a math wizard myself, I was both intrigued and slightly frightened by where this conversation with my new author friend was going to go.

Sure, I was aware of the Bill James-like movement in hockey, but at this point, it was much maligned and misunderstood by me and most of my media peers. For the record, I was less "maligned" and much more in the "misunderstood" camp. I thought my use of the NHL's real time stats was cutting edge, but in my heart, I knew I was in over my head.

As we talked it became clear that I was dealing with someone who had found his calling. The passionate conversation quickly eased my fears that I needed to understand physics, operate an abacus, or do long-division math problems to understand what was being said. All I really needed to do was be open-minded and listen.

We talked a little about analytics, but it was really the conversation about being a self-published author that opened me up to the world of Rob Vollman.

Remember that thought about who carries around copies of his books to a fundraiser? As we talked, he wowed me with the heart and soul he poured into the book. It was his life's work, except that it wasn't. Turns out, Rob was an author by night and an oil and gas professional by day. Through him, I learned that if you create and publish your own book, you are responsible for all aspects of the project including the distribution and promotion.

As we continued to chat, I learned that Rob was really just looking for a vehicle to spread his message that analytics is for everyone and that they add so much more to any hockey discussion. The book allowed him the means to distribute his thoughts and ideas. Whatever he could do to promote the book gave him another opportunity to discuss hockey on his terms.

It was during this meeting that I was also introduced to Rob's patience, because as I got more comfortable with the topic, the dumber and more crass my questions became.

"Do you guys really want to predict the scores and not play the games?"
"Do you guys really understand what heart is?"
"Do you guys really think you know more than a hockey professional?"

I mean seriously, I think back to these kinds of queries and the thinly-veiled shots at what I didn't understand, it's a minor miracle that Rob didn't throw his arms in the air and bolt for the nearest exit.

He didn't. Instead, he took the time to dispel the crap that I was regurgitating in a very calm and rational matter. As he did, I began to listen and not talk. Before you know it, he led me to my own personal statistical awakening. In my first meeting with Rob, he debunked the myth of the 'stats nerd' and gave me another tool to help me do my job.

This was the day that I learned I could use analytics to ask better questions. I could use analytics to better understand the games I was supposed to be analyzing. This was the day I learned I could use analytics to help confirm what my eyes were telling me, and visa versa. After our initial meeting, Rob and I began to do the occasional radio interview. He was the perfect guest because he made the topic accessible. His ability to take somewhat complex ideas and explain them in an easy to understand manner is a real skill.

Over time, the occasional interview turned into a regular weekly radio appearance named after this book. While I am quick to point out that our initial meeting was a real learning experience for me, the learning has never stopped. He challenges me to think about things in hockey from different points of view. My fear of numbers, fear of not knowing or understanding a certain stat isn't anywhere near as crippling as it used to be. I know that If I run across something that I don't comprehend, I have Hockey Abstract the book, or Hockey Abstract the website, or even better, Hockey Abstract's author just a phone call away.

While I hate to put words into his mouth, I would suggest Mr. Vollman has grown too in the time that I have known him. Not from our association as much as from his own success. He is a passionate person who wants to invite as many people as possible into his hockey world.

A world that isn't angry, preachy, or condescending and to be honest, that's a rare feat in this day and age.

I consider Rob a friend, I have attended a couple of his conferences and was made to feel like I had a small role to play. He has been a consistent volunteer in charity events that we run to help disadvantaged youth hockey players. He is by all definitions just a really good dude!
So if you are new to the Hockey Abstract books, welcome. I know you will get something out of it that is going to make hockey more enjoyable for you, or challenge you, or ideally both. If you have been part of the Hockey Abstract family from the get-go, then clearly you have good taste.

I eagerly await digging into this latest copy and learning something new.

Introduction

By Rob Vollman

And we're back!

It is with great pleasure that I welcome you all back to another print edition of *Hockey Abstract*, after a two-year hiatus to write *Stat Shot*.

To be clear, it didn't take me two years to write *Stat Shot*. I wrote the book in 2015, which is why that year's edition of *Hockey Abstract* was available in electronic format only, and was only half as many pages as usual. Then, *Stat Shot* was published in 2016, and it didn't make sense to self-publish a competing book, so the 2016 edition was also half-length and electronic.

But now, we're back. The only problem is that *Stat Shot* was so successful that everybody wanted me to write another, so I have spent 2017 doing just that. With my luck, that will also be a big hit, and I'll never get the chance to write *Hockey Abstract* again.

Rather than put *Hockey Abstract* on the back burner indefinitely, I reached out to some of my favourite colleagues to fill the second half of the book. In fact, doing this is very much in spirit of *Hockey Abstract*, which was always meant as a platform for the work of the entire community, not just mine.

That's why I'm thrilled to introduce you to a whole new batch of contributing authors to join me, Tom Awad, and our esteemed illustrator Joshua Smith this year. Regrettably, our partner Iain Fyffe wasn't free to contribute this year.

First, there's Matt Cane, who contributed a chapter on what makes a good power play. I met Matt at the first Ottawa Hockey Analytics conference in 2015[1], where he was perfectly representative of the brilliant new generation in hockey analytics.

Matt and I collaborated on a history-based player projection guide for *Dobber Hockey*[2], he has been invaluable in keeping the NHL translation factors (NHLe) and the annual super-spreadsheets up to date, and he almost got us kicked off the Ottawa-to-Toronto train after the second Ottawa Hockey Analytics conference in 2016 with our rousing conversation. His work can be found regularly on the outstanding *Hockey Graphs* website[3] and his own website[4], and it's a pleasure to include his latest work here.

I've also asked my old friend Charles Mousseau to contribute a chapter, on the game's best clutch shooter. Chuck and I go all the way to the mid-1990s, and the pure mathematics classes at the University of Calgary whose grading curves we absolutely destroyed. Some of

---

1   Website for the Ottawa Hockey Analytics conference is http://statsportsconsulting.com/ottanalytics/.
2   Dobber Hockey website is http://www.dobbersports.com, but this guide is no longer for sale.
3   Matt Cane's author archives at Hockey Graphs is https://hockey-graphs.com/author/mattcane/.
4   Matt Cane's website is Puck Plus Plus, https://puckplusplus.com/.

my fondest memories of those days are getting together with Chuck, grabbing a couple of Super Big Gulps, and playing one math-based strategy game or another – including Strat-o-Matic hockey. Boy, did he love the players with an intimidation rating of 12 or better.

High intimidation ratings brings us to Allan "Lowetide" Mitchell, and his chapter on failed rebuilds. For those who aren't familiar with the host of the *TSN 1290* radio show, the humour of describing someone so friendly and jovial as being intimidating is probably lost. In these parts, Allan's show is well-known for being accessible and high-spirited, even in the pre-McDavid days when being a hockey fan in Edmonton wasn't very much fun.

Lowetide was one of the first people to really believe in my work, and in me personally, and originated the use of the phrase "Vollman sledgehammer" in reference to player usage charts. He brings an important voice to our conversation, including the perspective that comes with a thorough knowledge of the game's history, the ideal balance between analytics and the eye test, and an undeniable passion for the game, and those who play it.

While on the topic of local radio show hosts, Rob Kerr is well known for being one of the best interviews in the business, as well as for his tireless charity work in Calgary. In fact, as he explains in the foreword, we first met at an annual charity event for PREP called "Let's Talk Hockey." I showed him my player usage charts from the original *Hockey Abstract*, and he was hooked. Not only did he help with the very first hockey analytics conferences, but he has included me with a weekly spot on his Sportsnet FAN 960 radio show for the past three seasons. He really gets what we're trying to do with hockey stats, appreciates our passion for the sport and what we do, and has a keen sense about how it can best be shared with a broader audience.

Perhaps the greatest pleasure is to include the work of Helmut Neher of the University of Waterloo, and Jeremy Sylvain of St. Lawrence University. They are the respective graduate and undergraduate winners of a student paper competition held by Michael Schuckers and Shirley Mills at the third annual hockey analytics conference at Carleton University on May 6, 2017. Including their work gives us a glimpse of what's to come in this field.

Finally, I want to welcome our new lead copy editor, Sydney Stype. She's one of the bright young people who responded when I reached out to anyone who was looking for a future in hockey analytics[5], who were interested in hearing about any opportunities I stumble upon, and being placed in touch with those who can make use of their passion. Her existing collection of hockey books is truly something to behold, and she was even in a position to help complete my own.

Without exception, everybody was excited to be a part of this project, and eager to contribute. To help coordinate all of our voices into one, I compiled a list of 10 tips and philosophies that have served Tom, Iain, and me well over the years. It was reportedly quite interesting and insightful, and it was recommended that our readers would enjoy reading it, too.

---

5   Rob Vollman, "Do you want an NHL job in hockey analytics?", *Hockey Abstract,* February 9, 2016, Web, http://www.hockeyabstract.com/thoughts/dowantannhljobinhockeyanalytics.

1. Have Fun

First and foremost, remember that this book is for entertainment, and it's meant to bring the joy of hockey stats to a larger audience. Whatever you write, make it fun, and let your passion for the topic shine through.

2. Ask Questions

In true Bill James fashion, the title should be a question, and chapters should begin by defining the problem without a pre-conceived solution in mind. Showing how stats can be used to understand and enjoy hockey is far more engaging to the readers than the end results, and it helps make the book timeless.

3. It's a book!

Take advantage of the medium. Online articles have to be short and snappy, but books can really dive into a topic. Take as many pages as you need to explore a topic, be candid and thorough about any limitations, and your work can ultimately serve as both a timeless record and a reference for the subject at hand.

4. Promote our field

Seek out and summarize all existing work in the field, and include lots of footnotes to the work of others. This is good for the readers, who get exposed to different perspectives and have a starting point to research the area further; it's good for you, as it demonstrates a more complete understanding of the topic and spares you from having to go over previously proven concepts in detail; and it's good for our community, by making our work seem like an important part of a far greater whole, and not just a novelty. Above all else, *Hockey Abstract* has always been meant as a platform to generate exposure for everybody's work, not just our own.

5. Credit your sources

Every single table or chart should have a footnote with the details of where the data comes from, even if the source is the same in each case, or comes directly from the NHL. Also, remember that our data sources have a nasty habit of disappearing every season, so include all the information that the readers need in order to play with the numbers themselves. Also, don't forget to credit the innovator of any particular stat or concept upon its first mention – I can help you figure out who that is if you don't know.

6. Consistent formatting

Check out previous editions for examples of how to format the tables and charts. Briefly, every table and chart should have a descriptive title, with the seasons the data covers, and the preceding paragraph should explicitly spell out any new abbreviations used in the table or chart. Don't forget to label your axes. Also, the *Hockey Abstract* standard is to use three seasons worth of data when it comes to individual player evaluation, not just one, so stick to that whenever possible.

7. Target the mainstream

Break things down into steps, explain your concepts in simple terms, and take nothing for granted, even when dealing with material that has been covered in previous editions. Provide lots of footnote references where readers can go for additional detail. For readers who may suffer from math anxiety, some effective techniques to keep the readers engaged include giving examples, putting things in charts and tables, and repeating key concepts in different ways. Always make sure that it's clear why you're doing something.

8. Share your work

Be completely transparent every step of the way. Readers should be able to completely reproduce your work for themselves (although not necessarily without great effort). If there's something you don't understand well enough to explain, or if you want to keep certain details a trade secret, then it's probably best not to write about that at all.

9. Peer review

Accuracy is critical. Nothing will destroy our credibility faster than a dumb math error. It is your responsibility to find someone to review the accuracy of your data and your calculations, and to make sure that your interpretations are clear and defensible. I can help you if you can't find an expert in a particular area.

10. Canadian spelling

Set your word processor spell check to Canadian English. You may stumble into a few other stylistic questions, like whether to use Corsi or SAT, but just make your choice, stay consistent, and I'll change it in the final edit if it's significantly at odds with the rest of the book. There will also be a copy editor to fix up whatever spelling and grammar mistakes get through the auto-check.

This list helped all of our new authors avoid some of the mistakes we have learned the hard way over the years, and take advantage of some of the best practices that we have learned[6]. Hopefully, it has also provided you with some insight into how we approach our work, and why.

Finally, I'm extremely excited to announce that this edition will also be available *en français*. Growing up bilingual in Ottawa, I know how easy it is for francophones to feel left out of a conversation, and also how their passion for the sport easily matches our own. While our bilingual authors like Tom Awad were happy to submit their contributions in both official languages, we relied heavily on passionate hobbyists like Christophe Perreault, Jean-Michel Côté, and Thomas Woloch to translate the rest.

---

6   I would also add that writing a quality chapter is a lot more work than most first-time contributors realize, and that they leave far too much of an eight-month project for the final weeks.

With that, it's time to kick off the fifth and latest edition of *Hockey Abstract*. It is a privilege and a pleasure to be in a position to share this particular stage with so many passionate and insightful people, which brings me to the answer one of the most common question that we get these days: Why do we do this? Not just why do we write books like these, but why do we organize conferences, share our data, make guest appearances on podcasts and radio, promote other people's work, and even help them find jobs? Why do we do any of this?

It's to grow this field.

I'll be honest, I'm really jealous of other major sports, especially baseball. They have countless statistical websites with every number you can imagine, and the bookstores' shelves are just full of great books. Tune in to a telecast, and you'll often see and hear brilliant statisticians providing fascinating insights on any number of aspects of their sport. On TV, you'll even see a little diagram in the corner that records the speed and accuracy of every pitch. And the teams themselves have an entire staff of MIT grads crunching numbers like crazy, and assembling the most competitive lineups possible.

Add it all up, and it's enough to make me wish baseball was the sport that captured my heart, but it isn't. Hockey is my passion. And I want all these great things for my beloved sport.

I can't necessarily speak for the others, but that's why I write books about hockey analytics, because I want there to *be* books about hockey analytics. I want to read a book by Matt Cane, but until he writes one, all I can do is publish my own, and invite him to write part of it.

In the end, that's the motivation behind everything that I do. That's why I write books, why I kicked off the hockey analytics conferences[7], why I go on radio[8], why I write for the NHL's official website, why I freely distribute my data[9], why I help people place people in front office jobs, and so on. It's because I want these things to happen, and they just weren't happening on their own.

I'm often asked why I don't work in a front office, but now it's probably obvious why I restrict myself to brief consulting arrangements. I would only take on a full-time assignment if I could help a GM create an analytics breakthrough in hockey the same way that Billy Beane did for baseball. I want to prove that it can be done, so that all the other teams would follow suit. Short of that lofty ambition, I'm far more useful to the sport when I'm writing books like these.

I want to build the field by getting people hooked, and giving them the tools to create. After all, if you wanted more fish, then you could go fishing and hand out the fish, or you could distribute fishing poles to as many people as possible. In your hands, you hold a proverbial fishing pole, *Hockey Abstract 2017*. Now, let's cast our reels!

---

7   A complete history of our hockey analytics conferences is maintained here,
    http://www.hockeyabstract.com/thoughts/abriefhistoryofhockeyanalyticsconferences.
8   An account of my various TV and radio guest spots is maintained here,
    http://www.hockeyabstract.com/products.
9   All my data is available for download on my website, http://www.hockeyabstract.com/testimonials.

How Good is Your Team, Really?

By Tom Awad

What makes a team good?

Professional sports, ultimately, are about winning. Sports establish a set of sometimes arbitrary rules with the objective of determining a winner (and, by extension, a loser). Therefore, it is no surprise that the only metric by which we judge pro sports teams are whether they win.

However, we sometimes take that too far. While we know that better teams win more often, it does not follow that the team that wins a single game is the better team, or even was the better team that night. All sports involve a heavy dose of luck. Hockey, in particular, is heavily infused with luck. There are two major reasons for this. The first is fundamental to the nature of the game: with its bounces, posts, split-second movements and gray zones in officiating, there will always be a certain amount of luck in any hockey game. The second is organizational: the salary cap and better management have wrought more parity across the NHL, making teams more evenly matched and making the winner of a single game – or, dare I say it, even a seven-game series – more of a toss-up than it used to be.

This doesn't matter to hockey fans one whit. Fans are narrative-driven, and whoever won is necessarily the "best" team. We write glowing memorials of how winning teams managed to overcome adversity to triumph over insurmountable odds, while losing teams "choked", "don't know how to win" or "couldn't take their game to the next level". All this because of a single lucky bounce in overtime after the two teams had played each other to a standstill. History is written by the winners.

I am in complete agreement that the only thing that matters when judging a hockey team is their ability to win; it is the very reason for a team's existence, their only purpose. But I disagree that what makes a good team is whether they have won in the past; what matters to me is using past information to determine how many games they will win in the future. To use terminology borrowed from economics, I am not looking for coincident indicators, but leading indicators.

Every general manager in the NHL understands this, or should: when they acquire a player, they do so based on what they feel that player can contribute in the future. Inasmuch as they overvalue a player's Stanley Cup rings or a single 40-goal season, they do so only because they misjudge how much this guarantees about the player's future performance, not because they are backwards-looking.

I will attempt to characterize which statistics best allow us to predict future performance. To simplify both data gathering and allow other people to easily reproduce my work, I will use full-season data, and use the data from a single season to predict a team's performance the next season. This is obviously imperfect: teams do have personnel movement and changes that make them different from year-to-year, but since the bulk of a team's core stays constant from one year to the next, it remains a fairly accurate measure. It also has the advantage that this is often what hockey fans are looking for. For example, by the time you are holding this book, one big question on your mind will be: "How well is my team going to do this year?"

The Data

I will be using the data of every NHL team for the last decade, starting in 2007–08 and finishing in 2016–17. This gives me 10 seasons for each team, which means nine predictions for each team, or 270 predictions in total. What I am trying to predict is team points in the next season. Since we all agree that wins are the objective, this is my target variable. My source variables could be anything that can be quantitatively measured about the team. I will start with official NHL statistics, then broaden my horizons as we delve deeper[10].

I would like to include playoff data; however, it comes with a host of issues. Because teams play against a very biased cross-section of teams in the playoffs, their performance in the playoffs is often not representative of their true talent level, the way an 82-game regular season, against all 29 other teams, is[11]. For simplicity's take, I have ignored playoff data in the first version. I will discuss later how to integrate it.

Theoretically, this should be simple. Predicting teams should be somewhat easier than predicting players, whose ice time and linemates can vary tremendously from one season to the next. While there is some personnel movement from one year to the next, most things are constant. Let's jump in!

The Basics: Goals and Shots

Many analyses of hockey statistics start with something like "goal differential explains 94% of win percentage[12]". In fact, over the last decade, same-season goal differential has indeed explained 90% of win percentage. Hockey is about scoring and preventing goals, of course, so this is no surprise. By contrast, shot differential, which is often cited as being a more representative "true skill", only explains 32% of win percentage[13].

---

10 Acknowledgement: All data in this chapter has been taken from Hockey Reference, http://www.hockey-reference.com and the NHL, http://www.nhl.com.

11 Note: There are now 30 other teams, but the data in question is before the addition of the Vegas Golden Knights expansion team, so there are only 29 other teams.

12 Alan Ryder, "The Ten Laws of Hockey Analytics", *Hockey Analytics,* January, 2008, Web, http://hockeyanalytics.com/2008/01/the-ten-laws-of-hockey-analytics/.

13 This assertion, and other similar ones throughout the following sections, are based on author's calculations. Generally they are the coefficient of determination, or r^2, between my source and dependent variables.

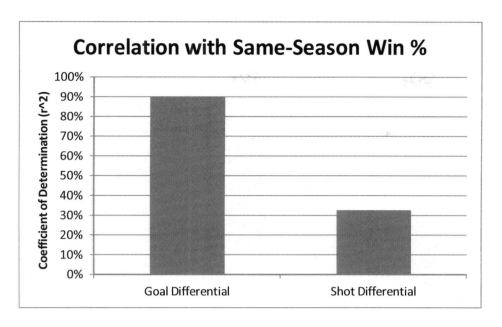

Surely, then, we'd expect goal differential to be equally useful in predicting the next season's performance. We don't expect 90%, but we do expect significant predictive power. In practice we see this:

While shot differential is only slightly weaker in predicting the next season's results, with a 25% explanatory power, goal differential has completely collapsed, explaining only 27% of win percentage. This, in a nutshell, is the reason why shot-based metrics have gained such a wide following in the last years: shot-based metrics measure a skill that is easily measurable and repeatable over the time frame of a single season. By contrast, converting shots into goals and preventing them through goaltending is a skill that takes years of data to be able to assess correctly.

What's even more interesting is what goal differential and shot differential tell you together. When predicting current-season win percentage, shot differential adds virtually nothing to goal differential: the predicted amount goes from 90.15% to 90.17%, a completely negligible improvement. But when looking at next season's results, using goal differential and shot differential together can predict 32% of a team's success, a significant improvement on using either statistic separately.

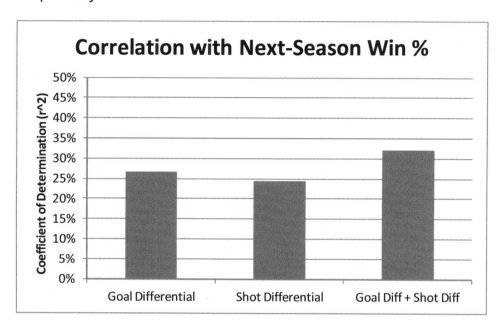

Adding More Statistics

Beyond goal differential and shot differential, I tried many other statistics to see if they helped the quality of my predictions, and few of them helped. I attempted to break out special teams goals – the total of power-play goals for and against, as well as shorthanded goals for and against – and they didn't help at all. It seems that when it comes to predicting a team's future ability, a goal is a goal. Interestingly, this means that one common method of relying only on even-strength goals, on the basis that they are more consistent, is superfluous.

I attempted to factor in this season's points, on the theory that the ability to win close games, and to somehow generate points in excess of what goal differential would predict, could be a repeatable skill. It was not, and factoring in points did not yield better results[14]. I tried certain "out there" statistics as well, such as shootout wins minus shootout losses, that yielded no additional predictive power either.

One of my biggest disappointments was finding out that playoff success did not in any way help predictions for next season's success. This was surprising to me because at an

---

14 Geek note: whenever I say "did not yield better results" or "did not add predictive power", this is not strictly true. Adding another dependent variable to an equation will always yield slightly better predictive power when looking at the same data. My criterion in this particular case was to improve the amount of predictive power by at least 0.1%.

individual level, playoff statistics *do* help. This is likely because players, especially young players, can develop in the course of a single season, and their statistics in May indicate much better what kind of player they will be in October than the numbers from the regular season.

For teams, however, there was no improvement. We can see this at a high level: the 27 teams that made the Conference Finals or better from 2008 to 2016 averaged 103.6 points during the regular season (normalizing to 82 games for the 2012–13 season), but only achieved 99.5 points the following year. In fact, as recently as 2015, the defending Stanley Cup champions Los Angeles Kings failed to make the playoffs entirely following their second Cup. Whether this is due to the accumulation of fatigue following a long season finishing in June, I won't venture.

Two statistics, however, did yield a mild improvement in my predictions. Factoring in a team's average age improved the predictive power from 32.2% to 32.9%, which seems small but is actually a large effect[15]. The effect was in the direction you would expect: younger teams tended to improve the next year, while older teams tended to regress. Age is an interesting variable because by itself it predicts in the opposite direction: if you knew nothing else about a team, you should predict that older teams will be better than younger teams. But older teams will underperform this season's statistics, while young teams will outperform them.

Factoring in even-strength expected goals[16] – which are shots weighed by shot quality – also improved the prediction by a small amount, to 33.3%. In fact, even-strength expected goals, by themselves, slightly outperformed shot differential when predicting next season's results.

Amazingly, team discipline, which I proxied using power play opportunities minus times short-handed, did yield some additional predictive power – but in the opposite direction of what was expected. Teams that were more penalized than their opponents had better results than those that were less penalized, all else being equal. Don't forget that I already factored in goal differential, so the "goal effect" of those extra power-play opportunities has already been taken into account.

I don't quite understand why this is, but the effect is measurable. We know that teams that are behind in the third period get more penalty calls against their opponents[17], but again this would be captured in goal differential. My theory is that we are capturing team-specific effects: the most penalized team of the last decade is the Anaheim Ducks, a very strong percentage team, and the next two are Boston and Washington, equally strong. The most disciplined team has been the Carolina Hurricanes, a fairly weak percentage team. Overall, team discipline added 0.3% to our predictive power.

One last statistic that is worthy of mention when discussing future performance is Cap Hit of

---

15 I used average age as defined by hockey-reference.com, which is weighted by ice time. This is probably the best measure possible, better than weighing by GP.

16 The concept of expected goals was first introduced by Alan Ryder in 2004 and has since been redeveloped by a number of analysts. Any roughly accurate measure of expected goals should give similar results. See: http://hockeyanalytics.com/Research_files/Shot_Quality.pdf

17 Tom Awad, "What Are Score Effects?", *Hockey Abstract 2014*, 2014, pgs 45-52.

Injured Players (CHIP). CHIP is a statistic measured by hockey analyst LW3H, and represents exactly what its name says: the amount of Cap Hit each team has among its injured players. CHIP can be consulted at the NHL Injury Viz website[18]. I expected that CHIP would be a kind of hidden treasure when it came to prediction, since everyone knows that some teams' performance suffers due to unexpected injuries, only to bounce back the next year. CHIP turned out to be very good at helping predict team performance; sadly, it was same-season CHIP that had predictive power. In other words, I can use this season's CHIP to explain why my team underperformed what was expected of them based on last season's statistics, but I cannot use it as a predictive tool to estimate what will happen next year[19]. Integrating this season's CHIP improved the predictions from 33.27% to 33.31%, a completely negligible amount, and I eliminated it from the final equation for simplicity's sake.

Why Can't I Do Better?

Needless to say, predicting only 33.6% of next season's win percentage is fairly disappointing, and I don't think I'm getting hired for my prognosticating skills based on these results. So there are two questions: is there anything else I can do to improve the quality of these predictions, and if not, why can't I do better?

I'll address the second question first. There is actually a huge amount of luck involved in the final NHL standings, even at the end of an 82-game season. To understand why, let's start with a premise: imagine all the teams in the NHL were perfectly matched. What would the final standings look like?

To simulate this, let's assume both teams score and allow an average of 2.6 goals per game, following a Poisson distribution[20]. What are the odds of a tie after regulation between these two perfectly matched teams?

Only 18%. This means that in 82% of the games, there will be a clear winner and loser, even though the teams are of identical strength. And even when there is a regulation tie, we know that one team will eventually escape with two points and the other with only one.

One interesting aside: while two perfectly matched teams will finish regulation in a tie only 18% of the time, NHL teams do so about 23% of the time. There are two effects at play here. One is that NHL teams clearly "play for the tie" whenever they can, which is a perfectly rational response to the NHL's ridiculous charity point system. The other is that they take risks when trailing by one goal, which leads to a greater number of tie games than if they simply played in a constant fashion for 60 minutes. To take one obvious example, pulling the goaltender with two minutes left will certainly lead to a higher number of ties, as well as a higher number of 2-goal games, than we would otherwise see.

---

18 The NHL Injury Viz website is http://nhlinjuryviz.blogspot.ca/p/index-page.html.

19 Later in this book, Jeremy Sylvain studies to what extent injuries can be predicted.

20 A Poisson distribution is a probability distribution. It is used on the field of statistics to figure out the probability of getting a certain number of events, like wins, within a known time, like 82 games, based on an average rate.

Put all of this together, we see that even among perfectly matched teams, a team will have 41% wins, 41% losses and 18% ties. The average number of points per game will be 1.09 under the NHL's point system (an average of 89 points over an 82-game season), and the standard deviation of points on a single game will be 0.95[21]. The standard deviation of points over an entire season is therefore 0.95 times the square root of 82, which is 8.6 points. Put another way: assuming an average of 91 points per team, which is the observed NHL average over the last decade, about 1/6th of teams will obtain 100 points or more, while 1/6th of teams will obtain 82 points or less. I am still assuming that all teams are of exactly the same calibre.

Given this, we can see that about 39% of a single-season's win percentage is luck, while we are predicting 33% of it, leaving 28% still "unmeasured".

These results match the estimates made by others. The late JLikens did an analysis all the way back in 2011 showing that, with the talent spread that existed in the NHL at the time, the best team would only finish first in the league roughly once out of every three seasons, and they would even miss the playoffs 2.2% of the time![22]

To clarify, luck has only represented 39% of win percentage over the last decade. In years past, when the difference between weak teams and strong teams was starker, luck represented a much smaller fraction. What interests us here is the NHL of today.

Digging up the Past

One of the keys to obtaining an even better estimate is understanding what our problem is. In particular, shooting percentage and save percentage over a single season are highly affected by randomness[23][24], and thus not very reliable at predicting next season's shooting percentage and save percentage. One of the ways of overcoming randomness is to take a larger sample size. In this case, I can look more than one season in the past to predict next season's results[25].

This has its own problems, obviously: as we look at more than one season, the team starts to change more and more, which makes it a less reliable model of what we are trying to predict. But the power of large sample sizes is strong, and this may overcome whatever other issues

21 Standard deviation is a statistical term intended to figure out to what extent a set of data is likely to vary from the average result. For a simple example of how to calculate standard deviation, see https://www.mathsisfun.com/data/standard-deviation-formulas.html.
22 JLikens, "How often does the best team win?", *Objective NHL,* June, 2011, Web, http://objectivenhl.blogspot.ca/2011/06/how-often-does-best-team-win.html.
23 Gabriel Desjardins (Hawerchuk), "PDO and regression to the mean", *Arctic Ice Hockey,* December 20, 2011, Web, https://www.arcticicehockey.com/2011/12/20/2648333/pdo-regression-to-the-mean-or-why-you-should-ignore-shooting.
24 Kent Wilson, "Wilson: Don't know Corsi? Here is a handy-dandy primer to NHL advanced stats", *Calgary Herald,* October 6, 2014, Web, http://www.calgaryherald.com/Sports/Wilson+know+Corsi+Here+handy+dandy+primer+advanced+stats/10265096/story.html.
25 Indeed, one of Hockey Abstract's legacies is the use of three seasons to study individual players and teams, not just the mainstream standard of one.

we may have. Again, we are helped by the nature of the current NHL: while depth players move freely from team to team, the salary cap encourages teams to sign their best players to long-term contracts, which means that team cores are fairly consistent from one season to the next.

In practice, the addition of an extra season's goal differential improved our predictive ability from 33.6% to 35.6%, which is a huge jump considering the difficulty we've had in improving out predictions otherwise. At this point we are predicting 35% of win percentage and 39% is luck, leaving 26% unmeasured.

Player Movement

At this point, my readers will tell me: "Tom, you're a fool! It's obvious why teams change so much from one season to the next and you can't measure it. The players change!" Well, you might be right, but we'll have to prove it.

First of all, let me clarify what I am measuring here: I am measuring year-to-year performance prediction in the post-2005, salary cap NHL. We know what the salary cap era has led to: long contracts and a focus on RFAs, as teams lock up their franchise players as soon as they can, and a dearth of high-end free agents since many of them end up playing for the same team for over a decade. Look at the players who have led their teams to the Stanley Cup over the last decade: Jonathan Toews and Patrick Kane, Anze Kopitar and Drew Doughty, Sidney Crosby and Evgeni Malkin, Henrik Zetterberg. All of them will have spent their entire prime, and possibly their entire career, with the same team.

This is not to say that there are no free agents, or that no players change teams and help their new teams. The last decade has seen the trading or signing of Joe Thornton, Marian Hossa, Ilya Kovalchuk, Rick Nash, and Phil Kessel, among others. All of these players helped their new teams get at least to the Stanley Cup Final and contributed significantly to making their organisations contenders. But we remember these signings because they were successful. There is also a litany of failed free-agent signings too numerous to list.

To figure out the impact of player movement, I created a list of 35 major free-agent signings, retirements or trades for draft picks and young players. The objective was to isolate cases where a major player was moving from one team to another without equivalent on-ice assets going the other way. Trading away an established player for prospects and draft picks may be a very good organizational move in the medium to long term, but the team receiving the established player should win in the very short term.

To determine the impact of free agents signings, unbalanced trades and retirements, I drew up a list of major transactions of this type between 2008 and 2015. The majority of them were free agent signings: in some cases, the player was formally traded a few days before July 1st for a 3rd round draft pick or something similar to give the receiving team a few days of exclusive negotiation rights; I counted these transactions. I also counted players who played the majority of the previous season with another team, were traded and then signed with their new team, like Martin St. Louis did with the New York Rangers. There were only two major "retirements" of players in their primes during this period, Jaromir Jagr in 2008 and Ilya Kovalchuk in 2013. Jagr wasn't really in his prime but, at 36 years old, was still better than most top forwards in the NHL. The proof is that he was still playing in the NHL in 2017, nine years later.

To determine the value of these players, I used the average GVT of the previous two seasons. Many of these players were injured or had otherwise problematic seasons before leaving their teams, and an average of two seasons gives a more accurate estimate of the player's value. In every case, I also pro-rated by the number of games. For example, in St. Louis's case, he played 62 games with the Lightning and 19 games with the Rangers in 2013-14, so I assumed the Rangers would only improve by 62/81 of St. Louis's total value.

I intentionally excluded goaltenders because their statistics are much more erratic and, because of the limited number of goaltending jobs on a single team, a new goaltender is much more likely to be replacing existing talent rather than adding to the team.

For reference, the "best" free agent of the last decade was Marian Hossa, who signed in 2008 with the Detroit Red Wings after a two-year average GVT of 17.6. Hossa was also the fourth-best free agent of the decade when he signed with the Blackhawks a year later. The weakest free agent on my list is Jason Spezza, who had certainly been considered an elite player during his tenure with the Senators, but signed with the Stars in 2014 after missing almost the entirety of the 2012–13 season, giving him a two-year GVT of only 5.5. He produced 62 points (and 9.4 GVT) for the Stars in his first season with them.

Noteworthy Player Moves, 2008–09 to 2016–17[26]

Player	Season	Old Team	New Team	Value
Marian Hossa	2008–09	Pit/Wpg	Detroit	17.6
Ilya Kovalchuk	2010–11	Winnipeg	New Jersey	17.0
Brad Richards	2011–12	Dallas	NY Rangers	16.0
Jaromir Jagr	2008–09	NY Rangers	KHL	15.9
Marian Hossa	2009–10	Detroit	Chicago	15.6
Ilya Kovalchuk	2013–14	New Jersey	KHL	14.0
Martin St. Louis	2014–15	Tampa Bay	NY Rangers	13.5
Patrick Sharp	2015–16	Chicago	Dallas	13.4
Alexander Semin	2012–13	Washington	Carolina	13.0
Marian Gaborik	2009–10	Minnnesota	NY Rangers	12.8
Rick Nash	2012–13	Columbus	NY Rangers	12.7
Tomas Vanek	2014–15	Mon/NYI/Buf	Minnesota	12.5
Phil Kessel	2015–16	Toronto	Pittsburgh	12.2
Alex Tanguay	2008–09	Calgary	Montreal	11.9
Brian Campbell	2011–12	Chicago	Florida	11.2
Brad Richards	2008–09	Tampa Bay	Dallas	11.1
Ryan Suter	2012–13	Nashville	Minnesota	11.0

26 Note: I have used the current franchise names for the teams in this table, so the Atlanta Thrashers show up as Winnipeg (Wpg) and the Proenix Coyotes are listed as Arizona (Ari)

Jeff Carter	2012–13	Columbus	Los Angeles	10.6
Jeff Carter / Jakub Voracek	2011–12	Philadelphia	Columbus	10.6
Jason Pominville	2013–14	Buffalo	Minnesota	10.4
Jarome Iginla	2014–15	Boston	Colorado	10.0
Zach Parise	2012–13	New Jersey	Minnesota	10.0
Mike Ribeiro	2013–14	Washington	Arizona	9.9
Dan Boyle	2008–09	Tampa Bay	San Jose	9.8
Mike Green	2015–16	Washington	Detroit	9.0
Daniel Alfredsson	2013–14	Ottawa	Detroit	8.4
Jarome Iginla	2013–14	Cgy/Pit	Boston	8.4
Justin Williams	2015–16	Los Angeles	Washington	8.3
Paul Stastny	2014–15	Colorado	St. Louis	7.9
Jaromir Jagr	2013–14	Bos/Dal	New Jersey	7.4
Brent Burns	2011–12	Minnesota	San Jose	7.4
Vincent Lecavalier	2013–14	Tampa Bay	Philadelphia	6.6
Brad Richards	2014–15	NY Rangers	Chicago	6.5
Brad Richards	2015–16	Chicago	Detroit	5.7
Jason Spezza	2014–15	Ottawa	Dallas	5.5

After integrating a "free-agent change" factor into my model, I found that it improved out prediction percentage by... 0.3%! We are now at 35.9% of predictability. I will admit, while I was not expecting a huge impact on the model, I was expecting a greater impact than that. The impact was estimated at about 0.14 points per free agent GVT, whereas we would have expected at least twice as much, since 1 GVT = 1 goal and hockey's 3-1-1 rule stats that three goals equals roughly one point in the standings[27].

Why is this? Why does adding good players not lead to a greater improvement throughout the entire team? I have a few theories, but they are just theories. I don't believe it is because free agents underperform on their new team, although there are obviously some well-known examples of this, such as the Jeff Carter trade to Columbus. There is no doubt that teams *overpay* for free agents, but that is a salary issue, not a hockey one. But it touches on what I think is the real reason: in the salary cap era, you can never just "add" a new player without disturbing the rest of your salary structure. You may have to make a series of other hockey moves to make room for a new $8.0 million salary, which means that your team doesn't improve as much as we would have expected it to.

The bottom line is that player movement is not usually a significant factor in explaining why teams improve or decline from one season to the next. We're not likely to ever see another Gretzky-to-LA type trade as we did in 1988, which led to a 23-point improvement in the Kings' fortunes.

Who's the Best? Who's the Worst?

One very interesting aspect of my approach is that, to the extent that it is accurate, it allows

---

27 Rob Vollman, "What's the Best Way to Build a Team?", *Stat Shot,* 2016, pg 38.

us to filter out the effects of luck and noise to discover who have been the truly best teams of the past decade. While the approach is not perfect, it has the advantage of not relying on any arbitrary weights and instead simply being based on whatever best predicts future success.

The following table has the top 20 teams of the past decade, as measured by how they performed relative to my model's expectations, with stats from the lockout-shortened 2012–13 season extrapolated to an 82-game schedule.

Best teams, 2007–08 to 2016–17[28]

Rnk	Team	Season	GP	PTS	vs Avg	vs Exp	Luck
1	Chicago Blackhawks	2009–10	82	112	20.0	22.3	-2.3
2	Chicago Blackhawks	2013–14	82	107	14.8	19.1	-4.4
3	Chicago Blackhawks	2012–13	48	77	40.3	16.7	23.6
4	Pittsburgh Penguins	2011–12	82	108	16.0	15.9	0.1
5	San Jose Sharks	2010–11	82	105	13.1	15.6	-2.5
6	Boston Bruins	2013–14	82	117	24.8	15.5	9.2
7	San Jose Sharks	2013–14	82	111	18.8	14.8	4.0
8	Washington Capitals	2016–17	82	118	26.4	14.7	11.7
9	Detroit Red Wings	2008–09	82	112	20.6	14.3	6.3
10	Washington Capitals	2009–10	82	121	29.0	14.0	15.0
11	San Jose Sharks	2008–09	82	117	25.6	13.9	11.7
12	Washington Capitals	2010–11	82	107	15.1	13.9	1.2
13	Detroit Red Wings	2007–08	82	115	23.9	13.7	10.2
14	St. Louis Blues	2014–15	82	109	16.8	13.6	3.2
15	Boston Bruins	2012–13	48	62	14.7	13.2	1.5
16	Los Angeles Kings	2013–14	82	100	7.8	13.0	-5.2
17	Boston Bruins	2011–12	82	102	10.0	13.0	-3.0
18	Pittsburgh Penguins	2012–13	48	72	31.8	12.7	19.1
19	Chicago Blackhawks	2010–11	82	97	5.1	12.5	-7.4
20	St. Louis Blues	2011–12	82	109	17.0	12.5	4.5

Any doubts about the Chicago Blackhawks being the best team of the last decade can be laid to rest after looking at this table. The top three teams are all Blackhawks teams from their golden 2010–2015 run, including the single-best team from 2010 that won the Stanley Cup. While those Blackhawks didn't even win the Presidents' Trophy, finishing third overall behind the Washington Capitals (#10 on this list) and the San Jose Sharks, they were clearly the best team in the NHL that season and their Stanley Cup was richly deserved. Those Blackhawks were so good that they won two more Stanley Cups after losing Andrew Ladd, Dustin Byfuglien, and Antti Niemi.

What jumps out from this table is the dominance of the blue-chip organizations of the last decade. As I mentioned previously, despite the salary cap, teams manage to keep their cores together for years at a time: this top 20 contains four Chicago teams, three San Jose Sharks, three Washington Capitals, three Boston Bruins, two Pittsburgh Penguins, two St. Louis Blues and two Detroit Red Wings, with only one lone Los Angeles Kings entry, the 2014 Cup

28 Acknowledgement: Raw standings data for these calculations from the *NHL*, http://www.nhl.com.

champions.

Of the 10 Cup champions, only four came from this list: the 2010 and 2013 Blackhawks, the 2014 Kings, and the 2008 Red Wings. The other champions are: the 2017 Penguins (#41, +9.2), the 2016 Penguins (#42, +9.2), the 2012 Kings (#48, +8.4), the 2015 Blackhawks (#60, +7.4), the 2009 Penguins (#86, +5.1) and the 2011 Bruins (#90, +4.7). Two more of these teams – the 2009 Red Wings and the 2013 Bruins – were Stanley Cup finalists.

Those last Bruins certainly are a case study in how hard it is to determine if percentages are reliable: those Bruins were backed by phenomenal goaltender Tim Thomas, who had bounced around the NHL, the AHL, and several European leagues before solidly establishing himself at the Bruins No. 1 in 2007. During the 2008–09 season, Thomas emerged as an unlikely Vezina winner at age 35, leading the league in save percentage and leading the Bruins to the top of the Eastern Conference. He struggled the next season, and it wasn't clear if he'd be remembered as a one-hit wonder, but in 2010–11 he bounced back, breaking the league's single-season save percentage record with .938, and again being the best goaltender in the league. He continued his strong play in the playoffs, and the Bruins won a seven-game final against the Vancouver Canucks, with Thomas winning the Conn Smythe. Age and other issues would eventually take their toll, but the Bruins would find another elite goaltender in Tuukka Rask, and would continue to get some of the best goaltending in the league for the next four seasons, with Rask helping them return to the Stanley Cup Final in 2013.

The point is, it is almost impossible to know ahead of time if this level of performance will be maintained. You don't know ahead of time if a talented goaltender will end up being a rock like Henrik Lundqvist, a one-hit wonder like Jose Theodore or Mike Smith, or somebody in between like Pekka Rinne, talented and inconsistent. The same is true to a lesser extent with position players, due to injury, chemistry or other factors.

The best teams at least seem to match our expectation. What about the worst teams?

Worst teams, 2007–08 to 2016–17[29]

Rnk	Team	Season	GP	PTS	vs Avg	vs Exp	Luck
1	Buffalo Sabres	2014–15	82	54	-38.2	-31.0	-7.2
2	Buffalo Sabres	2013–14	82	52	-40.2	-19.9	-20.3
3	Colorado Avalanche	2016–17	82	48	-43.6	-18.7	-25.0
4	Arizona Coyotes	2016–17	82	70	-21.6	-18.5	-3.2
5	Arizona Coyotes	2014–15	82	56	-36.2	-18.4	-17.8
6	Vancouver Canucks	2016–17	82	69	-22.6	-17.8	-4.8
7	Atlanta Thrashers	2007–08	82	76	-15.1	-17.5	2.4
8	Edmonton Oilers	2010–11	82	62	-29.9	-17.3	-12.6
9	Edmonton Oilers	2014–15	82	62	-30.2	-17.0	-13.2
10	Florida Panthers	2012–13	48	36	-29.7	-16.3	-13.4
11	Florida Panthers	2013–14	82	66	-26.2	-16.2	-10.0
12	New York Islanders	2008–09	82	61	-30.4	-16.2	-14.2

29 Acknowledgement: Raw standings data for these calculations from the *NHL*, http://www.nhl.com.

13	Arizona Coyotes	2015–16	82	78	-13.2	-15.1	1.9
14	Edmonton Oilers	2013–14	82	67	-25.2	-14.6	-10.7
15	New Jersey Devils	2014–15	82	78	-14.2	-14.2	0.0
16	Edmonton Oilers	2009–10	82	62	-30.0	-13.3	-16.7
17	Minnesota Wild	2010–11	82	86	-5.9	-13.3	7.4
18	Tampa Bay Lightning	2008–09	82	66	-25.4	-13.2	-12.2
19	Toronto Maple Leafs	2014–15	82	68	-24.2	-13.0	-11.2
20	Edmonton Oilers	2011–12	82	74	-18.0	-12.9	-5.1

For those who followed the Buffalo Sabres from 2013–14 to 2014–15, you remember the pain, and it is no surprise to find them atop of the list here. Those two seasons saw the Sabres in full rebuild mode, and it showed in the numbers. On the positive side for Sabres fans, the team's numbers have improved over the past two seasons, and there is hope for the future.

The suffering of Sabres fans may seem like nothing next to the suffering of Oilers fans, who see their team appear on this list five times over a six-year stretch from 2009–10 to 2014–15. This is another team that has finally turned the corner, moreso over the last season with the emergence of Connor McDavid as a generational talent, Cam Talbot's presence as a solid No. 1 goaltender after years of instability in the crease, and the continued building of a solid blue line with Adam Larsson and Oscar Klefbom.

The three most recent editions of the Arizona Coyotes appear here. Unlike the Oilers and Sabres, the current makeup of the Coyotes presages that the team has another painful season or two ahead of it before it can return to contention.

The last two teams that are worthy of mention are the 2016–17 Avalanche and the 2016–17 Canucks, both of whom rank among the six worst teams of the last decade. Both of these teams show all the hallmarks of teams that will continue to struggle persistently: very weak puck possession numbers (they were among the four worst teams in the NHL last season, along the Coyotes and the Sabres) combined with a lack of top-end talent that could generate good percentages to compensate, either on the front end or between the pipes. This can and will change over the next few seasons, as the teams draft, trade and develop new talent, but things don't look good for either team for 2017–18. But, we'll save most of the detailed analysis on the coming season for the next chapter.

Luck vs. Skill

Ok, come on, Tom. Give us the juicy stuff. We already knew who were the best and worst teams of the last decade; we do follow hockey, after all. You claim to be able to measure luck: tell us who the luckiest teams of the last decade were?

Ok, fine. But before I do, I want to insist on one thing: my system classifies a fair portion of percentages as luck, because that's what they are for most teams. For a few teams that have proven to be persistently skilled, the system will overestimate the impact of luck. Therefore, certain elite teams – think Washington, Pittsburgh, and Anaheim in particular – will be seen as lucky when they are in fact good. This doesn't mean they weren't also lucky, but simply that the share of their success due to luck may be slightly inflated. On to the list!

Luckiest teams, 2007–08 to 2016–17[30]

Rnk	Team	Season	GP	PTS	vs Avg	vs Exp	Luck	Pred	Actual
1	Colorado Avalanche	2013–14	82	112	19.8	-4.8	24.6	86.7	90
2	Chicago Blackhawks	2012–13	48	77	40.3	16.7	23.6	108.2	107
3	Anaheim Ducks	2012–13	48	66	21.5	1.3	20.3	92.8	116
4	Pittsburgh Penguins	2012–13	48	72	31.8	12.7	19.1	104.2	109
5	Boston Bruins	2008–09	82	116	24.6	5.9	18.7	97.4	91
6	Montreal Canadiens	2014–15	82	110	17.8	0.7	17.1	92.2	82
7	Washington Capitals	2015–16	82	120	28.8	12.0	16.8	103.5	118
8	Chicago Blackhawks	2016–17	82	109	17.4	0.8	16.6	92.3	TBD
9	Anaheim Ducks	2010–11	82	99	7.1	-7.9	15.0	83.6	80
10	Washington Capitals	2009–10	82	121	29.0	14.0	15.0	105.5	107
11	Arizona Coyotes	2009–10	82	107	15.0	1.3	13.7	92.8	99
12	San Jose Sharks	2009–10	82	113	21.0	7.5	13.4	99.0	105
13	Vancouver Canucks	2010–11	82	117	25.1	11.9	13.2	103.4	111
14	Anaheim Ducks	2007–08	82	102	10.9	-2.1	13.0	89.4	91
15	Montreal Canadiens	2007–08	82	104	12.9	0.0	12.9	91.5	93
16	Anaheim Ducks	2013–14	82	116	23.8	11.4	12.4	102.9	109
17	Vancouver Canucks	2014–15	82	101	8.8	-3.5	12.3	88.0	75
18	New York Rangers	2014–15	82	113	20.8	8.7	12.1	100.2	101
19	Washington Capitals	2016–17	82	118	26.4	14.7	11.7	106.2	TBD
20	Dallas Stars	2015–16	82	109	17.8	6.1	11.7	97.6	79

It is no surprise to see three teams from the lockout-shortened 2012–13 season among the top four luckiest teams on my list. As has been discussed extensively here and elsewhere, larger sample sizes help to filter out the effect of luck; conversely, smaller sample sizes amplify it, so a shorter season will increase the impact of luck as each one-goal game, overtime goal, or shootout loss has a larger impact on the standings.

My luck measurement does seem to give accurate predictions for the future. The 20 luckiest teams on my list averaged 112.5 points during their lucky seasons (again, normalizing 2012–13 to 82 games). I predicted that they would achieve an average of 97 points the subsequent year, a decline of 15.5 points. In practice they averaged 98 points, a decline of 14.5 points. Once again, I will state that my system slightly overstates luck for some elite teams.

The Anaheim Ducks show up four times on my lucky list and beat my predictions by an average of seven points. Either they have had the luckiest stretch of any team in recent history, or Ryan Getzlaf, Francois Beauchemin, Corey Perry, and Jonas Hiller were just really good, and able to exceed expectations over several seasons. I'm a statistics guy and I value evidence above all else: the consistency of Anaheim's success indicates that true talent has been at least partly responsible for their achievements.

---

30 Acknowledgement: Raw standings data for these calculations from the NHL, http://www.nhl.com.

A few teams on this list are worthy of specific comments. The top team is the 2013–14 Colorado Avalanche, and they are a worthy champion as no team has been as lucky as them over the course of a full season. The Avalanche had finished last in the Western Conference the previous season (the 2012–13 Avalanche will be listed later as the 10th unluckiest team of the decade), but they went from an 8.1% to a 10.1% shooting percentage, while their save percentage increased by a similar amounts, from 90.1% to 91.9%. The arrival of Nathan MacKinnon, their reward for their terrible 2012–13 season, gave an air of legitimacy to the improvement, especially since MacKinnon had an excellent rookie season. During this time, the Avalanche were outshot by 248 shots, almost three per game, a sure sign that they were not as dominant as their record indicated. They finished an amazing 26-12 in one-goal games, which is how they managed 112 points in the standings despite only outscoring their opponents by 30 goals.

As a Montrealer, I can also comment on the 2007–08 and 2014–15 editions of the Canadiens, as I remember them personally. I can guarantee you that most hockey fans are not aware of how much luck is involved in their favourite team's success. In Montreal, whenever the Canadiens are doing well, there's an expression you hear: "Ca sent la coupe!", meaning "It smells like the Cup!". I heard this in 2007–08, when the Canadiens unexpectedly finished atop the Eastern Conference with 104 points after having missed the playoffs the previous season; they did so by leading the league with 262 goals thanks to a 10.8% shooting percentage, but still got outshot by 2.5 shots per game. As was the case with the Avalanche, the arrival of a young star – in this case Carey Price – made the improvement feel more real. The Canadiens fell back down to Earth the following season.

An even starker manifestation of this phenomenon occurred in 2014–15, when the Canadiens earned 110 points mostly thanks to a .933 save percentage by Price, by now an established elite netminder, and thanks to good luck in one-goal games. Unfortunately for them, they still got outshot by 136 shots, and the next season, with Price injured, the wheels fell off and the team fell to 13th place in the East with only 82 points. What luck giveth, luck taketh away.

Cross-Checking

Characterizing luck is a fraught exercise, so one way to verify if I have done it correctly is to compare it to someone else's measure of luck; ideally, someone else who calculated it in a completely different way from me. Luckily, Rob has done exactly that.

In the original *Hockey Abstract*, he wrote a chapter called "Who is the Luckiest Team?[31]" In it, he characterized team luck as the sum of five factors: shooting and save percentages, special teams, injuries, post-regulation record, and record in one-goal games. The good news is that Rob's approach is completely different from mine: while he tried to identify elements that are due to luck, I have identified the elements that are due to skill, and assumed everything else is luck. If our measurements line up roughly, this is a good sign that I am on the right track.

---

31 Rob Vollman, "Who is the luckiest team?", *Hockey Abstract,* 2013, pgs 62-75.

Top 30 Luckiest Teams, 2008–09 to 2012–13[32]

Season	Team	PDO	STI	CHIP	OT/SO	1-Goal	Luck Index
2012–13	Toronto	1036	106.6	2763	2-5	9-3	29.7
2012–13	Pittsburgh	1030	104.4	5399	5-0	8-2	27.3
2012–13	Chicago	1024	103.9	3852	11-5	8-3	26.2
2008–09	Boston	1036	106.0	7045	7-10	11-10	23.5
2011–12	Nashville	1024	105.2	3619	8-8	12-10	21.7
2010–11	Vancouver	1026	109.9	8553	8-9	11-7	21.5
2012–13	Anaheim	1016	103.0	1660	7-6	7-2	20.7
2010–11	Anaheim	1016	104.8	5963	13-5	16-10	20.6
2009–10	San Jose	1019	106.0	3349	8-11	12-6	20.2
2009–10	Washington	1027	104.0	5202	11-13	9-8	19.5
2011–12	Vancouver	1019	105.8	6948	15-9	12-9	19.5
2012–13	Washington	1025	104.7	5173	7-3	6-7	18.2
2011–12	NY Rangers	1019	101.9	6190	12-7	9-5	17.6
2009–10	Buffalo	1013	104.2	3885	10-10	11-9	14.6
2009–10	Phoenix	1006	99.1	3979	19-7	10-6	14.3
2011–12	New Jersey	1007	106.8	8240	16-6	8-7	13.2
2010–11	Boston	1023	98.8	5715	3-11	13-7	12.8
2010–11	Dallas	1012	98.1	3239	10-11	13-6	12.7
2008–09	Minnesota	1019	107.7	9138	8-9	11-13	12.6
2008–09	San Jose	1004	107.5	6095	10-11	16-7	12.6
2011–12	Boston	1019	100.7	7568	11-4	8-12	12.5
2009–10	Colorado	1021	98.3	7853	9-9	14-10	12.2
2009–10	Vancouver	1019	102.5	10055	8-5	9-8	11.7
2008–09	Vancouver	1018	100.2	5307	8-10	9-9	11.3
2008–09	Florida	1021	99.2	8363	7-11	9-4	10.8
2008–09	New Jersey	1005	98.8	6909	15-4	10-5	10.6
2008–09	Anaheim	1005	103.3	3617	12-7	11-14	9.9
2009–10	Los Angeles	1006	101.1	4766	14-9	11-10	9.8
2009–10	St. Louis	1005	103.7	4068	10-10	11-9	9.7
2010–11	Los Angeles	1004	101.6	5083	11-6	11-9	9.2

As you can see, among the teams that overlap Rob's 2009–2013 analysis period, there is a huge amount of agreement between us. Both of us have three teams from the lockout-shortened 2012–13 season at the top, both agreeing on Pittsburgh and Chicago while I have Anaheim at #2 and he has them at #7 while having Toronto at #1 (more on them later). My next three teams – the 2008–09 Boston Bruins, the 2010–11 Anaheim Ducks and the 2009–10 Washington Capitals – also show up in Rob's top ten. It seems that we are indeed measuring mostly the same things.

This is not surprising. Two of Rob's factors – post-regulation record and record in one-goal games – are explicit ways in which teams' performance in the standings exceeds their goal differential, which we know to not be sustainable, and shooting and save percentages are

32 Acknowledgement: For Rob's calculations, raw PDO and STI data came from *Hockey Reference* http://www.hockey-reference.com, CHIP data came from *Springing Malik* http://springingmalik.blogspot.ca, and win/loss records came from NHL's website http://www.nhl.com.

known to not be fully maintained from one season to the next, as shown in my analysis of goal differential's predictive power earlier in this chapter. I found earlier that CHIP (Cap Hit of Injured Players) did not have any predictive power on next year's standings so I don't factor it into my calculations[33]. The only area in which we truly disagree is with regards to special teams, which he considers to be mostly luck and I consider to be mostly skill. The reason why I consider them to be skill is simple: overall goal differential has more power in predicting next season's standings than even-strength goal differential alone, although the difference is small. Therefore, teams that do well on special teams – like the 2012–13 Toronto Maple Leafs – will look "lucky" to Rob but "skilled" to me.

Just Some Bad Luck

The flip side of the luckiest teams is, of course, the unluckiest teams. These are the teams whose performance had their fans questioning both their loyalty and, sometimes, their sanity, wondering if everything that could go wrong in a single season would go wrong. The only positive side of knowing how unlucky your team has been is the hope that it should only get better from there.

Unluckiest teams, 2007–08 to 2016–17[34]

Rnk	Team	Season	GP	PTS	vs Avg	vs Exp	Luck	Pred	Actual
1	Colorado Avalanche	2016–17	82	48	-43.6	-18.7	-25.0	72.8	TBD
2	Buffalo Sabres	2013–14	82	52	-40.2	-19.9	-20.3	71.6	54
3	Carolina Hurricanes	2014–15	82	71	-21.2	-1.7	-19.5	89.8	86
4	Colorado Avalanche	2010–11	82	68	-23.9	-5.2	-18.7	86.3	88
5	Columbus Blue Jackets	2011–12	82	65	-27.0	-8.9	-18.1	48.3	55
6	Arizona Coyotes	2014–15	82	56	-36.2	-18.4	-17.8	73.1	78
7	Nashville Predators	2012–13	48	41	-21.2	-3.8	-17.4	87.7	88
8	Tampa Bay Lightning	2012–13	48	40	-22.9	-5.7	-17.2	85.8	101
9	Edmonton Oilers	2009–10	82	62	-30.0	-13.3	-16.7	78.2	62
10	Colorado Avalanche	2012–13	48	39	-24.6	-8.1	-16.5	83.4	112
11	Tampa Bay Lightning	2007–08	82	71	-20.1	-3.6	-16.5	87.9	66
12	Colorado Avalanche	2008–09	82	69	-22.4	-6.0	-16.4	85.5	95
13	Toronto Maple Leafs	2009–10	82	74	-18.0	-3.1	-14.9	88.4	85
14	Toronto Maple Leafs	2015–16	82	69	-22.2	-7.7	-14.5	83.8	95
15	New York Islanders	2008–09	82	61	-30.4	-16.2	-14.2	75.3	79
16	Winnipeg Jets	2015–16	82	78	-13.2	1.0	-14.2	92.5	87
17	Florida Panthers	2012–13	48	36	-29.7	-16.3	-13.4	75.2	66
18	Florida Panthers	2010–11	82	72	-19.9	-6.6	-13.3	84.9	94
19	Edmonton Oilers	2014–15	82	62	-30.2	-17.0	-13.2	74.5	70
20	Calgary Flames	2015–16	82	77	-14.2	-1.4	-12.7	90.1	77

Rejoice, Avalanche fans: who else can claim to have both the luckiest *and* unluckiest team of

---

33 Note from Rob: Including injuries so prominently was one of my key errors, and why I overrated the Senators when Karlsson and Spezza were injured. Other players tend to step up more than I had expected.
34 Acknowledgement: Raw standings data for these calculations from the *NHL*, http://www.nhl.com.

the last decade, and only three years apart? The 2016–17 edition of the Avalanche was officially the unluckiest team we have found, which is not surprising given that they also had the lowest win percentage (0.293) of the decade. In fact, the Avalanche's talent level should allow them to return to semi-respectability next season with 73 points.

The Avalanche did indeed have quite a run of bad luck, with the 2010–11, 2012–13, and 2016–17 teams making the top 10. No other team made the top 10 more than once, although we see quite the string of basement-dwellers here. It is no surprise that the shortened 2012–13 season is overrepresented here as well, with three teams in the top 10.

On average, these are teams that "should" have obtained 81 points, but averaged only 65. They also averaged 81 points the subsequent season, indicating that their luck bounced back perfectly the next year. In fact, 11 of the 19 teams improved by 15 points or more.

Here is the full list of teams by luck for the 2016–17 season.

Luckiest Teams, 2016–17[35]

Rnk	Team	GP	PTS	Vs Exp	Luck
1	Chicago Blackhawks	82	109	0.8	16.6
2	Washington Capitals	82	118	14.7	11.7
3	Columbus Blue Jackets	82	108	6.1	10.3
4	Pittsburgh Penguins	82	111	9.2	10.1
5	Montreal Canadiens	82	103	2.1	9.2
6	Edmonton Oilers	82	103	3.5	7.8
7	New York Rangers	82	102	2.6	7.8
8	Ottawa Senators	82	98	-1.4	7.8
9	Anaheim Ducks	82	105	6.2	7.1
10	Calgary Flames	82	94	-2.6	5.0
11	Minnesota Wild	82	106	10.0	4.4
12	New York Islanders	82	94	-1.3	3.6
13	St. Louis Blues	82	99	4.0	3.4
14	Toronto Maple Leafs	82	95	0.3	3.0
15	San Jose Sharks	82	99	5.8	1.6
16	Tampa Bay Lightning	82	94	3.0	-0.6
14	Nashville Predators	82	94	4.4	-2.1
18	Winnipeg Jets	82	87	-1.8	-2.8
19	Arizona Coyotes	82	70	-18.5	-3.2
20	Philadelphia Flyers	82	88	0.1	-3.8
21	Carolina Hurricanes	82	87	-0.6	-4.0
22	Vancouver Canucks	82	69	-17.8	-4.8
23	Detroit Red Wings	82	79	-7.5	-5.1
24	Buffalo Sabres	82	78	-7.7	-5.9
25	Boston Bruins	82	95	9.7	-6.3
26	Florida Panthers	82	81	-3.1	-7.5
27	New Jersey Devils	82	70	-12.3	-9.4

35 Acknowledgement: Raw standings data for these calculations from the *NHL*, http://www.nhl.com.

28 Dallas Stars	82	79	-1.4	-11.3
29 Los Angeles Kings	82	86	6.8	-12.4
30 Colorado Avalanche	82	48	-18.7	-25.0

Obviously, the presence of Chicago, Washington, and Pittsburgh near the top of the list looks suspiciously like "good teams making their own luck", and I believe that is partially true, although both Chicago and Pittsburgh increased their point totals, by six and seven points respectively, from the 2015–16 season.

Looking at the bottom, nobody can dispute the Avalanche's bad luck last year, while the Dallas Stars had just dominated the Western Conference with 109 points the previous season, and the Los Angeles Kings were coming off a 102-point season and were just two years removed from winning the Stanley Cup. The vagaries of chance govern the lives of both Kings and paupers.

Next Season

I'm obviously not cruel (or stupid) enough to show you all of this without giving you the predictions for next season's standings.

Please keep in mind that the standard deviation of points, even with a perfect model, is 8.6 points, and the standard deviation on my model is about 11 points. This leaves a lot of room for error, so when you reread this in June 2018 (you will do that, right?) judge me on whether I had most of the good teams on top and most of the bad teams on the bottom, and not on the fact that I predicted your team to miss the playoffs when they actually finished 2nd in the division:

Projected Standings, 2017–18

Rnk	Team	High	Avg	Low
1	Washington Capitals	117.4	106.3	95.2
2	Minnesota Wild	112.7	101.6	90.5
3	Boston Bruins	112.4	101.3	90.2
4	Pittsburgh Penguins	111.9	100.8	89.7
5	Los Angeles Kings	109.5	98.4	87.3
6	Anaheim Ducks	108.9	97.8	86.7
7	Columbus Blue Jackets	108.8	97.7	86.6
8	San Jose Sharks	108.5	97.4	86.3
9	Nashville Predators	107.1	96.0	84.9
10	St. Louis Blues	106.7	95.6	84.5
11	Edmonton Oilers	106.2	95.1	84.0
12	Tampa Bay Lightning	105.7	94.6	83.5
13	New York Rangers	105.3	94.2	83.1
14	Montreal Canadiens	104.8	93.7	82.6
15	Chicago Blackhawks	103.5	92.4	81.3
16	Toronto Maple Leafs	103.0	91.9	80.8

14	Philadelphia Flyers	102.8	91.7	80.6
18	Carolina Hurricanes	102.1	91.0	79.9
19	New York Islanders	101.4	90.3	79.2
20	Dallas Stars	101.3	90.2	79.1
21	Ottawa Senators	101.3	90.2	79.1
22	Winnipeg Jets	100.9	89.8	78.7
23	Calgary Flames	100.1	89.0	77.9
24	Florida Panthers	99.6	88.5	77.4
25	Detroit Red Wings	95.2	84.1	73.0
26	Buffalo Sabres	95.0	83.9	72.8
27	New Jersey Devils	90.4	79.3	68.2
28	Vancouver Canucks	84.9	73.8	62.7
29	Arizona Coyotes	84.2	73.1	62.0
30	Colorado Avalanche	84.0	72.9	61.8

I have to admit, I wasn't expecting to see the Blackhawks and Flyers neck and neck in the standings. The Blackhawks were the major downside surprise to my eyes; the two major upside surprises were the Boston Bruins and Los Angeles Kings, two aging teams whose predictions were bolstered by their stellar puck possession numbers.

— MOTOR CITY CEPHALOPODS —

"WELL BOYS, IT LOOKS LIKE IT'LL BE A FEW MORE YEARS TOGETHER BEFORE ANY OF US HIT THE ICE!"

Remember, I didn't choose these numbers; I have to do what the data tells me. Also, remember that I expect about five teams out of thirty to overshoot the "High" prediction and five teams to undershoot the "Low". Either way, I'll be back here next year to either bask in my glory, or eat crow.

Astute readers[36] will notice that I have not made any predictions for the Vegas Golden Knights, as this system is based on predicting team performance in the aggregate from the previous season and there are, obviously, no previous seasons to base ourselves on. At a high level, the Knights have put together a weak but nevertheless NHL-calibre team, and I believe that their first season could resemble that of the 2000–01 Columbus Blue Jackets (71 points in 82 games), but will probably be a bit weaker, in the 60-70 point range. At the very least, the expansion draft rules guaranteed that we won't have a rerun of the 1991–92 San Jose Sharks (39 points, and 24 the next season) or the 1992–93 Ottawa Senators (24 points, followed by 37 the next year).

VEGAS UNIFORMS

HOME   ROAD   ALTERNATE

Closing Thoughts

It is somewhat disappointing that we were only able to predict 36% of next season's performance using our model, but given that we knew from the start that luck represents 39% of single-season performance, it's not as bad as it seems.

We learned that both goal differential and shot differential have significant predictive power in predicting team performance, and that even the previous season's goal differential also helps

---

36 Which, of course, is all of you!

us. We learned that, beyond these basic statistics, there are many statistics that we value in analytics that don't add any predictive power: even-strength goals, injuries, and playoff success all had no impact. It was also reassuring to confirm that shootout wins had no predictive power either. On that note, it was interesting to learn to what extent teams play for the regulation-time tie. In the end, we only used six statistics in our model: goal differential, shot differential, goal differential of previous season, age, even-strength expected goals, and power-play opportunity differential.

Understanding a team's true talent is important for both fans and general managers, but especially for GMs who need to understand if their team is really as good, or bad, as the numbers say, and if their "window" to win a Stanley Cup is still open. While this is in no way the last word on the subject, the fact that my estimate of luck matches up so well with Rob's indicates that we are likely both doing a fairly good job of characterizing luck – and, by extension, skill.

How Can Stats be Used to Evaluate Teams?

By Rob Vollman

Is this the age of parity?

Ostensibly, the salary cap and rules changes introduced in 2005–06, along with the absence of expansion prior to this coming season, has led to an age in parity that makes it almost pointless to project the standings. But, is this really the case?

In *Hockey Abstract*, we challenge conventional wisdom using objective measures. The traditional views often prove to be correct, but there are some fascinating insights to be learned when they're not.

The task begins with clear definitions. In this case, one way to define parity is that the best teams in the league aren't that much better than the worst, which gives every team a good chance of winning on any given night, of making the playoffs, and driving towards the Stanley Cup.

To test whether that definition is correct, we can compare the three best and the three worst teams from every season, to see if the gap between them is any closer today than it was in the past.

Because of the way points are earned has changed over the years, goals will be used to compare teams. Throughout the NHL's entire history, scoring and preventing goals has always been the primary means to achieve a team's objectives. And, because the number of games in a season and league scoring levels have changed over the years, the comparison will be made using each team's goal percentage rather than each team's goal differential. Goal percentage is calculated by dividing goals scored by the sum of goals scored and goals allowed.

When placing the data all the way back to the 1967–68 expansion on the following chart, our current definition of parity means that we should see the two lines representing the average goal percentage of the top three teams and the bottom three teams come closer together – but we don't. It appears that the gap between the best teams and the worst teams is really no different now than it has been since the late 1970s. By this definition, there's no increased level of parity in the modern age.

NHL Parity, 1967-68 to 2016-17

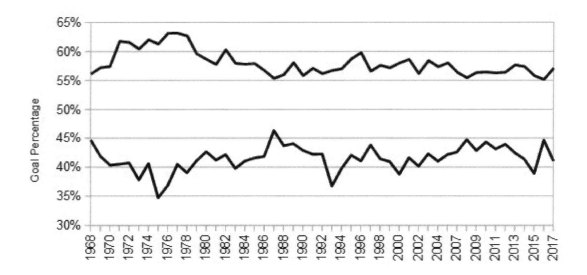

This doesn't necessarily disprove the theory that the NHL has achieved greater parity, because the problem could be with our chosen definition. Maybe the gap between the great teams and the bad teams is no smaller, but there's more mobility in and out of those groups than there used to be. That is, the best teams in one year aren't necessarily the best teams in the next, like they used to be.

Take the 1986–87 season, for example. According to the chart, it appears that the gap between the best teams and the worst teams was at its smallest point. No team finished more than six points out of the playoffs that year, and only one team won more than 46 games in the 80-game schedule. It was a very tight pack.

However, I remember that season well, and it certainly doesn't feel like there was parity, because it was right in the heart of the Edmonton Oilers dynasty. They had just topped 100 points for the sixth straight season, won their third Stanley Cup in four years, and remained one of only three teams to have won the Stanley Cup over the course of my entire life to that point – 12 years. By comparison, the NHL has crowned seven different Stanley Cup champion in the past 12 years.

Another definition of parity can be crafted by looking at what happens to the teams in each of these two three-team groups. If we are in an age of parity, then by calculating the average change in goal percentage the following season, we should see the best teams getting worse, and the worst teams getting better, and to a greater extent than ever before. However, there doesn't appear to be much of a change at all.

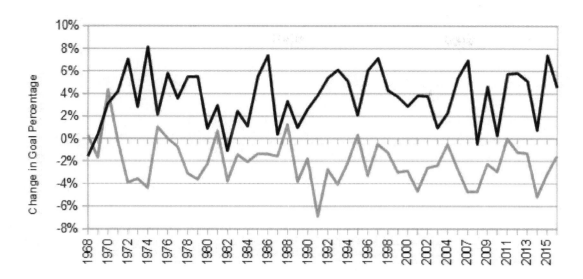

Fate of Extreme Teams, 1967-68 to 2016-17

If you squint, maybe the top teams are getting worse to a slightly greater extent than before, but the worst teams certainly aren't improving to any greater extent.

Besides, you shouldn't have to squint. If there really was more mobility, then the bad teams would be improving at much higher rate than before, and the decline of the stronger teams would be far more obvious.

We could go on crafting more and more definitions for parity until we found one that worked, but the point has already been reasonably illustrated. We haven't disproved the notion that the NHL is in an age of parity, but we have demonstrated that if that theory is true, then it sure is difficult to capture objectively to any meaningful extent. Specifically, the gap between the good teams and the bad teams is the same as it has been for 30 years, and the best and worst teams rise and decline at roughly the same rate as they always have.

None of this alters the eternal fact that predicting the standings is difficult. Without the benefit of hindsight, it was hard in the 1980s, and it remains hard today. Even if an expert has somehow constructed an accurate picture of a team in the current day, so many things can happen over the course of 82 games to throw things off.

Unlike in the 1980s, today's advantage is that we are now armed with a new weapon. We have access to a lot of fancy data that can make it a little easier to sort out which teams were boosted by external factors, and to figure out the impact of certain roster changes. All we have to do is figure out how to use this new weapon. And that's exactly what we strive to do in these pages.

Before we begin, let me make it clear that the team-level analysis contained in the following section is *not* about making predictions. After all, hockey analytics are about probabilities, and not destinies.

The real purpose of the following two-page team breakdowns is to get a deeper understanding of a team's strengths and weaknesses, and not where they'll ultimately finish in the standings. It achieves this by avoiding narratives and speculation, and focusing on what is measurable and predictable, and what has a provable relationship with winning. In a way, it's as much about how to use numbers in an analysis, as it is about the numbers themselves.

You often hear fans and pundits argue that stats have their place, but that they aren't the be-all, end-all. That is a straw man argument, because no statistician has ever claimed that they are, or that they should be. Heck, Tom even put a number on it in the opening chapter – 36%.

Statistical analysis was never, ever meant to replace anything. Our take isn't even meant to be *better* than other perspectives, only different. So, continue to listen to those who have played and/or coached the game, to the local media who have access to the players and coaches, and to the local websites that can keep all the information up to date. Trust me, you have our blessing.

To most fans, the real value of this statistical perspective is its scarcity. Fans are constantly surrounded by the traditional perspectives, but these pages are one of the few places where some of those views can be either confirmed or challenged, and where some of the overlooked teams, players, and factors can get the proper attention.

Before we dive in, we want to strike the right balance with getting new readers up to speed, while avoiding being overly repetitive to those who are already familiar with the previous editions.

In the following pages, we'll walk through the key concepts, but some of the more detailed examinations and explanations will only be referenced to the other books in this series. The two key sections are the player usage charts, and the Hockey Abstract Checklist. Let's begin with the latter.

The Hockey Abstract Checklist

It's quite common for various hockey publications to break down its analysis into categories. In *Hockey Abstract*, our approach is only different in the slightly different choice and ordering of the categories, and the objective way in which they are measured.

Those who are already familiar with our work will be able to jump right in, because the methodology hasn't changed from previous editions. Just flip through the following pages to check out the updated data and a few new observations about each category, before diving right into the team analysis.

New readers will find the team analysis just as insightful, but will want to read the following overview more carefully, and may need to consult either the 2014 edition or the 2015 update to get more detail on why certain categories were chosen, and how they're being measured.

The concept behind the checklist is pretty simple. In all, there are 13 categories, and as a nod to the imprecise nature and high-level nature of this process, there are only three possible scores for each one:
- A star if the team is an elite leader in the given category,
- A checkmark if they have it covered at roughly the same level as a playoff team,
- Otherwise, it is left blank.

Some of our reasoning is explained below, some of it in the individual team analysis, and the rest is based on our experience doing this type of work in a variety of different publications over the years.

But, if you don't like our own interpretation of the data, or if things change, feel free to get out a pencil, and edit the assigned scores to your own liking. Or, hop on Twitter and let us know which animal's biological waste is apparently in place of our brains. Whatever works for you.

Puck Possession

Puck possession is a sloppy shorthand. In fact, it's so sloppy, that most statisticians don't even use that term at all anymore, and that's probably for the best.

In reality, when you hear or read about puck possession in statistical terms, it's normally based on shot-based metrics, and not on an actual time-based measurement of puck control or zone time.

The good news is that shot-based metrics are actually better than puck possession. They encapsulate not only the ability to gain control of the puck, retain that control, and prevent the opponent from doing so, but also the capability to translate that possession into shot attempts. That's why shot-based metrics aren't favoured because of their relationship with puck possession, but because of their relationship with scoring and winning.

There's no need to re-hash the entire topic again here, having been covered in an introductory fashion in the original *Hockey Abstract*[37], and then in unsurpassed detail in *Stat Shot*[38]. As such, most readers have already become quite familiar with the proper applications and limitations of the data below.

We have made one change for this edition. To address score effects, which were covered in the 2014 edition[39], this data used to be based on the first two periods, and on tied games in the third period. That reduces the skewing effect that occurs when teams who are frequently protecting leads sit back into a defensive shell, and those who are frequently chasing them

37 Rob Vollman, "Shot-based Metrics", *Hockey Abstract,* 2013, pgs 112-121.
38 Tom Awad, "Everything you ever wanted to know about shot-based metrics (but were afraid to ask)", *Stat Shot,* September 2016, pgs 228-281.
39 Tom Awad, "What are Score Effects?", *Hockey Abstract 2014,* 2014, pgs 45-52.

opening things up and getting a lot of extra shot attempts.

Using close-game data was always just for simplicity, and for accessibility for the common fan. For statisticians, useful data should never be thrown away. Instead, a team's shot-based data should be adjusted for the calculated impact of score effects, so that all of it can be included. In fact, there are other adjustments that can refine the view even further (the details of which are in *Stat Shot*[40]), but these score effects are really the main one.

After five seasons, I believe we have all reached the point where we can officially adopt the slightly more precise model, and use score-adjusted shot attempt percentages, rather than those that set aside close game data.

Score-Adjusted Shot Attempt Percentages[41]

Team	2014–15	2015–16	2016–17	Weighted Average
Los Angeles	55.0	56.8	53.8	54.8
Boston	52.3	49.9	55.3	53.3
Washington	52.0	51.5	53.0	52.4
San Jose	51.5	51.8	52.2	52.0
Nashville	52.7	52.5	51.2	51.8
Pittsburgh	53.8	53.1	50.5	51.7
Montreal	48.5	51.2	52.6	51.6
Chicago	54.3	51.6	50.9	51.6
Tampa Bay	53.3	52.2	50.8	51.6
Carolina	51.4	51.4	51.1	51.3
Anaheim	51.1	53.2	50.3	51.2
St. Louis	52.4	52.2	50.3	51.1
Dallas	52.4	52.5	49.8	50.9
Philadelphia	49.2	50.1	50.8	50.4
Florida	50.8	49.8	50.3	50.2
Toronto	45.2	50.5	51.3	50.2
Winnipeg	53.6	51.1	48.9	50.2
Minnesota	51.0	47.9	50.4	49.8
Detroit	53.5	51.7	47.8	49.7
Columbus	46.9	47.6	51.1	49.5
Edmonton	47.3	48.1	50.7	49.5
NY Islanders	53.4	49.5	48.0	49.2
Calgary	44.4	48.1	50.5	48.9
NY Rangers	50.6	48.0	48.3	48.5
Ottawa	50.6	47.0	48.4	48.3
Vancouver	49.0	46.8	46.9	47.2
New Jersey	46.8	45.5	46.4	46.2
Colorado	43.2	44.5	46.8	45.6
Buffalo	36.2	46.8	47.0	45.4

40 Tom Awad, "Everything you ever wanted to know about shot-based metrics (but were afraid to ask)", *Stat Shot,* September 2016, pgs 228-281.
41 Acknowledgement: Shot attempt data comes from *Puck on Net* http://www.puckon.net.

| Arizona | 47.2 | 46.5 | 44.2 | 45.3 |

As can be observed by noting that the top-ranked team, the Los Angeles Kings, missed the playoffs, along with consistently strong performers like the Tampa Bay Lightning and Carolina Hurricanes, obviously shot-based metrics aren't everything. But, they are something.

In addition to noting where a team ranks within the NHL, it's also important to note which direction it is heading. In this case, Winnipeg, Detroit, the New York Islanders, and Arizona have been trending down, possibly along with the Lightning and last year's Stanley Cup finalists, Pittsburgh and Nashville.

At the other end of the spectrum, teams like Montreal, Columbus, Edmonton, Calgary, Toronto, Colorado, Buffalo, San Jose, and Philadelphia are trending up. Other teams are bouncing around, and some teams never change, like Carolina.

The Vegas Golden Knights can't be included in this chart, but given their unusual blue line selections in the expansion draft, I suspect that they would rank right near the bottom.

And remember, this is not a prediction, it is a weighted average of the past, and there's a difference between the two. That's why it's important to consider significant roster changes that can impact a team's shot-based metrics, such as the big roster shake-up in Chicago, and a handful of key moves made by the Islanders this summer.

The Shootout

This checklist was originally put together in order of importance, which was established through a statistical combination of each category's correlation with winning, and how persistent the measurements were from season to season. Given its value in the first component of that equation, a team's shootout abilities was ranked second.

With the advent of three-on-three overtime, the shootout is now of reduced value. The number of games decided in the shootout has dropped from 160 in 2014–15 to 100 in 2015–16 and 99 in 2016–17. As such, the opportunity to add a few points with a low-cost shootout specialist like P.A. Parenteau or goalie Jhonas Enroth has really dwindled.

There are those who are grateful for its reduced importance. The shootout can create an artificial illusion of greater parity than actually exists. It messes with the standings, reduces the chances that the league's top 16 teams actually make the playoffs, and shuffles the order of those who do.

While a skills competition is admittedly an arbitrary way to decide a hockey game, and has virtually no relationship to a team's ability to play the sport, it still has an important impact on the final standings, and should be studied.

Since the shootout was introduced for the 2005–06 season, the Colorado Avalanche have a

64.7% winning percentage in 105 games. They have scored on a league-leading 39.2% of their shots, way more than Minnesota Wild, in second place with 36.5%. Their .717 save percentage is just shy of Boston's league lead, .718. Consequently, they have a 68-37 record, which works out to around two or three extra points per season, relative to an average team.

Then there's Philadelphia, whose save percentage of .601 is well back of Toronto's .620 in 29th, and Calgary .634 in 28th. Their 27.7% shooting percentage is 28th, leading to an overall record of 40-75, which has effectively cost them two to three points per season. And, some seasons, they missed the playoffs by even less.

So, teams can ignore the shootout at their own peril. Despite the reduced important, it could make sense to keep an eye out for one or two secondary players who bring shootout talent to the table.

Shootout data can be scarce, but the following table can serve as a rough guide. It's rather crude ranking is based on each team's number one goalie, and its three main shooter options. Players who are new to their teams are *italicized* for easy reference of potentially significant changes.

Career Totals of Top Team Shootout Options[42]

Team	Goalie	SV%	Shooter 1	SH%	Shooter 2	SH%	Shooter 3	SH%
San Jose	Jones	.816	Pavelski	37.0	Couture	45.7	Burns	34.6
NY Rangers	Lundqvist	.738	Nash	36.5	Zuccarello	50.0	Zibanejad	43.8
Colorado	Varlamov	.752	Duchene	37.5	MacKinnon	50.0	Landeskog	33.3
Anaheim	Gibson	.727	Perry	33.0	Getzlaf	36.2	Silfverberg	52.8
Detroit	Mrazek	.762	Nielsen	48.9	Zetterberg	25.8	Nyquist	35.5
Dallas	*Bishop*	.694	Spezza	36.4	Seguin	48.9	*Radulov*	45.0
Chicago	Crawford	.729	Toews	48.3	Kane	40.0	Anisimov	30.4
Florida	Luongo	.680	Barkov	51.7	*Vrbata*	43.3	Bjugstad	34.5
Washington	Holtby	.659	Oshie	54.9	Backstrom	34.4	Kuznetsov	42.9
NY Islanders	Greiss	.754	*Eberle*	38.5	Ladd	36.7	Tavares	27.8
St. Louis	Allen	.770	Steen	42.9	Tarasenko	34.4	Berglund	20.0
Vegas	*Fleury*	.740	*Neal*	35.4	*Shipachyov*	TBD	*Perron*	34.7
Columbus	Bobrovsky	.724	Atkinson	35.5	Johnson	28.9	*Panarin*	71.4
Nashville	Rinne	.722	*Bonino*	37.5	Ribeiro	34.9	Johansen	32.4
Arizona	Domingue	.857	Duclair	42.9	*Stepan*	33.3	Perlini	66.7
Ottawa	Anderson	.677	Turris	38.2	Ryan	34.5	Burrows	37.2
Vancouver	Markstrom	.737	*Gagner*	31.9	Eriksson	22.7	Horvat	40.0
Minnesota	Dubnyk	.645	Koivu	41.8	Parise	40.4	*Ennis*	34.9
Pittsburgh	Murray	.615	Crosby	41.4	Letang	37.1	Malkin	35.6
Buffalo	Lehner	.529	*Pominville*	41.2	Moulson	39.0	*Josefson*	52.4
Los Angeles	Quick	.694	Kopitar	37.9	Brown	30.2	*Cammalleri*	29.1
Boston	Rask	.727	Bergeron	29.4	Krejci	29.2	Marchand	25.9
Edmonton	Talbot	.589	Draisaitl	57.1	Letestu	41.7	*Jokinen*	39.1
Tampa Bay	Vasilevskiy	.826	Callahan	31.3	Kucherov	30.4	Stamkos	21.6

42 Acknowledgement: Raw shootout data came from *NHL.com* http://www.nhl.com.

Winnipeg	*Mason*	.655	Wheeler	34.9	Little	29.4	Laine	75.0
Montreal	Price	.714	*Hemsky*	33.3	Galchenyuk	25.0	Pacioretty	26.7
Philadelphia	*Elliott*	.675	Giroux	32.9	Voracek	33.3	Simmonds	30.4
Calgary	*Smith*	.633	Monahan	36.0	Versteeg	32.1	Gaudreau	21.4
Carolina	Ward	.628	Stempniak	32.7	Skinner	17.1	Aho	40.0
Toronto	Andersen	.606	Bozak	36.8	van Riemsdyk	28.6	Kadri	20.0
New Jersey	Schneider	.613	Zajac	22.2	Hall	27.8	Henrique	12.5

I'm quite comfortable with the results of high-level method including teams like San Jose, the NY Rangers, and Anaheim at the top of the list with Colorado. Each team has a solid goalie, and more than the three excellent shooter options listed in the preceding table.

I also have a fair deal of comfort that teams like Toronto, Calgary, and New Jersey were all included at the bottom with Philadelphia. They all have below-average goaltending, and only three above-average shooters between them.

As for Vegas, they have probably the third best shootout goalie in Marc-Andre Fleury, two solid shooters in James Neal and David Perron, but not a lot of shooting depth beyond that. That should still be enough to pick up a few extra points this season.

Goaltending

Of these various categories, goaltending can have a disproportionately significant impact on a team's season, but it can also be very hard to predict over a single season.

Furthermore, goaltending is one area where the NHL has achieved a great deal of parity, relative to previous seasons. Later in this book, we have devoted an entire chapter to an exploration of all the different techniques that are used to help make distinctions between one team's goaltending and another's, but for now we'll start with the simple, high-level picture that can be crafted by looking at a three-year average of the even-strength save percentage of every team's goaltending tandem, in a 3-to-1 ratio between the starter and the backup (assuming their save percentage is based on a reasonable number of games). Once again, those who have changed teams are *italicized*.

Even-Strength Save Percentages, 2014–15 to 2016–17[43]

Team	Starter	ESSV%	Backup	ESSV%	3:1 Avg
Montreal	Price	.938	Montoya	.914	.932
Washington	Holtby	.931	Grubauer	.929	.931
Pittsburgh	Murray	.933	*Niemi*	.918	.929
Florida	Luongo	.929	Reimer	.928	.929
Arizona	*Raanta*	.931	Domingue	.922	.929
Winnipeg	*Mason*	.930	Hellebuyck	.924	.929
Minnesota	Dubnyk	.931	*Svedberg*/Stalock	.917	.928
Columbus	Bobrovsky	.928	Korpisalo	.924	.927

43 Acknowledgement: Raw goaltending data from the *NHL*, http://www.nhl.com.

New Jersey	Schneider	.928	Kinkaid	.923	.927
Ottawa	Anderson	.931	Condon	.912	.926
NY Rangers	Lundqvist	.928	*Pavelec*	.920	.926
Carolina	*Darling*	.929	Ward	.913	.925
Nashville	Rinne	.925	Saros	.923	.925
Philadelphia	*Elliott*	.925	Neuvirth	.922	.924
Anaheim	Gibson	.925	*Miller*	.921	.924
Vegas	*Fleury*	.924	*Pickard*	.922	.924
Los Angeles	Quick	.927	*Kuemper*	.911	.923
NY Islanders	Greiss	.923	Halak	.920	.922
Chicago	Crawford	.931	*Forsberg/Berube*	.895	.922
Edmonton	Talbot	.925	Brossoit	.913	.922
Tampa Bay	Vasilevskiy	.921	Budaj	.923	.922
Buffalo	Lehner	.922	*Johnson*	.919	.921
Toronto	Andersen	.923	McElhinney	.914	.921
Dallas	*Bishop*	.923	Lehtonen	.913	.921
San Jose	Jones	.920	Dell	.946	.920
Detroit	Howard	.919	Mrazek	.922	.920
St. Louis	Allen	.921	Hutton	.915	.920
Boston	Rask	.925	Khudobin	.902	.919
Calgary	*Smith*	.921	*Lack*	.914	.919
Vancouver	Markstrom	.918	*Nilsson*	.923	.919
Colorado	Varlamov	.917	*Bernier*	.918	.917

It comes as more than a shock to see the Arizona Coyotes near the top of the list with Montreal, Washington, and Pittsburgh, and ahead of the New York Rangers and Columbus Blue Jackets.

On one hand, Antti Raanta's numbers do suggest that he has been the league's best backup, and most fans don't realize how solid Louis Domingue's stats have been, once the impact of Arizona's weak special teams are removed. On the other hand, these goalies have played 94 and 77 games respectively, and it's unlikely that they will actually sustain these numbers over the long run. So, they may not be at the elite level, but the Coyotes do have the potential for great goaltending.

There is some controversy at the other end of the spectrum, where teams with excellent starters, like Tuukka Rask, are being ranked below teams without one, like Detroit. In most cases, this is a consequence of their backups, Anton Khudobin in Boston's case. While it's important to have a quality backup, this low ranking is probably overly pessimistic. That's why the checklist isn't filled out blindly, but carefully based on a number of factors, and a lot of experience with the underlying stats.

As for Vegas, they'll be just fine. Everybody knows that Marc-Andre Fleury is a capable starter, and Calvin Pickard happens to be an above-average backup. It must sting the established teams that the Golden Knights will be ahead of half the league in year one.

Bear in mind that there are a number of useful metrics that can expand on this simplistic view, and help adjust for all the factors that can influence save percentage (which are broken down in full detail in *Stat Shot*[44]), or that can simply provide a completely different perspective. Later in this book, there's a chapter dedicated to the exploration of all the different statistics introduced throughout the *Hockey Abstract* series, and elsewhere in the community.

Penalty Kill

Despite an inexperienced blue line, an absence of big names up front, and finishing outside the playoffs for the seventh straight season, the Carolina Hurricanes are believed to be one of the league's best at killing penalties.

As the Hurricanes have ably demonstrated, how well a team performs shorthanded isn't necessarily related to how well it plays at even strength. That's because killing penalties isn't like playing regular hockey down a player; it is a completely different game, with completely different strategies. Some otherwise bad teams will have the tools to excel at it, while otherwise great teams will not.

Predicting how well teams will kill penalties isn't easy to do. Each season, a team's penalty killing percentage can bounce up and down for no obvious reason. For example, Dallas finished dead last with a penalty killing percentage of 73.9% last season, which was well behind Colorado, who were in 29th with 76.6%. But, the Stars ranked 10th in 2015–16 with 82.3%, with virtually the exact same roster.

Maybe you have read or heard some good explanations about what happened in Dallas, because fans and pundits can be very good at explaining the results after the fact. Unfortunately, those insights never seem to be useful in predicting what will happen in the future.

The truth is that penalty-killing percentages jump up and down because of Alan Ryder's third law of hockey analytics: goals are random events[45]. When an average of just 48 power-play goals are allowed per team over an 82-game schedule, it is very easy for a few bad bounces to completely disguise each team's true abilities.

That's why we prefer to stay focused on far more predictable shot-based data. In the long run, goal-based data will start to conform to the shot-based data anyway, depending on the level of goaltending the team receives. Admittedly, the goaltending in Dallas has been quite poor, which is why their fortunes could reverse with the arrival of Ben Bishop, whose career shorthanded save percentage of .897 ranks fourth among the 64 active goalies to have played at least 50 games[46].

As a high-level starting point, the following table is sorted by a three-year weighted average of

44 Rob Vollman, "Who is the best puck stopper?", *Stat Shot,* September 2016, pgs 169-227.
45 Alan Ryder, "The Ten Laws of Hockey Analytics", *Hockey Analytics*, January, 2008, Web, http://hockeyanalytics.com/2008/01/the-ten-laws-of-hockey-analytics/.
46 Acknowledgement: Shorthanded save percentage data came from the *NHL* http://stats.nhl.com.

how many shot attempts a team has allowed over 60 minutes of shorthanded play. From there, each individual team analysis can be completed by digging deeper into specific coaches, players, strategies, and situations involved.

Attempted Shots Allowed per 60 Minutes on the Penalty Kill[47]

Team	2014–15	2015–16	2016–17	Weighted Average
Carolina	86.8	80.6	80.4	81.4
Florida	95.9	93.2	86.5	89.8
Washington	105.5	99.4	83.0	90.9
Boston	96.5	94.4	89.1	91.7
St. Louis	89.7	95.7	90.3	91.8
Los Angeles	94.9	96.8	88.5	91.8
NY Rangers	84.4	98.6	92.2	92.9
Montreal	94.5	94.7	92.3	93.3
Nashville	92.6	89.8	97.7	94.7
Philadelphia	97.2	98.3	92.3	94.7
Calgary	93.4	102.8	91.7	95.1
New Jersey	96.2	90.8	98.5	96.0
Anaheim	92.6	94.1	98.9	96.6
Vancouver	90.6	97.0	99.3	97.4
Minnesota	90.7	97.4	99.8	97.8
Colorado	101.6	105.2	94.1	98.3
Columbus	98.4	99.2	98.1	98.5
Dallas	97.6	99.4	102.3	100.8
Pittsburgh	104.7	96.4	102.1	100.8
Tampa Bay	105.9	101.5	99.8	101.2
Toronto	104.2	85.5	109.4	101.8
Ottawa	96.2	102.5	104.1	102.5
Detroit	99.5	100.5	104.7	102.8
San Jose	101.9	99.8	105.5	103.4
Edmonton	95.0	102.8	106.5	103.8
Winnipeg	94.7	105.7	105.6	104.1
NY Islanders	101.5	97.3	108.9	104.5
Arizona	118.4	96.1	110.2	107.3
Chicago	99.0	107.0	111.7	108.5
Buffalo	109.6	100.6	113.7	109.4

As we can see, the number of shot attempts teams allow per 60 minutes is somewhat consistent from season-to-season, relative to goal-based data. Depending on how it is measured, scoring chances tend to line up closer to the shot-based data, too.

Even with the shot-based data, those with unexpected results should be examined closely. For example, last year we were caught off guard by the Toronto Maple Leafs, who turned around completely under new coach Mike Babcock. That's something of an unexpected

47 Acknowledgement: Penalty killing data came from *Hockey Analysis* http://stats.hockeyanalysis.com.

surprise, given that Detroit's performance was merely average when he coached there. Well, it turned out to be a very temporary boost, because they went right back down to normal last year. This year, the same fate could befall the Washington Capitals.

To me, the biggest surprise was the Florida Panthers, who rank second behind the Hurricanes in the preceding table. After they overhauled their blue line last summer, they only had one or two penalty-killing defencemen, Jason Demers and secondary option Alex Petrovic. Last season, they employed Mark Pysyk, rookie Michael Matheson, and the normally sheltered Keith Yandle alongside Demers, and ranked second in the NHL with a 85.3% penalty killing percentage. Even with an understanding of how unpredictable penalty killing can be, I was still taken aback by the team's unexpected success.

We have frequently been asked to include a team's penalty-killing percentage in this table, and not to leave readers with the false impression that goal-based data is entirely useless. We have resisted that suggestion because goal-based data is already *all* that we ever see. We have all seen it, we all know it, and its bias has already entrenched itself in our minds, and in the narratives of the mainstream. It doesn't need to be repeated here. It's more valuable to have this fresh, and separate perspective than it would be to supplement it with what we already know, and what could be clouding our judgment in a very challenging aspect of team evaluation.

Power Play

Having struggled our way through penalty killing, we have arrived to the simpler world of the power play. Unlike when shorthanded, teams tend to use their best players with the man advantage, and their contributions are clearly recorded in terms of goals and assists.

We can assemble a table with the same three-year weighted average of each team's shot attempts per 60 minutes, and produce results that are similar to what we would get with a subjective poll of the league's best power plays. Pittsburgh might be swapped with Los Angeles, but otherwise this is a ranking that most fans and pundits would agree upon.

Attempted Shots per 60 Minutes on the Power Play[48]

Team	2014–15	2015–16	2016–17	Weighted Average
Boston	113.6	118.3	108.3	111.9
Los Angeles	99.7	114.5	111.4	110.6
Anaheim	103.4	111.6	111.9	110.6
Philadelphia	108.8	107.4	112.4	110.5
Washington	115.4	109.2	108.2	109.5
Toronto	90.5	114.8	106.1	106.4
San Jose	115.2	102.0	105.4	105.8
Edmonton	99.5	95.3	107.7	103.0
Dallas	94.9	105.6	102.6	102.4

48 Acknowledgement: Power play data came from *Hockey Analysis* http://stats.hockeyanalysis.com.

NY Rangers	101.1	104.1	99.3	100.9
Carolina	97.8	102.9	99.7	100.3
Pittsburgh	98.8	96.4	101.9	99.9
Buffalo	79.7	97.4	105.2	99.3
Calgary	99.9	94.0	100.7	98.7
Florida	89.4	90.8	104.6	98.5
Minnesota	97.0	98.4	98.6	98.3
Winnipeg	101.3	90.0	97.5	95.9
NY Islanders	94.1	93.2	97.6	95.8
Ottawa	105.0	89.4	95.5	95.1
Nashville	93.0	89.9	95.2	93.4
Tampa Bay	78.7	89.1	98.3	92.9
Detroit	99.1	98.0	87.0	91.9
Arizona	109.3	97.7	84.2	91.6
Chicago	102.0	85.6	91.0	91.0
St. Louis	101.2	82.5	90.7	89.9
Vancouver	95.4	90.3	86.3	88.7
Columbus	93.1	90.6	86.2	88.4
Montreal	96.2	93.8	81.4	87.1
Colorado	88.7	89.4	84.4	86.4
New Jersey	76.9	83.3	87.1	84.6

Unlike with penalty killing, when a team jumps up in the power play rankings, it's a little bit easier to figure out if the improvement will be lasting. For instance, Toronto also improved on the power play in 2015–16, and the arrival of Auston Matthews made it safe to predict that most of that improvement would persist in to 2016–17. Likewise, Edmonton's huge vault forward with the development Connor McDavid and Leon Draisaitl has every chance to continue in 2017–18.

A lot of the more detailed analysis will be saved for Matt Cane's chapter on the power play, but for our purposes, rating a team's power play is statistically different from penalty killing in only three regards: it has a slightly lower correlation to winning percentage, it's a bit easier to identify the impact of individual players, and goal-based data is a little more useful.

Scoring Line

The line everybody already knows best is the team's top scoring line. Statistically, this is the line that is called upon for offensive zone faceoffs, and when trailing late in the game. In traditional terms, this is the line with the team's leading scorers and highest-paid players, and those who get most of the press. You definitely know which line this is for your local team, and have a pretty good idea for the other 30 teams, as well.

Sometimes it's not immediately obvious which one is the scoring line in every case, so let's use the Stanley Cup championship Pittsburgh Penguins as an example. Sidney Crosby's line had a combined cap hit of around $10.3 million, while Evgeni Malkin's was usually $20.3

million[49]. Crosby started 62.4% of his shifts in the offensive zone, Malkin started 70.4%[50]. So, even though Crosby outscored Malkin 64-49 at even strength, Malkin's line should be classified as the scoring line (for purposes of our analysis).

That's where the familiar territory ends, because the top lines are evaluated a little differently in these pages, and it may not always line up with mainstream thinking. For example, a player's reputation means very little in our analysis, including the immeasurable ability to raise his game in clutch situations. Since the power play is being evaluated separately, only even-strength data is considered, and it is assessed on a per-minute basis, to equalize the playing field with regards to opportunity. From there, fine-grain analysis is possible by looking at each player's ability to shoot, pass, draw penalties, win faceoffs, and so on. Yes, each line's ability to play defensively and to drive possession is also considered, but as a secondary concern to their primary responsibility, which is to score.

Shutdown Line

Identifying and evaluating defensive play with statistics is a little bit more challenging, but today's metrics do make it possible to accurately identify the league's best and worst shutdown lines, at a high level.

Simply put, each team's top shutdown line is that which is composed of the forwards who are matched up against the top scoring lines, as defined in the preceding section. Unlike strictly defensive lines, they play in both the offensive and the defensive zones, and more often whenever the team is protecting a late lead. This sort of information can be determined with player usage charts (explained in the next section), and with Micah Blake McCurdy's new score state deployment charts[51], both of which use data that is published in NHL play-by-play files and/or shift charts.

Evaluating such players can be a little bit trickier than those whose sole responsibility is scoring, but their bottom line is to suppress scoring in terms of shot attempts, scoring chances, and goals. There is also some fine-grain analysis here, like winning faceoffs and staying disciplined, but ultimately it doesn't really matter if a line's success is achieved by throwing hits, with solid positional play, or with pure speed.

As demonstrated in Selke Trophy voting every year, it's also important for a shutdown line to pose a possession-driving and scoring threat of its own. In fact, the most effective way to defend is to control the play and/or move the action to the offensive zone.

In fairness, some of the more cap-strapped teams don't really have a clear scoring or shutdown line, because they spread the responsibilities out over several lines, or may have a particularly effective checking line. These teams may not be as dangerous when chasing a late lead, and they may be more vulnerable when protecting one, but they also may not find

49 Acknowledgement: Cap data came from *NHL Numbers* http://www.nhlnumbers.com.
50 Acknowledgement: Zone Start data came from the *NHL* http://stats.nhl.com.
51 Score state deployment charts are available at http://www.hockeyviz.com.

themselves in such positions as often, if the rest of the lineup is well-constructed.

It's also not unusual for teams to blend these top two lines together, or even to spread them out over three lines. In these cases, the evaluation of one line might be higher than expected, while the other is a little bit lower, but ultimately it should average out with an accurate evaluation of the team's forward strength on the whole.

Forward Depth

Among the best teams, the top lines will often cancel themselves out, and games will be decided by the secondary lines. Or, in the case of the weaker teams, strong performances from the depth lines are required for them to have any chance to compete with the league's best teams.

That's why every team can achieve great value with a versatile, deep, and cost-effective collection of players who can provide difference-making secondary scoring, kill time with low-event hockey when the top six is resting, and be able to step up into the top six whenever injuries or other circumstances require it.

Finding these types of undervalued role players is where hockey analytics can really shine. Anyone can describe the strengths and weaknesses of superstars like Crosby or McDavid, but the statistical perspective is invaluable at classifying and rating the unheralded secondary players. For specific examples of all the different qualities and how they're measured, check out chapter nine in the original *Hockey Abstract*, "Who is the Most Undervalued Player?[52]"

Top Pairing and Second Pairing

In this year's Stanley Cup Playoffs, the Nashville Predators served as the latest example of the value of having a highly effective top-four. P.K. Subban, Ryan Ellis, Roman Josi, and Mattias Ekholm boosted an otherwise decent team to near-championship status. It's the same situation that was previously observed with the Tampa Bay Lightning, and which will soon be noted with the Carolina Hurricanes.

Some teams are lucky enough to have a single superstar around whom to build its blue line, like the classic historic examples of Nicklas Lidstrom, Chris Pronger, and Scott Niedermayer. This model works perfectly if you have the right player, if he stays healthy, and if he has the right complementary players around him. The best modern-day example would be 2015–16 Norris Trophy winner and three-time finalist, Drew Doughty of the Los Angeles Kings.

In pursuit of this single-star strategy, some teams build their blue line around the wrong player. For example, Dion Phaneuf was obviously not suitable for that role in Toronto. However, the Maple Leafs aren't the only team that has risked big money in the quest for one

52 Rob Vollman, "Who is the Most Undervalued Player?", *Hockey Abstract,* 2013, pgs 85-95.

of the few players around whom a blue line can legitimately be built.

That's why the safest model is to build a well-balanced blue line like Nashville's, with a mix of versatile and often cost-effective two-way players. While solid defencemen are admittedly hard to acquire, the keen front office can usually draft, sign, or trade for such players over time. This is a low-risk strategy, because no single injury or disappointing season will derail it, because there is a lot of upside if one of these secondary players break out, and because it usually requires a little bit less cap space overall.

Identifying a team's top four usually isn't that difficult, because there's not a lot of turnover from season to season. Of the 129 defencemen that could be classified as top-four options in 2016–17 based on ice-time and how often they face top-six opponents[53], 103 would be so classified in 2015–16, too. Of the 26 new members of the top four, 16 were previously third-pairing options, and 10 were rookies.

Some of the exceptions proved to be very significant, like rookies Zach Werenski in Columbus, Nikita Zaitsev in Toronto, and Ivan Provorov in Philadelphia, but for the most part we saw them all coming. In most of the few remaining cases, the new top-four opportunity was the result of an unexpected injury or transaction, and the defenceman didn't have a significant impact on the standings.

The top four itself may be reasonably easy to project, but it can be difficult to predict exactly how each team will organize it. That's why teams are ranked by whichever deployment results in the highest overall score.

As to how individual defencemen and pairings are evaluated, this is where shot-based metrics tend to be favoured over goal-based metrics, and with good reason.

As explained in a bit more detail in the team-building chapter in *Stat Shot*[54], defencemen tend to have a more limited impact on scoring than forwards. Defensively, a great goalie can make a mediocre blue line look good, and a weak goalie can make solid defencemen look terrible. Offensively, defencemen have virtually no control over whether the forwards score on 5% of their shots, or 10%. All that defencemen can do is help achieve control of the puck, move it up the ice, and help gain and keep the zone. Their performance in those areas can't really be measured in goals, assists, and plus/minus, but it can be estimated with a variety shot-based metrics, as Tom explained in more detail in *Stat Shot*[55].

Defensive Depth

It's surprising that teams play with 12 forwards and six defencemen. A combination of one or two mid-game injuries and penalties can deplete a team's blue line, and the lack of

53 Technically there should only be 120 top-four defencemen, but with a few injuries, the number swells by 9.
54 Rob Vollman, "What's the best way to build a team?", *Stat Shot*, September 2016, pgs 12-74.
55 Tom Awad, "Everything you ever wanted to know about shot-based metrics (but were afraid to ask)", *Stat Shot*, September 2016, pgs 228-281.

defencemen is intended to make room for what – an extra forward who plays six or seven minutes a game, and only in the first two periods?

Until the basic strategy changes, defensive depth will continue to be critical, even for teams that essentially shorten their bench to the top four late in the game.

In this category, the key factors are to have a strong third pairing, with players that are capable of stepping up into a top-four role when it becomes necessary. Teams also need to have plenty of additional players in order to absorb inevitable injuries, and to provide the versatility required for the coach to inject size, defensive play, or some secondary scoring, whenever it is required.

The final wrinkle is how to classify players like Shayne Gostisbehere and Justin Schultz. Subjectively, they're obviously not considered to be depth defencemen, but statistically they don't rank in their team's top four in minutes played, and are rarely used against top opponents, or in the defensive zone. In analytics circles, this used to be referred to as the Keith Yandle role, but he hasn't been used that way since he was signed in Florida.

An element of personal judgment is required in these cases, but it can also help explain cases where the defensive depth is scored higher than expected, and the top four a little bit lower.

Coaching

The Pittsburgh Penguins switched coaches mid-season from Mike Johnston to Mike Sullivan, finished strong, and won the Stanley Cup in back-to-back seasons. That was actually the third time in eight seasons that the Stanley Cup winner made an in-season coaching change.

What's more, Pittsburgh's Stanley Cup Final opponent that first season was the San Jose Sharks, who had switched from long-time coach Todd McLellan to Peter DeBoer the previous summer, climbed back into the playoffs, and came within a few goals of winning their first-ever Stanley Cup.

Despite the seemingly obvious impact of coaching changes, nobody really seems to include coaching as one of the key factors in team evaluation. It is the most undervalued and understudied aspect of team analysis this time of year.

In fairness, it can be challenging to objectively measure the performance of a coaching staff, which is why it is this low on the checklist – but that doesn't mean that we shouldn't try. There are obviously some staffs around the league that have far more experience and prior success than others, and it's worth the effort to identify them.

That's the reasoning behind our coaching metric, which was developed for *Hockey Prospectus* way back in 2009[56]. Simply put, the concept is to compare how well a team was

---

56 Rob Vollman, "Howe and Why: Coaches", *Hockey Prospectus,* October 26, 2009, Web,
    http://www.hockeyprospectus.com/puck/article.php?articleid=328.

expected to perform from their actual position in the standings, and over enough time a reasonably accurate picture of each coach's impact can be formed.

In this case, expectations are set by taking the previous season's points, and regressing them towards the league average by the historical average of 35%. That means that good teams need to stay good, bad teams need to improve by more than they would have with any other coach, and average teams just need to get better.

Applying it league-wide, and against the career NHL totals of everyone who has served as a head coach at any point in the past five seasons, here's the updated leader board. The best (or luckiest) coaches can regularly add an average of five or six points above expectations (PAX) to the standings, and an aberration like Bruce Boudreau adds almost 10 per season.

Active NHL Coaches for 2017–18, All-Time[57]

Team	Coach	GC	PTS	PAX	PAX/82
Minnesota	Bruce Boudreau	763	1004	91.5	9.8
NY Islanders	Doug Weight	40	52	4.7	9.6
	Dan Bylsma	565	695	46.4	6.7
Tampa Bay	Jon Cooper	344	413	24.7	5.9
Dallas	Ken Hitchcock	1454	1761	93.1	5.2
Edmonton	Todd McLellan	704	861	40.3	4.7
Chicago	Joel Quenneville	1539	1903	86.4	4.6
	Patrick Roy	246	284	13.3	4.4
Montreal	Claude Julien	1021	1236	55.4	4.4
Vegas	Gerard Gallant	327	339	17.0	4.3
Nashville	Peter Laviolette	1005	1160	51.0	4.2
Toronto	Mike Babcock	1114	1356	56.8	4.2
	Michel Therrien	814	926	37.6	3.8
Washington	Barry Trotz	1442	1613	66.3	3.8
NY Rangers	Alain Vigneault	1134	1352	47.6	3.4
	Darryl Sutter	1285	1435	49.6	3.2
Ottawa	Guy Boucher	278	312	7.9	2.3
	Paul MacLean	239	263	5.5	1.9
Pittsburgh	Mike Sullivan	300	360	6.9	1.9
	Bob Hartley	944	1046	21.4	1.9
Anaheim	Randy Carlyle	786	913	16.9	1.8
Philadelphia	Dave Hakstol	164	184	2.9	1.5
St. Louis	Mike Yeo	381	436	4.9	1.1
Calgary	Glen Gulutzan	212	231	2.5	1.0
Vegas-AHL	Craig Berube	161	178	1.6	.8
Columbus	John Tortorella	1093	1191	8.4	.6
Calgary-Asst	Dave Cameron	137	157	0.8	.5
NYR-Asst	Lindy Ruff	1493	1675	4.8	.3
Boston	Bruce Cassidy	137	147	0.3	.2
Florida-Asst	Jack Capuano	483	518	-0.2	.0

57 Acknowledgement: Raw coaching data for my calculations from *Hockey Reference*, http://www.hockey-reference.com.

Team	Coach				
	Dave Tippett	1114	1254	-4.1	-.3
San Jose	Peter DeBoer	658	708	-6.2	-.8
	Adam Oates	130	147	-2.1	-1.3
Tampa Bay-Asst	Todd Richards	424	445	-10.6	-2.0
Montreal-Asst	Kirk Muller	187	187	-5.0	-2.2
Winnipeg	Paul Maurice	1365	1392	-38.7	-2.3
Boston-Asst	Joe Sacco	294	290	-9.1	-2.5
Carolina	Bill Peters	246	244	-8.1	-2.7
	Ralph Krueger	48	45	-1.9	-3.3
WHL	Mike Johnston	110	131	-4.6	-3.4
New Jersey-Org	Claude Noel	201	204	-8.4	-3.4
Chicago-Asst	Kevin Dineen	146	140	-7.4	-4.2
Detroit-Asst	John Torchetti	66	66	-3.7	-4.6
	Ted Nolan	471	431	-34.3	-6.0
Detroit-AHL	Todd Nelson	51	43	-4.0	-6.4
	Willie Desjardins	246	245	-19.4	-6.5
New Jersey	John Hynes	164	154	-15.4	-7.7
Detroit	Jeff Blashill	164	172	-17.5	-8.8
Los Angeles	Scott Gordon	181	151	-21.3	-9.7
	Ron Rolston	51	44	-10.8	-17.3
New Jersey-Org	Peter Horachek	108	79	-23.3	-17.7
Anaheim-AHL	Dallas Eakins	113	86	-24.6	-17.8
Florida-Org	Tom Rowe	61	58	-15.6	-21.0
Colorado	Jared Bednar	82	48	-37.3	-37.3

As always, there are a few teams that are starting the season with coaches who have no NHL experience, like Phil Housley of the Buffalo Sabres, Bob Boughner of the Florida Panthers, and Travis Green of the Vancouver Canucks. There are also several teams with coaches who have very limited NHL experience, like Boston's Bruce Cassidy, Colorado's Jared Bednar, and NY Islanders Doug Weight.

In these and other cases, the analysis includes a weighted average of the coach's entire history in other leagues, like the AHL, U.S. College, and the Canadian major juniors.

Current NHL Coaches, 2017–18[58]

Coach	Team	NHL GC	NHL PAX	Other GC	Other PAX	PAX 82
Doug Weight	NY Islanders	40	4.7	0	0.0	9.6
Bruce Boudreau	Minnesota	763	91.5	865	75.4	7.6
Jon Cooper	Tampa Bay	344	24.7	221	47.4	6.6
Gerard Gallant	Vegas	327	17.0	204	58.3	6.0
Ken Hitchcock	Dallas	1454	93.1	432	65.6	5.4
Joel Quenneville	Chicago	1539	86.4	80	1.4	4.5
Peter Laviolette	Nashville	1005	51.0	230	32.0	4.3
Todd McLellan	Edmonton	704	40.3	752	52.5	4.1

58 Acknowledgement: Raw coaching data for my calculations from *Hockey Reference*, http://www.hockey-reference.com.

Claude Julien	Boston	1021	55.4	487	23.6	4.0
Mike Babcock	Toronto	1114	56.8	736	35.2	3.6
Barry Trotz	Washington	1442	66.3	400	23.8	3.6
Mike Sullivan	Pittsburgh	300	6.9	94	29.7	3.4
Dave Hakstol	Philadelphia	164	2.9	459	43.2	2.9
Travis Green	Vancouver	0	0.0	350	23.2	2.7
Alain Vigneault	NY Rangers	1134	47.6	741	4.2	2.7
Guy Boucher	Ottawa	278	7.9	430	27.3	2.4
Glen Gulutzan	Calgary	212	2.5	593	44.3	2.2
Randy Carlyle	Anaheim	786	16.9	80	13.7	2.0
Peter DeBoer	San Jose	658	-6.2	878	117.0	1.7
Mike Yeo	St. Louis	381	4.9	80	14.9	1.7
Bruce Cassidy	Boston	137	0.3	730	24.5	1.0
John Tortorella	Columbus	1093	8.4	160	8.3	0.7
Bob Boughner	Florida	0	0.0	544	9.3	0.7
Scott Gordon	Los Angeles	181	-21.3	700	49.2	0.3
Phil Housley	Buffalo	0	0.0	0	0.0	0.0
Bill Peters	Carolina	246	-8.1	456	24.9	-0.3
John Hynes	New Jersey	164	-15.4	384	33.7	-1.6
Paul Maurice	Winnipeg	1365	-38.7	212	21.2	-1.9
Jeff Blashill	Detroit	164	-17.5	228	28.2	-3.1
Rick Tocchet	Arizona	148	-5.9	0	0.0	-3.3
Jared Bednar	Colorado	82	-37.3	451	21.4	-8.5

From this perspective, it's a little bit easier to identify the third of the league that are taking risks, and the third that has a bit of an advantage. In my latest work, this coaching analysis also includes the experience and prior success of the entire staff, including the impact of goalie coaches, like Stephane Waite in Montreal, or Martin Brodeur in St. Louis.

In time, more involved coaching metrics will be developed that can produce a far more accurate assessment of each staff. Until then, this simple, high-level approach should be enough to make distinctions between teams with high experienced and accomplished coaching staffs, and those who are taking a little more risk.

Prospects

If you go back and look at the blown projections every year, teams usually defy the pundits because of some combination of hot goaltending, great coaching, or the sudden explosion of young talent. Those are the three key factors to keep in mind at this time of year, so there needs to be a way to account for each team's organizational strength.

For example, first-year players like Auston Matthews, Mitch Marner, William Nylander, Nikita Zaitsev, Zach Hyman, and Connor Brown obviously had a massive combined impact on Toronto's triumphant return to the Stanley Cup playoffs last season. Some of that was expected, and factored into the team's projection, but there was still an additional, unanticipated impact from these prospects.

Based on Tom's GVT statistic, rookies contribute about 300 extra goals scored or prevented, which works out to a combined shift of about 100 points in the standings every year.

Most importantly, these points are not evenly divided among the 30 teams. For most teams, rookies aren't that big a factor in the standings. They may have one or two solid regulars, or a backup goalie, or maybe a handful of depth players, but nothing that really moves the needle in the standings. However, there are always about six teams whose organizational strength helps them move up the standings by six to 10 points.

It's not always easy to predict which teams it will be. Traditional analysis and scouting is helpful, along with metrics like NHL translation factors[59] and the Projectinator[60], but it's not an exact science. Among those teams whose rookies are expected to make significant contributions, half of them usually do, like last year's Maple Leafs and Blue Jackets. However, there are usually a couple of teams whose rookies develop faster than expected, like perhaps those in Pittsburgh last year.

To provide at least some data in this final section, I like to compile how each team's AHL affiliate performed last season, along with the most recent organizational rankings by sites like *The Score*[61], *ESPN*[62], *the Hockey Writers*[63], and *Last Word on Sports*[64]. However, going to print August 1 means using year-old rankings. Since most of their rookies broke out last season, I doubt that Toronto still tops the list. To supplement this perspective, we have added a chapter after the team analysis that takes a closer look at notable rookies.

Subjective Assessments of Organizational Strength, 2017–18

Team	AHL	The Score	ESPN	Hockey Writers	Last Word	Total
Toronto	13	1	1	3	1	19
Arizona	23	2	2	2	2	31
Columbus	16	5	4	4	4	33
Winnipeg	25	3	3	1	3	35
Philadelphia	5	15	6	5	5	36
Carolina	15	4	5	6	6	36
NY Islanders	11	6	7	7	7	38
Calgary	14	12	9	8	11	54
Boston	8	8	12	10	24	62

59 Rob Vollman, "Translating data from other leagues", *Hockey Abstract,* 2013, pgs 159-182.
60 Iain Fyffe, "What do a player's junior numbers tell us?", *Stat Shot,* September 2016, pgs 75-120.
61 Craig Hagerman, "Ranking the 30 NHL farm systems", *The Score,* August 1, 2016, Web, https://www.thescore.com/news/1064617.
62 Corey Pronman, "Ranking every NHL team by prospect pipeline", *ESPN,* August 29, 2016, Web, http://www.espn.com/nhl/insider/story/_/id/17327996/nhl-prospect-pipeline-rankings-ahead-2016–17-season-led-toronto-maple-leafs.
63 Brett Slawson, "The NHL's Best Farm Systems: A 1-30 Ranking", *The Hockey Writers,* August 3, 2016, Web, http://thehockeywriters.com/nhl-prospect-pools-the-complete-ranking/.
64 Ben Kerr, "NHL Organizational Prospect Pool Rankings (Top 10)", *Last Word on Sports,* September 16, 2016, Web, http://lastwordonsports.com/2016/09/16/nhl-organizational-prospect-pool-rankings-top-10/.

Anaheim	3	16	22	16	8	65
Montreal	18	9	15	11	13	66
Detroit	6	10	18	21	17	72
Edmonton	20	7	8	19	20	74
Nashville	9	23	10	14	19	75
New Jersey	17	11	19	9	21	77
St. Louis	4	14	23	23	14	78
Vancouver	21	18	13	17	10	79
Tampa Bay	12	21	14	18	18	83
San Jose	2	13	24	27	22	88
Buffalo	26	17	11	12	23	89
Washington	7	24	26	22	15	94
Dallas	24	22	25	13	12	96
Ottawa	29	29	16	15	16	105
Pittsburgh	1	26	27	26	26	106
Colorado	28	28	21	25	9	111
Minnesota	19	27	17	28	25	116
Chicago	27	19	20	24	29	119
Florida	22	20	30	20	28	120
Los Angeles	10	30	29	30	30	129
NY Rangers	30	25	28	29	27	139

Other Categories

There are other possible categories for the checklist, but the line had to be drawn somewhere. Of the remaining possibilities, the categories were either too difficult to measure, or just weren't important enough to the final results. So, categories like faceoffs and discipline were rolled into the other sections.

The category that just missed the cut-off is an evaluation of the front office. After all, the teams that make the right moves throughout the season could get boosted in the standings to an extent that can't be measured today.

However, it is very difficult to evaluate the quality of each team's front office. And, even if we could, a skilled front office would likely have already built a competitive roster before the season even began, and it would therefore be reflected in all the other categories.

For what it's worth, I've put together the following table based on an equal combination of three perspectives:
- The subjective opinion of Justin Cuthbert of *the Score*[65],
- An impressively careful analysis conducted by Carolyn Wilke and Chris Watkins of *Hockey Graphs*[66], and

65 Justin Cuthbert, "Ranking the 31 NHL General Managers", *the Score,* August 3, 2016, Web, https://www.thescore.com/nhl/news/1064619-ranking-the-31-nhl-general-managers.
66 Carolyn Wilke and Chris Watkins, "The 2017 NHL GM Report Card", *Hockey Graphs,* May 3, 2017, Web,

- The results of the annual survey conducted by Dominik Luszczyszyn[67] on the subjective impression that his readers had on a front office's ability to build the roster, manage the cap, draft and develop prospects, make trades, and navigate free agency, not to mention their overall vision.

Subjective Assessments of NHL Front Offices, 2017–18

Team	Cuthbert	Wilke Watkins	Model	Total
Tampa Bay	1	2	3	6
Nashville	4	1	1	6
Pittsburgh	3	3	2	8
Dallas	6	4	8	18
Toronto	11	6	4	21
Winnipeg	8	7	11	26
Chicago	2	9	16	27
Anaheim	7	8	12	27
St. Louis	10	11	9	30
Carolina	22	5	5	32
Calgary	13	16	7	36
Washington	5	10	23	38
Arizona	16	13	13	42
Vegas	17	14	14	45
Florida	9	18	24	51
San Jose	14	17	21	52
Philadelphia	21	15	18	54
Columbus	30	20	6	56
Minnesota	28	21	10	59
NY Rangers	25	19	19	63
NY Islanders	12	24	27	63
Buffalo	18	25	20	63
New Jersey	20	23	22	65
Montreal	26	12	28	66
Edmonton	27	27	15	69
Ottawa	23	30	17	70
Los Angeles	19	28	25	72
Detroit	15	29	29	73
Boston	24	26	26	76
Colorado	29	22	31	82
Vancouver	31	31	30	92

These are three very different and admittedly arbitrary evaluations, but Nashville ranks first, and David Poile did win the GM of the Year award in 2016–17.

---

https://hockey-graphs.com/2017/05/03/the-2017-nhl-gm-report-card-part-2/.

67 Dominik Luszczyszyn, "Front office confidence rankings, part 2: Fans weight in on how each team is doing", *Hockey News,* July 28, 2017, Web, http://www.thehockeynews.com/news/article/front-office-confidence-rankings-part-2-fans-weigh-in-on-how-each-team-is-doing.

However, the other two finalists were Edmonton's Peter Chiarelli and Ottawa's Pierre Dorion, who ranked 24th and 25th, respectively. Voting is done by the GMs themselves, along with some league executives and journalists, who may very well have a very different perspective on this matter. Maybe someday we'll figure out how to capture their perspective, too.

Player Usage Charts

What can we possibly write about player usage charts that hasn't already been written?

To briefly summarize the volumes written on the subject over the years, player usage charts are a great way to visualize a team's depth charts by incorporating three modern statistics into a single graph.

- Is the player offensively-minded, or defensively-minded? The horizontal axis is the percentage of faceoffs for a which a player has lined up in the offensive zone, relative to the defensive zone.
- Is he a top-six forward, a top-four defenceman, or a secondary player? The vertical axis has an estimate of the player's average quality of competition.
- What were his team's results? The sized and shaded circles represent how well the team has done from a shot-based perspective when that player was on the ice, relative to when he wasn't.

Put it all together, and it's easy to see at a glance what holes might exist on any given team, which roles players has been assigned, what to expect of each player's or line's performance, and how to compare similar players across teams.

Player usage charts are one of the most popular innovations in this field, and they can be found practically everywhere. They're available in *Hockey Abstract* books, at *Hockey Prospectus*, *Dobber Sports*, *McKeen's* magazine, several online statistical websites[68], and all the leading hockey fansites[69]. They have also been featured in a variety of mainstream publications, from *the Hockey News*, *the Globe and Mail*, and *the Washington Post*, to Czech magazines and Swiss newspapers.

Player usage charts are also a very space-efficient way to illustrate a team's current set of strengths and weaknesses – a picture is worth a thousand words, after all.

For example, this season affords us the unique opportunity to see what we can figure out from the following player usage chart of an expansion team, the Vegas Golden Knights. The data within is a weighted average of the previous three seasons, since a single season is simply not enough data on which to evaluate individual player data, and is measured relative to the rest of each player's team.

---

68 Most recently at Corsica.Hockey, http://www.corsica.hockey/skaters/ (then choose usage charts).
69 Although Kent Wilson of Flames Nation and Garret Hohl of Hockey Graphs like to rag on us by calling them player *deployment* charts.

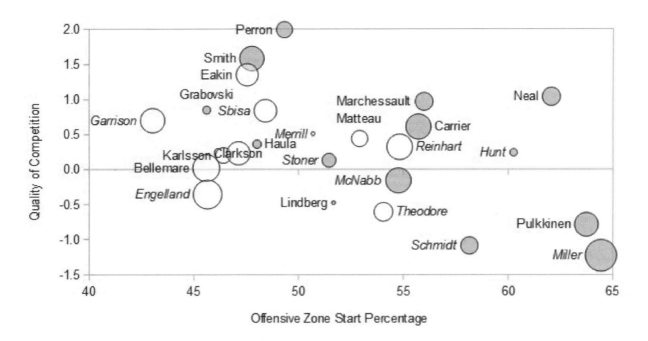

Vegas Golden Knights - Player Usage

What do all of these white and shaded circles actually mean? Basically, a team's top scoring line is on the far right, angling down towards the horizon, like James Neal, and Jonathan Marchessault. The shaded circles means that their teams have better shot-based metrics when they're on the ice relative to when they don't, which makes perfect sense for skilled players who get to start their shifts in the offensive zone all the time.

The top shutdown line will be at the top of the chart, and to the left of the top scoring line, like David Perron, Reilly Smith, and Cody Eakin. In cases like Eakin's, this can lead to the white circles that denote that the team's shot-based metrics drop when these players on the ice, which makes sense given that they're taking on top opponents like Crosby and McDavid. However, this isn't always the case, because sometimes the team's best players are assigned these roles.

The checking line is always on the left side, generally hovering around the horizon or below, and they tend to have big white circles, like Pierre-Edouard Bellemare, William Karlsson, and David Clarkson. Those ugly white circles are partly a consequence of their demanding defensive responsibilities, but it's also a reflection of the fact that if they were more complete players who could drive possession, then they probably wouldn't be on the checking line in the first place.

Those at or even below the horizon are generally depth players, such as enforcers, rookies, and AHL call-ups. In the case of players like Teemu Pulkinnen, those tasked exclusively with providing secondary scoring appear on the far right.

Also notice that the defencemen are marked with italics, to make them easier to spot. Those with defensive responsibilities will be at the top of the chart and trending to the left, like Jason Garrison, and Luca Sbisa. Notice that both defencemen have the white circles that denote poor shot-based metrics. That's not a good indication.

As with forwards, depth defencemen are closer to or below the horizon, and those on the right side, like Colin Miller, are generally those assigned a more offensive-minded role.

Beyond these quick and easy impressions of the NHL's newest team, experience has taught us a handful of more subtle insights, such as the following:

- Look for players with unusually out-of-place circles, such as shutdown players with nicely shaded circles, like Smith, or sheltered players with white ones, like Griffin Reinhart.
- Question the value of players that are assigned the tough minutes but have huge white bubbles, like Eakin, Garrison, and Sbisa. Just because someone plays the tough minutes doesn't mean that he should!
- Likewise, don't be too dismissive of nice, shaded circles just because someone has easy minutes, like Miller and Pulkkinen. Often, that success translates well even when these players are assigned a more challenging role.
- Regardless of whether the circle is white or shaded, be skeptical of the results for any players who are anywhere near the minimum cut-off (roughly 20 games, in our case), because their results could be badly skewed by the small sample size. In this case, we can remain cautious about Reinhart's (37 games) poor results, and restrain our enthusiasm for Carrier's (41 games) encouraging start.
- Dive deeper and ask local experts when studying anyone whose usage has changed considerably over the past three years, including both young players who are getting tougher assignments, and older players who don't really carry the tough minutes anymore.
- Since these charts use a weighted average of three seasons worth of data, be alert for those who played most of that time on a different team with either very different zone start percentages, or a much different possession-based standard. Everybody here is on a new team, but some players will be playing with a particularly different partner.
- Also remember that the circles are calculated relative to one's teammates, so be mindful of with whom players are being compared. A shaded circle on a solid team like Nashville and St. Louis was a lot more difficult for players like Neal and Perron to achieve than similar shaded circles for Carrier and Pulkkinen, for instance.
- While forwards are commonly assigned shifts based on the zone in which a play is about to start, most defencemen are assigned shifts primarily to match up against certain opponents. That's why there's usually a bigger spread for defencemen in terms of quality of competition (the vertical axis) than for zone starts (horizontal).
- While discussing defencemen, be aware that rookies are rarely used in a top-four fashion – maybe 10 per season. While it's impressive when they do so effectively, it shouldn't be taken too seriously when they don't.
- The scale can be different from team to team so that the charts are easier to read, so be very, very mindful of that when flipping between pages. The Vegas chart is pretty

typical, but coaches with more extreme deployment strategies may have the axis stretched out – like Peter Laviolette's Nashville Predators, for instance.

- Occasionally, players of very low significance will be left out, in order to avoid stretching the chart to accommodate him. These players are normally situated (very far) off the lower part of the chart.
- Lastly, get out a pencil, and be ready to draw in any changes that occur after this book went to print[70]. Unsigned RFAs should already be included, but not UFAs.

And that's about it! For more information, consult the cheat sheet on the next page, which was first published in the *Hockey Abstract 2015 Update*, or run through the detailed chapter in the original *Hockey Abstract*[71].

There's even more wisdom that can extracted from these player usage charts, which we will strive to point out throughout the course of the following team essays. Hopefully, you will learn to use and love these charts as much as we do.

Closing Thoughts

Team-level predictions are notoriously unreliable, whether they're based on analytics or on traditional analysis. Too many things can occur throughout the course of a season to confound a team projection, such as injuries, major transactions, hot goaltending, quickly developing rookies, unusual coaching decisions, and puck luck, just to name a few. Only an online website that can be updated with all the major developments throughout the course of a season can have any chance of accurately projecting what is to come.

That's why the focus of this next section isn't so much on forecasting the outcome of the next season, but on interpreting the player usage charts, and providing demonstrations on how certain analytics can be used to shed light on what might come to pass in 2017–18.

Between the quick interpretation of team player usage charts and the adaptable Hockey Abstract checklist, a reasonably useful view can be crafted for each team, and in such a way that it can be easily updated with new information, or to reflect any traditional analysis that goes beyond the level of insight that this analytic perspective can provide.

It's easy to get too fixated and worked up on the results, but try to relax and enjoy the process. If you have additional data, or an alternative interpretation of the existing data, then it is perfectly reasonable to take out a pencil and adjust the checklist appropriately. Enjoy!

---

70 Assuming you printed this out. Pencils aren't advisable if you're reading this on a tablet.
71 Rob Vollman, "Understanding Context with Player Usage Charts", *Hockey Abstract*, 2013, pgs 122-126.

Player Usage Chart Cheat Sheet

The horizontal axis features the player's **offensive zone start percentage**, which is the percentage of all shifts he started in that zone, relative to the rest of the team. It's important to remember that the perhaps poorly-named statistic does not include shifts that started in the neutral zone, nor on-the-fly changes. Think of it more as a representation of whether a player is used primarily for his offensive or defensive talents.

The advantage of an offensive zone start is obvious. Starting in the offensive zone means that subsequently winning a face-off generally leads directly to a shot on goal, whereas in the defensive zone, it would need to be carried out and the offensive zone gained before a shot could even be attempted. As such, each offensive zone start has been calculated to be worth an extra 0.8 shot attempts in a player's shot-based plus/minus (0.4 shots for and the 0.4 that goes against the opponents).

On the vertical axis, you'll find the player's **quality of competition**, which is the average plus/minus of one's opponents over 60 minutes, except that it is based on attempted shots (Corsi or SAT) instead of goals. This plus/minus is also measured relative to the team's other players, giving each team roughly the same number of players over zero as there are under (although the latter tend to lose their jobs). Those who face the top lines will be at the top of the chart, while those with the easier task of facing mostly depth lines will be at the bottom.

Other methods of measuring the average quality of one's competition do exist, like those that use goals, shots, or shots weighted by location and other quality factors. There's also a growing trend to use the average ice time of one's opponents, instead of their average shot-based or goal-based plus-minus, as innovated by Eric Tulsky (now of the Carolina Hurricanes). This year, these alternative views have been blended into the estimate in equal portions.

Finally, there are those big circles around each player's name. This is a representation of how well the team did with that player on the ice, in terms of puck possession (kind of). A big, shaded circle means that the team does very well, while a white one means that they're frequently getting stuck in their own zone, and/or playing without the puck.

More accurately, these circles are based on the team's attempted shot differential (per minute) when that player is on the ice relative to when he's not. That means that there should be roughly the same number of shaded bubbles as white bubbles. A player on a great team has to be even better than his teammates in order to earn a shaded bubble, while a player on a far weaker team would have a much lower bar over which to climb.

For all the details, consult chapter 12 of the original *Hockey Abstract* (2013).

Anaheim Ducks

Last summer, Anaheim surprisingly fired one of the league's best coaches after four straight division titles, and it actually worked! The Ducks improved by two points in the standings, won their fifth straight title, and advanced to the Western Conference Finals. What can be written about that? Good call.

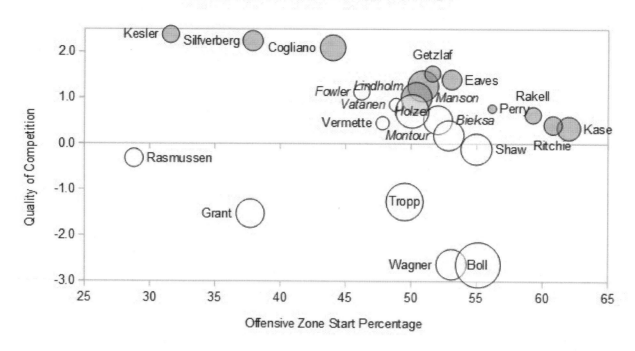

Anaheim Ducks - Player Usage

In fairness, credit for Anaheim's perennial contention must be shared by GM Bob Murray, who won the GM of the Year Award in 2014, in recognition of building and maintaining an almost perfectly balanced rotation of players at various points of their careers.

As usual, the top three players in Anaheim's scoring race were the team's veterans, including Ryan Getzlaf and Corey Perry, who will be playing together for the 13th consecutive season. However, a quick glance at the player usage chart shows that the team is competitive because of its shutdown line, not their increasingly average scoring line. Selke finalist Ryan Kesler, the highly underrated Jakob Silfverberg, and speedy iron man Andrew Cogliano are all at the top-left corner of the chart because they take on top competition in both zones, and they also have the shaded circles that denote solid shot-based metrics. Very few teams can match that second line.

And then there's Anaheim's wealth of young defencemen. The rest of the player usage chart is a little bit smashed together, but let your eyes focus on the seven italicized names in the middle, which denote defencemen. The Ducks have several players who can take on top opponents, in both zones. In particular, Hampus Lindholm and Josh Manson stand out as one of the league's most underrated second pairings.

And then what about the goaltending? It hardly seems possible in the salary cap era, but the Ducks have the above-average goaltending tandem of 23-year-old John Gibson and 2010 Vezina winner Ryan Miller for a combined cap hit of just $4.3 million. That's a huge advantage.

The main question with this lineup appears to be its top pairing. The Ducks have invested heavily in Cam Fowler as their No. 1 defenceman, and while he clearly had a breakout season, it may have been too early for that huge an endorsement. As for his potential partner, there are indications that Sami Vatanen might be better in a more sheltered and offensive-minded role (like Gostisbehere or Schultz), rather than in taking on top opponents with Fowler. As for Kevin Bieksa, he's 36, and already being transitioned to a depth pairing where he can help develop someone like Brandon Montour, 23, or Jacob Larsson, 20.

Depending on how quickly those young players develop, blue line depth could be an issue, too. While it's not necessarily a weakness, teams positioning themselves for legitimate Stanley Cup contention usually don't have the likes of Korbinian Holzer and Steven Oleksy so high on the depth chart.

In terms of the raw count of available options, forward depth is less of an issue. However, the player usage chart does highlight the fact that only Patrick Eaves, Nick Ritchie, and rookie Ondrej Kase have nicely shaded circles. Among Cup contenders, depth lines can be the difference-makers. While shot-based metrics aren't everything, those big white circles don't do much to ease these concerns.

Score	Category	Notes
✔	Possession	In this area, they took a step back under Carlyle, but they're still above average, thanks to the top lines.
✔	The Shootout	The Ducks are among the best in the shootout.
✔	Goaltending	Anaheim has the most cost-efficient goaltending tandem.
✔	Penalty Kill	Kesler is one of the game's best penalty killers.
✔	Power Play	Anaheim is starting to build a secondary threat behind Getzlaf and Perry.
✔	Scoring Line	Getzlaf and Perry are on the cusp of losing this checkmark.
✔	Shutdown Line	In this area, they have been leaders for a decade, or more.
✔	Forward Depth	Young players prevent this from being a weakness, but it is not a strength.
	Top Pairing	Is Fowler a legit No. 1 defenceman?
☆	Second Pairing	The young duo of Lindholm and Manson is one of the most underrated second pairings.
	Defensive Depth	Even if Montour and Larsson are ready, they're still thin.
✔	Coaching	It was a tough act to follow, but Carlyle did a fine job.
✔	Prospects	There are several young players with potential to break out.

Assessment: A sixth straight division title? Well, that's up to McDavid.

Arizona Coyotes

There's definitely potential for the Coyotes to take a few teams by surprise this year. After a relatively quiet first season as Arizona's GM, John Chayka had a busy summer making improvements in virtually every corner of the team's lineup. Factor in the potential upside if the team's younger players have breakout seasons, and they could really turn things around.

Arizona Coyotes - Player Usage

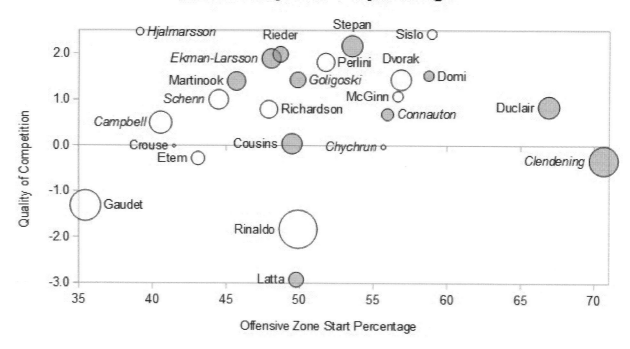

In nets, Antti Raanta has never been a starter, but he has the potential to be a big improvement over Mike Smith. Flip to the goaltending chapter, and see how Raanta ranks top-3 in most statistical categories, among goalies who aren't already established starters.

On the blue line, team MVP Oliver Ekman-Larsson and reserve option Kevin Connauton are the only defencemen who remain from the 2015–16 season. Chayka added Alex Goligoski in 2016, and Niklas Hjalmarsson in 2017, giving the team three solid top-four veterans who can take on top opponents in both zones, and with decent shot-based metrics and scoring totals. Jakob Chychrun, 19, will have the opportunity to stretch forward past the defensive-minded Luke Schenn into a No. 4 role.

Behind them, the Coyotes have the potential to develop a player like Adam Clendening or big rookie Kyle Wood into one of those sheltered, puck-moving defencemen on the right-middle side of the chart, like Philadelphia's Shayne Gostisbehere. Wood won the hardest shot competition at last year's AHL All-Star Game.

Up front, the Coyotes added Derek Stepan. Normally a solid, two-way second-line centre,

Arizona is one of the few places where he'll be called upon to play a top-line role. If used in that capacity, Stepan would play with Max Domi, 22, and Anthony Duclair, 21, who combined for 96 points in their rookie 2015–16 season, but just 53 in 2016–17.

The key to the second line is Tobias Rieder, 24, one of the league's best-kept secrets. The chart demonstrates how he can effectively face top opponents in both zones. He has averaged only 31 points per season, but is the team's top penalty-killing forward, alongside checking line centre Jordan Martinook, 25.

Given the departure of Arizona's veteran forwards, Radim Vrbata, Martin Hanzal, and Shane Doan, the team will have an exciting reliance on strong performances from Dylan Strome, Lawson Crouse, Clayton Keller, Christian Fischer, Brendan Perlini, and Christian Dvorak, who are all age 21 or younger, and have a combined 224 NHL games between them. There could be big trouble if they falter, because the remaining veterans Brad Richardson and Jamie McGinn are meant only as complementary players, and Nick Cousins and Emerson Etem are suitable for the depth lines only.

The key to unlocking this enormous potential is in the hands of new coach Rick Tocchet. While it's risky to go off the board and pick a coach with just 148 games of experience, all at the NHL level and without much success, Dave Tippett wasn't exactly getting results lately. Effectively, there's only upside potential here.

Score	Category	Notes
	Possession	The Coyotes have a long way to go on this front.
✔	The Shootout	The goalies and shooters are relatively untried, but they could have their noses above water in the shootout.
✔	Goaltending	Statistically, Raanta is one of the best goalies who isn't already an established starter.
	Penalty Kill	Hjalmarsson will help improve one of the league's worst PK.
	Power Play	Among the 138 forwards with 20 power play points over the past two years, Stepan and Domi are the only Coyotes.
	Scoring Line	They desperately need Domi and Duclair to bounce back.
	Shutdown Line	If Strome can centre the scoring line, then Stepan could lift the shutdown line instead, alongside Rieder.
✔	Forward Depth	There are 16 forwards on that chart, plus at least three more rookies. They're bound to craft a decent bottom six.
✔	Top Pairing	For the second straight season, Chayka has added a solid top-four defenceman.
	Second Pairing	They are still one player short of a complete top four.
✔	Defensive Depth	There's potential for a strong third pairing.
	Coaching	There were safer and more proven options available.
☆	Prospects	Half of their lineup includes players with 0-2 NHL seasons.

Assessment: The Coyotes are a few breakout seasons from their fourth fourth-place finish in six seasons – otherwise they'll remain in the draft lottery.

Boston Bruins

For years, the Bruins forged a winning identity around a great coach, elite goaltending, the ultimate shutdown defenceman, and the best two-way line in the business. With the departure of Claude Julien, the gradual decline of Tuukka Rask, and Zdeno Chara hitting 40, they're left with only one of those four advantages. It's time to forge a new identity around its wealth of promising young talent.

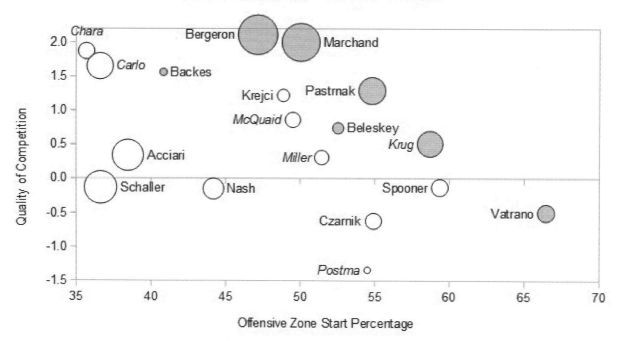

Boston Bruins - Player Usage

Every year, we marvel at those huge shaded circles at the top of the chart for Patrice Bergeron and Brad Marchand. They take on top opponents in both zones, and dominate their opponents to an extent that we haven't seen since Pavel Datsyuk left for the KHL. Since these shot-based metrics are measured relative to the rest of the team, either they're crushing it, or the rest of the team has struggled – or maybe a bit of both.

The problem with having Bergeron and Marchand is that it skews the results for everybody else. On Boston, a large shaded circle might mean that they frequently play with Bergeron and Marchand, and not that they're playing particularly effectively. Indeed, failing to take quality of linemates into account is one of the top criticisms of player usage charts.

As you can tell from his shaded circle, David Pastrnak spent most of the season on that top line, but new coach Bruce Cassidy used him on the scoring line with David Krejci instead. He was replaced on the top line by David Backes, who is much more similar to Bergeron and Marchand in style and usage.

63

There are some interesting options to complete Krejci's scoring line. The default choice used to be Matt Beleskey, but he topped out a career high of 37 points in 2015–16, and tumbled to eight points last season. The new default option became Ryan Spooner, who has averaged 44 points over the past two seasons. However, he may be needed to centre the third line. That leaves the more interesting choice of one of last year's 5-foot-9 rookies, Frank Vatrano or Austin Czarnik. For the AHL's Providence Bruins, Vatrano scored 36 goals in 36 games in 2015–16, and Czarnik has 86 points in 93 career games. Last year, they combined for 31 points in 93 NHL games.

On the blue line, the two key players are Chara and Torey Krug. The captain is in the top-left corner because he plays the tough minutes against top opponents in the defensive zone. Krug is middle-right because he gets the more offensive-minded shifts against secondary opponents. Each player fills these roles quite effectively.

As usual, the Bruins lack depth. This has been a chronic problem in Boston, even when they were among the top Cup contenders. In graphical terms, there aren't many circles on that chart, and most of them are white. So, watch for first and second-year players to fill in a lot of those gaps, possibly including Anders Bjork, Jakob Forsbacka-Karlsson, Peter Cehlarik, and Sean Kuraly up front, and certainly including Brandon Carlo and Charlie McAvoy on defence.

Score	Category	Notes
✔	Possession	There aren't a lot of shaded circles, but the top players are just downright dominant, and lift the whole team.
	The Shootout	Rask is great in nets, but they need some shooters.
	Goaltending	That was Rask's second mediocre season in a row, and there are questions about who will back him up.
☆	Penalty Kill	Strong special teams are one of Boston's trademarks. Backes, Bergeron, and Chara are all outstanding on the PK.
☆	Power Play	The team's offence is highly reliant on their underrated PP.
	Scoring Line	The Bruins need a breakout season from someone new.
☆	Shutdown Line	I think Tina Turner was singing about Boston's shutdown line.
	Forward Depth	Rookies may address the team's long-ignored depth issues.
	Top Pairing	At 40, Chara may no longer be able to carry a top pair all by himself.
✔	Second Pairing	The Bruins have bled defencemen for years, and Krug is the only other proven top-four option that remains.
	Defensive Depth	It's not a promising sign when the seventh name on the depth chart is Paul Postma (who always rings twice).
	Coaching	Cassidy developed many of these players in Providence.
✔	Prospects	Half of the opening night lineup could feature players with fewer than 100 games of NHL experience.

Assessment: Boston may look like a disaster beyond the top line, but that top line is very good, and the team's younger players hold enough promise to grab a wild card spot.

Buffalo Sabres

In 1972–73, the Sabres vaulted up the standings by 37 points, then slid back by eight points in 1973–74. They replaced coach Joe Crozier with the untried Floyd Smith, and then leapt to 113 points and a surprise appearance in the Stanley Cup Final in 1974–75. If the Sabres keep following that pattern, then they'll stun us all again in 2017–18.

Buffalo Sabres - Player Usage

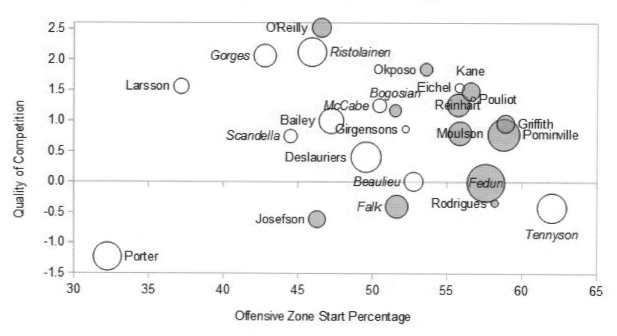

Buffalo's key strength is down the middle. Jack Eichel has the potential to factor into the race for the Art Ross Trophy this season, Ryan O'Reilly is among the league's best two-way second-line centres, and Johan Larsson and Zemgus Girgensons are promising defensive line options.

That strength at centre is supplemented by the team's considerable forward depth, which was built up even further by new GM Jason Botterill with the acquisition of Jason Pominville from the Minnesota Wild, and free agents like Benoit Pouliot and Jacob Josefson. These three players join Matt Moulson as veterans who can provide secondary scoring and help improve the team's shot-based metrics from the bottom six, although one of them will likely play on the top lines, to fill the remaining slot left by wingers Sam Reinhart, Evander Kane, and Kyle Okposo.

However, the Sabres lack the defensive tools to fully capitalize on their depth of scoring. Up front, none of these top-six forwards are as obvious an asset to a shutdown line as O'Reilly. Furthermore, the giant white circles around the defencemen playing the toughest minutes, Josh Gorges and Rasmus Ristolainen, suggest that Buffalo doesn't have anyone who is truly suited for that role on the blue line, either.

Above all, the Sabres need to address those defensive deficiencies. For the third time in five seasons, Buffalo allowed the most shots, and were among the six worst teams in penalty-killing percentage. This wouldn't be an issue if they had great goaltending, but Robin Lehner and Chad Johnson is the type of tandem that can get a team by, not one that will steal games.

To that end, defencemen Jake McCabe, Zach Bogosian, and the newly acquired Marco Scandella will have to rise up the chart and share more of the defensive load, especially since the summer's other arrivals, Nathan Beaulieu and KHL First Team All-Star Viktor Antipin, will be on the middle-right side of the chart, and focused on scoring.

Up front, Kane will have to shift more to the left and complete his transformation into an effective two-way winger, and checking line players such as Josefson and Evan Rodrigues will have to shift up the chart, and take on tougher opponents.

Score	Category	Notes
	Possession	There are a lot of shaded circles on the chart, but the Sabres are starting from a big hole.
	The Shootout	Pominville and Josefson solve their shooting problem, but Lehner is one of the league's weaker shootout goalies.
	Goaltending	Lehner/Johnson appears to be an average tandem, at best.
	Penalty Kill	Buffalo has been among the league's worst at killing penalties.
✔	Power Play	Their power play has steadily improved for years.
✔	Scoring Line	The Sabres have quite a few options to play with Eichel.
	Shutdown Line	Beyond O'Reilly, the Sabres lack shutdown forwards.
✔	Forward Depth	There are some pretty decent forwards who will be fighting for spots in the lineup.
	Top Pairing	Ristolainen is being used far too ambitiously, and needs help.
	Second Pairing	The Sabres need their blue line to step up.
✔	Defensive Depth	Scandella, Antipin, and Beaulieu are nice pickups, and the Amerks are loaded with defencemen, including Guhle.
	Coaching	Swapping in Housley and Payne for Bylsma and Murray gives up a fair bit in terms of experience and past success.
	Prospects	The bulk of the team's organizational strength is already on the ice, and the rest will have to fight their way in.

Assessment: Much stronger defensive play is the only remaining major obstacle between Buffalo and the playoffs.

Calgary Flames

Calgary's captain Mark Giordano has won one playoff series in his career, which has been spent entirely with the Flames. While he's certainly pleased that they made the playoffs for the second time in three seasons, he's likely eager for the next step in the rebuild, which is to actually advance by a round or two.

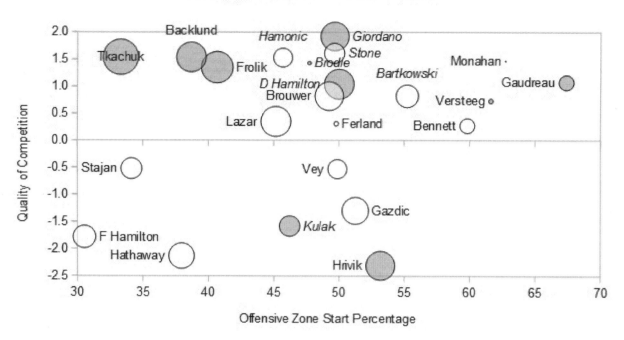

Calgary Flames - Player Usage

The rest of the league is finally catching on to Backlund, who finished fourth in Selke voting, and was centre on one of the most underrated second lines in the NHL. Flanked by Michael Frolik and gritty rookie Matthew Tkachuk, Backlund took on top competition in both zones, and his big, shaded circle indicates just how well he does in terms of shot-based metrics.

The other big, shaded circles at the top of the chart belong to Giordano and his first pairing partner, Dougie Hamilton. Not only do they have great shot-based metrics, but they combined for 89 points, and averaged 1.10 points per 60 minutes at even-strength, both of which rank near the top of the league's best pairings.

On the second pair, Giordano's former partner T.J. Brodie appeared to struggle on his off-side, and without an effective partner, but the Flames sacrificed a first-round and two second-round picks in a serious bid to address that. Travis Hamonic's white circle was a result of a terrible 2016–17 season, but he has clearly established himself as a solid top-four option in the past.

The players who surprisingly don't have large shaded circles are those on the top line, Johnny Gaudreau and Sean Monahan, who are on the right, offensive-minded side of the chart. Even in terms of scoring, they took a step back from a combined 141 points in 2015–16 to 119 in 2016–17.

Actually, there aren't many shaded circles at all, beyond the top lines. In fact, if Kris Versteeg is used to complete the top scoring line, then the only secondary players with shaded circles have a combined 51 NHL games, Marek Hrivik and defenceman Brett Kulak. Shot-based metrics aren't everything, but all of those white circles could indicate the kind of depth issue that prevents deep playoff runs. To compete, the Flames need Sam Bennett and Curtis Lazar to realise their full potential, and for Troy Brouwer to become the complete, two-way player in which they invested $4.5 million per season in the 2016 off-season.

In the end, the most important factor in Calgary is usually the goaltending. They tried Jonas Hiller and Karri Ramo in 2015–16, Brian Elliott and Chad Johnson in 2016–17, and now it's Mike Smith and Eddie Lack for 2017–18. If this new tandem succeeds, then it will be an interesting vindication for those who argue for the importance of shot quality on save percentage. As detailed in the upcoming chapter on goalie analytics, Smith and Lack are two of the three goalies whose stats have been dragged down to the greatest extent by shot quality recently. Then again, even if shot quality plays a big factor in a goalie's save percentage, who is to say they're going to be better off in Calgary?

Score	Category	Notes
	Possession	Calgary has been backing off its over-emphasis on grit, and had great shot-based metrics in the second half.
	The Shootout	The Flames had better win their games in regulation or OT.
	Goaltending	Will the third new tandem in three years be the charm?
✔	Penalty Kill	The Flames went from one of the least penalized teams to one of the most. The extra practise must be paying off.
✔	Power Play	Calgary has Gaudreau, Monahan, and puck-moving D.
	Scoring Line	Surprisingly, Gaudreau and Monahan rate lower than most scoring lines in usage, scoring, and shot-based metrics.
☆	Shutdown Line	Calgary had one of the league's best second lines last year.
	Forward Depth	Versteeg is the only established NHLer in the bottom six with a shaded circle.
☆	Top Pairing	Calgary has one of the league's best top three.
✔	Second Pairing	Hamonic had a dreadful season, but has proven himself to be a more than capable top-four defenceman in the past.
	Defensive Depth	They have only six defencemen with more than 30 games of NHL experience, and half of them have white circles.
✔	Coaching	Gulutzan deserves some credit for Calgary's playoff return.
	Prospects	They have some organizational strength, but this is predominantly a veteran lineup.

Assessment: The Flames rebuild might get stalled, but it's unlikely to go in reverse.

Carolina Hurricanes

After years of being fawned over by statisticians, Nashville's appearance in the Stanley Cup Final added more credibility to this type of analysis, and has drawn some attention to which team is predicted to break out next. Though they might still be a year and a Subban-like trade away, Carolina is the latest love interest in the world of hockey analytics.

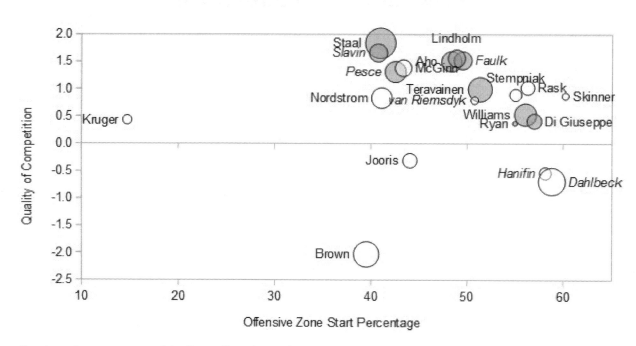

Carolina's primary appeal is its collection of strong, young, two-way defencemen. If you can ignore how the chart was stretched out by checking-line centre Marcus Kruger, who was buried in the defensive zone by the Chicago Blackhawks, then you'll see Justin Faulk, who is 25, Jaccob Slavin, 23, and Brett Pesce, 22, all being used against top competition, in both zones, and with the nicely shaded circles that denote good shot-based metrics. This summer, the Hurricanes added Trevor van Riemsdyk, 26, to complete a young top four that carries a combined cap hit of just $7.21 million.

And, that's not all. Noah Hanifin, 20, could be poised for a breakout season, and prospects like Haydn Fleury, 21, could be ready to crack the lineup, and relieve coach Bill Peters of the need to rely on replacement-level depth options, like Klas Dahlbeck.

After a puzzling $6.05 million investment in Eddie Lack and Cam Ward last season, who had ranked 38th and 43rd in career save percentage (minimum 50 games), the Hurricanes wisely acquired and signed Scott Darling, who ranks fifth. Flip to the chapter on goalie analytics, and you'll see the potential upside for Carolina if he successfully transitions into a No. 1 goalie.

That just leaves scoring as Carolina's primary hurdle. The team's only established scoring threat is Jeff Skinner, 25, who set new career highs of 37 goals and 63 points last season, and was identified as the league's best clutch scorer in an upcoming chapter. The newly acquired Justin Williams is the only other player on this roster who has topped 52 points in a season, and he hasn't done so since 2011–12.

However, Victor Rask, 24, Teuvo Teravainen, 22, Elias Lindholm, 22, and Sebastian Aho, 20, each scored between 42 and 49 points last season, while playing top-six minutes and mostly posting good shot-based metrics. Add in veterans Jordan Staal and Lee Stempniak, and the Hurricanes have a depth of scoring that will continue to grow, even if they may not have a single, elite scoring line at the moment.

The same situation applies to the shutdown line. Staal is the team's only established shutdown player, as indicated by that giant shaded circle at the top of the chart. But, again, the team has a depth of responsible two-way players throughout its lineup, and the shaded circles at the top of the chart suggest that players like Aho and Lindholm may already be effective in this role.

Carolina's opening day lineup may feature only five skaters who were alive when GM Ron Francis last played for their predecessor in 1990–91, the Hartford Whalers, but make no mistake – this young team is already starting to become competitive.

Score	Category	Notes
✔	Possession	They're one of five teams with score-adjusted shot-based metrics above 51% in each of the past three seasons.
	The Shootout	Carolina is one of the easier teams to beat in the shootout.
✔	Goaltending	Darling should at least provide league-average goaltending.
☆	Penalty Kill	Carolina is possibly the league's best at killing penalties.
✔	Power Play	Faulk is the key to a power play that features a depth of scoring.
	Scoring Line	Skinner is the team's only true scoring line threat, for now.
✔	Shutdown Line	Staal may finally have some quality wingers to work with.
✔	Forward Depth	Carolina has a depth of scoring and two-way play.
✔	Top Pairing	The Hurricanes could one day have the league's best top four.
	Second Pairing	Carolina could use a bit more scoring from the point.
	Defensive Depth	They have a wealth of prospects but, at the moment, Dahlbeck is sixth on the depth chart.
	Coaching	Peters is still hunting for his first taste of success since the Spokane Chiefs were WHL champs in 2008.
✔	Prospects	This is a very young team with loads of breakout potential.

Assessment: After eight long seasons, it's time for Carolina to get back into the playoffs.

Chicago Blackhawks

The experts were stunned when the Chicago Blackhawks were swept aside in the first round of the playoffs, but they really shouldn't have been. Despite 50 wins and 109 points, there were already signs that Chicago was finding it increasingly difficult to manage their cap situation and remain dominant as their core players continue to age.

Chicago Blackhawks - Player Usage

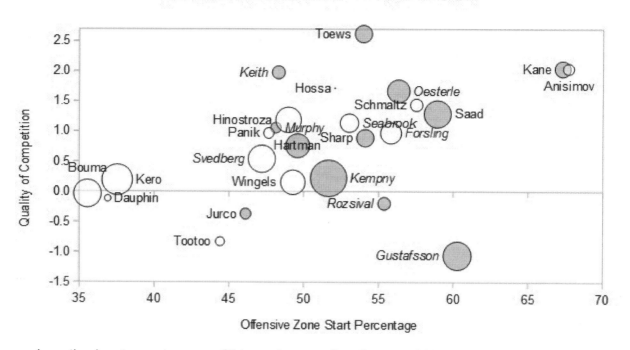

In our view, the best way to ease Chicago's cap situation would be to move Brent Seabrook. He is highly respected, and a premium has been placed on defencemen lately. So, start the bidding war of trade offers, and let some other team handle his $6.75 million annual cap hit until age 39. Given his white circle, and his position in the middle of the chart, his cap space might be better invested in someone else anyway.

Instead, GM Stan Bowman moved Niklas Hjalmarsson to the Arizona Coyotes, in exchange for Connor Murphy. Their playing style and cap hits are about the same, but Murphy is six years younger and more physical, but hasn't really faced the tough minutes to the same, great extent. His success may depend on whether or not he is paired up with Chicago's perennial Norris candidate, Duncan Keith. In case you're new to hockey, he's the nicely shaded circle handling the tough minutes in the top-left area of the chart.

Bowman's other big move was to trade Artemi Panarin to the Columbus Blue Jackets in a deal for Brandon Saad. Again, they are very similar players in style, in cap hit, and in the giant shaded circles that represent solid shot-based metrics, but Saad may have a bit more of a defensive upside.

71

For Saad, the default option is to simply replace Panarin on the top scoring line with Patrick Kane and Artem Anisimov, whose position on the chart demonstrate that they frequently handle power-vs-power matchups, but with among the highest offensive zone start percentages in the league. However, with the news that Marian Hossa may not compete this season, Saad might be deployed on the top shutdown line with Jonathan Toews instead, whose position at the top of the chart indicates that he takes on top opponents, and in both zones.

Beyond those seven players, it's hard to predict how the lineup will fall into place. Based on their shaded circles, it appears that Jordan Oesterle, Michal Kempny, and Erik Gustafsson would be good choices on the blue line, but they have played a combined total of just NHL 116 games. And, at age 39, Michal Rozsival is just a depth option. Only time will tell, but the Blackhawks might be better off with Gustav Forsling, Jan Rutta, rookie Ville Pokka, or 6-foot-8 Viktor Svedberg. At least they have plenty of options.

Up front, Chicago needs Patrick Sharp to bounce back into top-six form, because there are no other obvious candidates for the top lines. Chances are that one of the secondary players will step forward, like Richard Panik did last season, with 44 points in 82 games after scoring 47 in his first 181, as well as rugged rookie Ryan Hartman, who scored 31 points and had the second-best shot-based metrics among the team's forwards. This year, the likeliest candidate for a breakout is Nick Schmaltz.

Score	Category	Notes
✔	Possession	They're on the decline, but still above average.
✔	The Shootout	Chicago is excellent in the shootout.
✔	Goaltending	The only question is if Forsberg or Berube can be a reliable backup for Crawford.
	Penalty Kill	Nobody can explain why the Hawks struggle shorthanded.
✔	Power Play	Kane is great, but they could use more shots and depth.
✔	Scoring Line	Losing Panarin could impact Kane.
✔	Shutdown Line	Toews finished top-6 in Selke voting for the 8th straight season, but will he have effective, two-way wingers?
	Forward Depth	It's a challenge to make the most of limited cap space.
✔	Top Pairing	Keith is one of the world's best defencemen, and they could stretch the lineup by pairing him with a depth option.
	Second Pairing	The Blackhawks need one more top-four defenceman.
✔	Defensive Depth	Chicago has only three established NHL defencemen (plus Rozsival), but a wealth of viable third pair options.
✔	Coaching	There are few (if any) active coaching staffs with a superior track record of success than Quenneville and company.
	Prospects	They can fill holes, but they won't move needles.

Assessment: Chicago will actually need to break a sweat to make the playoffs this year.

Colorado Avalanche

We're not going to dump on the Avalanche, no pun intended. Over the years, statisticians have scored almost as many points on Colorado as its opponents have, and it's time to move on. Using stats to point out mistakes is easy, but this year we're going to use them to show how Colorado might try to rebuild itself from the ashes.

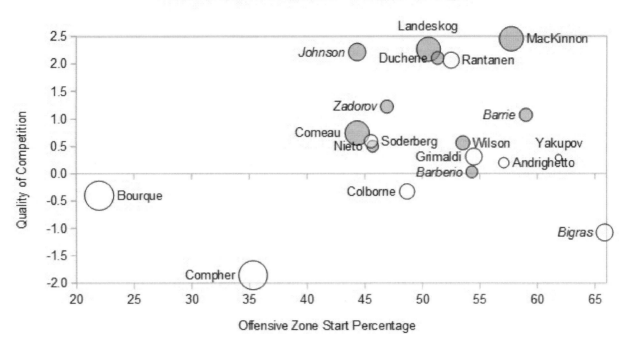

Colorado Avalanche - Player Usage

There are rumours of trading Matt Duchene, but the key is to rebuild around the team's greatest existing assets, which are highlighted on the player usage chart with the large, shaded circles at the top of the chart belonging to Nathan MacKinnon, Gabriel Landeskog, and Duchene. That means that they take on top opponents, and help drive the shot clock in the right direction. However, their average even-strength scoring rate dropped to an inadequate 1.50 points per 60 minutes, from an impressive 2.09 over the three preceding seasons.

In the past, Duchene has helped many linemates to career highs, and could help re-ignite the career of Nail Yakupov, who led rookies with 31 points in 48 games after being drafted first overall in 2012 (the year before MacKinnon was drafted first overall). Another possibility is to match Duchene up with Sven Andrighetto, who scored 15 points in 19 games after being acquired from Montreal at the trade deadline.

There's also the possibility that prospects like Tyson Jost and JT Compher could have an immediate impact in the top six, just like Mikko Rantanen, who scored 20 goals and 38 points last year.

On the blue line, Colorado has already started to rebuild around Erik Johnson, Nikita Zadorov, and Tyson Barrie, all of whom are in the upper part of the chart reserved for those who take on top-six opponents, and who have the shaded circles that indicate the advantage they're providing the Avalanche, in terms of shot-based metrics. In particular, Colorado would be lost without Johnson, who is relied upon to handle all the tough minutes. He was also drafted first overall, back in 2006.

For scoring, the Avalanche rely on Barrie, who is more of an offensive specialist, and ranks ninth among the 261 defencemen to play at least 1,000 minutes over the past four seasons with an average of 1.13 points per 60 minutes at even-strength. As for the 6-foot-5 Zadorov, he's the type of heavy hitter who might normally play on the third pairing on a deeper team, but deserves a shot in the top four in Colorado.

As for depth, there are only 19 players on that chart. Up front, they do have veterans like Colin Wilson, Blake Comeau, Joe Colborne, and Carl Soderberg, but the blue line will have to rely on Mark Barberio, and a handful of prospects like Chris Bigras, Anton Lindholm, and the hard-hitting Duncan Siemens.

In nets, it's obviously not ideal for the goalie with the ninth greatest cap hit at his position to rank 26th in career save percentage (minimum 50 games), but Varlamov has an upside, given that he was the runner-up for the Vezina in 2013–14. They also added Jonathan Bernier this summer, who ranks 33rd in cap hit, and 34th in save percentage. So, at least they nailed the cap hit on that one.

Score	Category	Notes
	Possession	At times, it seems that they go out of their way to avoid having the puck.
☆	The Shootout	Colorado remains possibly the best shootout team in the NHL.
	Goaltending	It was a really tough season for Varlamov.
	Penalty Kill	This is one area where they have already started to improve.
	Power Play	Barrie is excellent, but that's about it.
	Scoring Line	With the right wingers, Duchene could climb back to 70 points.
✔	Shutdown Line	MacKinnon and Landeskog have a very high upside.
	Forward Depth	Their player usage chart looks pretty barren, and without many players who could reasonably play top-six minutes.
	Top Pairing	They'd be lost without Johnson to handle the tough minutes.
✔	Second Pairing	Offensively, Barrie is one of the league's top-10 defencemen.
	Defensive Depth	Bigras ranks fifth in NHL experience, with 31 games.
	Coaching	Going off the board doesn't always work.
✔	Prospects	On any given night, they'll have about four rookies on the ice.

Assessment: Gentlemen, we can rebuild them. We have the technology.

74

Columbus Blue Jackets

Given their wild swings, it's hard to get an accurate read on the Columbus Blue Jackets. One moment they're last in their division, then they close the calendar year with 16 straight wins, then they go ice cold and win only four of their last 16 games, including getting dumped in a five-game, opening-round playoff series. Where does the team's true talent lie?

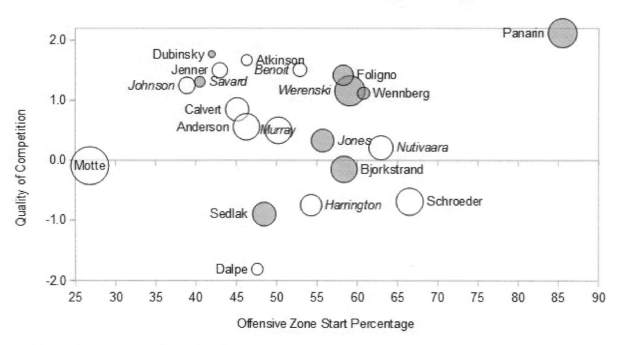

Columbus Blue Jackets - Player Usage

Even without hot goaltending, the Blue Jackets still would have been a winning team. If he had matched his previous career save percentage of .917, then Sergei Bobrovsky would have allowed 27 more goals. Even with a resulting loss of 10 points in the standings, Columbus would still have broken its franchise record, and made the playoffs with four points to spare.

So yes, Columbus has become a legitimately competitive playoff team, even if Bobrovsky doesn't bag a third Vezina Trophy. While a lot of the credit deservedly went to John Tortorella, who won the Jack Adams for the second time, the real turning point could be the team's new top pairing of rookie Zach Werenski, who is 20, and Seth Jones, 22. They're easy to spot on the chart, because they're the ones with the big shaded circles that denote good shot-based metrics. They also combined for 89 points, became the third and fourth defencemen in franchise history to score more than 40 points in a season, and made Columbus the only team with two such defencemen last season.

A pleasant consequence of this new top pairing is that Jack Johnson has been able to transition into a second pair role in which he has been far more effective (or, less ineffective). He and David Savard are on the left side of the chart, because they tend to take on the defensive assignments, especially against top opponents.

As for the big shaded circle way up in the right-hand corner, that's for Artemi Panarin, who was acquired this summer in a trade involving Brandon Saad. He could be just the player to finally complete a legitimate top scoring line by helping to unleash Alexander Wennberg's considerable playmaking potential, and boosting captain Nick Foligno back up to the career high of 73 points that he scored in 2014–15.

The shutdown line will likely include the forwards on the top left side of the chart, Brandon Dubinsky, Boone Jenner, and team scoring leader Cam Atkinson. However, only Dubinsky has a shaded circle, and together they rank 29th in shot-based metrics, among projected shutdown lines. In fact, there are only two other shaded circles on the entire chart, belonging to rookie depth forwards Lukas Sedlak and the highly promising Oliver Bjorkstrand.

Does that mean that the Blue Jackets have a depth problem? Possibly on defence, given the white circles surrounding rookie Markus Nutivaara and the still-promising Ryan Murray, and the recruitment of depth options like Andre Benoit and Cameron Gaunce.

However, depth could be less of an issue up front, where more prospects appear to be on the verge of contributing, like Pierre-Luc Dubois, Markus Hannikainen, and Sonny Milano. At the very minimum, the team's organizational strength means that any depth issues will be short-lived.

Score	Category	Notes
✔	Possession	Only three teams have fewer shaded circles.
✔	The Shootout	Panarin adds a much-needed shooter to the lineup.
✔	Goaltending	What a bounceback-ski by Bobrovsky.
✔	Penalty Kill	There are no major concerns here.
	Power Play	They ranked 27th in shot attempts per 60 minutes last year.
	Scoring Line	It'll be exciting to see Panarin and Wennberg play together.
	Shutdown Line	Shot-based metrics aren't everything, but they can be a signal of larger issues.
	Forward Depth	They will be relying on a lot of prospects to fill the holes.
☆	Top Pairing	Werenski and Jones are sensational for their age.
✔	Second Pairing	The scoring success of the top pair is facilitated by Johnson and Savard, who handle the defensive assignments.
	Defensive Depth	Even if Murray finally realizes his considerable potential, Columbus is still short a few defencemen.
✔	Coaching	Tortorella is the only active coach with 2 Jack Adams awards.
✔	Prospects	Werenski demonstrated the projection-defying impact that a prospect can have. There could be another this year.

Assessment: They're no threat for the divisional crown, but the Blue Jackets can secure back-to-back playoff appearances for the first time in franchise history.

Dallas Stars

Guess who's back? After its first place finish in 2015–16, Dallas appeared to ignore its weaknesses, and predictably tumbled to its worst points percentage since 1995–96. Complacent no longer, the Stars have turned to the same coach who lifted them up to five consecutive division titles the last time they struggled, Ken Hitchcock.

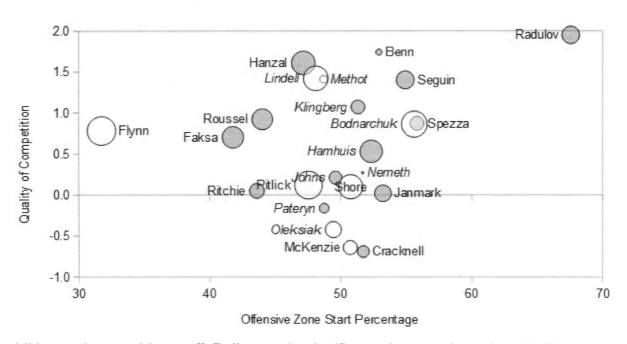

In addition to the coaching staff, Dallas made significant changes throughout its lineup. Frustrated with the league's worst save percentage despite the greatest cap hit, the Stars bought out Antti Niemi (now of the Penguins), and acquired two-time Vezina finalist Ben Bishop. His career save percentage of .919 ranks 14th among active goalies, and his new cap hit just under $5.0 million ranks 17th.

Up front, Alexander Radulov and Martin Hanzal were brought in for the combined cap hit of $11 million. This summer's free agent market appeared soft for forwards in their early 30s – but obviously not in Dallas. Radulov, whose position on the far-right side of the chart is reflective of his usage in a strictly offensive capacity, will likely have the good fortune to play on the top scoring line with Jamie Benn and Tyler Seguin.

The second line, which is traditionally responsible for taking on top opponents in both zones, will be built around Hanzal. Though not positioned quite as perfectly on the chart, Antoine Roussel, Radek Faksa, and Jason Spezza each have nicely shaded circles, and are all reasonable candidates to join him in that role. Spezza would add scoring, Roussel adds physicality, and Faksa may be the team's best defensive forward.

On the blue line, Marc Methot was the summer's big investment. While he's unlikely to earn his $4.9 million cap hit without the incomparable Erik Karlsson at his side, he's certainly the kind of second-pair, stay-at-home defenceman that the Stars have needed for years.

In addition, the team's organizational strength has developed to the point that it can finally address the remaining (and longstanding) blue line deficiencies. Last season, rookie Esa Lindell played on the the top, puck-moving pair with John Klingberg. He has a nice offensive upside, but the white circle suggest that he needs a bit more time to develop into that role. This season, prospect Julius Honka is another skilled, puck-moving defenceman that could enter the lineup. As long as there are responsible veteran defencemen like Methot and Dan Hamhuis to guide them, the Stars should have an effective blue line. Finally.

Lastly, GM Jim Nill tweaked the depth lines, adding checking-line wingers Brian Flynn and Tyler Pitlick. They may have giant white circles, but Flynn can kill penalties, Pitlick is a big hitter with some offensive upside, and the team's depth otherwise could have been a little thin. As it now stands, there's a great mix of different types of forwards, almost all of whom are in their prime, and several of whom have nicely shaded circles. They'll be fine.

Score	Category	Notes
✔	Possession	No team has more shaded circles on their chart than Dallas.
✔	The Shootout	No goalie wants to face Benn, Seguin, and Radulov in the shootout.
	Goaltending	Bishop replaces Niemi. Is that the answer?
	Penalty Kill	Flynn, Hanzal, and Methot should help.
✔	Power Play	The star forwards should get even deadlier with the new wave of young, puck-moving defencemen.
✔	Scoring Line	McDavid might get some competition for the Art Ross Trophy.
✔	Shutdown Line	Hanzal is a good centre around whom to build this line.
✔	Forward Depth	They have a young and versatile collection of forwards.
	Top Pairing	Klingberg is the only legitimate top pair defenceman, but he isn't the kind who can carry someone.
✔	Second Pairing	They have two solid veterans who can guide young talent.
✔	Defensive Depth	It would take a lot of injuries to run out of decent players.
☆	Coaching	Hitchcock could win the Jack Adams that he should have won with Dallas back in 1996–97.
✔	Prospects	A big boost from its young defencemen is a distinct possibility.

Assessment: They paid a premium, but the Stars absolutely acquired the players they needed to re-establish themselves as contenders.

Detroit Red Wings

Yes, Detroit's miraculous playoff streak may have come to an end, but it does free up the Red Wings to finally embrace a rebuild. However, their efforts to keep that streak alive has pushed them into last place in the long-term cap model laid out in *Stat Shot*. So, it could take some time to dig themselves out of their hole.

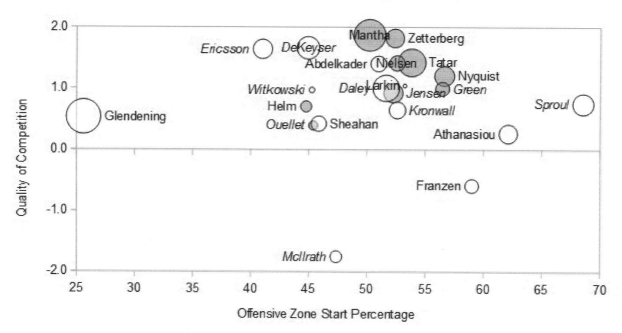

Detroit Red Wings - Player Usage

Every time I see all those white circles around the italicized names on Detroit's player usage chart, like defensive specialists Danny DeKeyser and Jonathan Ericsson at the top, I always wonder why the Red Wings never fixed their blue line. They may have thrown a lot of money at it, and currently rank second in the total blue line cap charge, but they never invested in the right players. I know that quality, top-four defencemen are at a premium these days, but Detroit has had over five years to identify and correct the problem. Heck, Ian White was on the top pair (with Nicklas Lidstrom) as far back as 2011–12.

As illustrated by his own white circle, free agent Trevor Daley is unlikely to help the situation, especially through his mid-30s, and Luke Witkowski and Dylan McIlrath are the type of hard-hitting defencemen who don't even seem to fit in with a modern game that's built around speed and skill.

Whatever happened to the possession-based play for which Detroit was once famous? The only shaded circles on the blue line belong to Mike Green, who has admittedly made a successful (if expensive) transition from a sheltered offensive specialist to a more balanced top-four defenceman, and depth-pair rookies Nick Jensen and Xavier Ouellet.

In nets, Detroit ranks third in total cap charge, and that investment hasn't worked out much more favourably than on defence. Jimmy Howard ranks 15th among goalies in cap hit, and 28th in career save percentage, and Petr Mrazek is 25th and 37th, respectively.

So, Detroit is going to have to rebuild around the talent that they have up front, which in turn is built around centres Henrik Zetterberg, who is still going strong at age 37, and one of the league's most complete, do-it-all players, Frans Nielsen. They are right next to each other at the top of the chart, and with nicely shaded circles. However, Zetterberg scores at the top-six rate of 1.64 points per 60 minutes over the past three years, and Nielsen is only 1.37.

Based on their scoring, and the position and size of their shaded circles on the chart, Tomas Tatar, Gustav Nyquist, and rookie Anthony Mantha makes sense on the wings. That leaves the final spot for Dylan Larkin, who could have a breakout season at age 21.

In terms of depth, Darren Helm is the star of the bottom six. He's fast, can win faceoffs, kills penalties, is one of the league's best at drawing penalties, and is the only remaining shaded circle on the chart.

There are other useful secondary forwards, like rugged winger Justin Abdelkader, the versatile Riley Sheahan, and the promising young Andreas Athanasiou, but there are only 11 (active) forwards on the chart. Rookie Tyler Bertuzzi is likely to find a role, but it wouldn't take very many injuries to derail what will already be a very challenging season.

Score	Category	Notes
✔	Possession	Detroit was once the archetype of possession-based hockey.
✔	The Shootout	Mrazek is better in the shootout than Howard. Nielsen is their best shooting option.
	Goaltending	They made the third greatest investment in cap space, but ranked 25th in team save percentage.
	Penalty Kill	Detroit needs more defensive specialists to work with Helm.
	Power Play	The Red Wings weren't a threat without Pavel Datsyuk.
✔	Scoring Line	Zetterberg is still getting it done.
	Shutdown Line	Neilsen is the only true top-six shutdown forward.
	Forward Depth	Helm is good, but Detroit is short on NHL-calibre forwards.
	Top Pairing	Too many defencemen are higher on the depth chart than they should be.
	Second Pairing	Detroit isn't getting an adequate return on its investment.
✔	Defensive Depth	Jensen and Ouellet are a solid third pair, and the AHL Griffins have a wealth of usable depth options.
	Coaching	As former coach of the Griffins, Blashill has experience with these players in the AHL.
✔	Prospects	Mantha leads a list of several players who could break out.

Assessment: Happy fun time is over.

Edmonton Oilers

Will all due respect to GM Peter Chiarelli, why was he among the finalists for the GM of the Year Award? The winner, David Poile, had to build and claw his team together from scratch, whereas everything positive in Edmonton has directly or indirectly been a consequence of winning the golden ticket on April 18, 2015 – six days before Chiarelli was hired.

Edmonton Oilers - Player Usage

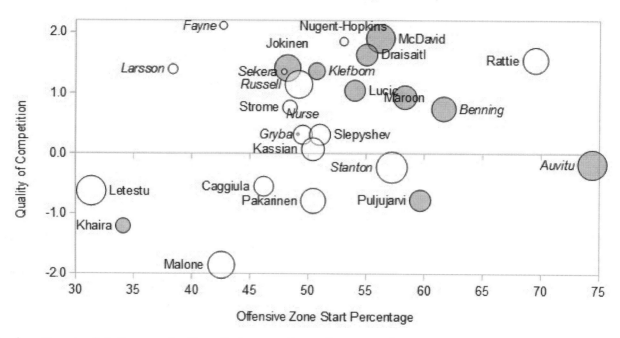

Winning the draft lottery set off a chain reaction of events that completely reversed course for the Edmonton Oilers. First, after years of failing to attract experienced NHL coaches, the Oilers hired Todd McLellan on May 19, 2015. Last season, he was a finalist for the Jack Adams.

Then, after years of failing to attract any top-four free agent defencemen despite a willingness to pay hefty premiums, Andrej Sekera signed a long-term deal on July 1, 2015. After a dismal decade, that was the turning point that helped lead to today's respectable blue line, which currently includes Oscar Klefbom and Adam Larsson, who are both 24, and at the top of the chart with Sekera. Larsson is to the left and more defensive-minded, while Klefbom is a complete, two-way defenceman with a nicely shaded circle. Klefbom agreeing to a seven-year extension on September 19, 2015 was probably no coincidence, either.

Skipping ahead a few months, another key move was on January 17, 2016, when goalie Cam Talbot agreed to a three-year extension, which ended a revolving door of mediocre goalies. He started 73 games and finished fourth in Vezina voting last year. McDavid had to be a key factor in fueling Talbot's interest to remain an Oiler.

81

Even Leon Draisaitl, who has the large shaded circle right next to McDavid's huge one, broke out with 77 points last season largely thanks to McDavid. Draisaitl scored 27 of his points on the power play last year, and his career even-strength scoring rate increases from 1.83 points per 60 minutes without McDavid to 2.22 with him. The other scoring line winger, rugged veteran Patrick Maroon, went from 1.63 to 2.36 – and he played with Ryan Getzlaf and Corey Perry when he was in Anaheim.

None of this is to suggest that Chiarelli deserves no credit at all - simply that McDavid has made his job far easier than Poile's. He even agreed to take a slight discount on his own eight-year extension to help Chiarelli make room for one more player.

McDavid also changes the way that this entire player usage chart can be interpreted. For example, drawing so much attention from opposing teams makes the job of second-line centre Ryan Nugent-Hopkins that much easier. Milan Lucic can boost the physicality, scoring, and shot-based metrics on that line, but at significant long-term expense.

Based on his big, shaded circle, and his position at the top of the chart, it appears that bargain free agent Jussi Jokinen would be a good fit on that second line. However, he scored just 28 points last year, and he may be used to bolster the bottom six instead, which is almost completely void of shaded circles, and players who can take on top opponents.

Score	Category	Notes
	Possession	The Oilers have started heading in the right direction.
	The Shootout	Jokinen adds yet another good shooter, but Talbot is among the worst goalies in the shootout.
	Goaltending	Talbot is solid, but the Oilers needs a reliable backup.
	Penalty Kill	This is one area that McDavid can't improve.
✔	Power Play	McDavid and Draisaitl are an effective combination.
☆	Scoring Line	It's not often that $100 million contracts look like bargains.
	Shutdown Line	Edmonton could use one more really strong two-way winger.
✔	Forward Depth	The Oilers have so many options that it's hard to imagine a scenario where they'd be short-handed.
✔	Top Pairing	Klefbom will be a solid No. 1 defenceman for years to come.
	Second Pairing	The numbers have never been kind to Kris Russell, though he is the league's best shot-blocker.
✔	Defensive Depth	It helps to have two developmental teams, the Bakersfield Condors and the New Jersey Devils.
✔	Coaching	Other than Pat Quinn's season, this is the team's most experienced and accomplished coaching staff in a long time.
✔	Prospects	The Oilers have a huge upside, when you consider all the young players who could break out.

Assessment: The Stanley Cup is always a possibility with McDavid on the roster.

Florida Panthers

Given that the Panthers are perceived to be one of the more enthusiastic adopters of hockey analytics, their struggles last year were seen as a strike against our field. However, if organizations are judged not by what they say, but by what percentage of their moves met with agreement from within the analytics community, then the Panthers can't be seen as our ambassadors. While it's great that statisticians have a seat at Florida's table, it doesn't appear to be at the head.

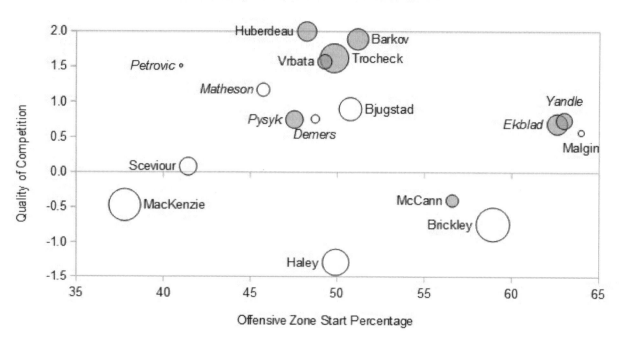

Florida Panthers - Player Usage

For example, last year we criticized the signing of free agent Keith Yandle, because $44.45 million over seven years was a lot of money for a 30-year-old who has never really played top-four minutes. Look at him – he's way over there on the right side of the chart and near the horizon, with Aaron Ekblad. They may be great defencemen, but for the 7th and 16th highest cap hits at their position, it's reasonable to expect them to be at the top and middle of the chart, taking on top opponents in both zones, and killing penalties.

If not them, then who will play the tough minutes in the defensive zone, and against top opponents? According to the numbers, that appears to be Alex Petrovic and rookie Mike Matheson, on the top-left side of the chart. They appear to have done ok, but does that deployment make sense? It better, because Jason Demers and Mark Pysyk are the team's only other defencemen. They need a top-four defensive specialist, or two.

The Panthers also went off the board in selecting San Jose assistant Bob Boughner as the team's new head coach. Of the 53 individuals to have coached at least one full season in the

OHL since 2010, Boughner ranked 19th in average points above expectations.

That's not to argue that the statisticians *never* agree with Florida's moves. In fact, they have clearly made some rather clever decisions lately, despite the disappointing season. But, we haven't been any more likely to agree with them than any other team.

One of the more interesting moves this summer was signing Evgeni Dadonov, who had the NHL equivalent of 31 goals and 69 points in 72 games in the KHL last year. While there's the risk that he may revert to his previously established level of 20 goals and 45 points, that's the sort of creative move that could really pay off.

Similarly, the Panthers added the 5-foot-9 Henrik Haapala, an extraordinary 23-year-old playmaker who led Finland's SM-Liiga in scoring last year. Dadonov and Haapala are likely to join the top six with the four players with the big, shaded circles at the top of the chart. Based on the player usage chart, there really isn't anyone who will be pressing them for a job on the top two lines. The only possibility appears to be Nick Bjugstad, who actually led the Panthers in scoring as a rookie in 2013–14, and carries a cap of $4.1 million. However, he scored just 14 points last season, and didn't score well by shot-based metrics, nor by any other measurement.

In nets, Florida is sticking with the steady tandem of Roberto Luongo and James Reimer, and there's nothing wrong with that. Since Luongo was re-acquired from the Vancouver Canucks on March 4, 2014, they rank 13th with a save percentage of .912. That's a welcome improvement from the .892 over the two preceding seasons, which ranked last.

Score	Category	Notes
	Possession	Florida are almost exactly average in shot-based metrics, but only one team has fewer shaded circles on its chart.
✔	The Shootout	Vrbata further bolsters a depth of great shooters.
✔	Goaltending	Luongo and Reimer are a perfectly acceptable tandem.
✔	Penalty Kill	Florida ranks second to Carolina in shot prevention.
	Power Play	They took a huge stride in the right direction, but lost four of their six highest-scoring forwards this summer.
✔	Scoring Line	Assuming good health and successful transitions from Europe, scoring shouldn't be a problem.
	Shutdown Line	The centres, Barkov and Trocheck, are the only top-six forwards in whose defence we can be truly confident.
	Forward Depth	There are only 17 names on the player usage chart.
✔	Top Pairing	Yandle and Ekblad enjoy highly favourable deployment.
	Second Pairing	They have far more heavy lifting to do than most second pairs.
	Defensive Depth	The Panthers have a good third pair, but don't have the depth to withstand any injuries.
	Coaching	This will be a challenging situation for a rookie NHL coach.
	Prospects	There are opportunities, but not many prospects to grab them.

Assessment: Florida appears to have neither the depth nor the defence to make the playoffs.

Los Angeles Kings

If there has been a strike against statistical analysis, then it's from the Los Angeles Kings. They were among the earliest known adopters of analytics, were the first organization to provide a endorsement quote for these books, and are always among the league's leaders in our beloved shot-based metrics. However, they have made the playoffs just once since winning the Stanley Cup in 2013–14, and were tossed in the first round. There's obviously a blind spot here, but where is it?

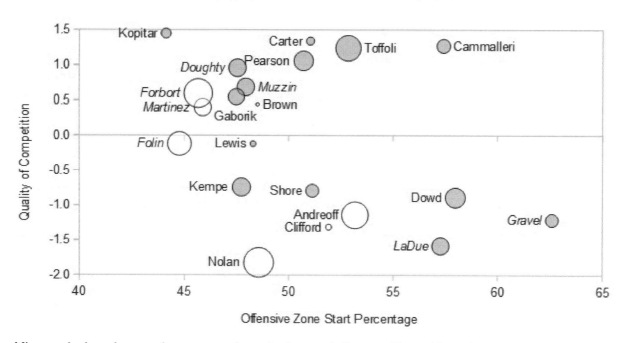

Los Angeles Kings - Player Usage

The Kings obviously need some serious help on defence. Drew Doughty may be in the conversation as the best defenceman in the world, but Jake Muzzin is the only other legitimate top-four defenceman on the roster. All the other defencemen on the player usage chart either have giant white circles, like Alec Martinez and rookie Derek Forbort, or are depth options at the bottom-right corner of the chart. Even by itself, that might have probably been enough to explain the team's poor showing.

Captain Anze Kopitar may have had an off year, but the top six appears to be adequate. With career lows of 12 goals and 52 points (ignoring the lockout-shortened 2012–13 season), Kopitar's franchise record of nine seasons leading the team in scoring came to an end, as did his three-year streak as a Selke finalist. Even in that reduced state, he's still an adequate centre for the team's top scoring line, especially with the low-cost addition of Michael Cammalleri for the wing.

Jeff Carter picked up the slack as the team's new scoring leader. He centres L.A.'s famous "70s Line" with Tyler Toffoli and Tanner Pearson, who have the nicely shaded circles at the top of the chart. As a group, they don't generate a ton of scoring, but each of them are strong defensively.

There are those who argue that it was a long-term injury to Jonathan Quick that derailed the season, but Peter Budaj (now of the Lightning) was just fine in his absence, with a .917 save percentage. Quick has an amazing reputation that helped make him a two-time Vezina finalist, but his career .916 save percentage ranks 27th among active goalies. Given how Budaj rekindled his career as his backup last year, there could be quite a battle between Darcy Kumper, Jeff Zatkoff, and Jack Campbell as his replacement for 2017–18.

Given that the team's forward depth is an obvious area of great strength, that just leaves coaching to blame. That's obviously how the organization felt, because Darryl Sutter was fired on the same day as GM Dean Lombardi, and was replaced by someone without nearly the same credentials. Of the 69 individuals who have coached in the AHL at some point in the past five seasons, Scott Gordon's career coaching stats rank 19th in average points added per season, two spots behind Bruce Cassidy of the Bruins. Unless they acquire and/or develop another defenceman or two, it's hard to see how Gordon will fare much better than Sutter.

Score	Category	Notes
☆	Possession	Even in a bad season, they still had great shot-based metrics.
	The Shootout	The Kings are below average in shooting and goaltending.
✔	Goaltending	Statistically, Quick doesn't measure up to his elite reputation, but he is still a solid starter.
✔	Penalty Kill	The Kings are quite effective at killing penalties.
✔	Power Play	Cammalleri may help boost an already solid power play.
	Scoring Line	Age, injuries, and disappointing seasons cast doubt on L.A's top scoring line.
✔	Shutdown Line	That 70s Line is still going strong.
✔	Forward Depth	The Kings have a very strong bottom six, but there are teams with longer lists of names.
✔	Top Pairing	Doughty could be the league's best defenceman.
✔	Second Pairing	The Kings are trying to stretch the lineup with only two legitimate top-four defencemen.
	Defensive Depth	Folin, Gravel, and Ladue round out the blue line.
	Coaching	Gordon has an opportunity to establish his NHL credentials.
	Prospects	There doesn't appear to be anyone of note on the horizon.

Assessment: With a better blue line, the Kings would be in the mix for a wild card spot.

Minnesota Wild

As predicted, the Wild's new coaching staff helped them jump back almost 20 points in the standings, set a franchise record with 106 points, and secure a home seed in the playoffs. However, they still got tossed in five games in the opening round. Will they build on this?

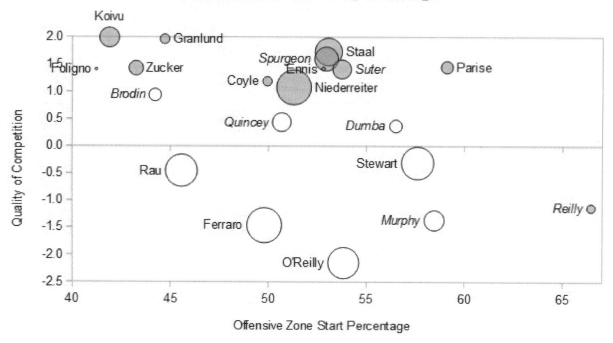

Minnesota Wild - Player Usage

All these player usage charts can start to blur together after a while, but if you draw a horizontal line through Minnesota's chart about halfway through the upper section, then you can get a pretty good idea of what the Wild are all about.

Above the line, they have a variety of players from left to right with the shaded circles that denote good shot-based metrics. Below the line, there are very few players, all but one of whom have white circles. It's just a theory, but that means that they have the top lines to compete with anyone in the league, but may lack the kind of depth that can often make the difference in the playoffs.

Assuming the theory is correct, the problem is most significant on the blue line. Nobody needs a player usage chart to know that Ryan Suter and Jared Spurgeon are highly effective at handling the tough minutes against top opponents in both zones, both in terms of scoring and shot-based metrics, but what about those rare times when they're catching their breath?

There's unquestionably great potential in Jonas Brodin, who is 24, and Matt Dumba, 23. On the left, Brodin's defensive play is highly respected, while Dumba's 34 points was tied for fifth among defencemen aged 22 or younger last year. But, if Minnesota is to be a true contender, both players need to break out right now. What's the alternative if either one of them needs more time, journeyman stay-at-home defenceman Kyle Quincey?

Forward depth is less of an issue, because nine of the 13 listed forwards are above our imaginary horizontal line, and most of them are in their prime.

Even if there's no big-name players who will compete for the Art Ross Trophy, Minnesota is not without its scoring-line weapons. At age 24, Mikael Granlund broke out with a team-leading 26 goals and 69 points last season, while serving as one of the team's top penalty-killers, and taking on top opponents in both zones at even-strength. Based on his solid shot-based metrics, he has the shaded circle in the upper-left corner of the chart next to his linemates, captain and Selke finalist Mikko Koivu and Jason Zucker – who broke out with 22 goals, 47 points, and a league-leading plus-34.

Granlund and Zucker weren't the only 24-year-olds to set new career highs. There's also Charlie Coyle and Nino Niederreiter, who is actually the team's best scorer on a per-minute basis. He averaged 1.93 points per 60 minutes at even strength over the past three seasons. Thanks to his great shot-based metrics, he has the giant shaded circle in the middle of the chart, just below Eric Staal, who had a great bounceback season while centring the top scoring line. Plus, there's Zach Parise, and the two secondary forwards acquired in a summer trade with Buffalo, the defensive-minded Marcus Foligno on the left, and Tyler Ennis towards the right.

In the end, most fans think Minnesota's fate comes down its goaltending. Minnesota was unbeatable when Devan Dubnyk appeared to be in Vezina form with a .941 save percentage as 2016 came to an end, after which they were quite beatable when he fell to .908 in 2017. Since they are essentially without a backup, the Wild better hope to get the former version.

Score	Category	Notes
✔	Possession	Their top lines are great, their depth lines are not.
✔	The Shootout	They have the shooters, but Dubnyk is weak in the shootout.
✔	Goaltending	Dubnyk has a great upside, but is without a proven backup.
✔	Penalty Kill	It's nothing to write home about, but it does the trick.
✔	Power Play	Minnesota is roughly average in almost every category, including the power play.
✔	Scoring Line	Staal really helped bring the scoring line back to life.
✔	Shutdown Line	Koivu was a Selke finalist, and Granlund could be next.
	Forward Depth	They have a very strong third line, but not much after that.
✔	Top Pairing	Suter finished top-10 in the Norris race for the sixth straight season, and Spurgeon finished 13th.
	Second Pairing	The Wild need breakout seasons from Brodin and Dumba.
	Defensive Depth	Just one injury, and Quincey is in the top four.
☆	Coaching	Boudreau and his staff are experienced and accomplished.
	Prospects	Joel Eriksson Ek could be a factor, but that's about it.

Assessment: Minnesota remains a strong candidate for a home playoff seed.

Montreal Canadiens

Over the past three seasons, the Canadiens have earned 193 points in the 140 games that Carey Price has played, which is 1.38 points per game, and 102 in the 106 that he has not, which is 0.96. At face value, that makes Price worth 26 points per 62-start season. That would have to be a four-fold exaggeration before his $10.5 million cap hit becomes an overpay. So, it's reasonable to argue that Montreal's fate rests predominantly on his shoulders.

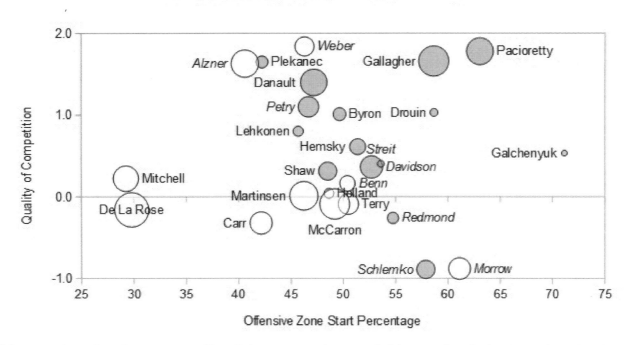

Montreal Canadiens - Player Usage

With a goaltending investment like Price, an understandable emphasis is placed on having the right defencemen in front of him. While it never appeared to be an issue in the past, the blue line has been completely overhauled. Of the 15 defencemen Montreal used in the 2015–16 season, only Jeff Petry remains.

Petry will continue to anchor the second pair as a reliable two-way defenceman with good shot-based metrics. It's uncertain who his partner will be, but Brandon Davidson, David Schlemko, Mark Streit, and even journeyman Zach Redmond have all had periods of success in third pair roles, and could perform well with Petry. So, it will probably be Jordie Benn or Joseph Morrow.

In place of P.K. Subban and Andrei Markov, the Canadiens now have Shea Weber and Karl Alzner at the top of the chart, taking on top opponents in both zones. However, they both have big white circles, which demonstrates the philosophical shift taking place in Montreal that places far less emphasis on shot-based metrics in that particular role.

The philosophy doesn't apply to the top lines, however, where Max Pacioretty and Brendan

Gallagher have big shaded circles. Pacioretty is a great goal-scorer who just led the team in scoring for the sixth straight season. Rather than Gallagher, there's the possibility that Pacioretty will play with the highly skilled Jonathan Drouin, who has the potential to de-throne him. If Alexander Galchenyuk centres that line, then he could be in the mix as well.

Historically, the second line was centred by Tomas Plekanec, who is appropriately located in the top-left corner of the chart. However, Philip Danault developed into that role last year, and responded with 40 points, sound defensive play, and exceptional shot-based metrics. This allowed Plekanec to boost the bottom six, by working with rookie Artturi Lehkonen and helping hard-working defensive specialist Paul Byron to a breakout, 43-point season.

The arrival of Ales Hemsky adds even more veteran experience, secondary scoring, and shot-based success to the bottom six, which includes about a dozen options, according to their player usage chart.

As for coaching, there was nothing obviously wrong about the team's numbers under Michel Therrien. However, Claude Julien has a strong NHL track record, and would have been snapped up pretty quickly if Montreal hadn't acted fast when he became available.

Score	Category	Notes
✔	Possession	With the exception of the top two defencemen, Montreal has developed an emphasis on strong shot-based metrics.
	The Shootout	Price is a good goalie, but Hemsky is the only good shooter.
☆	Goaltending	If any goalie deserves that kind of money, then it's Price.
✔	Penalty Kill	The Canadiens were practically built to kill penalties.
	Power Play	Montreal finished last in power play shot attempts per minute.
✔	Scoring Line	Drouin could have a breakout season if he plays with a consistent top goal-producer like Pacioretty.
✔	Shutdown Line	Montreal has a mix of skilled, young, two-way forwards.
✔	Forward Depth	Only one team has more forwards on its player usage chart.
	Top Pairing	If shot-based metrics are to be believed, then Montreal could have a vulnerability here.
	Second Pairing	Petry is a reliable second pair defenceman.
✔	Defensive Depth	There is no shortage of solid third-pair options.
✔	Coaching	Julien is one of only a handful of active coaches with a stronger NHL track record than Therrien.
	Prospects	The team's organizational strength won't be felt this year.

Assessment: Montreal remains a solid playoff team.

Nashville Predators

It was highly rewarding to watch the Predators compete in last year's Stanley Cup Final. Given that my first radio guests spots were with Nashville back in 2011, I developed a certain attachment to the team – despite being nicknamed Buzzkill for my frequent criticisms.

In the years that followed, I watched and reported with satisfaction as more and more of the organization's decisions lined up with our viewpoints. Last year's playoff success was not only a pleasing summit for that journey, but it felt like something of a vindication for our perspective. Now the question is if this was all a fluke, or if that success will continue.

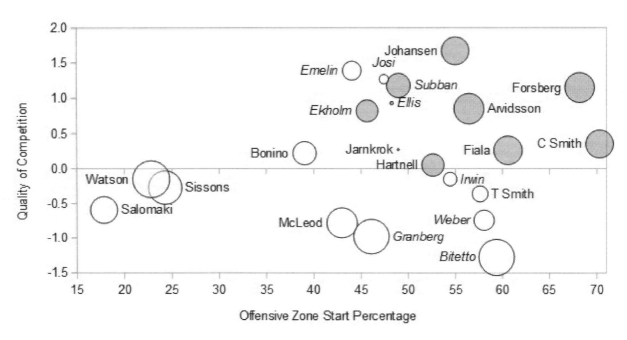

Nashville Predators - Player Usage

Looking back, the earliest and strongest signal of impending success was Nashville's blue line. Built primarily through the draft, and then cut loose with the bold acquisition of P.K. Subban last summer, the Predators may have the best top four in the league. On the chart, Subban, Mattias Ekholm, Roman Josi, and Ryan Ellis are all in the same spot, taking on top opponents in both zones, and with particularly good shot-based metrics in the case of the Subban-Ekholm pairing.

Aware of a potential depth issue, GM David Poile also added defensive-minded veteran Alexei Emelin to fill in whenever one of the big four is out of the lineup, and to otherwise boost the least-used third pair in the league (those with all the white circles below the horizon).

Up front, Nashville assembled one of the league's best two-way top lines mostly through trade. Ryan Johansen, Filip Forsberg, and Victor Arvidsson are all between ages 23 and 25, scored between 58 and 61 points, play in all three manpower situations, take on top

91

opponents, and have the big, shaded circles that indicate very strong shot-based metrics.

With the loss of the team's next three highest-scoring forwards, Nashville's summer challenge was to assemble a second line that can score. Based on even-strength scoring rates, they do have some interesting options, even if none of them are have established themselves in top-six roles, at the top of the chart.

The big shaded circle on the far right side belongs to Craig Smith, whose average even-strength scoring rate of 1.81 points per 60 minutes over the past three seasons actually exceeds Johansen's, 1.74, and matches free agent centre Nick Bonino's. The highest scoring rate on the team actually belongs to 35-year-old free agent power forward Scott Hartnell, 2.16, who has a nicely shaded circle of his own. Rookie Kevin Fiala's scoring rate was just 1.38, but there are hopes that he can break out this year, at age 21.

After them, all those white circles among depth-line forwards appear ominous. However, they do have a solid third-line centre in Calle Jarnkrok, and everybody saw what players like Pontus Aberg, Colton Sissons, Austin Watson, and Frederick Gaudreau were capable of in the playoffs. So, it's possible that forward depth won't be an issue for much longer.

In nets, Nashville is engaging in a fascinating experiment. Backup goalie Juuse Saros is just 5-foot-11, but had a save percentage of .929 in Finland's SM-liiga, .924 in the AHL, and .922 in 22 NHL games. Just in case, the Predators also brought back Anders "the Giant" Lindback, and still have 6-foot-4 third-string goalie Marek Mazanec.

Score	Category	Notes
✔	Possession	Nashville is one of the league's stronger possession teams.
✔	The Shootout	They are roughly average at shooting and goaltending.
✔	Goaltending	Rinne's not elite over the long term, but he's capable.
✔	Penalty Kill	Even without Fisher, their PK will be just fine.
	Power Play	The Predators could use more scoring punch.
	Scoring Line	Nashville only has three established top-six forwards
✔	Shutdown Line	Those three each happen to be effective two-way players.
	Forward Depth	There is only one or two shaded circles outside the top six.
✔	Top Pairing	Despite being a Cup Finalist, Josi is the only Predator to get a first or second place vote for the NHL All-Star Teams.
☆	Second Pairing	Subban and Ekholm are among the best second pairs.
✔	Defensive Depth	Even if they all have white circles, Nashville has several more defencemen. Emelin could play in the top four, if necessary.
✔	Coaching	The underrated Laviolette is effective at zone matching.
✔	Prospects	The Predators have Fiala and Saros, plus some late bloomers up front who could break out this year.

Assessment: Last year was no fluke. Nashville will remain in the mix for years to come.

New Jersey Devils

Ok, this is starting to get ridiculous. In 2015–16, the New Jersey Devils finished last with 184 goals, and yet they somehow managed to get worse, scoring 183 last year. They haven't scored 200 goals in a season since 2011–12, which was the season that they reached the Stanley Cup Final – and the last time they made the playoffs.

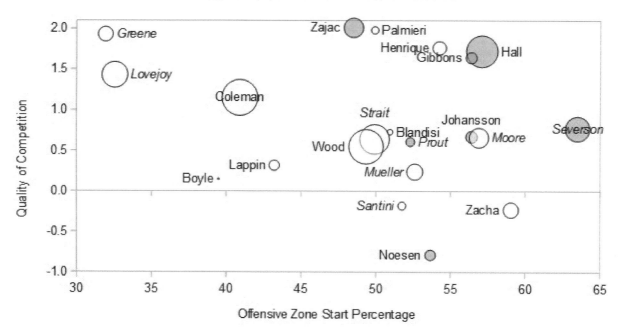

New Jersey Devils - Player Usage

The good news for the Devils is that they won the lottery for the first overall selection, which has certainly proved helpful to other teams. Last season, Auston Matthews led the Toronto Maple Leafs with 40 goals and 69 points, and second overall pick Patrik Laine scored 36 goals and 64 points for the Winnipeg Jets. That would be a welcome boon for the Devils.

With the pick, the Devils selected Nico Hischier, but he is more of a prospect for the longer term. In fact, he didn't even lead his own QMJHL team in scoring last year, the Halifax Mooseheads. However, Hischier is only one of many prospects who could crack the lineup and break out this year, like John Quenneville, Pavel Zacha, Stefan Noesen, Miles Wood, Blake Speers, Blake Coleman, and Nick Lappin.

This isn't to argue that the Devils are completely devoid of established scorers. The best example is Taylor Hall, who has the giant shaded circle in the top-right side of the chart, because of his great shot-based metrics. He led the Oilers in scoring in three of his six seasons there, finished second in another two, and tied Kyle Palmieri last year with 53 points.

The two other key circles near Hall and Palmieri belong to Travis Zajac and Adam Henrique, the only other two Devils to score more than 31 points last year. They're also the team's top two penalty-killing forwards, and their location at the middle-top of the chart make them ideal for more of a shutdown line.

Further down the chart and on the right, New Jersey also added free agent Marcus Johansson, who scored 24 goals and 58 points on Washington's second scoring line with Evgeny Kuznetsov and Justin Williams last year.

How about scoring from the blue line? Judging from his position on the far right side of the chart near the horizon, there is the possibility that Damon Severson is being developed into a scoring-focused No. 4 defenceman like Shayne Gostisbehere or Justin Schultz. If so, he could continue to build on his 31 points last year, which led the team's defencemen.

There doesn't appear to be any other defencemen who can contribute to the scoring, save a little bit from John Moore. Dalton Prout is a hitter, Michael Kapla probably isn't ready, depth-pair prospects like Yaroslav Dyblenko, Steven Santini, and Mirco Mueller don't have much offensive upside, and captain Andy Greene is way up in the top-left corner of the chart because he is absolutely buried with all the defensive zone minutes against top opponents. His only company is Ben Lovejoy, whose giant white circle suggests that he's not nearly as suitable for those kinds of tough minutes.

All of this puts Schneider into a hopeless situation. His career save percentage of .922 is exactly the same as Braden Holtby's, but he has a lower winning percentage (.700 to .532) because of his much lower goal support (2.99 to 2.19). No Vezina recognition for him!

Score	Category	Notes
	Possession	Long ago, the Devils were a model for shot-based metrics.
	The Shootout	New Jersey may be the worst team in the shootout.
✔	Goaltending	On a team with more goal support, Schneider would be a multi-time Vezina finalist.
✔	Penalty Kill	The Devils are solid at killing penalties.
	Power Play	They may be the worst team with the man advantage.
	Scoring Line	The less written about this, the better.
	Shutdown Line	It feels odd for to leave this box blank for New Jersey.
	Forward Depth	The team is deep in organizational strength, but it's always a crapshoot to predict when prospects will be ready.
	Top Pairing	Greene will get buried with all the tough minutes and an inadequate partner, yet again.
✔	Second Pairing	There is potential to build a solid puck-moving pair around Severson.
	Defensive Depth	They're counting on rookies and an injury-free season.
	Coaching	It was a setback for Hynes, who had a promising first season.
✔	Prospects	Their only chance to be competitive is if Hischier and several of their numerous prospects break out this year.

Assessment: Unless they can find a way to score, the Devils return to the draft lottery.

New York Islanders

There are those who dismiss the success of certain teams on the grounds that it is easy to be successful with a first overall pick in the lineup. Well, it has been eight years since the New York Islanders drafted John Tavares first overall, and what do they have to show for it? Three playoff appearances, in which they have won only a single series.

To help them be competitive, Tavares even agreed to a discount contract in 2011, which currently carries a cap hit that is matched or exceeded by four of his teammates. Well, there is only one year left before that golden opportunity ends, so winning isn't nearly as easy as some people seem to think, with or without a franchise player.

New York Islanders - Player Usage

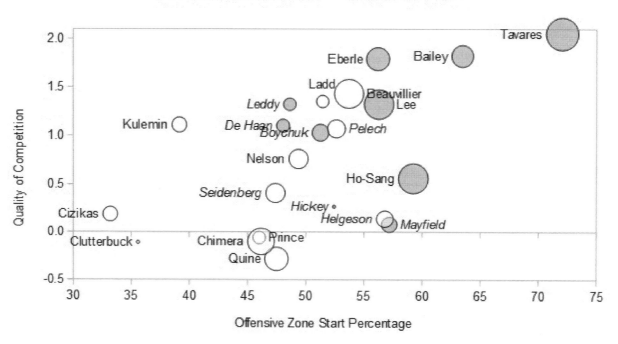

On the chart, Tavares is way out there on an island in the top-right corner. That means that he is understandably used in the offensive zone to a greater extent than all but a few NHL players, and has to face each team's top opponents.

His scoring line wingers will likely include two of the three nicely shaded circles closest to him on the chart, Joshua Bailey, Anders Lee, and Jordan Eberle, who was acquired from the Edmonton Oilers this summer, to make cap space for a first overall pick of their own. There's little question that virtually any combination of them will be effective in terms of both scoring, and shot-based metrics.

Most successful teams with a franchise player like Tavares have a second top forward around whom to build a second line. Depending on who it is, this is either a scoring line that takes advantage of the easier matchups that occur while opponents are focused on the top line, or a shutdown line that aims to handle the tough minutes itself. In the case of the Islanders, the intention was clearly the latter, but the white circles demonstrate how players like Andrew Ladd and Brock Nelson aren't having the greatest success in that regard. They are not even located at the top-left side of the chart, which would relieve more of the pressure on Tavares.

This season, the Islanders hope to develop one or more of their young forwards, Joshua Ho-Sang, Anthony Beauvillier, Mathew Barzal, and Michael Dal Colle into key roles. Their development could be critical in maintaining the perception that the Islanders are competitive. Even if none of them prove to be a solution for the second line, they are the key to building a bottom six that already includes effective (but overpaid) veterans like Jason Chimera, Nikolai Kulemin, Cal Clutterbuck, and Casey Cizikas.

On the blue line, much has been written about top defencemen Johnny Boychuk and Nick Leddy, but consider Calvin de Haan, who has a similar shaded circle and location on the chart. That means that de Haan has been handling the same kind of minutes as Boychuk and Leddy, against top-six opponents, in both zones, and has done just as well from a shot-based perspective. That's why he is the reasonable choice to replace Travis Hamonic in the top four, and why he should be effective in doing so.

It's unclear who will complete the top four. Veterans Dennis Seidenberg and Thomas Hickey are probably best suited for a third pair, defencemen Seth Helgeson and Scott Mayfield are of the more hard-hitting depth variety, and Adam Pelech probably still needs a little bit more time to develop. While it's not particularly common for rookies to step directly into the top four, the pressure could be on Ryan Pulock to fill that hole.

Score	Category	Notes
	Possession	I knew it was a mistake to give them a checkmark last year.
✔	The Shootout	Eberle gives the team a second good shooter.
✔	Goaltending	Greiss and Halak are both fine goalies.
	Penalty Kill	The Islanders have struggled at shutting down top opponents, in any manpower situation.
	Power Play	It's hoped that Eberle will help boost the Islanders' power play.
✔	Scoring Line	Tavares is certainly the team's greatest strength.
	Shutdown Line	A good shutdown line, like when Nielsen was in town, takes a lot of pressure off the top line.
✔	Forward Depth	The veterans are overpaid, but effective, and are supplemented by a lot of talented youth.
✔	Top Pairing	Leddy and Boychuk are an effective top pair.
	Second Pairing	The Islanders only have three top-four defencemen.
✔	Defensive Depth	They have a total of nine reasonable blue line options.
	Coaching	Despite no coaching experience at any level, assistant GM Doug Weight is taking over himself.
✔	Prospects	The Islanders have up to five players who could break out.

Assessment: The Islanders can compete for a wild card spot.

New York Rangers

The New York Rangers have remained competitive for longer than any team based outside California. However, they have yet to win a Stanley Cup in this extended window of contention, and time is bound to start running out. Is there anything more they can do?

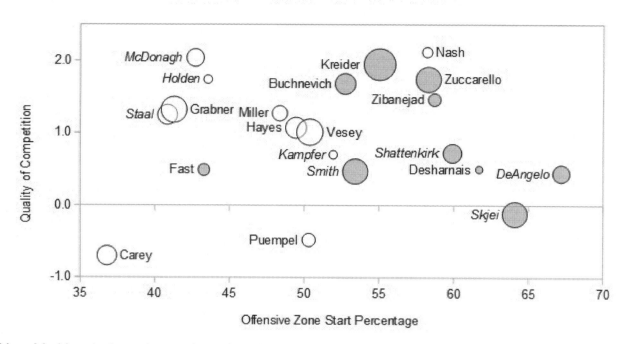

New York Rangers - Player Usage

If New York's window slams shut, then it will be on the fingers of GM Jeff Gorton, who has spared no expense in keeping it open. This summer, the big investments were on the blue line, to sign power play specialist Kevin Shattenkirk, and renew Brendan Smith. Instead, they may have wanted to pursue some defensive specialists who can play the tough minutes, rather than more firepower.

As can be seen from their shaded circles on the chart, these moves are solid from a shot-based perspective. However, both players are near the horizon and towards the right side of the chart, meaning that they generally don't take on top opponents, and are generally meant for offensive-minded duty in the bottom half of the lineup. That's not necessarily a problem, but they also have players like rookie Brady Skjei and prospect Anthony DeAngelo as excellent candidates for those roles, plus journeyman Steven Kampfer as injury insurance.

Several of those players are going to have to switch roles, and start taking on the tough minutes against top opponents and in the defensive zone, in the top-left side of the chart. Based on their white circles, Ryan McDonagh, Nick Holden, and Marc Staal could probably use some assistance in this regard.

The issue is even greater up front, where they have plenty of forwards who can score, but not as many who can defend. Though without any potential Art Ross candidates, Jesper Fast and prospect Vinny Lettieri are the only forwards on their roster who aren't plausible candidates to score 20 goals and 50 points. Even depth forward Paul Carey scored 55 points in 55 games for the AHL Hershey Bears last year, so the Rangers will literally be rolling four lines that all pose at least a modest scoring threat.

So, there are plenty of players who can score, but it's not clear who will be tasked with shutting down top opponents, especially in the absence of Derek Stepan. Fans might point to Fast or Michael Grabner, but they're on the secondary lines. Here, we're not just referring to defensive players on the left of the chart, but those who can be used at the top of the chart, against players like Alex Ovechkin or Sidney Crosby. But, there's really nobody there, and especially none with the shaded circles that denote shot-based success.

To potentially exaggerate this shortage of players who can effectively handle the tough minutes, starting goalie Henrik Lundqvist had the first below-average season of his entire life at age 34. Then, Gorton traded away solid backup Antti Raanta, and replaced him with Ondrej Pavelec. Add it all up, and the Rangers should be a very strong team offensively, but they could be vulnerable defensively.

Score	Category	Notes
	Possession	They are establishing a reputation as a non-possession team.
✔	The Shootout	The Rangers are among the best in the shootout.
✔	Goaltending	Lundqvist will bounce back.
✔	Penalty Kill	The Rangers are excellent at killing penalties.
✔	Power Play	By himself, Shattenkirk could boost any team to a checkmark.
✔	Scoring Line	Though without a single Art Ross-contending superstar, the Rangers are always a threat to score.
	Shutdown Line	With Stepan gone, the Rangers lack obvious candidates to take on top opponents, up front or on defence.
☆	Forward Depth	Strong depth lines has long been a philosophical choice.
✔	Top Pairing	McDonagh is highly underrated, and Shattenkirk can evolve into a complete, two-way defenceman.
	Second Pairing	New York can get a lot of scoring from the point, but has very few players who can effectively handle the tough minutes.
☆	Defensive Depth	They have several young, excellent, puck-moving options.
✔	Coaching	With Ruff joining Vigneault, no coaching staff has more combined games of experience than the New York Rangers.
	Prospects	Though not at the top of the league, there is potential that a couple of players could break out for New York this year.

Assessment: The Rangers are on the decline, but remain a playoff-calibre team.

Ottawa Senators

Rather than go off the board and select a new head coach without any experience and/or success at any level, the Ottawa Senators went with coaches with proven track records, like Guy Boucher and Marc Crawford. The results? They wound up bouncing back 13 points in the standings, and advancing to within a double overtime goal of making the Stanley Cup Final. Just some food for thought.

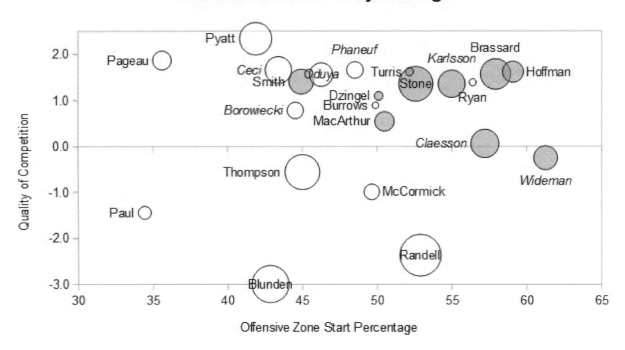

Ottawa Senators - Player Usage

The notion that Erik Karlsson is weak defensively is one of the myths that hockey analytics has been helping to dispel. Yes, he is an offensive-minded defenceman on the right side of the chart, but he's near the top because he takes on the best opponents, and he has the kind of large, shaded circle that demonstrates that he generates far, far more offence than he permits. Flip through the other charts, and you won't find any defencemen positioned similarly who don't have solid defensive reputations.

If there is an issue on Ottawa's blue line (and there is), then it's with the rest of it. Karlsson has proven that he can carry practically anyone on the top pair, but the second pair of Dion Phaneuf and Cody Ceci both have white circles, as does Johnny Oduya, and all the other names on the chart are depth players who averaged 14 minutes a night, or less.

In fairness, the shaded circles do suggest that Fredrik Claesson and Chris Wideman performed quite well last season, but they played very sheltered minutes in the bottom right, against secondary competition, and in the offensive zone. Someone will have to break out this year, whether it's one of those two, or rookie Thomas Chabot, or one of the team's many tough prospects who are cast from the same mold as Mark Borowiecki.

Given that mediocre blue line, it's safe to argue that Ottawa's deep playoff run was mostly driven by the team's forwards (and Karlsson). As showcased in the Eastern Conference Final, one of the team's key assets is its strength down the middle. From right (offensive) to left (defensive) on the chart, the Senators have Derick Brassard, Kyle Turris, Zack Smith, and Jean-Gabriel Pageau. They're each at the top of the chart and capable of playing against top-six opponents, they each scored at least 32 points and took at least 137 shots in the regular season, and only Brassard didn't take at least an occasional shift killing penalties.

Offensively, Ottawa's top wingers are Mike Hoffman and Mark Stone, based not only on the huge shaded circles based on their shot-based metrics, but also on their even-strength scoring rates of 2.22 and 2.12 points per 60 minutes over the past three seasons combined.

To that, the Senators added some depth for the playoffs, with Alex Burrows, Viktor Stalberg (now in Switzerland), Tommy Wingels (now with Chicago), a healthy Clarke MacArthur, and a rejuvenated Bobby Ryan. If Ryan truly is reborn, and MacArthur is healthy, and Ryan Dzingel continues to develop, then the Senators could have a real depth of scoring on the wings, which can help the team overcome its blue line deficiencies, and make the playoffs again.

Score	Category	Notes
	Possession	They're a possession team with Karlsson on the ice, and something entirely different when he's not.
✔	The Shootout	They have at least three excellent shooters.
✔	Goaltending	The Senators have perfectly acceptable goaltending.
	Penalty Kill	Given how many strong defensive forwards they have, it's odd that they give up so many shorthanded shot attempts.
	Power Play	Karlsson and Hoffman have been effective.
✔	Scoring Line	If Ryan is reborn, then Ottawa should be in good shape.
✔	Shutdown Line	Stone finished sixth in the Selke race last year.
✔	Forward Depth	The depth chart starts to look a little sketchy on the fourth line, but the third line is excellent.
✔	Top Pairing	They can stretch their lineup by playing anyone with Karlsson.
	Second Pairing	By comparison, Karlsson probably makes Phaneuf and Ceci look worse than they really are.
	Defensive Depth	This is probably the team's primary concern.
✔	Coaching	Choosing coaches with experience and prior success has its advantages.
	Prospects	Out of necessity, a few young defencemen will get a shot.

Assessment: While another deep run is unlikely, the Senators can battle for a wild card.

Philadelphia Flyers

While the Flyers have had their struggles over the past five seasons, drafting Nolan Patrick second overall this summer added to the kind of organizational strength that can turn things around quite quickly.

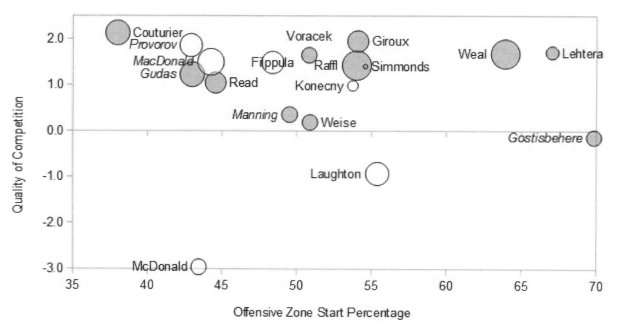

When studying a prospect's scoring totals, it's important to consider age. When Patrick broke out with 41 goals and 102 points in 72 games for the Brandon Wheat Kings, he was only 17 years old. All the other players in the WHL scoring race that season were two or three years older.

The same situation applied to Jordan Weal, who was 17 when he scored the same 102 points in 72 games for the Regina Pats six years earlier. Weal closed the season on a line with Wayne Simmonds and either Claude Giroux or Valtteri Filppula, and scored 12 points in 23 games.

Another prospect who could find himself in the top six is Travis Konecny, who started last season on a top line with Sean Couturier and Jakub Voracek, and scored 12 points in the first 20 games.

Despite how the chart might look, the Flyers desperately need these three prospects to break out. Claude Giroux may rank third in total points over the past six seasons combined, but most of that is on the power play. At even-strength, his average scoring rate is an alarmingly low 1.37 points per 60 minutes over the past three seasons.

Giroux may have a nicely shaded circle that denotes good shot-based metrics, but the Flyers need more scoring on his top line. Currently, the top options are Jakub Voracek and Wayne Simmonds, but their scoring rates are a mediocre 1.69 and 1.50, respectively. At a glance, it may appear that players like Michael Raffl and Jori Lehtera can help, but they are secondary contributors only.

Second-line centre Sean Couturier has a similar issue on the shutdown line. While he is certainly a capable two-way player, he's not much of a scoring threat, and the Flyers are short on players in the top-left corner, who can take on top opponents in defensive situations. Matt Read is more of a secondary player, and Valtteri Filppula's white circle signals that he should be, too.

Philadelphia's organizational strength is also badly needed on the blue line. There are only five names on that chart, only two of whom have more than two NHL seasons under their belts (and one of whom is Andrew MacDonald). They need prospects like Travis Sanheim and Samuel Morin to make the jump this year. Morin is in the same style as hard-hitting defensive options like Radko Gudas and Brandon Manning, while Sanheim has the offensive upside to play a more of a two-way role, like Ivan Provorov.

This summer, Philadelphia locked down Shayne Gostisbehere to a long-term contract. He's way on the right side of the chart and on the horizon, because he plays a very specific kind of role. He is carefully deployed against secondary lines, and in offensive situations only. He performs that role very well, but be mindful of how that requires everybody else to shift to the left side of the chart, and up, in order to pick up the defensive slack.

If coach Dave Hakstol succeeds in developing these prospects and making the playoffs, then it might help overcome the NHL's inexplicable resistance to hiring NCAA coaches. But, if they falter, then keep an eye on new assistant coach Kris Knoblauch. Of all coaches outside the NHL under age 40, Knoblauch's coaching metrics are among the best.

Score	Category	Notes
✔	Possession	It's reasonable to classify Philadelphia as a possession team.
	The Shootout	Philadelphia is below average in shooting and goaltending.
✔	Goaltending	The Flyers replaced Mason with Elliot. Is that a wash?
✔	Penalty Kill	Couturier and Read headline a decent penalty kill.
☆	Power Play	Giroux and the Flyers are outstanding on the power play.
	Scoring Line	Despite appearances, they don't generate enough scoring.
	Shutdown Line	Couturier is excellent, but needs more scoring, and wingers.
✔	Forward Depth	Philadelphia's depth lines should be solid.
	Top Pairing	They don't have anyone to effectively take on tough minutes.
✔	Second Pairing	Gostisbehere is a highly effective puck-moving 4th D.
	Defensive Depth	There are only five names on that chart.
✔	Coaching	Why more teams don't mine NCAA for coaches is beyond me.
☆	Prospects	Patrick boosts them from a checkmark to a star.

Assessment: The Flyers should be in the mix for a wild card spot.

Pittsburgh Penguins

At 30, what does Sidney Crosby need to do in his remaining years to finish his career within the conversation as the greatest player of all-time? Last year, he added another Rocket Richard, Conn Smythe, and Stanley Cup to his already impressive list of credentials, and was runner-up for the Art Ross and the Hart. How many more years does he have to keep that up before Gretzky, Lemieux, Orr, and Howe have competition?

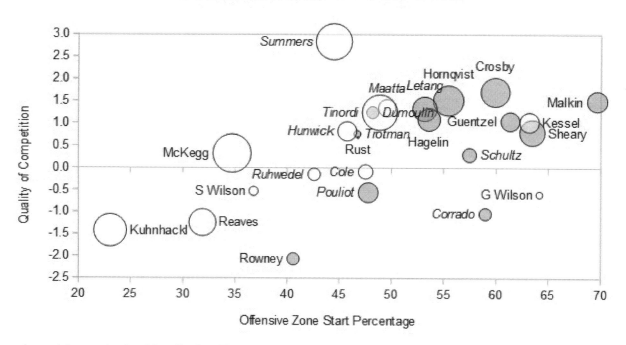

Pittsburgh Penguins - Player Usage

You almost have to feel badly for Evgeni Malkin, who is destined to rank no better than the fourth best player in Penguins history, no matter what he does. Despite his own incredible list of achievements, he was mysteriously left off the NHL's list of Top-100 players of all-time.

As for the team analysis at hand, the Penguins are defined by Crosby and Malkin, who give the Penguins the best one-two punch down the middle in hockey today, and one of the best of all-time. With two such dominant players, the Penguins employ a power-vs-power strategy, which can be seen by the way the circles flow from the bottom-left to the top-right. That is, the more skilled players are used both offensively and against top competition, while the more defensive players are used against the depth lines. Unlike almost all other teams, they don't have anyone in the top left corner who takes on top opponents in defensive situations, nor anyone in the bottom-right getting sheltered.

This philosophy doesn't necessarily extend to the blue line, where they are without superstars of the same magnitude. They do have Kris Letang, who plays a lot of minutes in all manpower situations, in both zones, and against top competition, and generates a lot of points and great shot-based metrics, but he's the only do-it-all blue line superman in town.

So, beyond Letang, the defencemen have assigned roles, which includes Olli Maatta and the highly underrated Brian Dumoulin towards the top-left, playing the tough minutes against top opponents in the defensive zone, while players like Justin Schultz on the right and near the horizon, because they are used more carefully in the offensive zone and against secondary competition. Beyond that, the Penguins have extraordinary blue line depth which can effectively bolster their strength in either of these areas.

Up front, the Penguins don't have quite as much depth, despite having been able to stretch out the lineup by playing prospects like Jake Guentzel and Conor Sheary on the top lines. This is largely a consequence of the salary cap, which doesn't permit teams to accumulate too many marquee players at once. The Penguins have chosen to invest their remaining dimes on Phil Kessel and Patric Hornqvist for the top six, and defensive-minded winger Carl Hagelin for the third line. Beyond that, they pretty much have to rely on players like Tom Kuhnackl, Carter Rowney, Scott Wilson, and Bryan Rust (and, hope that nobody gets hurt).

In nets, Matt Murray's solid play has taken some of the edge off losing a solid goalie like Marc-Andre Fleury in the expansion draft – especially since he had his worst year in seven seasons. Flip to the chapter on goaltending analytics to see how effective Murray might be.

Score	Category	Notes
✔	Possession	They took a dip last year, but the Penguins are still a strong possession team.
	The Shootout	They have the shooters, but not the goaltending.
✔	Goaltending	Murray has demonstrated that he can be a solid No. 1 goalie.
✔	Penalty Kill	Losing Bonino, Cullen, and Hainsey could sting.
✔	Power Play	Crosby, Malkin, Kessel, Letang, oh my.
✔	Scoring Line	Four of the players in the three-year, top-10 even-strength scoring rates play for the Penguins.
☆	Shutdown Line	Pittsburgh doesn't have a shutdown line persay, but whatever you call Crosby's line is obviously sensational.
	Forward Depth	The cap space only extends so far.
✔	Top Pairing	Only his injuries have kept Letang out of the Norris mix.
✔	Second Pairing	Schultz has found a role in which he can be effective.
☆	Defensive Depth	There are 12 defencemen on that chart, half of whom have shaded circles.
✔	Coaching	Pittsburgh's a good example of how the right coach can make all the difference.
	Prospects	We're not expecting any significant rookie impacts.

Assessment: The Penguins remain a Stanley Cup contender.

San Jose Sharks

The Vegas Golden Knights should study the San Jose Sharks as one of the modern era's most successful, and least successful, expansion teams. On one hand, they have made the playoffs in 17 of the past 19 seasons, but on the other hand, they have never won the Stanley Cup, and have made the Final only once.

San Jose Sharks - Player Usage

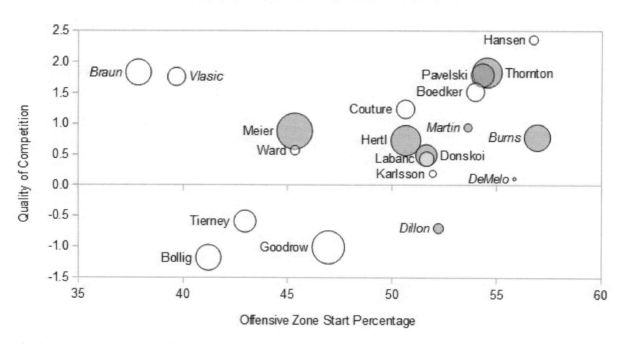

For whatever reason, Joe Thornton often gets the blame for San Jose's post-season disappointments, when really he should get more credit for the regular season success. Even on this chart, the shaded circles are often a consequence of who got to play with him and Joe Pavelski. For example, it's obvious that Tomas Hertl has enjoyed his fair share of ice time on that line over the past few years.

An interesting exception is rookie Timo Meier. Although it's only based on 34 games on the depth lines, Meier's shot-based metrics were fantastic. Given the team's troubling lack of forward depth, they'll be counting on some breakout seasons from him, and others.

In particular, one or more of these young players may be relied upon for the second line, which has an opening with the departure of Patrick Marleau to the Toronto Maple Leafs. Typically, this assignment involves players located on the top-left side of the chart, because it requires taking on top opponents in both zones, but none of the remaining players fit that description. Logan Couture and Jannik Hansen both take on top opponents, are strong defensively, kill penalties, and have the scoring rates required to play in the top six, but are located more to the right, and have the white circles that denote weaker shot-based metrics.

105

The same description roughly suits Mikkel Boedker and defensive-minded veteran Joel Ward, but they don't have top-six scoring rates.

On the blue line, the assignments are quite clear, and effective. Brent Burns and Paul Martin are the offensive-minded pair, as demonstrated by their position on the far-right side of the chart. That leaves the tough minutes to Marc-Edouard Vlasic and Justin Braun, who are consequently on the far left, and towards the top, because they take on the top opponents. Yes, they have white circles that denote weaker shot-based metrics, but they do have a challenging assignment, and one that doesn't allow for a lot of ice time with Thornton.

As for defensive depth, Brenden Dillon and Dylan DeMelo should form a decent third pair, but the depth chart is pretty barren beyond them. The team's seventh defenceman appears to be prospect Tim Heed, who scored 56 points in 55 games in the AHL last season, but has only a single game of NHL experience.

There's also a potential depth issue in goal. Martin Jones has been a reliable No. 1 goalie for the past two seasons, but his possible backups Aaron Dell, Troy Grosenick, and Antoine Bibeau have a combined 24 games of NHL experience. So, the Sharks could easily get into trouble if the injury bug bites either Jones, or one of the team's top four defencemen – not to mention Thornton or Pavelski.

Score	Category	Notes
✔	Possession	Thanks mostly to Thornton and Pavelski, San Jose's shot-based metrics are safely above average.
☆	The Shootout	Statistically, San Jose is the best in the shootout.
	Goaltending	Jones is adequate, but has no backup.
	Penalty Kill	The Sharks appear to have the players to be effective killing penalties, but they haven't been.
☆	Power Play	San Jose has a highly effective power play, thanks to Burns, Thornton, and Pavelski.
✔	Scoring Line	Even at 38, Thornton can still get the job done.
	Shutdown Line	Only three of these forwards scored 30 points last year.
	Forward Depth	There aren't many names on this chart, and too many of them have big white circles.
✔	Top Pairing	Burns could be the game's best offensive defenceman.
✔	Second Pairing	And Vlasic could be one of the game's best, defensively.
	Defensive Depth	The Sharks can't absorb any blue line injuries.
✔	Coaching	OHL coaches have never had a lot of success in the NHL, but Peter DeBoer and his staff are working to change that.
	Prospects	While the Sharks certainly need some breakout performances, they are without any obvious blue chip prospects.

Assessment: The Sharks are on the decline, but can still battle for a wild card spot.

St. Louis Blues

At this time of year, the contribution hockey analytics can make to team analysis is to help establish where teams currently are, and in which direction they're headed. The Blues have been a Cup contender for most of this decade, but with the loss of coach Ken Hitchcock, defenceman Kevin Shattenkirk, and forwards Jori Lehtera and David Perron, they appear to be on a gradual decline.

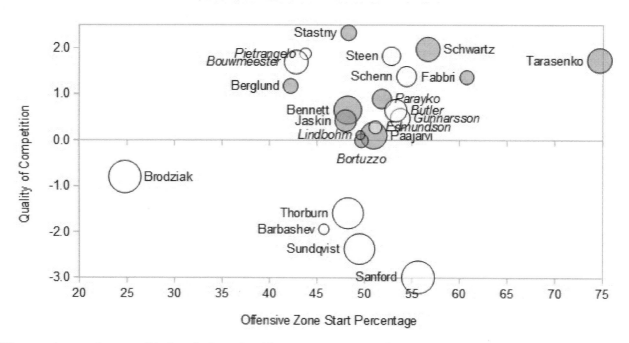

St. Louis Blues - Player Usage

Of the various players St. Louis has lost in recent years, Shattenkirk's could be the most notable. Not only will his absence be felt on the power play, but it weakens the team's top four close to its breaking point.

It seems uncomfortable to criticize a blue line that includes such a skilled and accomplished player as captain Alex Pietrangelo, but he's increasingly alone in an unenviable situation. Jay Bouwmeester is 34 years old, hasn't scored 20 points in a season in four years, and his sliding shot-based metrics have started to produce an alarmingly large white circle. Burdened by all the tough minutes and an aging partner, Pietrangelo has flipped to white, as well.

Obviously, big Colton Parayko has developed into an excellent two-way defenceman, but Shattenkirk's absence forces them to keep Bouwmeester in an overly challenging role, and forces a player like Joel Edmundson to play in the top four. There's a depth of five defencemen near Parayko on the depth chart, plus prospect Jordan Schmaltz, but the Blues need someone who can play tough minutes, and take pressure off the top pair.

The loss of Lehtera and Perron isn't as immediately troubling, because they were not critical players, and the team did acquire Brayden Schenn. However, they (and Nail Yakupov) are a noticeable part of the slow erosion that has been going on for years, which included David Backes and Troy Brouwer the year before.

The Blues still have plenty of talent up front, mind you. They have Vladimir Tarasenko, who scored in the 40-goal, 75-point neighbourhood for the third year in a row. In fact, that's more of a rich, gated community than a neighbourhood. He's on the far-right side of the chart because he's used in a strictly offensive fashion. Schenn was used a similar way in Philadelphia, where he was particularly useful on the power play. However, his white circle reveals some poor shot-based metrics.

Their big, shaded circles at the middle-top of the chart also demonstrate how useful Jaden Schwartz and Paul Stastny have been, because they can take on top opponents in both zones, and still produce points and good shot-based metrics. Alexander Steen is the same type of forward, but has curiously fallen into white-circle territory lately. Finally, there's hope that Robby Fabbri can complete the top six.

Even with the erosion of forward depth, the Blues have some useful secondary forwards like Beau Bennett, Magnus Paajarvi, and Vladimir Sobotka, plus Patrik Berglund should be back after shoulder surgery by the calendar year's end. Based on their giant white circles, it's not clear how much Kyle Brodziak and Chris Thorburn have left to offer, but there's certainly hope for the development of Ivan Barbashev, Oskar Sundqvist, and Zach Sanford.

Score	Category	Notes
✔	Possession	The Blues shot-based metrics are consistently above average.
✔	The Shootout	St. Louis could use one more shooter.
	Goaltending	You could make a good tandem of former Blues goalies.
✔	Penalty Kill	Even with the loss of so many great defensive forwards, the Blues are still effective when shorthanded.
	Power Play	The loss of Shattenkirk will hurt the team's power play, but the addition of Schenn should help.
	Scoring Line	Tarasenko is one of the game's most effective scorers.
✔	Shutdown Line	The Blues have a lot of money invested in their top two-way players.
✔	Forward Depth	Even with the annual loss of quality forwards, the Blues still have some pretty good bottom-six options.
	Top Pairing	Pietrangelo is excellent, but Bouwmeester is on the decline.
✔	Second Pairing	Can someone step up, and play with Parayko?
✔	Defensive Depth	There's a big clump of third-pair defencemen on the chart.
	Coaching	The Blues were red hot with Yeo, but he doesn't have an established track record of success.
✔	Prospects	There will be several 1st- and 2nd-year players in the lineup.

Assessment: I'm not saying that it's been a long time since the Blues made the Stanley Cup Final, but Jaromir Jagr has never seen them do it.

Tampa Bay Lightning

Are they contenders, or aren't they? There are some who argue that a healthy Stamkos is all that is required to resume the team's deep playoff runs. And, there are others who believe that the fallout from their cap issues drops the Lightning out of contention. Maybe a look at some of the underlying numbers will help establish what to expect from Tampa Bay.

Tampa Bay Lightning - Player Usage

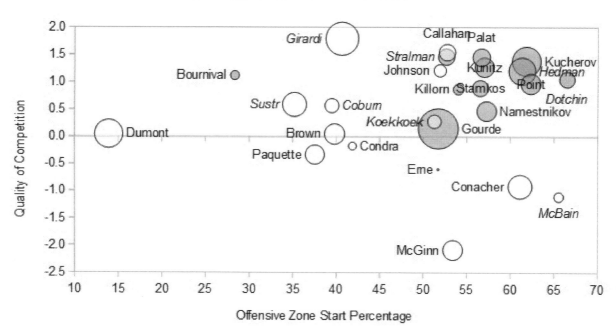

Every successful team has to deal with cap issues eventually, and the Lightning has navigated theirs pretty well, all things considered. It was a foregone conclusion that they would lose Ben Bishop, but Andrei Vasilevskiy, who is 23, was promising in his first season as the team's No. 1 goalie. At first glance, veterans Peter Budaj and Michael Leighton may appear to be curious choices as backups, but they have each been rock solid in the AHL, and certainly don't use up very much cap space.

Jonathan Drouin might be destined to be a star for Montreal, but the Lightning simply couldn't afford everybody. At the very least, GM Steve Yzerman made the best of the situation by acquiring picks and prospects for Drouin, Bishop, and the various veterans that had to be moved at last year's trade deadline.

Even without Drouin, Tampa Bay appears to have plenty of scoring, especially with Stamkos back from injury, and the emergence of rookie Brayden Point. They should take some pressure off of Nikita Kucherov, who led the team's forwards in scoring by a wide margin.

While those three players are on the right, offensive-minded side of the player usage chart, Tampa Bay also has a few two-way players who are more to the left, and taking on top opponents higher up the chart. Most notably, that includes the other members of the Triplets line, Ondrej Palat and Tyler Johnson, both of whom Yzerman managed to extend for a combined $10.3 million. That's not bad at all.

Despite the fact that veterans Chris Kunitz and Ryan Callahan are located right in the mix with those other players on the chart, they're at the point of their careers where they'll be transitioning into secondary roles. Instead, Alex Killorn can be inserted into that kind of top-six, two-way role, although he's not quite at the same level as Johnson or Palat at either end of the ice.

On the blue line, the Lightning curiously signed free agent Dan Girardi to replace Jason Garrison, who was lost in the expansion draft. While his giant white circle looks ominous, at least Tampa Bay didn't overpay for a marginal defenceman to the same extent as so many other teams this summer, and at least he's not required to play a top-pair role for which he no longer appears to be suited.

There's really no need for Tampa Bay to rely on any of their veteran, white-circled defencemen for more than secondary purposes. Tampa Bay has Anton Stralman to handle the tough minutes, many of which can also be handled by Vezina finalist Victor Hedman, albeit in a more offensive-minded capacity. Also, it looks like Jake Dotchin might be able to push his way into the top four, while Slater Koekkoek could start pushing Braydon Coburn and Andrej Sustr for ice time on the third pair.

Score	Category	Notes
✔	Possession	The Lightning have a pretty clear commitment to shot-based metrics – the Girardi signing notwithstanding.
	The Shootout	Vasilevskiy has had promising success in the shootout so far, but they could use another shooter.
	Goaltending	I think they'll be just fine, but statistically there is a bit of risk.
	Penalty Kill	The Lightning have improved, but have more work to do.
✔	Power Play	The return of Stamkos should help boost the team.
✔	Scoring Line	Few teams have as strong a duo as Stamkos and Kucherov.
✔	Shutdown Line	Palat and Johnson are solid two-way forwards.
✔	Forward Depth	Despite the team's cap-related losses, Tampa Bay's forward depth is as strong as ever.
✔	Top Pairing	Hedman can do it all, and will remain in the Norris race.
	Second Pairing	Even in a reduced role, Girardi might struggle
✔	Defensive Depth	The Lightning do have options if injuries strike their blue line.
✔	Coaching	Cooper is an excellent coach, but their staff-wide metrics are pulled down by Bowness's data from the 90s.
✔	Prospects	Yzerman has been focused on replenishing the team's organizational strength.

Assessment: It a reasonably safe bet that Tampa Bay makes the playoffs, and another deep run certainly appears possible.

Toronto Maple Leafs

Last year, Toronto proved just how quickly teams can rebuild. I doubt that any team will ever find itself in a larger hole than Toronto was after the 2013–14 season. Saddled with many ill-advised long-term contracts, a decade of mediocrity, terrible shot-based metrics, and a depleted prospect pool, things looked grim. Three seasons later, they're back in the playoffs, with their best points total since before the 2005 lockout.

Toronto Maple Leafs - Player Usage

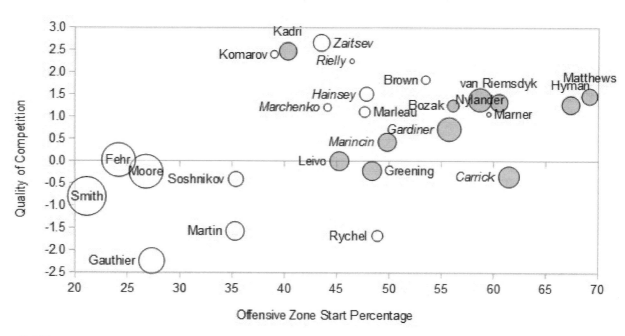

How did Toronto recover so quickly? The short answer is that they adopted possession-based hockey, invested in an experienced and accomplished coaching staff, had excellent results in the NHL Entry Draft, and enjoyed a little bit of luck. The longer answer...well, that could probably fill an entire chapter.

Toronto also serves as an example of the kind of impact prospects can have when they all break out at once. The Maple Leafs improved from 69 points to 95 last year, and the largest factor in that improvement was probably the team's rookies.

Studying the chart, most of the rookies were offensive-minded forwards. Four of them are to the right of the chart, and Auston Matthews and Zach Hyman are even beyond Toronto's established scoring-line veterans, James van Riemsdyk and Tyler Bozak. The positioning is actually a little bit unusual for Hyman, who is a defensive specialist who kills penalties and scored just 28 points, but he did often serve as the defensive conscience on the scoring lines.

While this gives Toronto a world of scoring depth, it also means that the Maple Leafs need a shutdown line that can handle the defensive-zone assignments, and against top opponents.

Those players are generally located on the top-left side of the chart, like Nazem Kadri and Leo Komarov. Kadri is particularly valuable, because he still manages exceptional shot-based metrics, and manages to remain among the team's scoring leaders. He's also among the best at drawing penalties, although he had an off-season in that regard.

Recognizing the importance of these types of players, Toronto invested heavily in free agent Patrick Marleau. And, while Connor Brown will never be the best player named Connor from the Erie Otters, he does have the potential to evolve into a great shutdown winger as well. The only issue here is that all of Kadri's possible wingers have the kind of white circles that denote below-average shot-based metrics, which goes against the team's new philosophy.

Amazingly, we've already listed 11 forwards, and haven't even started to scratch the depth lines, which also feature a number of interesting veterans, and promising prospects. Suffice it to say, Toronto is stacked up front.

The blue line isn't quite so lucky. Rookie Nikita Zaitsev and 23-year-old Morgan Rielly got burdened with all the tough minutes against top opponents, at the top of the chart. Free agent Ron Hainsey will help with that, given how effective he was in that role for the Stanley Cup champions last year. Based on his position in the chart, perhaps Alexey Marchenko has potential in this regard, as well.

That leaves Jake Gardiner to play in a more sheltered second pair situation, further down the chart against secondary opponents, and a little more to the right. He has exceptional shot-based metrics, and could probably handle a more challenging role. In terms of depth, the Maple Leafs have Martin Marincin and Connor Carrick. Their shot-based metrics are just fine, but the team could probably use a few more established players, in case injuries strike or some of the younger players struggle.

Score	Category	Notes
✔	Possession	The team's most startling transformation has been with its shot-based metrics.
	The Shootout	Bozak is the only good shooter, and Andersen struggles.
	Goaltending	Toronto has high expectations for Andersen.
	Penalty Kill	The team's leap forward in 2015–16 proved to be temporary.
✔	Power Play	It's safe to classify the team's PP woes as resolved.
✔	Scoring Line	Toronto led the NHL with five players with 60 or more points.
	Shutdown Line	Their shutdown line lacks scoring and good shot-based stats.
☆	Forward Depth	No team can match Toronto's forward depth.
	Top Pairing	Their top pair was overburdened with tough minutes.
✔	Second Pairing	Hainsey was a wise and much-needed addition.
✔	Defensive Depth	Only 4-5 of their defencemen were NHL regulars last year.
✔	Coaching	It pays to invest in an accomplished coaching staff.
✔	Prospects	Further development of the team's young players is possible.

Assessment: It's an uphill battle, but a second consecutive playoff appearance is likely.

Vancouver Canucks

In the preceding couple of seasons, it was hard to make sense of Vancouver's moves, and where the organization thought it was, and where it was headed. Then, in a summer where some teams appeared to be losing their minds, the Canucks had a solid draft, acted reasonably in free agency, and appeared to be making tangible strides in the right direction. With or without analytics, this is not an easy team to figure out.

Vancouver Canucks - Player Usage

After their thin blue line was hit hard by injuries, the Canucks were probably "saved" from the draft lottery by surprising performances in the top four from rookie Troy Stecher, now 23, and Ben Hutton, 24, as well as 6-foot-7 rookie Nikita "Do or do not, there is no" Tryamkin, 23, on the depth pair.

Their rapid development helps put the team's blue line in far better shape. In the top four, they still have two-way veteran Alexander Edler and underrated defensive specialist Chris Tanev, who each have shaded circles towards the top-left corner of the chart, because they take on top opponents, and often in the defensive zone. Plus, they added free agent defenceman Michael Del Zotto, who is to the right of those two, and has a similar shaded circle.

Even if injuries strike the blue line again, the Canucks have the depth to handle it. In addition to those six defencemen, they have big Erik Gudbranson, free agent Patrick Wiercioch, and prototypical injury reserve defenceman Alex Biega.

Up front, their scoring line remains in the experienced hands of the Sedin twins, Daniel and Henrik, who have the nicely shaded circles on the top-right side of the chart. Despite being perfectly sound defensively, they are obviously used in offensive situations, and certainly attract the primary focus of the team's top opposing players every night.

Last year, the second line was built around Bo Horvat, Sven Baertschi, and Alex Burrows (now of the Senators). While Horvat, 22, was the first non-Sedin to lead the team in scoring since Markus Naslund back in 2005–06, the white circles suggest that this line didn't have the greatest success from a shot-based perspective.

There don't appear to be any superior options on this chart, beyond versatile veteran Loui Eriksson, but his scoring dropped from 63 points to 24 last year. However, they do have almost $10.4 million invested long-term in him and Brandon Sutter, so the Canucks ought to involve them in more prominent roles.

Regardless of how the top six is constructed, the Canucks have a wealth of secondary forwards, like Sam Gagner and Markus Granlund, and several young prospects, like Brock Boeser, Nikolay Goldobin, and Jake Virtanen. So, the bottom six should be excellent.

While they're playing a conservative game in terms of depth, the Canucks have taken some gambles in nets, and behind the bench. Despite a career .906 save percentage as a backup, they have invested in Jacob Markstrom as the No. 1 goalie, presumably because of his impressive .920 save percentage in the AHL. That had better work out, because his backups are Anders Nilsson, .908, and Richard Bachman, .906.

Behind the bench, they're going with Travis Green, who has just over four years of experience as a head coach, mostly in the AHL. Even among recent AHL coaches, Green's coaching metrics rank only slightly above average, and most similar to Colorado's Jared Bednar. That's not a promising sign.

Score	Category	Notes
	Possession	The Canucks are not a possession-focused team.
✔	The Shootout	Gagner gives them another shooter, and Markstrom is good.
	Goaltending	Vancouver is taking a bit of a risk in nets.
	Penalty Kill	They'll miss Burrows and Hansen.
	Power Play	Vancouver doesn't have a lot of top-end offensive firepower.
	Scoring Line	At 37 (both of them), the Sedins aren't what they once were.
	Shutdown Line	For all that money, they need more from Sutter and Eriksson.
✔	Forward Depth	Their depth lines are young and solid.
	Top Pairing	Though capable defensively, Vancouver's top defencemen don't provide a lot of scoring.
✔	Second Pairing	Del Zotto was one of the more affordable free agent 4th-Ds.
☆	Defensive Depth	Even if injuries strike the blue line again, they should be ok.
	Coaching	It's become fashionable to go off-the-board these days.
✔	Prospects	Boeser is among several breakout candidates at forward.

Assessment: Vancouver is rebuilding, and the playoffs may remain out of reach this year.

Vegas Golden Knights

It was a missed opportunity, in my view. Based on the published protection lists, the Vegas Golden Knights could have easily assembled a playoff-calibre team in the expansion draft, whose scoring could have been supplemented through free agency, and been competitive from year one. Instead, it almost appears as if they were deliberately trying to build a non-competitive team that is destined to have been overhauled by year three.

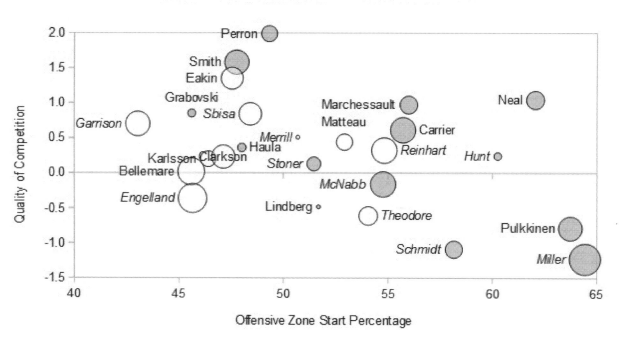

The greatest missed opportunity was on the blue line, where Vegas could have really constructed a top-10 blue line through the expansion draft. Instead, this player usage chart features the giant white circles of shot-based underachievers like Jason Garrison, Luca Sbisa, Deryk Engelland, and Griffin Reinhart. Flipping through the other charts, it doesn't appear as if any of these players would play in the top four on virtually any other team.

On the bright side for the Golden Knights, they did select seven high-quality third-pair defencemen, all but one of whom (Shea Theodore) have the shaded circles that denote good shot-based metrics. However, with the possible exception of Jon Merrill, their locations towards the bottom-right side of the chart suggest that they have played in sheltered roles in the offensive zone, and against the depth lines.

Based on the various mock expansion drafts, it was clear that scoring would be a problem, and that Vegas would have to rely on free agency and trades. And, indeed, they signed Vadim Shipachyov from the KHL, and made a deal with the Florida Panthers to secure both Reilly Smith and Jonathan Marchessault for the top six.

Based on the right side of the chart, the Golden Knights may craft a scoring line by adding James Neal to a line with Shipachyov and Marchessault, and it might not be that bad, from either a scoring or a shot-based perspective. Located towards the top-left, Smith can anchor a more defensive second line with David Perron and Cody Eakin. Their scoring could be a little light, and Eakin's white circle is a concern, but it also shouldn't be that bad.

Beyond that, the Golden Knights didn't have much of a problem building adequate forward depth. While prospects weren't eligible for the expansion draft, and teams were careful to protect those who were past the three-year threshold, the Golden Knights still managed to find some good, slightly older depth-forward prospects like William Carrier, Oscar Lindberg, Teemu Pulkkinen, and rookies Brendan Leipsic and Tomas Nosek.

In goal, GM George McPhee had his choice of several great options in the expansion draft. In the end, he went with a proven, reliable No. 1 goalie in Marc-Andre Fleury, and a solid backup in Calvin Pickard. There's nothing wrong with that combination.

As for coaching, Gerard Gallant is back behind an NHL bench, and he actually ranks fourth among coaches when his success in the QMJHL is also considered. However many points this team was destined to start with, Gallant will probably add another five.

Score	Category	Notes
	Possession	Their top defencemen don't have strong shot-based metrics.
✔	The Shootout	Fleury's excellent in the shootout, and Neal and Perron give the team at least two proven shooters.
✔	Goaltending	Fleury/Pickard is one of the best expansion team tandems.
✔	Penalty Kill	Bellemare will take the lead on a promising penalty kill.
	Power Play	Their power play stats could rank near the bottom of the NHL.
	Scoring Line	It's a lot better than expected, but still below average.
	Shutdown Line	Scoring could be a problem for Vegas in year one.
✔	Forward Depth	The team's forward depth could serve as an equalizer.
	Top Pairing	They have no defencemen who could play on the top pair anywhere else.
	Second Pairing	Stats probably didn't play any role in drafting their top four.
☆	Defensive Depth	They have six or seven solid third-pair defencemen.
✔	Coaching	Vegas is one of the few teams with coaching openings this year that didn't go off the board.
	Prospects	McPhee acquired a number of draft picks, and will build up strong organizational strength over time.

Assessment: Vegas could have built a contender, but seemed focused on semi-tanking.

Washington Capitals

As the team's cap-related issues start to catch up with them, the Ovechkin-era Washington Capitals are at risk of going down in history as one of the best teams that never won the Stanley Cup – or even reached the Conference Finals. But, there is still time.

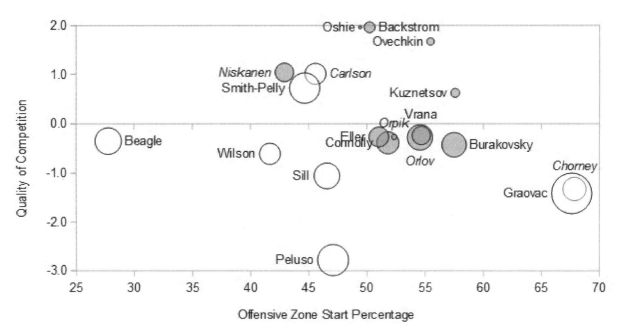

Washington Capitals - Player Usage

That statement wasn't meant as a criticism of the team, or of Alexander Ovechkin specifically. After all, it acknowledges just how great a team this has been – and that Ovechkin was the primary reason for their great success.

On the player usage chart, Ovechkin is right at the top, taking on top opponents just like established two-way forwards Nicklas Backstrom and T.J. Oshie, and isn't nearly as far to the right as most people expect. These are three exceptional players, but they'll soon all be in their 30s, and now carry a combined cap hit of almost $22 million.

Up front, the other big cap hit is scoring line centre Evgeny Kuznetsov, $7.8 million. Offensively, his position on the player usage chart is similar to Ovechkin's, but further down the chart, because he doesn't face the team's top opponents to the same extent.

Kuznetsov spent most of last season with the team's two greatest cap-related losses, Justin Williams and Marcus Johansson. Studying the chart, that leaves them without any more top-six forwards. So, coach Barry Trotz may split up that top lines, in order to help stretch players like Andre Burakovsky and rookie Jakub Vrana into the top six.

However, that move would create a problem with the depth lines – there are only eight other forwards on the chart, only two of which have the shaded circles that denote good shot-based metrics, Lars Eller and Brett Connolly. That might not hurt them much in the regular season, but that is the sort of issue that can make the difference in the playoffs.

This depth issue is even more serious on the blue line, where the Capitals have just five defencemen on the chart, the fifth of which is journeyman Taylor Chorney.

Cap-related issues meant that they couldn't keep both Dmitry Orlov and Karl Alzner. Noticing Orlov's giant shaded circle, their choice makes sense, but it does leave Matt Niskanen and John Carlson alone in the top-left part of the chart to handle all the tough minutes in the defensive zone, and against top competition. And, Carlson's white circle suggests that he struggles to maintain good shot-based metrics in that kind of role. However, their only other defenceman is Brooks Orpik who, at age 37, has already transitioned into a secondary role.

With Braden Holtby and Philipp Grubauer in nets, it is possible that Washington has the kind of elite goaltending that will bail them out of any shortcomings on defence. But, they will need to solve their potential depth issue before the playoffs, or they may make another early exit.

Score	Category	Notes
✔	Possession	Last year, they had their best shot-based metrics ever.
✔	The Shootout	Oshie and Kuznetsov are a combined 51 for 99.
☆	Goaltending	Holtby and Grubauer could be the league's best tandem.
☆	Penalty Kill	The Capitals are one of the best on special teams.
☆	Power Play	Ovechkin and Backstrom are among the league's best.
✔	Scoring Line	The Capitals are hoping that Burakovsky or Vrana are ready for top-line duty with Kuznetsov and/or Ovechkin.
✔	Shutdown Line	Backstrom and Oshie are potential Selke candidates.
	Forward Depth	Washington's depth issue could be serious.
✔	Top Pairing	The Capitals have three good two-way, top-four defencemen.
✔	Second Pairing	Everybody will have to stay healthy, and someone will have to step up to play on the second pair.
	Defensive Depth	Chorney is their fifth-most established defenceman.
✔	Coaching	In 18 seasons, Trotz's teams have won five playoff series.
	Prospects	Out of necessity, Washington will be dipping into organizational strength that may not be NHL-ready.

Assessment: The Capitals remain a Cup contender, but the window is closing.

Winnipeg Jets

For a team with this much young talent and core veterans who are still close to their primes, it's practically a crime against hockey that the Jets aren't more competitive. What is it going to take to get this franchise into the playoffs for the third time in its 18-season history, and to actually win its first playoff game?

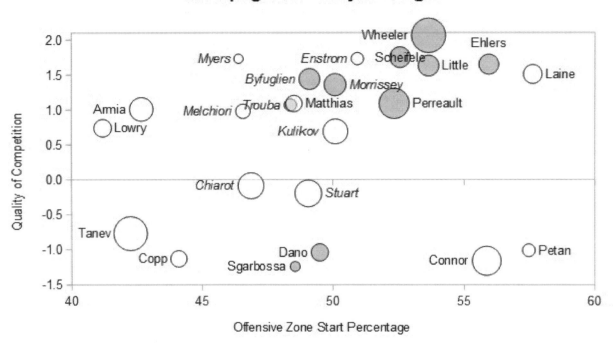

Winnipeg's most obvious need has always been goaltending. Ondrej Pavelec (now of the Rangers) was finally pushed out of top spot last year, but Connor Hellebuyck and Michael Hutchinson didn't fare much better, with save percentages of .907 and .903, respectively. There is hope that prospect Eric Comrie can eventually help, but the Jets wisely decided not to gamble on the rapid development of these three goalies, and instead invested in free agent goalie Steve Mason.

The Jets have also sought to improve the defence that plays in front of them. To that end, the (overpriced) addition of free agent Dmitry Kulikov gives the team six defencemen who are near the top-middle of the chart, with recent experience taking on top opponents in both zones. Of them, Dustin Byfuglien, Jacob Trouba, and rookie Joshua Morrissey are the best in terms of shot-based metrics and scoring.

If the defence and goaltending hold up, then the greatest remaining concern has been coaching. While statistical evaluation methods in this area are admittedly not very mature, it's not a lens through which Paul Maurice appears to be particularly effective. However, the Jets have decided to stick to their guns behind the bench, for better or for worse.

Up front, Winnipeg's top six forwards are pretty easy to identify, on the top-right side of the chart. Five of them have the giant shaded circles that denote strong shot-based metrics, but the surprising odd man out is Calder Trophy runner-up Patrik Laine. He may have led the team with 36 goals, but the Jets were surprisingly outshot 959-873 when he was on the ice at five-on-five. That difference of -86 was ahead of only Brandon Tanev, and depth defencemen Mark Stuart and Ben Chiarot.

Laine is also not yet very strong defensively, which is another reason why he is located so far to the right. Among the other five, Nikolaj Ehlers and Mathieu Perreault also play a more offensive-minded style. Veterans Blake Wheeler and Bryan Little are strong two-way players, and are regularly used to kill penalties, and would be ideal on more of a shutdown line. Team scoring leader Mark Scheifele is an underrated all-around player, and can essentially succeed in whatever role he is assigned to play.

As for depth, there are four interesting groups of two on the chart, after the more central Shawn Matthias. On the left defensive side, but still against above-average competition, is big Adam Lowry and Joel Armia, both 24. On the bottom right, there's Kyle Connor, 20, and 5-foot-9 Nic Petan, 22, who are skilled players with offensive upsides. At the middle-bottom, with shaded circles, are still-promising depth players Michael Sgarbossa and Marko Dano. Andrew Copp is with Tanev in the bottom-left corner. Even beyond this, the Jets still have prospects, like Jack Roslovic. Suffice it to say, Maurice has a lot of choices in the bottom six.

Score	Category	Notes
	Possession	They have been heading in the wrong direction, and fast.
	The Shootout	They need to add a few young players to the shootout.
✔	Goaltending	Statistically, their new goaltending combination actually ranks in the top third of the league.
	Penalty Kill	They have the talent, but aren't getting the results.
	Power Play	An effective power play would help the Jets make the playoffs.
✔	Scoring Line	They had four forwards with at least 25 goals, 64 points.
✔	Shutdown Line	Wheeler and Little are both legitimate Selke candidates.
✔	Forward Depth	They have a versatile wealth of options age 24 or under.
	Top Pairing	Enstrom's on the decline, and lost his offensive upside years ago.
✔	Second Pairing	They have six players who could arguably play in the top four.
✔	Defensive Depth	There are a lot of options on the blue line, although many of them have giant white circles.
	Coaching	In 20 seasons, Maurice has made the playoffs seven times, and escaped the first round twice.
✔	Prospects	The Jets do have the potential to explode up the standings.

Assessment: The Jets could be in the wild card race, even despite themselves.

What About Nico Hischier?

By Rob Vollman

Selected first overall in the 2016 NHL Entry Draft, Auston Matthews stepped right into the NHL, led Toronto with 40 goals and 69 points, won the Calder Trophy, and boosted the Maple Leafs into the playoffs.

As for Connor McDavid, who was selected first overall in 2015, it's fair to say that he has single-handedly changed course for the Edmonton Oilers.

As we keep going back in time, it becomes increasingly obvious how first overall picks can alter a team's projections for the following season. In fact, even those drafted second or third overall can have a similar impact.

That's why we've added this additional section right after the team essays, to specifically investigate how this year's first overall selection, Nico Hischier of the New Jersey Devils, and all of the other prominent new NHLers will impact their teams. This year, that includes the second overall pick Nolan Patrick, and even veterans like Vadim Shipachyov of the Vegas Golden Knights, and Evgeni Dadonov of the Florida Panthers.

As with all *Hockey Abstract* content, this will be more about the ways that we explore the subject matter, and not as much about the specific applications to players like Hischier. And, when studying the impact that first-year players might have, there are some well-established tools in the world of hockey analytics at our disposal.

The first thing we can do is to search the QMJHL's history for historical players with the same era-adjusted statistics at the same age as Hischier (or whomever is being studied), and to see what happened to them. Methods for doing that are explored in *Hockey Abstract*[72].

Instead of only searching the QMJHL, the pool of available data can be greatly expanded by finding a way to incorporate data from other leagues. That's where league translations come in, which are also explained in great detail in the original *Hockey Abstract*[73]. Essentially, they translate a player's scoring data from another league to a common, NHL equivalent (NHLe), based on the change in scoring of all those who had previously gone from that league to the NHL. To do that yourself, just multiply a player's scoring data by the multiplier in the table below.

NHL Translation Factors, as of 2016–17

League	Factor
Kontinental Hockey League (KHL)	0.77
Swedish Hockey League (SHL)	0.62
American Hockey League (AHL)	0.47

72 Rob Vollman, "Historical Player Projections", *Hockey Abstract,* 2013, pgs 183-187.
73 Rob Vollman, "Translation Data From Other Leagues", *Hockey Abstract,* 2013, pgs 159-182.

Finland SM-Liiga	0.46
Western Collegiate Hockey Association (WCHA, pre-2013)	0.44
National Collegiate Hockey Association (NCHC)	0.43
Switzerland (NLA)	0.43
Hockey-East	0.38
Big Ten	0.33
Central Collegiate Hockey Association (CCHA, Defunct)	0.32
Ontario Hockey League (OHL)	0.31
Western Hockey League (WHL)	0.28
Quebec Major Junior Hockey League (QMJHL)	0.25
ECAC	0.23

And, instead of only comparing players who are the same age as Hischier, the pool of available data can be expanded even further by adjusting each historical player's statistics, based on the average change in a player's stats as they age.

If you want to do this for yourself, here is the table used in Iain Fyffe's Projectinator, which is covered in the second chapter of *Stat Shot*[74]. Just multiply a player's stats by the given multiple to translate it to the standard of a player who is 17 years and 0 months old. And, if you want to build your own table, and even expand it to older ages, the best method is covered in the opening chapter of *Stat Shot*[75].

Point Multipliers by Age, in Years and Months

	0	1	2	3	4	5	6	7	8	9	10	11
15	1.436	1.420	1.404	1.389	1.374	1.359	1.344	1.330	1.316	1.302	1.288	1.275
16	1.262	1.249	1.236	1.223	1.211	1.198	1.186	1.175	1.163	1.151	1.140	1.129
17	1.000	0.995	0.990	0.986	0.981	0.976	0.971	0.967	0.962	0.958	0.953	0.949
18	0.840	0.832	0.824	0.817	0.809	0.802	0.795	0.788	0.781	0.774	0.767	0.760
19	0.674	0.665	0.657	0.648	0.640	0.632	0.624	0.616	0.608	0.600	0.593	0.585
20	0.520	0.512	0.503	0.495	0.487	0.479	0.471	0.464	0.456	0.449	0.442	0.435

If we blend all of these techniques together, then we can build a massive database of every player, adjusted for scoring levels, age, and league quality. Then, we can find all the players whose stats were similar to Hischier's, no matter when, where, or at what age they played.

In fact, that's exactly what Josh Weissbock and Cam Lawrence did when they designed the Prospect Cohort Success model[76], which allows them to estimate Hischier's probability of NHL success, and the level of that success, based on the performance of all of those with similar data in the past.

PCS is in use by the Florida Panthers, has inspired other NHL organizations to build similar

74 Iain Fyffe, "What do a Player's Junior Numbers Tell Us?", *Stat Shot,* September 2016, pgs 75-118.

75 Rob Vollman, "What's the Best Way to Build a Team?", *Stat Shot,* September 2016, pgs 32-36.

76 Josh Weissbock, "Draft Analytics: Unveiling the Prospect Cohort Success Model", *Canucks Army,* May 26, 2015, Web, https://canucksarmy.com/2015/05/26/draft-analytics-unveiling-the-prospect-cohort-success-model/.

models, and also inspired public models, like Garret Hohl's SEAL-Adjusted scoring[77], Lochlin Broatch's Projection Project[78], and Hayden Speak and Zac Urback's DEV model[79]. Later in this chapter, we'll even show you how to build a model of your own.

And models like these are essentially the leading edge in the evolution in our statistical analysis of prospects and rookies.

Since these sophisticated models feel a little bit like swatting a fly with a nuclear bomb, we're going to start with something simple – hockey cards. Using league translations, we're going to translate each prospect's scoring data from wherever they played in the past to an NHL equivalent. The process involves the following three steps:
1. Adjust for varying scoring levels by dividing each season of a player's data by the goals-per-game that year, and multiplying it by the 2016–17 standard.
2. Multiply that adjusted scoring data by the above league translation factors, which are based on all those players who went from that league to the NHL in the past.
3. Adjust for varying scoring levels once again, by multiplying it by the scoring levels in the NHL at the time, and the numbers of games played in a season.

The end result should be like the back of a hockey card, with what each player's scoring would have looked like had he played in the NHL his entire adult life.

We're not going to adjust for age, but it is included in every row of data. Just like with a regular hockey card, that means that it's up to us to interpret the impact age might have had on a player's scoring totals. In fact, it is up to us to consider *all* the additional factors that could have affected a player's scoring, like his role, his team, his linemates, how much power play time he likely received, and so on.

Without getting into the greater complexity of some of the aforementioned models, we will identify a few players with similar statistics, and briefly explore how that might help us set expectations for the rookie at hand. So, let's get started.

Player Cards

After all that build-up, Hischier's will actually be the most useless translation in this entire chapter.

The problem is that we have only two years worth of data with which to study Hischier, and one of them involves just 15 games, and a single point. Well, technically, we have eight seasons worth of data, but most of it is in Switzerland's junior leagues, for which we have absolutely no data on which to base a translation. For what it's worth, here's how his player card looks.

77 Garret Hohl, "SEAL-Adjusted Scoring and Why it Matters for Prospects", *Hockey Graphs,* June 15, 2016, Web, https://hockey-graphs.com/2016/06/15/seal-adjusted-scoring-and-why-it-matters-for-prospects/.
78 Lochlin Broatch, "Methodology and Definitions", *The Projection Project,* 2016, Web, http://www.theprojectionproject.com/Home/Methodology.
79 Zac Urback, "Introducing DEV", 2016, *Prospect Stats,* Web, http://prospect-stats.com/blog/Introducing_DEV/.

Nico Hischier's NHL-Equivalent Career Scoring[80]

Age	Team	GP	G	A	PTS	Season	GP	G	A	PTS
17	Bern SC	15	1	0	1	2015–16	25	1	0	1
18	Halifax	57	38	48	86	2016–17	69	11	14	25

In each player card, a player's actual stats will be on the left side, and then how it would have looked in the NHL, and in the season in question, is on the right side.

In this case, if Hischier had been playing the NHL at age 18 last year, then he would have scored 25 points in 69 games. A quick scan through recent history, and it appears to be most similar to Evander Kane, who scored 14 goals and 26 points in 66 games for the Atlanta Thrashers in 2009–10, at age 18.

While that appears to be surprisingly low, bear in mind that Hischier didn't even lead Halifax in scoring last season. Combing recent history for players with similar scoring totals at that age in the QMJHL, there are very few who went straight to the NHL.

Also, remember that even if he had played in the NHL, he probably would have been playing 10 minutes a night on a depth line, with no power play time, and with relatively weak linemates, much like Kane. It stands to reason that any such player could do much better at age 19, with that extra season of development, better linemates, and more opportunities. And, in fact, Kane himself improved to 19 goals and 43 points in 73 games at age 19. Depending on how he is used, it's possible that Hischier could do that well this season. And, obviously, much better in the long run.

Nolan Patrick, who was selected second overall by the Philadelphia Flyers, might be a better example of someone who will have a big impact in his rookie season. Here's his translated player card.

Nolan Patrick's NHL-Equivalent Career Scoring[81]

Age	Team	GP	G	A	PTS	Season	GP	G	A	PTS
14	Brandon	3	1	0	1	2013–14	3	0	0	0
16	Brandon	55	30	26	56	2014–15	63	11	9	20
17	Brandon	72	41	61	102	2015–16	82	15	22	37
18	Brandon	33	20	26	46	2016–17	38	7	9	16

Patrick's hernia injury last season and his face infection this summer make it impossible to chart his progression, but can you imagine how unbelievable it would be for a 17-year-old to score 37 points in 82 games in today's NHL (were it possible)? If so, can you imagine how many points such a gifted player could score two years later, at age 19?

The closest comparable I can find is Ryan Nugent-Hopkins, who scored 31 goals and 106 points in 69 games for the Red Deer Rebels at age 17. He went directly to the NHL at age 18, where he scored 18 goals and 52 points in 62 games. Perhaps Patrick would have scored the

80 Acknowledgment: Raw data for the translations from *Hockey DB,* http://www.hockeydb.com.
81 Acknowledgment: Raw data for the translations from *Hockey DB,* http://www.hockeydb.com.

equivalent last year, if not for the hernia.

Unfortunately, Nugent-Hopkins's age-19 season was derailed by the labour dispute, so we don't really have a solid basis on which to estimate how Patrick will do this coming year. However, he was on pace for the equivalent of 41 points in 68 games that year, so I think it's safe to expect at least as much for Patrick, depending on how he is used – which we will explore in the following section of this chapter.

As a basic point of comparison, consider how Patrick's old teammate, and Hischier's new teammate, performed in the WHL, John Quenneville. He appears to be trending towards 30 points or more in 2017–18, but he's also three years older than Patrick.

John Quenneville's NHL-Equivalent Career Scoring[82]

Age	Team(s)	GP	G	A	PTS	Season	GP	G	A	PTS
17	Brandon	47	8	11	19	2012–13	31	2	2	4
18	Brandon	61	25	33	58	2013–14	69	8	10	18
19	Brandon	57	17	30	47	2014–15	65	5	10	15
20	Brandon	57	31	42	73	2015–16	65	10	13	23
21	Albany/New Jersey	70	15	35	50	2016–17	72	8	19	27

The mainstream consensus appears to be that Arizona's Dylan Strome is Patrick's key rival for the rookie scoring race. Based on his playing card, it's easy to understand that opinion.

Dylan Strome's NHL-Equivalent Career Scoring[83]

Age	Team(s)	GP	G	A	PTS	Season	GP	G	A	PTS
16	Erie	60	10	29	39	2013–14	72	4	10	14
17	Erie	68	45	84	129	2014–15	82	16	31	47
18	Erie	56	37	74	111	2015–16	68	14	27	41
19	Erie/Arizona	42	22	54	76	2016–17	42	8	21	28

Scoring the equivalent of 47 points at age 17 is simply incredible, even if he did play with McDavid. Even without McDavid, Strome scored the equivalent of 41 points in 68 games the next season, and then had a season that was on pace for the equivalent of over 50 points at age 19. Given the lack of scoring options in Arizona, Strome will likely be given every opportunity on the top line and the first power play unit to strike out towards 60 points this year, or more.

There are a couple of other former OHL players who are frequently mentioned, like Joshua Ho-Sang of the New York Islanders and Alexander Nylander of the Buffalo Sabres. Let's take a quick look at their player cards before moving on.

Joshua Ho-Sang's NHL-Equivalent Career Scoring[84]

Age	Team(s)	GP	G	A	PTS	Season	GP	G	A	PTS
17	Windsor	63	14	30	44	2012–13	44	3	7	10

82 Acknowledgment: Raw data for the translations from *Hockey DB*, http://www.hockeydb.com.
83 Acknowledgment: Raw data for the translations from *Hockey DB*, http://www.hockeydb.com.
84 Acknowledgment: Raw data for the translations from *Hockey DB*, http://www.hockeydb.com.

		GP	G	A	PTS	Season	GP	G	A	PTS
18	Windsor	67	32	53	104	2013–14	81	12	25	36
19	Windsor/Niagara	60	17	64	62	2014–15	72	6	17	24
20	Niagara	66	19	63	82	2015–16	80	7	23	30
21	Bridgeport Sound/NYI	71	14	32	46	2016–17	75	9	19	28

Ho-Sang broke out a little bit later than Patrick and Strome, with the impressive equivalent of 36 points in 81 games at age 18. However, he hasn't built on that strong total, and seems to have leveled off at a 30-point pace in the three seasons since then. Furthermore, the Islanders have far more prospects than they have opportunities this season.

As for Nylander, his age-17 breakout was only to the equivalent of 28 points in 69 games, and then he took a bit of a step back in his age-18 season. It looks like he needs more time.

Alexander Nylander's NHL-Equivalent Career Scoring[85]

Age	Team(s)	GP	G	A	PTS	Season	GP	G	A	PTS
17	Mississauga	57	28	47	75	2015–16	69	10	17	28
18	Rochester/Buffalo	69	10	19	29	2016–17	74	5	10	15

Let's take a step back from the challenging task of studying prospects, and consider veterans who have a lot more seasons worth of solid data. On that front, the best place to start is Vadim Shipachyov of the Vegas Golden Knights.

Vadim Shipachyov's NHL-Equivalent Career Scoring[86]

Age	Team	GP	G	A	PTS	Season	GP	G	A	PTS
21	Cherepovets	29	4	5	9	2008–09	42	4	5	10
22	Cherepovets	55	14	30	44	2009–10	81	14	31	45
23	Cherepovets	51	13	25	38	2010–11	77	14	26	40
24	Cherepovets	54	22	37	59	2011–12	82	24	40	63
25	Cherepovets	51	17	23	40	2012–13	47	11	15	26
26	St. Petersburg	52	12	20	32	2013–14	79	14	23	37
27	St. Petersburg	49	12	42	54	2014–15	67	12	41	53
28	St. Petersburg	54	17	43	60	2015–16	74	17	44	62
29	St. Petersburg	50	26	50	76	2016–17	68	27	52	80

Shipachyov had a breakout season on the KHL's monster St. Petersburg team last year, which was easily the best team outside the NHL. They lost only eight games all year in regulation time, and their roster included Ilya Kovalchuk, Pavel Datsyuk, and Slava Voynov. In fact, I wonder how this team would have fared in the NHL. Surely they would have been better than the Colorado Avalanche, for example.

In my view, that means that Shipachyov is unlikely to score at that career high of 80 points in 68 games unless he were also on an NHL juggernaut, like perhaps playing with Sidney Crosby or Evgeni Malkin on the Pittsburgh Penguins. Playing with James Neal and Jonathan Marchessault on the Vegas Golden Knights, however, he is more likely to score at his previously established peak performance of 62 or 63 points, or less.

85 Acknowledgment: Raw data for the translations from *Hockey DB,* http://www.hockeydb.com.
86 Acknowledgment: Raw data for the translations from *Hockey DB,* http://www.hockeydb.com.

To take a similar example, consider the translated player card of his St. Petersburg teammate Evgeni Dadonov, who was signed by the Florida Panthers.

Evgeni Dadonov's NHL-Equivalent Career Scoring[87]

Age	Team(s)	GP	G	A	PTS	Season	GP	G	A	PTS
17	Chelyabinsk	24	4	1	2	2006–07	36	1	1	2
18	Chelyabinsk	43	7	13	20	2007–08	62	7	13	20
19	Chelyabinsk	40	11	4	15	2008–09	59	11	4	15
20	Rochester/Florida	80	17	23	40	2009–10	82	8	11	20
21	Rochester/Florida	60	16	17	33	2010–11	61	17	18	36
22	3 Teams	70	10	21	31	2011–12	74	7	14	21
23	Donbass	52	14	23	37	2012–13	48	9	15	24
24	Donbass	54	15	14	29	2013–14	82	17	16	34
25	St. Petersburg	53	19	27	46	2014–15	72	19	27	45
26	St. Petersburg	59	23	23	46	2015–16	81	24	24	48
27	St. Petersburg	53	30	36	66	2016–17	72	31	38	69

Just like Shipachyov, Dadonov broke out from his previously established high-water mark of 45 to 48 points to a new high of 69 points on that great St. Petersburg team. Since he's likely to play somewhere on Florida's top six with the likes of Aleksander Barkov and Jonathan Huberdeau, it's possible that he'll top his normal upside in the mid-40s, especially since he is a couple of years younger than Shipachyov. Not likely, but possible.

The Florida Panthers also signed Henrik Haapala from Finland's SM-liiga. He broke out at age 23 last season, leading the SM-liiga in scoring with 60 points in 51 games. While those would be very encouraging scoring totals if Haapala were a teenager, like when Patrik Laine and Sebastian Aho were in that league, we estimate that this great season is only the equivalent of about 38 points in 70 games at the NHL level at this slightly older age.

Henrik Haapala's NHL-Equivalent Career Scoring[88]

Age	Team(s)	GP	G	A	PTS	Season	GP	G	A	PTS
19	Tampere	32	3	10	13	2012–13	26	1	3	4
20	Tampere	36	1	3	4	2013–14	49	1	2	2
21	Tampere	25	4	6	10	2014–15	34	2	4	6
22	Tampere	47	12	18	30	2015–16	64	7	11	18
23	Tampere	51	15	45	60	2016–17	70	9	28	38

For Haapala, probably the closest comparison is with Joonas Donskoi, who scored 49 points in 58 games in SM-liiga when he was 22, followed by 36 points in 76 games in the NHL.

Haapala is a terrific playmaker, and may wind up playing with Barkov on the otherwise thin Florida top-six. Given the natural rate of development at age 24, he could continue to trend up. Then again, he's only 5-foot-8, and there's the risk he could get pushed out of the lineup altogether.

---

87 Acknowledgment: Raw data for the translations from *Hockey DB,* http://www.hockeydb.com.
88 Acknowledgment: Raw data for the translations from *Hockey DB,* http://www.hockeydb.com.

Heading back to North America, another name that sometimes pops up is Kenny Agostino, who signed with the Boston Bruins after he had a terrific season in the AHL, leading the league with 83 points in 65 games, at age 24. However, there are lots of players who scored buckets in the AHL, but never translated that to NHL success. Will Agostino join them?

Kenneth Agostino's NHL-Equivalent Career Scoring[89]

Age	Team(s)	GP	G	A	PTS	Season	GP	G	A	PTS
18	Yale University	31	11	14	25	2010–11	71	6	8	13
19	Yale University	33	14	20	34	2011–12	77	8	11	18
20	Yale University	37	17	24	41	2012–13	48	5	7	12
21	Yale/Calgary	41	15	19	34	2013–14	90	9	11	20
22	Adirondack	67	15	28	43	2014–15	72	7	13	21
23	Stockton/Calgary	67	23	34	57	2015–16	72	11	17	28
24	Wolves/St. Louis	72	25	61	86	2016–17	77	13	32	45

Agostino's AHL season works out to 45 points in 77 games at the NHL level, which would obviously make the Bruins quite happy. However, his previously established scoring level was between the equivalent of 20 and 28 points. Plus, his five actual points in 17 career NHL games works out to 24 points over a full, 82-game schedule.

To make the situation even tougher on Agostino, Boston has a lot of skilled young forwards who are going to be gunning for roster spots this season, including Anders Bjork of Notre Dame and Jakob Forsbacka Karlsson of Boston University, Providence Bruins rookies like Sean Kuraly and Peter Cehlarik, and a few players who have already had their NHL debut seasons, like Austin Czarnik. So, there's a real possibility that Agostino's rookie NHL season will have to wait a little longer.

Another top AHL player who has grabbed some attention lately is Pontus Aberg, thanks to his performance on Nashville's top line after Ryan Johansen was injured in the playoffs.

Pontus Aberg's NHL-Equivalent Career Scoring[90]

Age	Team(s)	GP	G	A	PTS	Season	GP	G	A	PTS
18	Stockholm	47	8	7	15	2011–12	70	7	6	14
19	Stockholm	52	12	28	40	2012–13	48	7	16	23
20	Karlstad	52	15	16	31	2013–14	78	13	14	27
21	Milwaukee	69	16	18	34	2014–15	74	8	9	17
22	Milwaukee	74	25	15	40	2015–16	80	12	7	20
23	Milwaukee/Nashville	71	32	22	54	2016–17	75	17	12	28

Aberg's upside is hinted at by his age-19 season, when he scored at the equivalent rate of a 40-point player. Since then, he has settled down to a level below 30 points, and even his five points in 18 career playoff NHL games works out to just 23 points in a full season.

Let's close this section by looking at many top names in college, where there has really been

89 Acknowledgment: Raw data for the translations from *Hockey DB*, http://www.hockeydb.com.
90 Acknowledgment: Raw data for the translations from *Hockey DB*, http://www.hockeydb.com.

a lot of growing interest lately. When looking at college data, the two key considerations are age, and conference. Statistically, that's how we knew that Jimmy Vesey would be a far different story in year one than Johnny Gaudreau and Jack Eichel. Specifically, that's because Vesey broke out at an older age, and from a weaker conference.

Here are the five most prominent names among this year's rookie forwards. In this case, the player's age is how old they were in their last college season, not how old they are now. The left side includes their combined scoring totals in college, and the right side is how that translates in the NHL, over a full season.

NHL-Equivalent College Scoring of Select Players[91]

Age	Player	Team	GP	G	A	PTS	Conference	GP	G	A	PTS
19	Kyle Connor	Michigan	38	35	36	71	Big-10	82	26	27	53
19	Brock Boeser	North Dakota	74	43	51	94	NCHC	74	18	21	38
18	Clayton Keller	Boston University	31	21	24	45	Hockey-East	65	17	19	35
20	JT Compher	Michigan	107	39	79	118	Big-10	80	10	21	31
18	Tyson Jost	North Dakota	33	16	19	35	NCHC	68	14	16	30

It appears that Connor is the real gem, but it's based on just 38 games worth of data, and it's hard to imagine him getting a lot of time on the top line and/or on the power play with Patrik Laine, Bryan Little, Blake Wheeler, Nikolaj Ehlers, and Mark Scheifele in town. The other four prospects play for Vancouver, Arizona, and Colorado, where there will probably be far more opportunities to score.

Again, this is just translated data from a player's past, without any context. How they perform in the NHL will have far more to do with how they are used than how they performed in college. So, let's look at that.

Rookie Usage

You'll notice that I didn't include any defencemen in the projections, and that's because their impact isn't really measured in scoring, but in their capacity to effectively play top-four minutes.

This season, the top rookie defencemen to watch include Boston's Charlie McAvoy, Dallas's Julius Honka, Tampa Bay's Mikhail Sergachev, Ottawa's Thomas Chabot, and Buffalo's Viktor Antipin. Their success will be evaluated not in goals and assists, but in whether or not they were able to take on top opponents, in both zones.

You might have already guessed where I was going with this, and yes, we're going to look at some of my beloved player usage charts. To help establish reasonable expectations for rookie defencemen in general, I selected the top 25 from last year in terms of total ice time, and put them on the following player usage chart.

---

91 Acknowledgment: Raw data for the translations from *Hockey DB,* http://www.hockeydb.com.

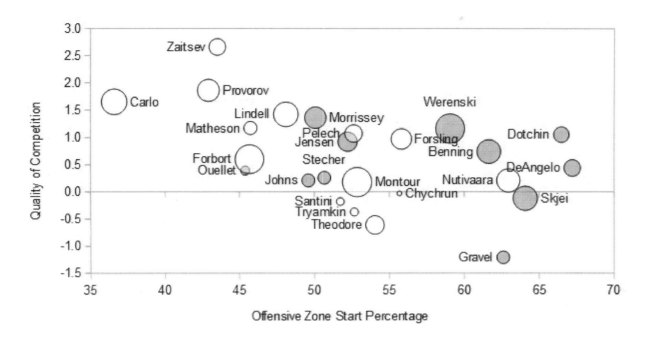

Rookie Defencemen - Player Usage

Last year, there were arguably only four rookie defencemen who played what could be described as the tough minutes, Nikita Zaitsev in Toronto, Boston Carlo in Boston, Ivan Provorov in Philadelphia, and Esa Lindell in Dallas. Based on those rather large white circles, none of them could be described as a smashing success, and were essentially used that ambitiously out of semi-desperation. Even Mike Matheson, who was arguably the most successful of the rookies who were assigned a shutdown role, was also used that way partly out of desperation, given that the team's top names, Aaron Ekblad and Keith Yandle, are mostly used in the offensive zone against the second lines.

So, if a team has other players to handle the tough minutes, it appears that rookie defencemen are best deployed in a more offensive capacity, on the right side of the chart, and against more secondary competition, closer to the horizon.

For example, having Jack Johnson and David Savard to handle the defensive minutes on the top left allowed Calder finalist Zach Werenski to have a truly fantastic season with Seth Jones on a more offensive-minded top pair. Likewise, Joshua Morrissey was surprisingly effective with Dustin Byfuglien on Winnipeg's offensive-minded second pair. In total, five of the 11 shaded circles that denote shot-based success are in the relatively sheltered quadrant of the chart. That seems to be the ideal location in which to introduce rookie defencemen.

For teams with adequate depth, the second alternative is to deploy rookie defencemen as two-way, No. 4 defencemen, like Detroit's Xavier Ouellet, Dallas's Stephen Johns, and Vancouver's Troy Stecher.

130

To get a similar sense of how rookies are used up front, I also put together the following player usage chart of the most prominent rookie forwards. It should include almost everybody who scored at least 25 points, or averaged at least 13 minutes per game.

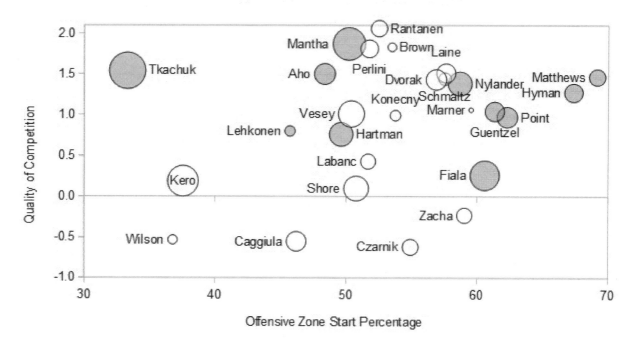

Rookie Forwards - Player Usage

Whether it's Aaron Ekblad in 2014–15, Artemi Panarin in 2015–16, or Auston Matthews in 2016–17, winning the Calder Trophy is often a matter of being on the far-right, offensive side of the player usage chart. Half of the other rookies with the shaded circles denoting shot-based success are also in that vicinity of the chart, and next year's Calder Trophy winner will be no exception.

The eyes are also drawn to the large shaded circles of Calgary's Matthew Tkachuk on the top-left, and of Detroit's Anthony Mantha and Carolina's Sebastian Aho at the middle-top. They may not finish among the Calder Trophy finalists, but the contributions that they make to their teams as rookies can be just as significant.

Building a Model

This chapter has been an admittedly high-level look at how Hischier and the NHL's other first-year players might perform this season. If you want to go even deeper, then how about building your own model?

Here's how to get started, step by step. Since nobody has the time to build a sophisticated model all at once, it has been laid out in such a way that you can do it bit by bit. This model is usable after each step, and will eventually grow to include all the components of the cutting-edge models that are actually used in the NHL today.

1. Build a database of traditional scoring stats for all players in a certain league, like the AHL. You can easily find this data on the league website and then just copy and paste it by hand, or build an automated solution, if you have programming skills. Then, when you want to get a better idea of what to expect from a player who played in that league, you can just search for anyone of the same age, with similar points per game.

2. To allow yourself to more accurately compare players from many years ago, add a simple era-adjustment to your database. The simplest way is to divide each player's points by the league average goals-per-game that season, and the multiply that by the modern league average goals-per-game.

3. Once you have a few leagues in your database, you can compare players to those in different leagues by multiplying every player's stats by the appropriate league translation factor. For starters, you can use the translation factors at the top of the chapter, but they will fall out of date, and you should eventually calculate them within your model itself, and possibly in more sophisticated ways.

4. Add an age adjustment so that you can compare players of different ages. That is, make an adjusted version of each player's scoring data to a common, standard age. Again, use the table at the top of the chapter for starters, but eventually the model should calculate the appropriate age adjustments, so that it doesn't fall out of date.

5. Expand the comparison criteria to use up three seasons of data, instead of using just one. A lot can happen in a single season, so we can get more accurate matches by looking at three years worth of data. You may even want to weight the data, so that the more recent seasons carry greater importance than the earlier seasons.

6. Rather than just looking for players whose adjusted points per game fall within a certain, hard-coded range, look online for some kind of "Nearest Neighbour" algorithm. Search for the statistical term k-Nearest Neighbour until you find a write-up that makes sense, and that you can apply to your ever-growing model.

7. Instead of just looking at points per game, add several different player stats to the comparison. If you have figured out the last step, then this step is pretty easy. For some leagues, you may only have the data for simple stats, like goals and assists. For others, you'll have ice time, data that is broken down by manpower situation, shot-based metrics, and so on. As you add more data to your model, the better your matches will be.

8. If you're looking for some final pieces of chrome, try applying statistical regression and an age curve, as described in *Stat Shot*[92], to create a statistical projection of the player's future over multiple seasons, and not just year one.

---

92 Rob Vollman, "What's the Best Way to Build a Team?", *Stat Shot,* September 2016, pgs12-73.

Yes, it is a lot of work to build models like these, but it's actually not that hard to do when it's broken down into steps.

You might need someone to help you build some kind of program to get the data from the league websites, and you might need a statistician to help you through step six, but there's really nothing to it. I've helped quite a few organizations build models like these, and if they can do it, so can you.

Closing Thoughts

Nothing foils a prediction of the standings quite like hot goalies, which are covered in the next chapter, and unexpected breakout seasons from rookies and other young players.

Every season, there are a few teams with a collection of prospects that all break out at once and make a surprise appearance in the playoffs, much like the Toronto Maple Leafs last season. There are also teams who have a single, breakout player who makes a particularly notable contribution, like Werenski or Tkachuk last year.

Even if it's almost impossible to predict which teams this will be, or who the specific players are who will break out, it's important to know how rookies can be used, and what kind of impact they can have. There are a number of ways that hockey analytics can play a key role in answering those types of questions, and the organizations who will be most successful are those who can implement these techniques most effectively, and incorporate them into their long-term planning.

Who is the Best Goalie?

By Rob Vollman

Despite all of the great statistical advances that has given us fascinating insights into virtually every aspect of team and player evaluation over the years, the analysis of goaltending has been left stagnant, and with no better method of evaluating talent than save percentage. At least, that's what you hear from so many pundits both inside and outside the hockey analytics community. But, it isn't true.

In reality, there's no area in hockey that has been subjected to closer scrutiny, has had more analysts exclusively dedicated to it, for a greater number of years, or has had more new metrics developed for its study.

Statistical goaltending analysis has a long and deep history that goes back over three decades to when the NHL finally starting using save percentage for the 1983–84 season. Shortly thereafter, two of the earliest statisticians, Jeff Z. Klein and Karl-Eric Reif, introduced Goalie Perseverance in their 1986 Hockey Compendium[93] as a combination of a goalie's efficiency (save percentage) and the volume of shots faced per game.

In 1999's revolutionary (and spider-squashing) 1878-page tome Total Hockey[94], Dan Diamond introduced era-adjusted statistics that measure certain statistics, including goals-against average, relative to the scoring levels of the day.

With the advent of shot location data in NHL game files for the 2002–03 season, legendary hockey statistician Alan Ryder introduced expected goals in 2004[95], which places a different weight on each shot, based on its likelihood of going in. This led to his shot quality neutral save percentage statistic (SQNSV%), which inspired a number of successors over the years, like Michael Schuckers DIGR in 2011[96], and modern-day xSV% models[97].

In January 2007, Phil "the Contrarian Goalie" Myrland launched his blog, Brodeur is a Fraud[98], which introduced countless advances to the field, and shaped most of what we know about goaltending today, statistically. Myrland tirelessly studied questions in every possible corner of the field, like the effect of workload on goaltending performance, where goalies should be drafted, rebound control, and clutch play.

---

93 Jeff Z. Klein and Karl-Eric Reif, "The Klein and Reif Hockey Compendium", 1986, pgs 131-159.
94 Dan Diamond, "Adjusted Scoring", *Total Hockey,* 1999, chapter 64, page 626.
95 Alan Ryder, "Shot Quality", *Hockey Analytics,* January 2004, Web,
   http://hockeyanalytics.com/Research_files/Shot_Quality.pdf.
96 Michael Schuckers, "DIGR: A Defense Independent Rating of NHL Goaltenders using Spatially Smoothed
   Save Percentage Maps", *St. Lawrence University and Statistical Sports Consulting,* March 4, 2011, Web,
   http://myslu.stlawu.edu/~msch/sports/Schuckers_DIGR_MIT_2011.pdf.
97 The xSV% statistic is available at Don't Tell Me About Heart,
   http://donttellmeaboutheart.blogspot.ca/p/xsv.html.
98 Myrland's Brodeur is a Fraud website http://brodeurisafraud.blogspot.ca/.

My own concrete contributions began in 2009 with the introduction of quality starts[99], which I followed up over the years with other concepts, such as home plate save percentage in 2014[100], which led to modern adjusted forms of save percentage, like those introduced by Sam Ventura and Andrew Thomas formerly of War on Ice[101], who now work in NHL front offices.

Even more recently, there are analysts like Nick Mercadante, Chris Boyle, Cat Silverman, and Clare Austin who devote their attention almost exclusively to the statistical analysis of goaltending, and who have been re-introducing a lot of these ideas in modern form.

And these are only the major highlights of the past 30 years. In its fullness, the field of goaltending analytics has been a long and thorough examination by a wide variety of gifted analysts. In fact, I can't think of any specific aspect of the game that has been examined to a greater extent, or where more insights have been discovered.

Applying these various perspectives to what's happening in today's NHL, the following summary table suggests that the debate for top starting goalie includes Montreal's Carey Price, Washington's Braden Holtby, Minnesota's Devan Dubnyk, and Chicago's Corey Crawford, with another half-dozen goalies on the fringes of the conversation. Among the unlisted backups and/or platoon partners, the most promising goalies include Carolina's Scott Darling, Pittsburgh's Matt Murray, and Arizona's Antti Raanta – so watch those three carefully this coming season.

Top Three No. 1 Goalies, by Various Measurements

Area	As Measured By	No. 1	No. 2	No. 3
Performance	Save Percentage	Price	Dubnyk	Holtby
Quality-Adjusted	Manpower-Adjusted Save Percentage	Price	Dubnyk	Holtby
	Home Plate Save Percentage	Greiss	Price	Schneider
	Quality-Adjusted Save Percentage	Price	Gibson	Halak
	Expected Goals Save Percentage	Price	Crawford	Mason
Importance	Game Stars	Price	Holtby	Bobrovsky
	Goalie Point Shares	Holtby	Dubnyk	Schneider
	Goals Saved Above Average	Price	Holtby	Dubnyk
	Expected Goals	Price	Crawford	Holtby
Consistency	Quality Start Percentage	Price	Crawford	Holtby

Let's dive in, and examine each category in a little more detail, including where each metric comes from, what it measures, its proper applications and limitations, and which goalies rank well.

---

99 Rob Vollman, "Howe and Why: Quality Starts", *Hockey Prospectus,* March 25, 2009, Web, http://www.hockeyprospectus.com/puck/article.php?articleid=54.

100 Rob Vollman, "Goaltending Analytics Re-visited", *Hockey Abstract 2014,* 2014, pgs 83-111.

101 Sam Ventura, "Adjusted Save Percentage: Taking into Account High, Medium, and Low Probability Shots", *War on Ice,* November 5, 2014, Web, http://blog.war-on-ice.com/adjusted-save-percentage-taking-into-account-high-medium-and-low-probability-shots/.

Overall Performance

Traditionally, goalies are evaluated using save percentage, which is saves divided by shots. Saves are defined as any shot that would have gone in if the goalie hadn't stopped it, in the subjective opinion of the scorekeeper. If it looks like the puck would have hit the post or missed the net, or if it was taken from outside the defensive zone, then a scorekeeper may not count it as a save. It's unfortunate that this statistic includes such a subjective component, but it remains a reasonable way of measuring a goalie's efficiency.

Statistically, the challenge is that most NHL goalies are equally efficient at making saves. With the exception of Price, who leads the following leader board by 4.3%, the goalies are so tightly clustered that we need four decimal places to start making distinctions. For example, the difference between Dubnyk and Holtby is only one goal in every 10,000 shots.

Save Percentage (SV%), 2014–15 to 2016–17[102]

Goalie	Team(s)	Shots	Saves	SV%
Carey Price	Montreal	4112	3820	.9290
Matt Murray	Pittsburgh	1805	1669	.9247
Antti Raanta	Chi/NYR	1701	1572	.9242
Devan Dubnyk	Ari/Min	5296	4890	.9233
Braden Holtby	Washington	5536	5111	.9232
Scott Darling	Chicago	2080	1919	.9226
Philipp Grubauer	Washington	1133	1045	.9223
Andrew Hammond	Ottawa	1505	1388	.9223
Corey Crawford	Chicago	5070	4675	.9221
Sergei Bobrovsky	Columbus	4535	4177	.9211
Craig Anderson	Ottawa	4296	3956	.9209
John Gibson	Anaheim	3103	2857	.9207
Cam Talbot	NYR/Edm	4803	4418	.9198
Roberto Luongo	Florida	4761	4378	.9196
Cory Schneider	New Jersey	5360	4927	.9192
Ben Bishop	TB/LA	4332	3979	.9185
Brian Elliott	StL/Cgy	3601	3306	.9181
Jonathan Quick	Los Angeles	4137	3797	.9178
Tuukka Rask	Boston	5475	5025	.9178
Marc-Andre Fleury	Pittsburgh	4677	4292	.9177
Steve Mason	Philadelphia	4648	4265	.9176
Robin Lehner	Ott/Buf	3323	3049	.9175
Henrik Lundqvist	NY Rangers	4923	4516	.9173
Frederik Andersen	Ana/Tor	4574	4194	.9169
Thomas Greiss	Pit/NYI	3196	2930	.9168
James Reimer	Tor/SJ/Fla	3351	3072	.9167
Pekka Rinne	Nashville	5308	4863	.9162
Jake Allen	St. Louis	3789	3471	.9161
Jaroslav Halak	NY Islanders	3542	3243	.9156

102Acknowledgement: Raw goaltending data from NHL's website http://www.nhl.com.

Andrei Vasilevskiy	Tampa Bay	2541	2326	.9154
Joonas Korpisalo	Columbus	1370	1254	.9153
Semyon Varlamov	Colorado	4250	3885	.9141
Peter Budaj	LA/TB	1442	1318	.9140
Martin Jones	LA/SJ	3766	3442	.9140
Ryan Miller	Vancouver	4569	4175	.9138
Calvin Pickard	Colorado	2511	2294	.9136
Jimmy Howard	Detroit	3004	2742	.9128
Anders Nilsson	Edm/Stl/Buf	1646	1502	.9125
Jacob Markstrom	Vancouver	1713	1563	.9124
Petr Mrazek	Detroit	3678	3355	.9122
Michal Neuvirth	Buf/NYI/Phi	2561	2336	.9121
Keith Kinkaid	New Jersey	1852	1689	.9120
Jonathan Bernier	Tor/Ana	3831	3493	.9118
Ondrej Pavelec	Winnipeg	2504	2282	.9113
Carter Hutton	Nsh/StL	1577	1437	.9112
Chad Johnson	NYI/Buf/Cgy	2727	2484	.9109
Mike Smith	Arizona	4695	4275	.9105
Eddie Lack	Carolina	2603	2370	.9105
Connor Hellebuyck	Winnipeg	2255	2053	.9104
Karri Ramo	Calgary	1886	1717	.9104
Louis Domingue	Arizona	2188	1991	.9100
Curtis McElhinney	CBJ/Tor	1982	1803	.9097
Al Montoya	Fla/Mtl	1630	1482	.9092
Michael Hutchinson	Winnipeg	2481	2254	.9085
Mike Condon	Mtl/Pit/Ott	2580	2343	.9081
Cam Ward	Carolina	4405	4000	.9081
Darcy Kuemper	Minnesota	1787	1621	.9071
Antti Niemi	SJ/Dal	3937	3569	.9065
Jonas Hiller	Calgary	2030	1838	.9054
Jhonas Enroth	Buf/Dal/LA/Tor	2043	1849	.9050
Kari Lehtonen	Dallas	4542	4105	.9038
Anders Lindback	Dal/Buf/Ari	1241	1121	.9033
Anton Khudobin	Car/Ana/Bos	1454	1312	.9023
Ben Scrivens	Edm/Mtl	1989	1777	.8934

Minimum 1000 Shots Faced

Even the difference between a Vezina-calibre goalie like Holtby and someone tossed aside, like Jaroslav Halak, is just one goal in every 130.8 shots. Halak ranked 29th in what was a 30-team league, and cleared waivers past all other 29 teams when he was sent down to the AHL by the New York Islanders last season. Given that there's an average of 30.2 shots per game, it would take an average of five games for the difference between these two goalies to manifest itself, and even then, only in the form of a single goal.

Even when basing the comparison on three full seasons, which is the tradition in the pages of *Hockey Abstract*, how can we even be sure that this small difference between goalies isn't just from certain outside factors, like playing conditions, team defense, or puck luck?

Even after 8,658 and 11,025 career shots respectively, we can only state with 95% statistical accuracy that Holtby's true save percentage lies in a broad range between .9160 and .9274, and that Halak's falls between .9119 and .9222[103]. So there's lots of overlap, and therefore plenty of uncertainty.

Repeating this exercise for all active goalies who have faced at least 2,000 career shots, and the true extent of the overlap becomes clear. Of the 57 other goalies, there are 45 whose confidence intervals overlap with the leader's, Boston's Tuukka Rask. That makes it virtually impossible to statistically argue that one goalie is truly better than another.

Save Percentage Confidence Intervals for Active Goalies[104]

Goalie	Team(s)	GP	Shots	Low	High	SV%
Tuukka Rask	Boston	395	10927	.9178	.9278	.9228
Scott Darling	Chicago	75	2080	.9111	.9341	.9226
Cam Talbot	NYR/Edm	186	5363	.9149	.9292	.9221
Cory Schneider	Van/NJ	330	9182	.9163	.9273	.9218
Braden Holtby	Washington	307	8658	.9160	.9274	.9217
John Gibson	Anaheim	118	3190	.9123	.9310	.9216
Carey Price	Montreal	509	15058	.9158	.9244	.9201
Sergei Bobrovsky	Phi/CBJ	330	9614	.9144	.9252	.9198
Henrik Lundqvist	NY Rangers	742	20992	.9161	.9234	.9197
Roberto Luongo	NYI/Fla/Van	966	28576	.9159	.9223	.9191
Ben Bishop	StL/Ott/TB/LA	270	7314	.9127	.9252	.9189
Corey Crawford	Chicago	381	10612	.9128	.9232	.9180
Frederik Andersen	Ana/Tor	191	5357	.9105	.9252	.9179
Robin Lehner	Ott/Buf	166	5220	.9102	.9251	.9176
Pekka Rinne	Nashville	508	14136	.9129	.9220	.9174
Jaroslav Halak	Mtl/StL/Wsh/NYI	395	11025	.9119	.9222	.9170
Antti Raanta	Chi/NYR	94	2311	.9057	.9282	.9169
Martin Jones	LA/SJ	164	4266	.9080	.9246	.9163
Craig Anderson	Chi/Fla/Col/Ott	506	15461	.9119	.9207	.9163
Devan Dubnyk	Edm/Nsh/Ari/Min	363	10435	.9109	.9216	.9162
Thomas Greiss	SJ/Ari/Pit/NYI	181	4896	.9083	.9238	.9161
Anton Khudobin	Min/Bos/Car/Ana	116	3097	.9063	.9258	.9160
Semyon Varlamov	Wsh/Col	348	10470	.9105	.9212	.9159
Jonathan Quick	Los Angeles	492	12892	.9110	.9206	.9158
Jimmy Howard	Detroit	401	11017	.9103	.9207	.9155
Andrei Vasilevskiy	Tampa Bay	90	2541	.9046	.9262	.9154
James Reimer	Tor/SJ/Fla	258	7549	.9089	.9215	.9152
Jake Allen	St. Louis	160	4135	.9066	.9236	.9151
Chad Johnson	NYR/Ari/Bos/NYI/Buf/Cgy	137	3689	.9059	.9239	.9149
Ryan Miller	Buf/StL/Van	709	21260	.9111	.9186	.9149

103This isn't exactly right, because goalie save percentages fall into more of a log-normal distribution than a normal distribution. After all, how can a goalie's save percentage be *above* 1.000? However, this is close enough to make the point.

104Acknowledgement: Raw goaltending data from NHL's website http://www.nhl.com.

Jonathan Bernier	LA/Tor/Ana	252	7171	.9082	.9211	.9147
Calvin Pickard	Colorado	86	2511	.9026	.9246	.9136
Brian Elliott	Ott/Col/StL/Cgy	372	9570	.9077	.9190	.9134
Petr Mrazek	Detroit	144	3907	.9041	.9218	.9130
Antti Niemi	Chi/SJ/Dal	423	11463	.9077	.9180	.9129
Mike Smith	Dal/TB/Ari	474	13952	.9079	.9173	.9126
Kari Lehtonen	Atl/Dal	612	17974	.9080	.9163	.9122
Marc-Andre Fleury	Pittsburgh	691	19487	.9081	.9161	.9121
Michal Neuvirth	Wsh/Buf/NYI/Phi	228	6270	.9045	.9185	.9115
Eddie Lack	Van/Car	136	3655	.9016	.9200	.9108
Steve Mason	CBJ/Phi	463	13167	.9060	.9157	.9108
Connor Hellebuyck	Winnipeg	82	2255	.8986	.9222	.9104
Carter Hutton	Nsh/StL	106	2611	.8994	.9213	.9104
Louis Domingue	Arizona	77	2188	.8980	.9220	.9100
Michael Hutchinson	Winnipeg	99	2569	.8986	.9208	.9097
Al Montoya	Ari/NYI/Wpg/Fla/Mtl	155	4072	.9008	.9184	.9096
Darcy Kuemper	Minnesota	102	2608	.8985	.9205	.9095
Jhonas Enroth	Buf/Dal/LA/Tor	153	4379	.9008	.9178	.9093
Cam Ward	Carolina	625	17802	.9050	.9134	.9092
Anders Nilsson	NYI/Edm/StL/Buf	78	2306	.8967	.9203	.9085
Mike Condon	Mtl/Pit/Ott	96	2580	.8970	.9193	.9081
Ondrej Pavelec	Winnipeg	379	10984	.9014	.9123	.9069
Jacob Markstrom	Fla/Van	109	2995	.8950	.9160	.9055
Curtis McElhinney	Cgy/Ana/Ott/Ari/CBJ/Tor	168	4296	.8967	.9142	.9055
Peter Budaj	Col/Mtl/LA/TB	357	9201	.8988	.9108	.9048
Jonas Gustavsson	Tor/Det/Bos/Edm	179	4717	.8927	.9097	.9012
Justin Peters	Car/Wsh/Ari	83	2313	.8884	.9128	.9006
Michael Leighton	Chi/Nsh/Phi/Car	110	2985	.8894	.9109	.9002

Minimum 2000 Shots Faced

Shot Quality Adjustments

Given the goaltending parity in today's NHL, it makes perfect sense to take a deeper dive into the data, because even the smallest insight can have a profound impact on the rankings.

For front offices, there's an incredible advantage to be gained in having an idea on which goalies might break out, and by making the right calculated gambles in nets. Readers of previous editions have already seen this with goalies like Dubnyk, Holtby, New Jersey's Cory Schneider, and NY Islanders Thomas Greiss. Who might be next?

The answer is to take a closer look at shot quality. It's an obvious fact that certain shots are more dangerous than others. For example, the average shot has about an 8% chance of going in, but we know that a player has a 31% chance of scoring on a penalty shot or a shootout, and just slightly less on a clear breakaway.

What we don't know is to what extent this impacts a goalie's numbers. That is, to what extent do these more dangerous types of shots even out over an entire season?

Let's start with something simple, like manpower adjustments. At even-strength, roughly 8% of shots go in, which goes up to 10% when a team is shorthanded, and 13% when on the power play. Whether that's because of using more skilled shooters, or because the shots are of higher quality is immaterial – the bottom line is that shots taken in each of these three situations shouldn't be treated equally when goalies are being compared using save percentage.

The simplest and most common adjustment to make is to break down a goalie's save percentages in each of these three primary manpower situations, and then re-combine them in the same, league-average ratio. Some analysts prefer to simply set special teams data aside and study only five-on-five play, but there's no reason to set aside valuable data when it also serves as an effective measurement of a goalie's ability to stop the puck.

Manpower-Adjusted Save Percentage (MASP%), 2014–15 to 2016–17[105]

Goalie	Team(s)	ES	SV%	PP	SV%	PK	SV%	MASP%
Carey Price	Montreal	3409	.938	107	.916	596	.878	.9287
Matt Murray	Pittsburgh	1470	.933	69	.899	266	.887	.9250
Antti Raanta	Chi/NYR	1427	.931	35	1.000	239	.874	.9239
Devan Dubnyk	Ari/Min	4407	.931	107	.944	782	.877	.9233
Philipp Grubauer	Washington	906	.929	24	.875	203	.897	.9231
Braden Holtby	Washington	4581	.931	152	.947	803	.877	.9229
Scott Darling	Chicago	1750	.929	51	.843	279	.900	.9222
Corey Crawford	Chicago	4223	.931	103	.922	744	.874	.9219
Sergei Bobrovsky	Columbus	3685	.928	101	.941	749	.883	.9218
John Gibson	Anaheim	2520	.925	57	.930	526	.901	.9212
Andrew Hammond	Ottawa	1270	.935	24	.917	211	.844	.9212
Craig Anderson	Ottawa	3568	.931	94	.936	634	.863	.9207
Roberto Luongo	Florida	3877	.929	118	.932	766	.872	.9202
Cam Talbot	NYR/Edm	4007	.925	103	.942	693	.885	.9197
Cory Schneider	New Jersey	4384	.928	144	.875	832	.879	.9196
Ben Bishop	TB/LA	3496	.923	104	.894	732	.900	.9189
Brian Elliott	StL/Cgy	2902	.925	90	.911	609	.887	.9188
Jonathan Quick	Los Angeles	3390	.927	87	.966	660	.867	.9185
Marc-Andre Fleury	Pittsburgh	3774	.924	118	.907	785	.890	.9183
Robin Lehner	Ott/Buf	2740	.922	77	.922	506	.891	.9176
Tuukka Rask	Boston	4577	.925	122	.951	776	.872	.9174
Frederik Andersen	Ana/Tor	3755	.923	118	.907	701	.887	.9171
Thomas Greiss	Pit/NYI	2656	.923	72	.861	468	.889	.9166
Steve Mason	Philadelphia	3894	.930	135	.911	619	.840	.9162
Jake Allen	St. Louis	3119	.921	82	.902	588	.893	.9162
Henrik Lundqvist	NY Rangers	4155	.928	109	.899	659	.851	.9160
Andrei Vasilevskiy	Tampa Bay	2056	.921	63	.921	422	.886	.9159

105Acknowledgement: Raw goaltending data from NHL's website http://www.nhl.com.

Jaroslav Halak	NY Islanders	2939	.920	71	.958	532	.887	.9157
Pekka Rinne	Nashville	4437	.925	120	.925	751	.860	.9156
James Reimer	Tor/SJ/Fla	2825	.928	72	.819	454	.863	.9155
Joonas Korpisalo	Columbus	1159	.924	26	.885	185	.865	.9142
Martin Jones	LA/SJ	3080	.920	102	.951	584	.875	.9141
Semyon Varlamov	Colorado	3516	.917	106	.953	628	.892	.9140
Peter Budaj	LA/TB	1198	.923	36	.917	208	.861	.9137
Calvin Pickard	Colorado	2076	.922	58	.966	377	.857	.9136
Anders Nilsson	Edm/Stl/Buf	1336	.923	37	.892	273	.864	.9134
Ryan Miller	Vancouver	3814	.921	110	.918	645	.868	.9133
Ondrej Pavelec	Winnipeg	1960	.920	76	.947	468	.868	.9131
Keith Kinkaid	New Jersey	1493	.923	40	.850	319	.868	.9130
Jacob Markstrom	Vancouver	1393	.918	43	.860	277	.892	.9128
Petr Mrazek	Detroit	2998	.922	78	.872	602	.869	.9128
Jimmy Howard	Detroit	2461	.919	88	.943	455	.873	.9127
Michal Neuvirth	Buf/NYI/Phi	2095	.922	61	.869	405	.869	.9126
Jonathan Bernier	Tor/Ana	3104	.918	114	.877	613	.884	.9124
Connor Hellebuyck	Winnipeg	1818	.924	53	.906	384	.849	.9119
Carter Hutton	Nsh/StL	1291	.915	42	.929	244	.889	.9113
Mike Smith	Arizona	3840	.921	118	.864	737	.866	.9110
Chad Johnson	NYI/Buf/Cgy	2259	.919	58	.931	410	.863	.9109
Louis Domingue	Arizona	1785	.922	63	.905	340	.850	.9104
Curtis McElhinney	CBJ/Tor	1609	.914	25	.880	348	.891	.9099
Michael Hutchinson	Winnipeg	1960	.916	67	.925	454	.874	.9098
Eddie Lack	Carolina	2222	.914	59	.949	322	.882	.9097
Al Montoya	Fla/Mtl	1368	.914	35	.914	227	.881	.9089
Karri Ramo	Calgary	1629	.917	40	.875	217	.871	.9087
Mike Condon	Mtl/Pit/Ott	2114	.912	80	.950	386	.876	.9079
Antti Niemi	SJ/Dal	3252	.918	118	.847	567	.854	.9066
Cam Ward	Carolina	3842	.913	83	.880	480	.873	.9062
Darcy Kuemper	Minnesota	1553	.911	42	.905	192	.875	.9056
Kari Lehtonen	Dallas	3747	.913	129	.891	666	.853	.9037
Jhonas Enroth	Buf/Dal/LA/Tor	1721	.915	56	.911	266	.838	.9035
Anders Lindback	Dal/Buf/Ari	1019	.912	32	.906	190	.858	.9035
Anton Khudobin	Car/Ana/Bos	1230	.902	27	.852	197	.909	.9022
Jonas Hiller	Calgary	1731	.919	59	.949	240	.800	.9015
Ben Scrivens	Edm/Mtl	1676	.903	41	.756	272	.853	.8922

Minimum 1000 Shots Faced

If you flip back a few pages (or take my word for it), then you'll notice that this adjustment didn't really change the picture much. That's probably because most teams spend roughly the same amount of time in each manpower situation, and because of the underlying goaltending parity.

As it turns out, 34 of the 58 goalies moved by no more than one position in the rankings. The biggest swing involved Winnipeg's Ondrej Pavelec moving up from 44th to 38th, and Detroit's Jimmy Howard falling from 37th to 42nd. It's interesting to contemplate how our opinions of

Pavelec and Howard would be interchanged if they had been playing on the other's team.

This simple adjustment may not have changed the picture much, but it did change it a little. With a few more strides in this direction, perhaps we can find an edge. So, let's press on.

The next most intuitive factor to consider is shot location. Obviously, shots from up close are far more dangerous than those from far away, or from a bad angle. In fact, that's part of the reason why shots are more dangerous on the power play.

This is exactly what was in mind when I introduced home plate save percentage in *Hockey Abstract 2014*[106], and it was useful enough to predict Dubnyk's breakout season the following year.

Briefly, home plate save percentage is simply the percentage of shots a goalie stops that were taken inside that dangerous area in front of the net that goes from the goal posts to the faceoff dots to the top of the faceoff circles, and straight between. Sometimes called "the House", we call it the home plate area, because it forms the same shape as the home plate in baseball.

Most goalies face about two in five shots from inside the home plate area, and post a save percentage of about .830. Like Dubnyk after his seemingly disastrous 2013–14 season, goalies who perform far better than that can often expect to have breakout seasons – once the blue line in front of them has improved.

If that pattern holds, then Andrei Vasilevskiy could have a breakout season for Tampa Bay this season, at age 23. His .945 save percentage from the outside is the worst among NHL goalies by a fair margin, but his .877 from up close leads the NHL.

Home Plate Save Percentage (HP SV%), 2014–15 to 2016–17[107]

Goalie	Team(s)	Outside Shots	Outside SV%	HP%	HP Shots	HP SV%
Andrei Vasilevskiy	Tampa Bay	1435	.945	43.5%	1106	.877
Thomas Greiss	Pit/NYI	1708	.958	46.6%	1488	.869
Matt Murray	Pittsburgh	1178	.955	34.7%	627	.868
Carey Price	Montreal	2486	.969	39.5%	1626	.868
Scott Darling	Chicago	1192	.966	42.7%	888	.865
Antti Raanta	Chi/NYR	956	.973	43.8%	745	.862
Andrew Hammond	Ottawa	890	.964	40.9%	615	.862
Cory Schneider	New Jersey	3007	.965	43.9%	2353	.861
Cam Talbot	NYR/Edm	2642	.970	45.0%	2161	.859
Martin Jones	LA/SJ	2097	.959	44.3%	1669	.857
Jaroslav Halak	NY Islanders	1865	.968	47.4%	1677	.857
Corey Crawford	Chicago	2989	.968	41.1%	2081	.856
Braden Holtby	Washington	3262	.970	41.1%	2274	.856

106Rob Vollman, "Goaltending Analytics Re-visited", *Hockey Abstract 2014,* 2014, pgs 83-111.
107Acknowledgement: Over the years, home plate save percentage data provided privately by friends like Greg Sinclair, Dawson Sprigings, and Micah Blake McCurdy.

Sergei Bobrovsky	Columbus	2640	.969	41.8%	1895	.854
Ben Bishop	TB/LA	2460	.967	43.2%	1872	.854
Ryan Miller	Vancouver	2442	.966	46.6%	2127	.853
Joonas Korpisalo	Columbus	765	.965	44.2%	605	.853
Philipp Grubauer	Washington	640	.977	43.5%	493	.852
Jacob Markstrom	Vancouver	884	.969	48.4%	829	.852
Frederik Andersen	Ana/Tor	2674	.963	41.5%	1900	.852
Carter Hutton	Nsh/StL	900	.956	42.9%	677	.852
Jonathan Quick	Los Angeles	2403	.967	41.9%	1734	.850
Jonathan Bernier	Tor/Ana	2215	.957	42.2%	1616	.850
Petr Mrazek	Detroit	2086	.960	43.3%	1592	.849
James Reimer	Tor/SJ/Fla	1937	.966	42.2%	1414	.849
Brian Elliott	StL/Cgy	2047	.970	43.2%	1554	.849
Semyon Varlamov	Colorado	2434	.963	42.7%	1816	.848
Peter Budaj	LA/TB	842	.961	41.6%	600	.848
Devan Dubnyk	Ari/Min	3268	.970	38.3%	2028	.848
Anders Nilsson	Edm/Stl/Buf	917	.964	44.3%	729	.848
Jake Allen	St. Louis	2148	.969	43.3%	1641	.846
Tuukka Rask	Boston	3278	.966	40.1%	2197	.845
John Gibson	Anaheim	1849	.972	40.4%	1254	.845
Robin Lehner	Ott/Buf	2105	.960	36.7%	1218	.844
Marc-Andre Fleury	Pittsburgh	2650	.974	43.3%	2027	.844
Henrik Lundqvist	NY Rangers	2870	.970	41.7%	2053	.844
Connor Hellebuyck	Winnipeg	1301	.960	42.3%	954	.843
Roberto Luongo	Florida	2949	.967	38.1%	1812	.842
Louis Domingue	Arizona	1240	.962	43.3%	948	.842
Keith Kinkaid	New Jersey	1092	.962	41.0%	760	.841
Michal Neuvirth	Buf/NYI/Phi	1510	.964	41.0%	1051	.838
Kari Lehtonen	Dallas	2516	.957	44.6%	2026	.837
Craig Anderson	Ottawa	2661	.973	38.1%	1635	.837
Calvin Pickard	Colorado	1475	.967	41.3%	1036	.837
Mike Smith	Arizona	2679	.966	42.9%	2016	.836
Steve Mason	Philadelphia	2810	.972	39.5%	1838	.835
Michael Hutchinson	Winnipeg	1432	.963	42.3%	1049	.834
Chad Johnson	NYI/Buf/Cgy	1543	.970	43.4%	1184	.834
Ondrej Pavelec	Winnipeg	1399	.976	44.1%	1105	.829
Jimmy Howard	Detroit	1834	.966	39.0%	1170	.829
Eddie Lack	Carolina	1480	.972	43.1%	1123	.829
Karri Ramo	Calgary	1103	.969	41.5%	783	.828
Pekka Rinne	Nashville	3345	.969	37.0%	1963	.827
Darcy Kuemper	Minnesota	1081	.959	39.5%	706	.827
Jonas Hiller	Calgary	1161	.965	42.8%	869	.826
Jhonas Enroth	Buf/Dal/LA/Tor	1242	.956	39.2%	801	.826
Mike Condon	Mtl/Pit/Ott	1506	.967	41.6%	1074	.825
Cam Ward	Carolina	2657	.963	39.7%	1748	.824
Al Montoya	Fla/Mtl	973	.967	40.3%	657	.823
Curtis McElhinney	CBJ/Tor	1199	.968	39.5%	783	.820

Antti Niemi	SJ/Dal	2330	.967	40.8%	1607	.820
Anton Khudobin	Car/Ana/Bos	813	.969	44.1%	641	.817
Anders Lindback	Dal/Buf/Ari	781	.960	37.1%	460	.807
Ben Scrivens	Edm/Mtl	1192	.954	40.1%	797	.803

Minimum 1000 shots faced

There's actually nothing new about studying shots taken inside the home plate area, because that idea has been around for decades. The difference today is that we are starting to measure results more objectively, and have started putting numbers to everything.

In just the past couple of seasons, home plate statistics have grown in popularity. They were featured in *Sportsnet*'s coverage of the 2015 World Junior Championships[108], and several statisticians have expanded on these ideas with location-adjusted metrics of their own.

Perhaps the greatest appeal of studying the home plate area is that the grip that parity has on save percentages starts to slip a bit. Consider the following chart, where the spread between goalies is almost three times wider inside the home plate area (on the horizontal axis) than the shots from the outside (vertical axis).

Save Percentage by Location, 2014–15 to 2016–17

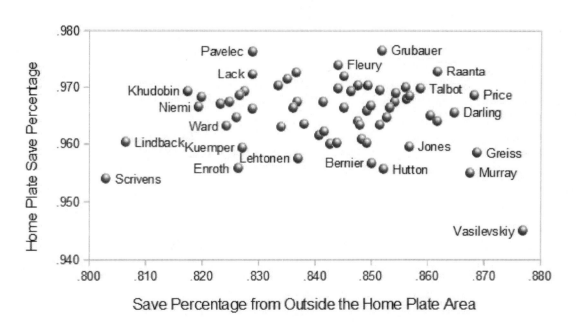

Next, just as we did with manpower situation, the logical step is to re-combine home plate data and outside shots back together in a league-average ratio. That's exactly what Thomas and Ventura did shortly after launching their War on Ice website for the 2014–15 season – after adding one more area.

Just as shots within the home plate area are more dangerous than those outside, shots taken in the slot immediately in front of the net are more dangerous than those elsewhere in the

---

108Screen capture: http://www.hockeyabstract.com/thoughts/oldideasmadenew.

home plate area. So, they broke down each goalie's save percentage into those taken inside a high danger zone in the slot, those taken in the medium danger zone elsewhere in the home plate area (plus a small section directly facing the net), and the outside, low-danger shots, and then re-combined all three zones back together in a league-average ratio[109].

From this perspective, Halak actually jumps ahead of Holtby, and all the way into fourth among starting goalies, and seventh overall. Now, we're getting somewhere.

Adjusted Save Percentage (AdjSV%), 2014–15 to 2016–17[110]

Goalie	Team(s)	Low	SV%	Med	SV%	High	SV%	AdjSV%
Antti Raanta	Chi/NYR	637	.984	607	.934	457	.827	.9280
Carey Price	Montreal	1671	.977	1473	.927	968	.848	.9278
Matthew Murray	Pittsburgh	653	.979	687	.937	465	.830	.9277
Scott Darling	Chicago	789	.970	759	.933	532	.838	.9245
John Gibson	Anaheim	1140	.984	1171	.939	794	.804	.9239
Philipp Grubauer	Washington	427	.986	430	.914	276	.837	.9236
Jaroslav Halak	NY Islanders	1188	.976	1304	.924	1050	.836	.9234
Cam Talbot	Edm/NYR	1761	.977	1797	.935	1249	.817	.9230
Corey Crawford	Chicago	1961	.979	1860	.930	1250	.822	.9230
Braden Holtby	Washington	2246	.982	1933	.925	1358	.824	.9229
Cory Schneider	New Jersey	1895	.972	2068	.924	1361	.838	.9222
Sergei Bobrovsky	Columbus	1731	.972	1724	.934	1080	.819	.9212
Andrew Hammond	Ottawa	613	.972	540	.924	352	.832	.9209
Thomas Greiss	Pit/NYI	1095	.974	1286	.925	815	.826	.9206
Marc-Andre Fleury	Pittsburgh	1769	.982	1684	.917	1224	.824	.9205
Henrik Lundqvist	NY Rangers	1895	.985	1724	.919	1304	.817	.9202
Ondrej Pavelec	Winnipeg	807	.988	1023	.914	674	.816	.9192
Jonathan Quick	Los Angeles	1624	.976	1487	.927	1026	.813	.9186
Brian Elliott	StL/Cgy	1389	.975	1346	.929	869	.810	.9185
Frederik Andersen	Ana/Tor	1671	.978	1815	.924	1089	.812	.9181
Roberto Luongo	Florida	1849	.982	1884	.921	1029	.806	.9169
Jacob Markstrom	Vancouver	568	.974	716	.926	430	.809	.9165
Martin Jones	LA/SJ	1400	.978	1405	.915	958	.818	.9164
Joonas Korpisalo	Columbus	561	.975	452	.914	357	.824	.9160
Ben Bishop	TB/LA	1748	.982	1614	.916	971	.809	.9160
Ryan Miller	Vancouver	1632	.974	1822	.922	1116	.813	.9159
Craig Anderson	Ottawa	1846	.984	1513	.917	937	.803	.9157
Steve Mason	Philadelphia	1911	.984	1645	.924	1092	.791	.9157
Eddie Lack	Van/Car	932	.984	968	.912	676	.809	.9154
Jake Allen	St. Louis	1496	.973	1402	.915	892	.823	.9154
Devan Dubnyk	Ari/Min	2399	.981	1819	.918	1075	.804	.9151
James Reimer	Tor/SJ/Fla	1367	.975	1214	.922	770	.805	.9146
Petr Mrazek	Detroit	1337	.984	1405	.908	895	.811	.9143

109Sam Ventura, "Adjusted Save Percentage: Taking into Account High, Medium, and Low Probability Shots", *War on Ice,* November 5, 2014, Web, http://blog.war-on-ice.com/adjusted-save-percentage-taking-into-account-high-medium-and-low-probability-shots/.
110Acknowledgement: Data obtained from *Corsica Hockey,* http://www.corsica.hockey.

Anders Nilsson	Edm/StL/Buf	593	.971	656	.915	399	.820	.9139
Semyon Varlamov	Colorado	1701	.974	1518	.922	1031	.804	.9139
Curtis McElhinney	CBJ/Tor	767	.980	672	.908	543	.812	.9132
Keith Kinkaid	New Jersey	658	.989	767	.905	426	.800	.9127
Anton Khudobin	Car/Ana/Bos	531	.983	498	.926	427	.775	.9119
Connor Hellebuyck	Winnipeg	897	.978	768	.918	563	.796	.9119
Mike Smith	Arizona	1761	.978	1789	.915	1145	.800	.9119
Michal Neuvirth	Buf/NYI/Phi	969	.974	1002	.919	590	.798	.9116
Peter Budaj	LA/TB	539	.972	597	.920	306	.801	.9116
Andrei Vasilevskiy	Tampa Bay	1030	.960	991	.916	520	.825	.9115
Jimmy Howard	Detroit	1221	.975	1073	.926	710	.785	.9115
Calvin Pickard	Colorado	1050	.978	868	.919	593	.791	.9114
Chad Johnson	NYI/Buf/Cgy	1078	.980	991	.921	659	.783	.9108
Tuukka Rask	Boston	2342	.981	2026	.915	1109	.791	.9107
Michael Hutchinson	Winnipeg	938	.977	922	.920	622	.789	.9106
Carter Hutton	Nsh/StL	595	.976	637	.901	345	.817	.9104
Robin Lehner	Ott/Buf	1517	.978	1098	.912	711	.797	.9102
Jonathan Bernier	Tor/Ana	1506	.966	1474	.909	851	.820	.9100
Al Montoya	Fla/Mtl	632	.981	608	.910	390	.792	.9093
Pekka Rinne	Nashville	2299	.980	1893	.926	1117	.770	.9092
Karri Ramo	Calgary	768	.983	673	.930	445	.755	.9088
Louis Domingue	Arizona	876	.966	802	.933	511	.779	.9087
Cam Ward	Carolina	1751	.978	1596	.919	1059	.776	.9077
Kari Lehtonen	Dallas	1725	.972	1625	.913	1193	.792	.9072
Mike Condon	Mtl/Pit/Ott	1024	.979	949	.905	607	.794	.9071
Antti Niemi	SJ/Dal	1664	.976	1288	.910	986	.785	.9057
Jonas Hiller	Calgary	828	.965	696	.915	506	.794	.9056
Jhonas Enroth	Buf/Dal/LA/Tor	796	.974	762	.907	486	.790	.9049
Darcy Kuemper	Minnesota	763	.967	641	.895	384	.807	.9023
Anders Lindback	Dal/Buf/Ari	540	.970	429	.907	272	.765	.8975
Ben Scrivens	Edm/Mtl	750	.968	783	.899	456	.761	.8928

Minimum 1000 shots faced

This perspective has caused some real movement in the leader board. Pavelec actually climbed up the leader board to a greater extent than Halak, going from 44th to 17th. Just as interestingly, a readily available replacement-level option like Anton Khudobin improved from 63rd to a respectable 38th.

In the opposite direction, Rask fell from 19th to 47th, and Dubnyk from 4th to 31st, which casts some doubt on their status among the elite. Also, Buffalo's Robin Lehner dropped from 22nd to 50th, and Nashville's Pekka Rinne, who is admittedly a frequent target of criticism within analytics circles, dropped from 27th to 53rd.

If very simple adjusted forms of save percentage can provide such insight, like those adjusted for manpower or with the shot locations broken down into three zones, what if there was a metric that went further, and incorporated absolutely everything that is known about the location and quality of each and every shot? Such a metric does exist, and was in fact introduced by Ryder way back in 2004 as shot-quality neutral save percentage (SQNSV%)[111].

Rather than break the ice into two or three zones, SQNSV% is based on expected goals, which assigns a weight to each and every shot based on the chances of it going in, which in turn is based on its exact location, and other quality factors, like whether or not it was a rebound. The number of goals a goalie actually allows is compared to the expected number of goals, which results in the best possible estimate of how many extra saves were made, relative to the league average. In a sense, it was designed to be the ultimate form of save percentage.

It has gone through a few iterations over the years, but the modern form of SQSNV% is called xSV%, with the x referring to that Expected Goals model, and not a statistic that belongs in Professor Charles Xavier's school of mutants.

This is also the station where we get off the train of statistics that everyone can calculate for themselves. While making it this far in the chapter can help everyone understand the concepts behind xSV%, the actual implementation can be quite complex. For this last metric, you're just going to have to trust us.

Fortunately, we have the highly trustworthy Dawson Sprigings available to handle all the math. He developed and maintains this statistic on his website *Don't Tell Me About Heart*[112], and is quite forthcoming about the underlying details for those who are curious. We also revealed many of the inner working in sometimes exhaustive detail in *Stat Shot*[113].

Price is way out in the lead from this perspective, with an even strength save percentage of 0.9403 that is far higher than expected based on the quality of shots faced, .9264. That difference of .0139 is almost double a tight pack of the next best batch of No. 1 goalies, Crawford, Mason, Lundqvist, Bobrovsky, Holtby, and Schneider.

Expected Save Percentage (xSV%) at Even Strength, 2014–15 to 2016–17[114]

Goalie	Team(s)	Shots	xGA	xSV%	GA	SV%	Diff
Carey Price	Montreal	3349	246.4	.9264	200	.9403	.0139
Matt Murray	Pittsburgh	1113	92.2	.9172	77	.9308	.0137
Andrew Hammond	Ottawa	1422	93.7	.9341	76	.9466	.0125
Scott Darling	Chicago	1918	133.9	.9302	112	.9416	.0114
Antti Raanta	Chi/NYR	1555	109.8	.9294	93	.9402	.0108
Corey Crawford	Chicago	4619	322.4	.9302	286	.9381	.0079
Steve Mason	Philadelphia	4216	287.7	.9318	258	.9388	.0070
Henrik Lundqvist	NY Rangers	4721	318.7	.9325	286	.9394	.0069
Sergei Bobrovsky	Columbus	3803	278.0	.9269	252	.9337	.0068

111Alan Ryder, "Shot Quality", *Hockey Analytics*, January 2004, Web,
   http://hockeyanalytics.com/Research_files/Shot_Quality.pdf.
112Acknowledgement: Data obtained from *Don't Tell Me About Heart*,
   http://donttellmeaboutheart.blogspot.ca/p/xsv.html.
113Rob Vollman, "Who is the best puck stopper?", *Stat Shot*, September 2016, pgs 169-227.
114Acknowledgement: Data obtained from *Don't Tell Me About Heart*,
   http://donttellmeaboutheart.blogspot.ca/p/xsv.html.

Braden Holtby	Washington	5033	335.3	.9334	302	.9400	.0066
Cory Schneider	New Jersey	4522	320.8	.9290	293	.9352	.0062
Philipp Grubauer	Washington	1042	66.5	.9362	61	.9415	.0053
Brian Elliott	StL/Cgy	3224	220.3	.9317	204	.9367	.0051
Joonas Korpisalo	Columbus	1408	87.4	.9379	81	.9425	.0045
James Reimer	Tor/SJ/Fla	3060	206.8	.9324	193	.9369	.0045
Cam Talbot	NYR/Edm	4354	299.8	.9311	283	.9350	.0039
Thomas Greiss	Pit/NYI	2987	208.0	.9304	197	.9340	.0037
Jonathan Quick	Los Angeles	3880	254.3	.9345	242	.9376	.0032
Marc-Andre Fleury	Pittsburgh	4103	280.8	.9316	268	.9347	.0031
Mike Smith	Arizona	4009	296.0	.9262	284	.9292	.0030
John Gibson	Anaheim	2788	189.2	.9321	181	.9351	.0030
Louis Domingue	Arizona	2114	137.1	.9351	131	.9380	.0029
Anders Nilsson	Edm/Stl/Buf	1537	103.3	.9328	99	.9356	.0028
Frederik Andersen	Ana/Tor	3932	275.9	.9298	266	.9323	.0025
Craig Anderson	Ottawa	3937	239.7	.9391	231	.9413	.0022
Petr Mrazek	Detroit	3274	222.5	.9320	217	.9337	.0017
Eddie Lack	Carolina	2439	179.8	.9263	176	.9278	.0016
Jaroslav Halak	NY Islanders	3126	231.4	.9260	227	.9274	.0014
Ondrej Pavelec	Winnipeg	2161	148.6	.9312	146	.9324	.0012
Devan Dubnyk	Ari/Min	4926	296.2	.9399	292	.9407	.0009
Peter Budaj	LA/TB	1139	88.7	.9221	88	.9227	.0006
Ryan Miller	Vancouver	4144	282.7	.9318	281	.9322	.0004
Connor Hellebuyck	Winnipeg	1909	130.7	.9315	130	.9319	.0004
Roberto Luongo	Florida	4304	275.0	.9361	274	.9363	.0002
Martin Jones	LA/SJ	3580	233.8	.9347	233	.9349	.0002
Jacob Markstrom	Vancouver	1627	109.0	.9330	109	.9330	.0000
Michal Neuvirth	Buf/NYI/Phi	2251	157.4	.9301	158	.9298	-.0003
Tuukka Rask	Boston	5032	323.5	.9357	326	.9352	-.0005
Calvin Pickard	Colorado	2172	151.8	.9301	153	.9296	-.0005
Keith Kinkaid	New Jersey	1590	108.2	.9320	110	.9308	-.0011
Ben Bishop	TB/LA	3972	261.3	.9342	266	.9330	-.0012
Antti Niemi	SJ/Dal	3549	249.7	.9296	254	.9284	-.0012
Jake Allen	St. Louis	3293	225.1	.9316	230	.9302	-.0015
Jonas Hiller	Calgary	1907	134.9	.9293	138	.9276	-.0016
Karri Ramo	Calgary	1926	123.5	.9359	127	.9341	-.0018
Jonathan Bernier	Tor/Ana	3360	235.8	.9298	242	.9280	-.0019
Kari Lehtonen	Dallas	4087	299.4	.9267	311	.9239	-.0028
Jimmy Howard	Detroit	2694	184.3	.9316	192	.9287	-.0029
Pekka Rinne	Nashville	4801	301.7	.9372	316	.9342	-.0030
Chad Johnson	NYI/Buf/Cgy	2575	171.3	.9335	179	.9305	-.0030
Jhonas Enroth	Buf/Dal/LA/Tor	1778	136.0	.9235	142	.9201	-.0034
Semyon Varlamov	Colorado	3942	261.4	.9337	278	.9295	-.0042
Curtis McElhinney	CBJ/Tor	1655	124.7	.9247	133	.9196	-.0050
Carter Hutton	Nsh/StL	1369	94.8	.9308	102	.9255	-.0053
Cam Ward	Carolina	4137	291.7	.9295	315	.9239	-.0056
Andrei Vasilevskiy	Tampa Bay	2145	138.5	.9354	151	.9296	-.0058

Al Montoya	Fla/Mtl	1511	100.4	.9336	110	.9272	-.0064
Mike Condon	Mtl/Pit/Ott	2458	156.6	.9363	173	.9296	-.0067
Robin Lehner	Ott/Buf	2818	185.3	.9342	205	.9273	-.0070
Michael Hutchinson	Winnipeg	2088	140.2	.9328	156	.9253	-.0076
Anders Lindback	Dal/Buf/Ari	1104	74.4	.9326	86	.9221	-.0105
Anton Khudobin	Car/Ana/Bos	1221	99.8	.9183	113	.9075	-.0108
Darcy Kuemper	Minnesota	1669	108.5	.9350	130	.9221	-.0129
Ben Scrivens	Edm/Mtl	1727	125.2	.9275	154	.9108	-.0167

Minimum 1000 shots faced

Amazingly, two of the three goalies who made the biggest gains from these shot quality adjustments were both acquired by the Calgary Flames this summer. Mike Smith improved from 47th in overall save percentage to 20th in save percentage above expectations, while Lack improved from 48th to 27th.

The largest jump up the rankings was Arizona's other goalie, Louis Domingue, who improved from 51st to 29th. Winnipeg's goalies Connor Hellebuyck and Ondrej Pavelec also shot up the rankings, which suggests a strong team effect. However, Winnipeg's other goalie, Michael Hutchinson, actually dropped down the standings. Buffalo's Robin Lehner had the greatest drop of all, from 22nd in absolute terms, to 59th from this quality-adjusted perspective.

Importance

An individual player's value is contextual. A great goalie will have far more value on a weak defensive team than on a great one, especially as he plays more games. Of course, a great goalie doesn't have much value on a truly horrible team, because all he will do is lift them out of a good draft lottery position. And, even on the perfect team, the world's second-best goalie won't have much value on a team that also had the best. Everything is contextual.

A purely subjective method of establishing a goalie's value is to look at the first, second, and third game stars that are awarded by local scorekeepers or broadcasters at the end of every game. In theory, goalies on great teams will have to share the game stars with other players, and goalies on losing teams won't have very man game stars to share. That means that great goalies on otherwise average teams should bubble to the top of the list.

From this perspective, it makes perfect sense that Price tops the list, and that goalies like Sergei Bobrovsky and Henrik Lundqvist aren't far behind. And, even though Washington is known for its great scorers and a solid blue line, Holtby is also high on the list.

This perspective also adds some credence to the notion that Darling has been the league's best backup, as he received a game star in 42.2% of his games, much more than Chicago's highly respected starter Corey Crawford, 29.4%. Carolina may have found itself a real gem.

Goalie Game Stars, 2014–15 to 2016–17[115]

Goalie	Team(s)	1st	2nd	3rd	Star%
Carey Price	Montreal	32	16	13	43.6%
Scott Darling	Chicago	10	7	10	42.2%
Braden Holtby	Washington	38	29	13	39.8%
Sergei Bobrovsky	Columbus	30	13	16	39.6%
Henrik Lundqvist	NY Rangers	38	12	14	38.8%
Calvin Pickard	Colorado	9	7	12	37.8%
Tuukka Rask	Boston	32	19	19	36.3%
Ondrej Pavelec	Winnipeg	11	6	13	35.3%
John Gibson	Anaheim	18	14	6	35.2%
Brian Elliott	StL/Cgy	14	20	11	35.2%
Pekka Rinne	Nashville	24	21	20	34.0%
Jonathan Quick	Los Angeles	23	19	11	34.0%
Antti Raanta	Chi/NYR	10	5	4	33.9%
Semyon Varlamov	Colorado	24	15	7	33.6%
Ryan Miller	Vancouver	23	13	14	33.3%
Roberto Luongo	Florida	15	19	19	33.1%
Mike Smith	Arizona	19	16	14	33.1%
Jake Allen	St. Louis	22	16	7	33.1%
Petr Mrazek	Detroit	13	12	14	32.8%
Andrei Vasilevskiy	Tampa Bay	8	10	8	32.1%
Carter Hutton	Nsh/StL	9	4	4	32.1%
Anton Khudobin	Car/Ana/Bos	8	6	3	32.1%
Al Montoya	Fla/Mtl	6	7	4	32.1%
Jimmy Howard	Detroit	10	13	11	31.8%
Cam Ward	Carolina	15	16	20	31.5%
Frederik Andersen	Ana/Tor	17	16	16	31.4%
Craig Anderson	Ottawa	16	10	16	31.1%
Jacob Markstrom	Vancouver	8	3	6	30.9%
Curtis McElhinney	CBJ/Tor	5	5	7	30.9%
Cam Talbot	NYR/Edm	27	14	8	30.6%
Devan Dubnyk	Ari/Min	21	21	14	30.4%
Marc-Andre Fleury	Pittsburgh	17	14	16	30.1%
James Reimer	Tor/SJ/Fla	10	10	11	30.1%
Steve Mason	Philadelphia	10	19	17	29.7%
Corey Crawford	Chicago	21	16	13	29.4%
Antti Niemi	SJ/Dal	17	9	13	29.1%
Chad Johnson	NYI/Buf/Cgy	13	5	9	29.0%
Keith Kinkaid	New Jersey	8	5	3	28.6%
Jonathan Bernier	Tor/Ana	16	10	9	28.2%
Cory Schneider	New Jersey	21	13	18	28.1%
Ben Bishop	TB/LA	15	11	18	28.0%
Darcy Kuemper	Minnesota	9	4	4	27.9%
Karri Ramo	Calgary	4	11	4	27.5%

115Acknowledgement: Game star data from Sporting Charts, http://www.sportingcharts.com/nhl/stats/first-second-third-star-statistics/2015/.

Louis Domingue	Arizona	7	3	8	27.3%
Mike Condon	Mtl/Pit/Ott	12	5	7	27.0%
Peter Budaj	LA/TB	4	7	4	26.8%
Jhonas Enroth	Buf/Dal/LA/Tor	6	5	5	26.2%
Thomas Greiss	Pit/NYI	7	9	11	25.7%
Jaroslav Halak	NY Islanders	19	6	6	25.6%
Martin Jones	LA/SJ	20	6	10	25.5%
Kari Lehtonen	Dallas	19	8	12	25.0%
Eddie Lack	Van/Car	10	6	5	25.0%
Michal Neuvirth	Buf/NYI/Phi	10	4	7	24.7%
Robin Lehner	Ott/Buf	9	8	8	24.3%
Connor Hellebuyck	Winnipeg	13	2	3	22.8%
Ben Scrivens	Edm/Mtl	8	5	2	22.4%
Matt Murray	Pittsburgh	3	6	3	20.0%
Jonas Hiller	Calgary	7	3	3	19.4%
Michael Hutchinson	Winnipeg	8	3	3	17.3%

Minimum 50 Starts

This is an interesting first glance, but there are obviously better ways to measure value than with a purely subjective and a reputation-based exercise like game stars.

Statistically, the simplest way to estimate a goalie's value is to calculate how many goals he prevented, by multiplying the league-average save percentage by the number of shots a goalie faced, and subtracting that from the actual saves. This statistic is known as Goals Saved Above Average (GSAA), and it requires that a goalie have a good efficiency (save percentage), and face a high shot volume.

Since GSAA doesn't take shot quality into account, the next step is to make adjustments for the varying average difficulty of the shots faced, much as we did previously with adjusted save percentage. One way to do that is with Adjusted GSAA per 60 minutes (Adj GSAA/60), which is the blending of Adjusted Save Percentage and GSAA, and is commonly known as Mercad[116] after its developer, Nick Mercadante. Unfortunately, this data requires going through the shot location in all the NHL play-by-play files, which is a time-consuming exercise that Mercadante has not yet had the opportunity to complete for last season.

Fortunately for us, the same goal can also be achieved by using the expected goals model. Instead of subtracting the league-average number of saves from actual saves, we can subtract the number of goals allowed from the number of expected goals.

From these perspectives, Price has prevented 60.3 goals above league-average over the past three seasons, or 46.4 when the quality of the shots are taken into account, both of which lead the league.

---

116 Nick Mercadante, "Goalies are Voodoo…But Improving Comparative Analysis Tools Can Help", *Blueshirt Banter,* August 12, 2015, Web, http://www.blueshirtbanter.com/analytics/2015/8/12/9136611/goalies-are-voodoo-but-improving-comparative-analysis-tools-can-help.

Goalie Catch-All Statistics, 2014–15 to 2016–17[117]

Goalie	Team(s)	GPS	GSAA	xGS
Carey Price	Montreal	31.8	60.3	46.4
Corey Crawford	Chicago	34.8	39.4	36.4
Braden Holtby	Washington	38.8	49.3	33.3
Henrik Lundqvist	NY Rangers	31.0	14.8	32.7
Steve Mason	Philadelphia	29.5	15.3	29.7
Cory Schneider	New Jersey	35.1	26.3	27.8
Sergei Bobrovsky	Columbus	30.6	30.6	26.0
Scott Darling	Chicago	14.4	17.2	21.9
Cam Talbot	NYR/Edm	31.7	26.5	16.8
Antti Raanta	Chi/NYR	12.1	16.7	16.8
Brian Elliott	StL/Cgy	23.0	13.5	16.3
Matthew Murray	Pittsburgh	13.0	18.7	15.2
James Reimer	Tor/SJ/Fla	20.9	8.1	13.8
Marc-Andre Fleury	Pittsburgh	29.7	15.7	12.8
Jonathan Quick	Los Angeles	26.2	14.5	12.3
Mike Smith	Arizona	25.9	-17.7	12.0
Thomas Greiss	Pit/NYI	19.9	7.8	11.0
Frederik Andersen	Ana/Tor	28.7	11.9	9.9
Craig Anderson	Ottawa	28.8	28.1	8.7
John Gibson	Anaheim	20.8	19.9	8.2
Louis Domingue	Arizona	11.8	-9.5	6.1
Petr Mrazek	Detroit	21.0	-7.9	5.5
Jaroslav Halak	NY Islanders	21.6	4.5	4.4
Devan Dubnyk	Ari/Min	37.2	47.8	4.2
Eddie Lack	Van/Car	14.3	-10.0	3.8
Ondrej Pavelec	Winnipeg	14.0	-7.4	2.6
Ryan Miller	Vancouver	26.8	-2.5	1.7
Roberto Luongo	Florida	31.2	24.9	1.0
Martin Jones	LA/SJ	22.2	-1.3	0.8
Peter Budaj	LA/TB	8.6	-0.4	0.7
Connor Hellebuyck	Winnipeg	12.4	-8.8	0.7
Jacob Markstrom	Vancouver	9.8	-3.2	0.0
Michal Neuvirth	Buf/NYI/Phi	14.6	-5.6	-0.6
Calvin Pickard	Colorado	14.8	-1.8	-1.2
Keith Kinkaid	New Jersey	10.5	-4.3	-1.8
Tuukka Rask	Boston	34.8	19.1	-2.5
Jonas Hiller	Calgary	9.9	-18.1	-3.1
Karri Ramo	Calgary	10.2	-7.4	-3.5
Antti Niemi	SJ/Dal	19.8	-30.7	-4.3
Ben Bishop	TB/LA	27.9	18.2	-4.7
Jake Allen	St. Louis	23.3	6.7	-4.9

117Acknowledgement: GVT data from Tom Awad and Hockey Prospects http://www.hockeyprospectus.com, GPS data from Hockey Reference http://www.hockey-reference.com, raw data for GSAA calculations came from the NHL's official website http://www.nhl.com, Mercad was provided by Nick Mercadante, and xGS was provided by Dawson Sprigings.

Jhonas Enroth	Buf/Dal/LA/Tor	9.9	-18.9	-6.0
Jonathan Bernier	Tor/Ana	21.6	-9.7	-6.2
Carter Hutton	Nsh/StL	8.8	-4.9	-7.2
Jimmy Howard	Detroit	17.3	-4.6	-7.7
Chad Johnson	NYI/Buf/Cgy	15.0	-9.3	-7.7
Curtis McElhinney	CBJ/Tor	10.7	-9.2	-8.3
Al Montoya	Fla/Mtl	8.7	-8.3	-9.6
Kari Lehtonen	Dallas	21.4	-47.8	-11.6
Andrei Vasilevskiy	Tampa Bay	15.5	2.7	-12.5
Anton Khudobin	Car/Ana/Bos	6.6	-17.4	-13.2
Pekka Rinne	Nashville	32.7	9.8	-14.3
Michael Hutchinson	Winnipeg	13.0	-14.4	-15.8
Mike Condon	Mtl/Pit/Ott	13.4	-15.9	-16.4
Semyon Varlamov	Colorado	25.1	-0.8	-16.6
Robin Lehner	Ott/Buf	21.1	10.7	-19.7
Darcy Kuemper	Minnesota	9.1	-12.9	-21.5
Cam Ward	Carolina	22.9	-27.6	-23.3
Ben Scrivens	Edm/Mtl	6.8	-41.6	-28.8

Minimum 50 Starts

You'll notice one extra columns here, GPS. What's that all about?

Fans of long-time and respected starting goalies like Cam Ward and Kari Lehtonen may have an issue with seeing a big fat negative number next to their stats. Without understanding the context, it looks like they're being described as terrible goalies.

The main issue is that these calculations are being done relative to the league-average. As talented as Ward, and Lehtonen are, they are not among the top 15 goalies in the world's most elite 30-team league. That's why they get the big fat negative number, even when compared to journeymen backups like Curtis McElhinney or Al Montoya.

That's where stats like Tom Awad's Goals Versus Threshold (GVT) have come in. Explained in far more detail in the original *Hockey Abstract*[118], GVT calculates how many goals were prevented relative to that of a replacement-level goalie. After all, if a starting goalie like Jonathan Quick is injured, he is replaced by a freely available AHL goalie like Peter Budaj[119], and not by a roughly a league-average starter like Martin Jones.

However, GVT is also a computationally intense statistic for which Tom hasn't had the time to complete. So, we're using Goalie Point Shares (GPS), which was introduced by Justin Kubatko[120]. From that perspective, GPS thrusts Ward and Lehtonen above the backup goalies, towards a more sensible position in the rankings, and without disrupting the otherwise sensible order at the top of the list.

118Rob Vollman, "Catch-All Statistics", *Hockey Abstract,* 2013, pgs 142-158.
119Of course, most replacement-level goalies don't play out of their minds, like Budaj did last year.
120Justin Kubatko, "Calculating Point Shares", *Hockey Reference,* Web, http://www.hockey-reference.com/about/point_shares.html.

Consistency

No matter how it's adjusted, there's more to goaltending than save percentage.

In particular, wins and losses seem to be of paramount importance when evaluating goalies, and has an undue influence over Vezina voting. For example, what business did Quick have among the 2015–16 finalists, with a save percentage hovering around league average? Well, he won 40 games.

Evaluating goalies based on wins and losses is a ridiculous thing to do. It doesn't take a background in math to understand that those are team statistics. After all, wins have as much to do with how many goals a team scored as how many goals were allowed – which is a function of both the goalie's performance and the team's own defensive play.

To take an easy example, consider Ben Bishop and Cory Schneider. They have identical .919 save percentages over the past three seasons, but Bishop's 93-49-14 win-loss record is far superior to Schneider's 73-83-26. Is this because Bishop just knows how to win? No, it is because he has received offensive goal support of 3.03 goals per game, which ranks third in the NHL, and well ahead of Schneider, whose offensive support of 2.19 goals per game is a decimal from being the league's lowest. Unless he's somehow contributing to the extra scoring, it's ridiculous to consider Bishop a superior goalie because of that.

Goal Support, 2014–15 to 2016–17[121]

Goalie	Team(s)	Starts	Goal Supp
Matthew Murray	Pittsburgh	60	3.32
Kari Lehtonen	Dallas	156	3.21
Ben Bishop	TB/LA	157	3.03
Frederik Andersen	Ana/Tor	156	3.00
Braden Holtby	Washington	201	2.99
Antti Raanta	Chi/NYR	56	2.98
Antti Niemi	SJ/Dal	134	2.96
Jonas Hiller	Calgary	67	2.96
Marc-Andre Fleury	Pittsburgh	156	2.93
Henrik Lundqvist	NY Rangers	165	2.88
Jaroslav Halak	NY Islanders	121	2.88
Karri Ramo	Calgary	69	2.86
Curtis McElhinney	CBJ/Tor	55	2.84
Craig Anderson	Ottawa	135	2.82
Pekka Rinne	Nashville	191	2.82
Thomas Greiss	Pit/NYI	105	2.80
Martin Jones	LA/SJ	141	2.79
Sergei Bobrovsky	Columbus	149	2.79
Brian Elliott	StL/Cgy	128	2.78

121Acknowledgement: Raw game-by-game data for my goal support calculations came from the *NHL* http://www.nhl.com.

Carey Price	Montreal	140	2.78
Darcy Kuemper	Minnesota	61	2.78
Connor Hellebuyck	Winnipeg	79	2.77
Jonathan Quick	Los Angeles	156	2.77
Cam Talbot	NYR/Edm	160	2.75
Tuukka Rask	Boston	193	2.75
Devan Dubnyk	Ari/Min	184	2.74
Michael Hutchinson	Winnipeg	81	2.73
Scott Darling	Chicago	64	2.72
Corey Crawford	Chicago	170	2.72
Chad Johnson	NYI/Buf/Cgy	93	2.71
Peter Budaj	LA/TB	56	2.71
Jonathan Bernier	Tor/Ana	124	2.70
John Gibson	Anaheim	108	2.70
Roberto Luongo	Florida	160	2.67
Cam Ward	Carolina	162	2.66
Jimmy Howard	Detroit	107	2.66
Petr Mrazek	Detroit	119	2.64
Jake Allen	St. Louis	136	2.64
Ondrej Pavelec	Winnipeg	85	2.64
Al Montoya	Fla/Mtl	53	2.62
Andrei Vasilevskiy	Tampa Bay	81	2.61
Ryan Miller	Vancouver	150	2.60
Eddie Lack	Van/Car	84	2.57
Semyon Varlamov	Colorado	137	2.56
Robin Lehner	Ott/Buf	103	2.56
Steve Mason	Philadelphia	155	2.55
Keith Kinkaid	New Jersey	56	2.55
Mike Condon	Mtl/Pit/Ott	89	2.50
Michal Neuvirth	Buf/NYI/Phi	85	2.50
Ben Scrivens	Edm/Mtl	67	2.49
James Reimer	Tor/SJ/Fla	103	2.49
Carter Hutton	Nsh/StL	53	2.42
Calvin Pickard	Colorado	74	2.36
Louis Domingue	Arizona	66	2.36
Jhonas Enroth	Buf/Dal/LA/Tor	61	2.23
Mike Smith	Arizona	148	2.21
Cory Schneider	New Jersey	185	2.19
Anton Khudobin	Car/Ana/Bos	53	2.18
Jacob Markstrom	Vancouver	55	2.18

Minimum 50 Starts

Placing too much emphasis on wins is not just a harmless error that can screw up Vezina voting, Hall of Fame choices and/or jersey number retirement, because it has also led to some disastrously overpriced contracts. So why is it done?

Whether voting for the Vezina or signing contracts, what general managers are actually

155

looking for is a goalie's ability to consistently give his team a chance to win. In the absence of alternatives, they have always used wins and losses. It would be far more effective to set shot volumes and team scoring aside, and simply count how often a goalie has played at or above the league average, and how many times he was blown away.

That's essentially the definition of a quality start, which was introduced at *Hockey Prospectus* in 2009[122], and explained in far more detail in the inaugural edition of *Hockey Abstract*[123].

From this perspective, Bishop does rank higher than Schneider, with quality starts in 62.4% of his games, compared to 59.5%, but it's not nearly as lopsided. Unsurprisingly, Price remains at the top of the list among established No. 1 goalies, followed by Crawford, Holtby, Lundqvist, and then Bishop.

Quality Starts, 2014–15 to 2016–17[124]

Goalie	Team(s)	Starts	QS	RBS	Pull	SV%	QS%
Antti Raanta	Chi/NYR	56	38	6	3	.9270	67.9%
Carey Price	Montreal	140	94	15	3	.9290	67.1%
Corey Crawford	Chicago	170	110	20	12	.9221	64.7%
Peter Budaj	LA/TB	56	36	7	5	.9141	64.3%
Braden Holtby	Washington	201	129	21	14	.9236	64.2%
Scott Darling	Chicago	64	40	6	1	.9237	62.5%
Henrik Lundqvist	NY Rangers	165	103	18	15	.9186	62.4%
Ben Bishop	TB/LA	157	98	18	12	.9195	62.4%
Frederik Andersen	Ana/Tor	155	96	24	13	.9179	61.9%
Brian Elliott	StL/Cgy	128	79	18	11	.9189	61.7%
John Gibson	Anaheim	108	66	14	11	.9213	61.1%
Al Montoya	Fla/Mtl	53	32	8	2	.9103	60.4%
Devan Dubnyk	Ari/Min	184	111	16	9	.9234	60.3%
Pekka Rinne	Nashville	191	115	25	7	.9162	60.2%
Thomas Greiss	Pit/NYI	105	63	15	9	.9173	60.0%
Sergei Bobrovsky	Columbus	149	89	16	10	.9208	59.7%
Jonathan Quick	Los Angeles	156	93	20	9	.9182	59.6%
Jaroslav Halak	NY Islanders	121	72	16	8	.9159	59.5%
Cory Schneider	New Jersey	185	110	21	14	.9189	59.5%
Martin Jones	LA/SJ	140	83	18	7	.9150	59.3%
Jake Allen	St. Louis	135	79	22	16	.9170	58.5%
Matthew Murray	Pittsburgh	60	35	4	5	.9242	58.3%
Roberto Luongo	Florida	160	92	18	12	.9199	57.5%
Tuukka Rask	Boston	193	110	32	14	.9183	57.0%
Jimmy Howard	Detroit	107	61	18	12	.9130	57.0%
Marc-Andre Fleury	Pittsburgh	156	88	16	7	.9176	56.4%
Jacob Markstrom	Vancouver	55	31	7	1	.9122	56.4%

122Rob Vollman, "Howe and Why: Quality Starts", *Hockey Prospectus*, March 25, 2009, Web, http://www.hockeyprospectus.com/puck/article.php?articleid=54.
123Rob Vollman, "Quality Starts", *Hockey Abstract*, 2013, pgs 189-195.
124Acknowledgement: Raw game-by-game data for my Quality Start calculations came from the *NHL* http://www.nhl.com.

Louis Domingue	Arizona	66	37	9	5	.9116	56.1%
Craig Anderson	Ottawa	135	75	14	6	.9209	55.6%
Cam Talbot	NYR/Edm	160	89	16	8	.9203	55.6%
Steve Mason	Philadelphia	155	86	20	14	.9180	55.5%
Petr Mrazek	Detroit	119	66	20	10	.9134	55.5%
Chad Johnson	NYI/Buf/Cgy	93	50	16	4	.9096	53.8%
Robin Lehner	Ott/Buf	103	55	11	7	.9172	53.4%
James Reimer	Tor/SJ/Fla	103	55	17	8	.9159	53.4%
Calvin Pickard	Colorado	74	39	13	5	.9122	52.7%
Cam Ward	Carolina	162	85	23	8	.9073	52.5%
Eddie Lack	Van/Car	84	44	15	2	.9081	52.4%
Karri Ramo	Calgary	69	36	10	9	.9099	52.2%
Andrei Vasilevskiy	Tampa Bay	81	42	9	5	.9135	51.9%
Keith Kinkaid	New Jersey	56	29	9	4	.9132	51.8%
Mike Condon	Mtl/Pit/Ott	89	46	16	5	.9077	51.7%
Jonathan Bernier	Tor/Ana	124	64	23	14	.9125	51.6%
Ryan Miller	Vancouver	150	77	17	10	.9138	51.3%
Kari Lehtonen	Dallas	156	79	29	20	.9039	50.6%
Semyon Varlamov	Colorado	137	69	21	15	.9152	50.4%
Michal Neuvirth	Buf/NYI/Phi	85	42	11	8	.9119	49.4%
Connor Hellebuyck	Winnipeg	79	39	15	12	.9102	49.4%
Antti Niemi	SJ/Dal	134	66	24	14	.9075	49.3%
Darcy Kuemper	Minnesota	61	30	12	8	.9060	49.2%
Ondrej Pavelec	Winnipeg	85	41	13	5	.9110	48.2%
Michael Hutchinson	Winnipeg	81	39	11	8	.9078	48.1%
Mike Smith	Arizona	148	71	26	16	.9106	48.0%
Carter Hutton	Nsh/StL	53	25	7	2	.9129	47.2%
Anton Khudobin	Car/Ana/Bos	53	25	14	4	.9010	47.2%
Jonas Hiller	Calgary	67	31	11	6	.9020	46.3%
Jhonas Enroth	Buf/Dal/LA/Tor	61	28	8	0	.9033	45.9%
Curtis McElhinney	CBJ/Tor	55	25	5	2	.9122	45.5%
Ben Scrivens	Edm/Mtl	67	25	15	5	.8919	37.3%

Minimum 50 Starts

Once again, there are a few unknown columns in this table, RBS and Pull. While there has always been a reluctance to include "negative" information in the pages of *Hockey Abstract*, there is value in knowing how many times goalies have been pulled, and how many times they were blown away with really bad starts (RBS).

Over the past three seasons, Dubnyk is the No. 1 goalie who is least likely to get blown away. His 16 RBS in 184 starts work out to 8.7%, which is a fair bit lower than the league average of 13.7%. On the flip side, the Stars old tandem of Antti Niemi and Kari Lehtonen are at the bottom, with really bad starts in 17.9% and 18.6% of their starts, respectively. That was probably a factor in the summer acquisition of Ben Bishop, who is blown away in 11.5% of his starts.

Getting pulled is another matter, because it's not just a reflection on the goalie's own play, but on the availability of a good backup, and the coach's tendency to shake things up mid game. For example, Carolina Hurricanes coach Bill Peters pulled Eddie Lack or Cam Ward just 10 times in a combined 246 starts. Compare that to Lindy Ruff and the Dallas goalies, who were pulled a combined 34 times in 290 starts.

Well, by this point of the chapter, we all know what the next step will be. As was the case with stats like save percentage and GSAA, quality start percentage doesn't take shot quality into account.

That's exactly why Mercadante devised Above Average Appearance Percentage (AAA%)[125], which is the percentage of games in which a goalie performs better than a league-average goalie would have performed against the same volume and quality of shots. However, as previously stated, hobbyists don't often have the time to update their numbers over the summer, so we won't be able to include them here.

Going to print without AAA% isn't actually as bad as it sounds. While stats like AAA% and quality starts are a big improvement over wins and losses for goalie evaluation, even these stats shouldn't be used when it comes time to sign contracts, because goalie consistency doesn't really appear to be a meaningful and persistent skill.

Just take Price, for example. By this point of the chapter, there appears to be sufficient evidence that he's the best goalie in the world. And yet, does the following chart of his 10-game rolling average save percentage suggest that he's consistent?

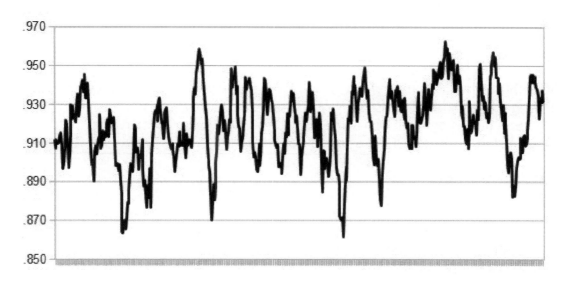

Carey Price's Career 10-Game Rolling Average

125Nick Mercadante, "Goalies are Voodoo...But Improving Comparative Analysis Tools Can Help", *Blueshirt Banter,* August 12, 2015, Web, http://www.blueshirtbanter.com/analytics/2015/8/12/9136611/goalies-are-voodoo-but-improving-comparative-analysis-tools-can-help.

Over the course of his career, Price's save percentage has fluctuated repeatedly and rapidly from a terrible .900 or below, to an exceptional .930 or above, and in a matter of *weeks*. Even in 2016–17, which is on the far right side of the chart, you can see his hot start, his mid-January plummet all the way down to .880, and then his late-season recovery to peak form.

Awarding contracts based on wins and losses makes no sense at all, but basing it on quality starts isn't a whole lot better. It's an interesting perspective on which to evaluate goalies, but we shouldn't get carried away with it.

Frivolities

One of the advantages of writing and publishing my own book is that I can write about whatever I want and you have to sit there and read it. Well, actually no I guess you don't, but please do.

With regards to goaltending, one of my little obsessions has been about why the starting goalies always play the entire game. In baseball, the starter normally only pitches five or six of the nine innings. Whether it's because of fatigue, poor performance, or wanting to strategically target part of the opposing lineup at a certain moment of the game, it's quite customary to bring in relief pitchers. In hockey, the starter completes the entire game, barring an injury or a blow-out.

Relief goalies are used in just 7.3% of games, which seems awfully low to me. I often ask former goalies and coaches why that is so, and they tell me that goalies need to be warm, flexible, and loose to play at their best, and that they also need to be "in the zone" mentally. Apparently, you're almost always better off sticking with the starter than bringing in someone who is cold. The goalies and goalies coaches among you are probably nodding your heads (or nodding off to sleep).

If that's true, then why does the backup goalie just sit there watching the game with a cap on? Why isn't he in the back stretching, staying loose, and doing both mental and physical exercises? Even if the coach doesn't care about having the option to bring him in, there's always the threat of an injury to the starting goalie. Why isn't he getting ready?

To this point, I'm told that the backup goalie takes the lion's share of practice shots before the game, so as not to wear out the starter, which means that he's usually too exhausted to play anyway. Again, why is that? Why not have a third-string practice goalie on hand to take the beating instead? You could even try to find a spare goalie who is similar to that day's opposing goalie in size, style, and handedness. It just seems like every answer that I get raises more questions.

Maybe I'm on to something, or maybe I'm not, but in today's NHL, it's important for teams to get an edge anywhere they can, and this might be it. Having a goalie who is warm, loose, and ready to play could be the deciding factor in a game, which could be the deciding factor in an entire season.

To that end, part of that strategy would be to identify backup goalies who *are* capable of coming into a game cold. That's why my whimsical look at relief goaltending over the years is more than just a frivolity, and possibly the first steps in a worthwhile exercise.

If I'm right, then that's yet another reason why Tampa Bay could really have something in Vasilevskiy. He may have only played nine games in relief over the past three seasons, but his save percentage is a league-leading .960 in such situations. There are plenty of goalies who have played almost as well as Vasilevskiy, most of whom are readily available on waivers, or as inexpensive free agents.

Relief Goaltending Statistics, 2014–15 to 2016–17[126]

Goalie	Team(s)	GR	GA	SV	Min	GAA	SV%
Andrei Vasilevskiy	Tampa Bay	9	4	97	216	1.11	.960
Chad Johnson	NYI/Buf/Cgy	7	3	68	197	0.91	.958
Eddie Lack	Van/Car	11	7	136	307	1.37	.951
Jonas Hiller	Calgary	11	7	135	335	1.25	.951
Reto Berra	Col/Fla	12	8	132	304	1.58	.943
Ben Scrivens	Edm/Mtl	5	4	61	191	1.26	.938
Jhonas Enroth	Buf/Dal/LA/Tor	11	8	112	285	1.68	.933
Jacob Markstrom	Vancouver	7	1	14	66	0.92	.933
Anton Khudobin	Car/Ana/Bos	6	4	56	139	1.73	.933
James Reimer	Tor/SJ/Fla	15	14	185	383	2.19	.930
Calvin Pickard	Colorado	12	14	184	428	1.96	.929
Jeff Zatkoff	Pit/LA	9	8	103	224	2.14	.928
Anders Nilsson	Edm/StL/Buf	8	12	149	266	2.71	.925
Mike Condon	Mtl/Pit/Ott	7	5	62	170	1.76	.925
Darcy Kuemper	Minnesota	9	9	108	257	2.10	.923
Ondrej Pavelec	Winnipeg	6	7	82	184	2.28	.921
Devan Dubnyk	Ari/Min	6	7	81	135	3.12	.920
Michal Neuvirth	Buf/NYI/Phi	7	7	79	206	2.04	.919
Michael Hutchinson	Winnipeg	15	17	186	452	2.26	.916
Anders Lindback	Dal/Buf/Ari	10	14	152	327	2.57	.916
Philipp Grubauer	Washington	11	9	97	278	1.94	.915
Peter Budaj	LA/TB	5	3	30	80	2.24	.909
Jimmy Howard	Detroit	9	10	99	263	2.29	.908
John Gibson	Anaheim	7	12	117	271	2.66	.907
Alex Stalock	SJ/Min	7	7	68	217	1.94	.907
Scott Darling	Chicago	11	10	92	256	2.34	.902
Kari Lehtonen	Dallas	11	18	164	371	2.91	.901
Steve Mason	Philadelphia	8	10	91	296	2.03	.901
Keith Kinkaid	New Jersey	12	15	132	355	2.53	.898
Jean-Francois Berube	NY Islanders	8	8	70	167	2.88	.897
Al Montoya	Fla/Mtl	11	14	122	348	2.42	.897
Thomas Greiss	Pit/NYI	7	8	69	195	2.46	.896

126Acknowledgement: Raw game-by-game data for relief goaltending calculations came from the *NHL* http://www.nhl.com.

Justin Peters	Wsh/Ari	5	9	77	236	2.29	.895
Brian Elliott	StL/Cgy	9	13	111	252	3.10	.895
Jake Allen	St. Louis	9	17	145	387	2.64	.895
Carter Hutton	Nsh/StL	12	14	117	294	2.86	.893
Petr Mrazek	Detroit	14	23	192	524	2.63	.893
Tuukka Rask	Boston	6	11	90	197	3.36	.891
Jonathan Bernier	Tor/Ana	11	14	113	280	3.00	.890
Niklas Backstrom	Min/Cgy	6	12	95	227	3.17	.888
Curtis McElhinney	CBJ/Tor	16	22	172	439	3.00	.887
Cam Talbot	NYR/Edm	5	7	54	139	3.02	.885
Antti Niemi	SJ/Dal	12	18	134	367	2.94	.882
Louis Domingue	Arizona	11	14	104	262	3.20	.881
Jonas Gustavsson	Det/Bos/Edm	7	9	66	165	3.27	.880
Antti Raanta	Chi/NYR	13	12	87	288	2.50	.879
Andrew Hammond	Ottawa	6	9	63	191	2.83	.875
Zane McIntyre	Boston	5	10	61	152	3.95	.859
Frederik Andersen	Ana/Tor	7	11	67	199	3.32	.859
Ben Bishop	TB/LA	5	10	60	198	3.03	.857
Ray Emery	Philadelphia	6	10	54	179	3.35	.844

Minimum 5 Relief Appearances

In fairness, there's really not much that can be read into this, given the atrociously small sample sizes involved. Chances are, the goalies at the top of the list were merely lucky, and don't necessarily have a particular talent for coming into the game cold.

Nevertheless, I have been identifying the league's best relief goalie with the Josh Harding Award ever since *Hockey Prospectus* first launched in the 2008–09 season. For whatever reason, Minnesota's old backup had the consistent ability to come into a game cold, and play just as well as the starter.

So, to close this chapter in traditional fashion, let's award this year's Josh Harding Award to James Reimer of the Florida Panthers. Reimer played four games in relief, and allowed just one goal in 43 shots, for a save percentage of .977 and a goals-against average of 1.01.

That may not sound like many games, but of the 14 goalies to enter more games in relief, the average save percentage was a lowly .878. The top save percentage were Jeff Zatkoff with 0.925 in five games, Kari Lehtonen with .914 in seven games, Peter Budaj with .909 in five games, and Jean-Francois Berube with .901 in seven games. So, Reimer was on top of a pretty weak field last season.

Josh Harding Award Winners, All-Time

Season	Goalie	Team(s)
2008–09	Josh Harding	Minnesota
2009–10	Yann Danis	New Jersey
2010–11	Joey MacDonald	Detroit
2011–12	Cory Schneider	Vancouver
2012–13	Steve Mason	CBJ/Phi

2013–14	Carter Hutton	Nashville
2014–15	Jonas Hiller	Calgary
2015–16	Chad Johnson	Buffalo
2016–17	James Reimer	Florida

Closing Thoughts

Despite the length of this chapter, we really only hit the highlights in the world of goalie analytics.

In the previous books, we've measured the value of goaltenders in a number of different ways, established what makes the good goalies good, identified the best goalies overall, and in a number of more isolated situations than just manpower situation and shot location. We've studied where they should be drafted, how much they should be paid, when they should be pulled for an extra attacker, whether they perform better after a bad start, and we've studied the effect of workload on save percentages. There has even been some quick looks at how to project their future, how to translate their data from other leagues, and which ones will make the Hall of Fame.

In addition to all of this analysis and hard-to-find data, these books have also included footnotes with links to additional research from everyone who has ever studied goalies statistically, and on virtually every topic imaginable. Trust all of us that this area has not been neglected, and we're doing far more than fiddling around with save percentage.

What does the future hold for goaltending analytics? As has been the theme of this entire chapter, the next step is shot quality. In the modern age of goalie parity, finding any way to create some separation from one goalie to the next is the secret to adding an extra win or two per season.

With shot location and statistical definitions of rebounds and shots off the rush, the first strides have already been taken. Right now, analysts like Ryan Stimson and former goalie Steve Valiquette have looked at the shot quality impact of passes, and cross-ice plays, using manually tracked data. It's only a matter of time before technology gives everyone access to the data required to look at additional factors, like shot velocity and screens.

Going forward, there will also be an attempt to bring in more data in goalie evaluation, whether that means going further back into each goalie's careers, including playoff data, or pulling in data from the AHL and other leagues. It will have to be translated and/or weighted differently, but more data is always better than less.

In the end, the argument could be made that *too much* emphasis has been placed on statistical goaltending analysis, relative to other areas of the game. After all, parity in goaltending means that a team could simply sign a couple of value-priced secondary options, and invest the extra money and attention in finding a great defenceman, or to tune their power play (which is coming up next). Whatever losses they experience in nets is bound to be made up by the superior team playing in front of them. Then again, maybe not. It's all food for thought.

What Makes a Power Play Successful?

By Matt Cane

For all of the progress the public analytics community has made in furthering our understanding of what leads to success in hockey, there remains a dearth of research on what makes a power play effective. Analysts to date have focused most of their work on player and team evaluation at full strength, and with good reason: 5-on-5 play has made up nearly 80% of the total time on ice played over the last three years[127]. But, we can't just toss aside any interest in the power play just because it makes up a much smaller portion of the game, since goal scoring rates are so much higher there. While just 8.3% of the game was played on the power play over the last three seasons, nearly 21% of the goals were scored during that time[128].

— SLASHING

"LOOKS LIKE TWO MINUTES FOR SLASHING, EH?"

This makes success on the power play crucial to a team's overall success. The New York Islanders missed the playoffs by a single point last year while scoring just 122 goals on the man advantage, well below the league median of 136.5. Their failure wasn't just a lack of opportunity either – the Isles led the league in 5-on-3 time on ice, but scored just two goals while up two skaters. Their failure to convert on the power play is a big reason why they were

---

127Acknowledgement: Raw data for this calculation from the *NHL*, http://www.nhl.com.
128Acknowledgement: Raw data for this calculation from the *NHL*, http://www.nhl.com.

watching from home rather than competing in the postseason in April[129].

While the amount of research done on special teams pales in comparison to our knowledge at even strength, there does exist a body of work that lays out a solid foundation for what helps teams succeed, or fail, on the power play. This chapter is meant to provide an overview of what the analytics community knows (or thinks we know) about what makes a power play successful.

We'll begin by defining what we mean by success: what measures we can use to evaluate a team's efforts on the power play.

Then, we'll then dive into what I'll call the three major pillars of power play design, the areas that a coach or general manager can influence to make their power play better. They are:

1. Player selection: How should you allocate your limited ice-time on the power play? How do we know which players are good at the power play, given that many players don't play on it? What does it mean to be a power play specialist, and should you look out for them?

2. Structure and formation: How important is play in formation?

3. Regrouping and entering the zone: How important is entering the zone with control? What is the best method for entering the zone? How can we measure a team's ability to successfully enter the zone without manually tracking zone entries?

Before we begin, however, I should note that while our knowledge on special teams is limited, a good deal of what we do know if through the efforts of Arik Parnass (now of the Colorado Avalanche) and his Special Teams Project. During the 2015–16 season, Arik watched and tracked every power play for six clubs (the Washington Capitals, Philadelphia Flyers, Toronto Maple Leafs, Montreal Canadiens, New York Islanders and Tampa Bay Lightning), recording everything from time in formation to zone entries to one-timers.

Throughout this chapter, I'll be referencing back to Parnass's work, as it forms the core of much of what we know about the power play. I sadly won't be able to do it full justice in the limited space we have available, but if what you read here piques your interest, I'd strongly encourage you to check out the full series[130].

How do we measure power play success?

Before we dig into how teams can be successful on the power play, we have to start by defining what success on the power play looks like.

The most commonly quoted measure of power play success is also one of the most flawed

---

129Acknowledgement: Islanders data from the *NHL*, http://www.nhl.com.
130Arik Parnass' Special Teams Project is online at http://www.nhlspecialteams.com.

metrics in the game. Power play percentage, for all its ubiquity, should be fired into the sun to ensure it can never be used by any analyst, writer, or commentator again (and, for safe measure, we should also consider exploding the sun afterwards, assuming that we have secured another source of light/heat/gravity).

What's the major problem with power play percentage? It treats all opportunities the same, regardless of the length or skater advantage. If a team gets a three-second power play before taking a penalty of its own, it is marked down for the same result as a team that fails to score during five full minutes of 5-on-3 play.

While a team's power play percentage will generally align with its goal scoring rates, there are cases where considering only power play percentage will change our view of its success: the Montreal Canadiens finished last season 13th in power play percentage[131], but rank three spots higher when ranked by power play goals scored per 60 minutes[132].

Given the somewhat obvious flaws of power play percentage, what should we be using instead? First, it almost always makes more sense to look at any statistic on a per 60 minutes basis, rather than "per opportunity". As we noted above, not all power play opportunities are created equal, especially given that an opportunity can last anywhere from one second to five or more minutes. By analyzing teams based on how long they actually play on the power play, we create a more even playing field on which to evaluate their abilities.

Another important distinction is to to break up our data by strength (5-on-4, 5-on-3, etc.). Lumping all our power play data into one bucket can obscure major differences in ice-time between strengths, which can heavily skew teams' stats. The difference last year between the league leaders in 5-on-3 time (the Islanders, with 15:30) and the last place team (the Canadiens, with 1:57) was over 13 minutes. At a league average rate of 20.3 goals scored per 60 at 5-on-3, that works out to roughly 4.6 extra goals for the Isles simply due to differences in opportunity (unfortunately, New York only managed to turn all that extra time into one extra actual goal)[133].

This will give us a better measure of a team's talent than power play percentage, since we're adjusting for the length of opportunities, but it may still be less than perfect due to the small sample sizes involved: on average, teams played just over 390 minutes at 5-on-4 last year[134]. That's not a tiny sample, but it's quite a bit less data than we have at full-strength, for either teams or skaters.

The next question is whether to use goals or shot attempts on the power play. While at full-strength we know that past shot attempts provide a better view of future success than past goals do, the evidence is a bit more mixed at 5-on-4. Following the 2012–13 season, Patrick D of Fear the Fin found that, much like at 5-on-5, shot attempts were a better predictor of power play success at the team level than any other metric, including past goal scoring and

131Acknowledgement: Canadiens data from the *NHL*, http://www.nhl.com.
132Acknowledgement: Data source is *Puckalytics,* http://www.puckalytics.com.
133Acknowledgement: Raw data for this calculation from the *NHL*, http://www.nhl.com.
134Acknowledgement: Data source is *Puckalytics,* http://www.puckalytics.com.

past shooting percentage[135]. This makes intuitive sense, and even has broad support amongst "old school" TV analysts: whenever a power play ends without a goal, you'll almost always hear them mention how many shots were taken as a measure of how well a team performed.

But those results are contradicted a bit by the work of Parnass, who in 2016 found that since the lockout-shortened 2012–13 season, past goals were often as good a predictor of future goals as past shot attempts were[136]. Why the discrepancy? As Parnass himself notes, it could be random variation in small samples, or it could be that there has been a widening in talent between teams over that period, making goals more indicative of true talent than they have been in the past.

Regardless of which metric you prefer, it's clear that 5-on-4 shot attempts per 60 minutes and 5-on-4 goals per 60 minutes are far superior to any commonly quoted metric. Both of these items correct the problems of mixing 5-on-4 and 5-on-3 play, and also take into account the length of any opportunity. And as long as you avoid using power play percentage, you'll have already taken away the most important thing you could learn from this chapter.

Step 1: Who should play on your power play?

The first question any coach needs to ask is who they should play on their power play. Some decisions are easier than others: Yes, you should play Alex Ovechkin and park him in the Ovi spot, no, you shouldn't have Jay Beagle feeding the puck to him[137].

But others aren't so obvious. Before any coach can start deciding which skaters to send out, they have to decide what their lineup will look like. And, generally, this comes down to deciding how many forwards to play on the power play.

Traditionally, teams have played with the same lineup on the man-advantage that they've used at full strength: three forwards up front, with two defencemen manning the points. But in recent years, more teams have been switching to a four forward, one defenceman setup to provide themselves with more offensive threats.

The four-forward approach is one that has been steadily growing in popularity in recent years. In 2009–10, teams played with four-forward units less than 40% of the time. This past season? Over 50%[138].

135Patrick D, "Special Teams Part II: What Drives Power Play and Penalty Kill Success?", *Fear the Fin,* July 14, 2013, Web, https://www.fearthefin.com/2013/7/14/4520832/special-teams-part-ii-what-drives-special-teams-success.

136Arik Parnass, "Special Teams Analytics in the 21st Century", *Hockey Graphs,* January 14, 2016, Web, https://hockey-graphs.com/2016/01/14/special-teams-analytics-in-the-21st-century/.

137Chris Gordon, "Jay Beagle is now a member of the Capitals power play", *Russian Machine Never Breaks,* December 5, 2016, Web, https://www.russianmachineneverbreaks.com/2016/12/05/jay-beagle-is-now-a-member-of-the-capitals-power-play/.

138Acknowledgement: Raw data for this calculation from the *NHL,* http://www.nhl.com.

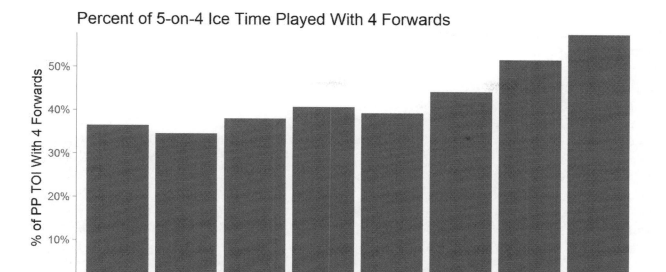

Percent of 5-on-4 Ice Time Played With 4 Forwards

The adoption of the four-forward strategy has been far from universal, however. Even this season, there were seven teams that played with four forwards at 5-on-4 less than 20% of the time[139].

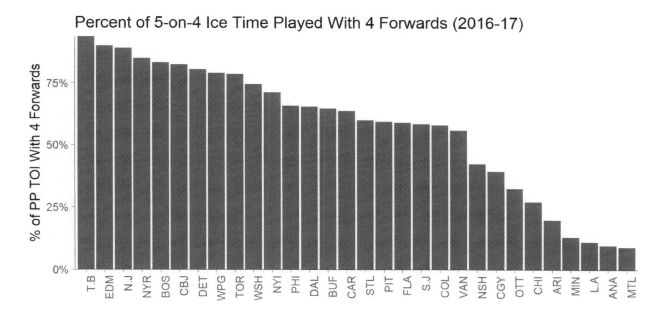

Percent of 5-on-4 Ice Time Played With 4 Forwards (2016-17)

With the increase in usage, a good question to ask is whether this strategy actually makes sense. Sure, it seems logical to trade offence for defence when your opponent is

139Acknowledgement: Raw data for this calculation from the *NHL*, http://www.nhl.com.

shorthanded, but do the numbers actually back up that thought? Perhaps that forward stuck defending a 2-on-1 is so inept at skating backwards that it cancels out any extra offensive opportunities your team may generate.

One of my strongest (and worst) hockey memories is watching Jason Pominville blow by Daniel Alfredsson in overtime of the 2006 Eastern Conference Finals to end the series[140]. While the Sens weren't actually using four forwards in that situation, it does illustrate pretty well every coach's worst nightmare about using a forward at defence. When you've got someone playing back there who doesn't do it often, the chances that they (and by extension, you) will look foolish almost certainly increase.

The question that needs to be asked, however, is whether that risk is anecdotal, or real. Are coaches just reliving their worst memories, or is there actually some truth to the idea that forwards are a risk defensively when they're put at the point?

And when we look at the data, it turns out that there is reason for coaches to worry defensively when they play with four forwards. Compared to a three-forward setup, teams using four forwards on the power play allow more shot attempts per 60 minutes, and post a lower save percentage.

Table 1: Power Play Results Against, by Lineup, 2009–10 to 2016–17[141]

Deployment	Shot Attempts per 60 Minutes	Save Percentage
Three Forwards, Two Defencemen	12.9	.924
Four Forwards, One Defenceman	13.2	.893

But that's only half the picture – we also have to look at whether that increased risk comes with a bigger reward. And the data shows that there's also a significant offensive benefit (as we'd expect) to playing with four forwards. Teams generate more shot attempts per 60 minutes using four forwards, while also scoring on a higher percentage of those shots.

Table 2: Power Play Results For, by Lineup, 2009–10 to 2016–17[142]

Deployment	Shot Attempts per 60 Minutes	Shooting Percentage
Three Forwards, Two Defencemen	90.7	11.5%
Four Forwards, One Defenceman	101.9	13.0%

This last point is a major feature of the four-forward power play: by taking out a defenceman, you're increasing the likelihood that any given shot is taken by a forward, who (in general) are more accurate shooters, no matter where they're shooting from.

Throw all these numbers together, and you'll see that four-forward units do in fact outperform three-forward groups in goal differential per 60 minutes, and by a fairly significant margin.

140 Don Brennan, "Alfie sums up Pominville's goal", *Ottawa Sun,* May 14, 2006, Web, http://slam.canoe.com/Slam/Hockey/NHL/Playoffs/Ottawa/2006/05/14/1579485-sun.html.
141 Acknowledgement: Raw data for this calculation from the *NHL*, http://www.nhl.com.
142 Acknowledgement: Raw data for this calculation from the *NHL*, http://www.nhl.com.

Table 3: Power Play Goal Differential, by Lineup, 2009–10 to 2016–17[143]

Deployment	Goals Scored per 60 Minutes	Goals Allowed per 60 Minutes	Goal Differential per 60 Minutes
Three Forwards, Two Defencemen	5.6	0.6	4.9
Four Forwards, One Defenceman	7.0	0.9	6.1

While some of this benefit can be explained by the fact that teams are more likely to use four forwards on their first unit and three forwards on their second, the advantage still persists when we take this into account. If we look only at teams that spent more than 80% of their ice-time using either four forwards or three forwards, we see that the four-forward teams generally outperform the three-forward teams.

Table 4: Power Play Goal Differential, by Deployment Preference, 2009–10 to 2016–17[144]

Team's Deployment at least 80% of the time	Number of Teams	Goal Differential per 60 Minutes
Three Forwards, Two Defencemen	57	5.3
Four Forwards, One Defenceman	24	6.1

If a four-forward setup is the way to go then, how big of an impact could teams see if they make the switch? If we assume that a team will see an increase of 1.2 goals per 60 minutes at 5-on-4, that translates to an extra goal on roughly one in 30 power plays. For an average team, that works out to an extra eight goals over the course of a season, if they were to switch from using three forwards and two defencemen for 100% of their power play minutes, to using four forwards and one defenceman at all times. That translates to about 2.5 points in the standings, using the standard conversion rate of three goals to one extra point, which is worth over a million dollars in today's NHL[145].

When should a team not play with four forwards? Some teams with particularly gifted offensive defencemen can get by with using two defencemen, because that offensive blueliner tends to act as a fourth forward anyways. Players like Ottawa's Erik Karlsson and Nashville's P.K. Subban may actually be better options than a team's fourth-best forward, in certain situations. We can see this in Table 4 above, as teams who used three forwards nearly exclusively outperformed the overall rate of three-forward units in total.

It also may make sense to play more cautiously when you have a lead late in the game. In that situation you want to reduce the total number of goals scored (both for and against), and so you may accept a decrease in your odds of scoring a goal if you also see a drop in your chances of giving up a shorthanded marker.

The flip side to that argument, of course, is that teams should be more aggressive in using four forwards late in a game when they're down. Since you often have little to lose from allowing a goal when you're trailing late (it doesn't matter if you lose by one or 10 goals),

---

143Acknowledgement: Raw data for this calculation from the *NHL*, http://www.nhl.com.
144Acknowledgement: Raw data for this calculation from the *NHL*, http://www.nhl.com.
145This is hockey's 3-1-1 rule, the first part of which is re-visited in the upcoming updates chapter, under the question about the game's best value contract.

teams should likely be more aggressive with their power play setups, using four forwards later in the power play (most teams will switch back to a two-defencemen setup towards the end of a man advantage when the penalized player is about to return).

Could Five Forwards Work?

The natural question that follows is whether a five-forward approach could make a power play even more dangerous. While there's limited data to make a full analysis, in small samples, it does seem to pay off.

In 2014–15, the St. Louis Blues played with five forwards for nearly 7% of their 5-on-4 time, posting an incredible 8.72 goal differential per 60 minutes when they did[146]. In fact, since 2009–10, teams playing with five forwards have posted a 6.6 goal differential per 60 minutes, just slightly higher than the rate for teams with four forwards. Though the sample here is limited, it does suggest that teams could get more aggressive with their deployments, particularly when trailing late.

Jack Han and Thomas Cote also found similar results when they used a five-forward power play on the McGill Martlets women's hockey team[147]. After graduations stole some of their power play options from the 2015–16 season, the Martlets experimented with a five-forward approach during the 2016–17 season with some success.

Their success reinforces the need for these decisions to be personnel specific – sometimes your best lineup will be using four forwards, while in other situations three or five will be ideal. These decisions should always be made with a consideration of the players available, and generally need to take into account your offensive depth (or lack thereof) on the blueline. Four forwards will generally be best, but as in every other area of hockey analytics, no rule is absolute for every club.

Which players are good at the power play?

Now that we know that we're probably better off using four forwards on the power play, we have to go about choosing which forwards we should use. Every offseason and every trade deadline, we hear over and over about how a team needs to find someone for their power play, whether it's a puck-mover to control play from the point, or a big body to clean up the mess in front. Teams seem to constantly be searching for help on the man advantage, and the most coveted skater of all is the power play specialist.

146Acknowledgement: Raw data for this calculation from the *NHL*, http://www.nhl.com.
147Relayed through conversation with Jack Han.

The Power Play Specialist

What exactly is a power play specialist though? A quick google search for "Power Play Specialist" yields dozens of articles listing off the top power play specialists in the NHL[148], but these lists are often full of players who are among the best in the league, period.

For example, a list of power play specialists from NHL.com published just prior to the 2014–15 season, had Alex Ovechkin, Erik Karlsson, and Steven Stamkos as the league's top power play specialists[149]. While all three of these players were, and still are, critical to their teams' power plays, they also were key players at even strength. They play top-line minutes, and their coaches depend on them to be the stars that lead their teams to success no matter what the situation.

The vast majority of power play units end up being created this way, as they get filled with top-six forwards and top-four defencemen. In theory, this is a decent way to select who to use on the power play – if you're a coach, you've likely filled your top two lines with your 10 best players, because if you haven't, you may not be putting together an optimal lineup at 5-on-5.

But, in reality, your six-to-eight best *offensive* forwards may not be your six-to-eight best *overall* forwards, and your two-to-four best *offensive* defencemen may not be your two-to-four best *overall* defencemen. There are a good number of teams who have offensively talented players who can contribute on the power play, but who just can't handle the defensive responsibility that playing in the top half of the lineup requires.

In order to truly define a player as a power play specialist we should be looking for these types of players, the skaters whose role on the team is primarily defined by their contributions away from even strength. In the same way that penalty killing specialists often would not have a roster spot if not for their ability to contribute while shorthanded, a true power play specialist should be a bottom of the roster player who may not be able to justify their inclusion in the lineup without their abilities on the man advantage.

The prototypical example of a team employing a modern day power play specialist may be Sam Gagner's 2016–17 campaign. After being cast aside by the Philadelphia Flyers following a lackluster 2015–16 season, Gagner signed a one-year deal at just above the minimum salary with the Columbus Blue Jackets. The Jackets, however, drastically changed Gagner's usage from what how he was deployed in Philadelphia. While he sat seventh among forwards in 5-on-5 time-on-ice percentage with the Flyers, he was the 11th-most used forward for Columbus, a significant drop[150]. Columbus figured out that even if they sheltered Gagner to protect him at even-strength, they could still get significant value by using his offensive talents on the power play[151].

148Rob Vollman, "Ranking the Top Power-Play Specialists in the NHL", *Bleacher Report,* October 9, 2013, Web, http://bleacherreport.com/articles/1798161-ranking-the-top-power-play-specialists-in-the-nhl.

149Dan Rosen, "Ovechkin rules top-14 power play specialists", *NHL.com,* September 6, 2014, Web, https://www.nhl.com/news/ovechkin-rules-top-14-power-play-specialists/c-729543.

150Acknowledgement: Raw data for this calculation from *Puckalytics,* http://www.puckalytics.com.

151Dimitri Filipovic, "Why the Columbus Blue Jackets are a case study in modern player usage", *Sportsnet,* December 29, 2016, Web, http://www.sportsnet.ca/hockey/nhl/columbus-blue-jackets-case-study-modern-

Gagner obviously isn't the only player to be placed is this kind of role, though he may be one of the more extreme cases. Thomas Vanek has also been cast this way for the last three years, being the ninth most used 5-on-5 skater on his team in each of the last three seasons, while playing nearly 50% of his teams' 5-on-4 ice-time[152].

Anecdotally, then, it would seem that teams are turning to the bottom half of their lineups more often on the power play in recent years, as more coaches figure out that players like Gagner and Vanek can be sheltered while still contributing on the man advantage. And, in fact, if you look at how often bottom-six forwards have been used on the power play over the last four seasons, we see a clearly increasing trend.

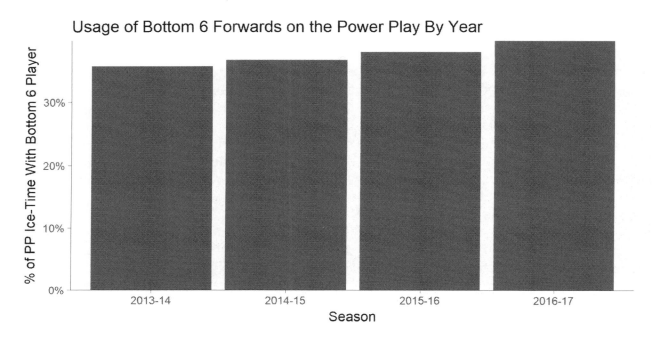

But, there's a slight wrinkle in the data we need to take into account – while it may seem like an increase in power play ice-time for bottom-six forwards would indicate that teams are getting more creative in their player deployment on the man advantage, there may actually be a simpler explanation for the rise: the four-forward power play.

We noted earlier that four-forward units were becoming more common in the NHL, but a side effect of that switch is that teams naturally have to dig deeper into their roster to fill out those units. If you consistently play four forwards on both your first and second power play units, by definition you'll have to choose players from your bottom six to fill out your power play.

This fact makes it a bit tricky to evaluate whether the power play specialist role is one that's useful to a team. To get around this problem, we'll have to narrow our definition of a power play specialist even further. We'll define a power play specialist as a player who:

player-usage/.

152Acknowledgement: Data source is *Puckalytics,* http://www.puckalytics.com.

1. Plays first-line minutes on their team's power play (ranking in the top five in power play time-on-ice percentage on their team, while playing at least 50 power play minutes in a season); and

2. Plays bottom-six or bottom-pair minutes at full-strength (ranking outside the top six among 5-on-5 time-on-ice percentage for forwards or outside the top four for defencemen)

This definition is significantly more limited than others, and as such we end up with very few power play specialists. Over the last four years, there have been just 23 forwards and nine defencemen who met our definition of power play specialists. Who exactly are they? The table below has all 32 specialists that our method identified, the season and team for which they played, as well as their team's 5-on-4 goals scored per 60 minutes with them on the ice during that season.

Table 5: Power Play Specialists, 2013–14 to 2016–17[153]

Season	Player	Team	Team Goals Scored per 60 Minutes
2016–17	Mark Letestu	Edmonton	10.0
2016–17	Patric Hornqvist	Pittsburgh	9.9
2016–17	Sam Gagner	Columbus	9.0
2016–17	Shayne Gostisbehere	Philadelphia	8.8
2015–16	Sami Vatanen	Anaheim	8.7
2016–17	Ryan Spooner	Boston	8.7
2015–16	Anders Lee	NY Islanders	8.6
2016–17	Anthony Deangelo	Arizona	8.4
2013–14	Kimmo Timonen	Philadelphia	7.9
2016–17	Tanner Pearson	Los Angeles	7.7
2014–15	Frans Nielsen	NY Islanders	7.7
2013–14	Torey Krug	Boston	7.5
2013–14	Patrik Elias	New Jersey	7.2
2015–16	Ryan Spooner	Boston	7.2
2014–15	Brock Nelson	NY Islanders	7.2
2016–17	Brandon Pirri	NY Rangers	6.9
2016–17	Kris Versteeg	Calgary	6.8
2013–14	Ray Whitney	Dallas	6.6
2013–14	Patrick Wiercioch	Ottawa	6.3
2013–14	Todd Bertuzzi	Detroit	6.3
2014–15	Andrew Shaw	Chicago	6.3
2013–14	Alex Chiasson	Dallas	6.2
2013–14	Nick Bonino	Anaheim	6.1
2015–16	Anthony Duclair	Arizona	6.1
2016–17	Thomas Vanek	Florida	5.8
2015–16	Thomas Vanek	Minnesota	5.7

153Acknowledgement: Data source is *Puckalytics,* http://www.puckalytics.com.

2014–15	Alex Burrows	Vancouver	5.5
2015–16	Noah Hanifin	Carolina	5.5
2014–15	Thomas Vanek	Minnesota	5.5
2013–14	Matt Cullen	Nashville	5.2
2016–17	Niklas Kronwall	Detroit	4.4
2013–14	Ryan Murphy	Carolina	2.1

The list is an interesting mix: there are a lot of older, offensive-minded forwards who may have lost a step at even strength, but who still have (or were thought to have) a lot to contribute on the power play. These are the Thomas Vanek's, the Ray Whitney's, and the Matt Cullen's of the world, and you'll generally find them towards the bottom of the list.

There are also a bunch of young defencemen, who may not have picked-up the NHL defensive game yet, but whose offensive talents are too great to leave on the bench on a man advantage. Carolina has done this twice, with limited success using Ryan Murphy, and slightly better results with Noah Hanifin.

And then there are what I'll call the "modern day" specialists – these forwards aren't yet past their prime, but they also haven't earned enough of their coaches' trust to get into the top six at even strength. This group includes the aforementioned Gagner, as well as Anthony DeAngelo, Ryan Spooner, Anders Lee, and Tanner Pearson, all of whom played the specialist role in the last two years. One interesting thing about this group is how well they've performed: the names towards the top of the list tend to be more from the "modern day" class, while the bottom of the list is filled with more of the aging stars.

Is this proof that power play specialists are useful, if you choose the right ones? It's a difficult question to answer. On the one hand, we don't have a lot of data from teams using a power play specialist. Just 18 of 32 players on the list above posted a goals scored per 60 minutes that was above the league average over the last four years of 6.42.

But, if we look at teams who use a power play specialist as a group, we see that they did in fact marginally outperform teams that did not use one.

Table 6: Teams Using a Power Play Specialist Vs. Those Who Didn't, 2013–14 to 2016–17[154]

Specialist Usage	Number of Teams	Goals Scored per 60 Minutes
Teams Using a Power Play Specialist	30	6.37
Teams Not Using a Power Play Specialist	90	6.29

The increase may not be significant, at least not statistically, but it is interesting. It's possible that this difference will wash out as time goes on, but it also may simply be that we don't have a large enough sample of power play specialists to make a claim about their effectiveness. After all, we only see about eight specialists per year, and we only get about 185 minutes of ice-time for each of them.

154Acknowledgement: Raw data for this calculation from *Puckalytics,* http://www.puckalytics.com.

But there are reasons to think that teams that find creative ways to construct their lineups and utilize their players would do better than teams that stick to a rigid, traditional method of lineup construction. Teams that have spent the time to place their players in the roles that take advantage of their specific skills likely spend more time on other tactical considerations and may just be the "smarter" teams overall. They may be the clubs that find many little advantages and turn them into a big overall advantage. The power play specialist may be a small piece of that, but it's one that shows how a coach or GM can squeeze a bit of extra value out of a lineup by considering specific strengths and weaknesses.

Identifying Power Play Talent

If the data we have indicates that there may be some benefit to using specialists on the power play, how can we know who might be a specialist? After all, our minutes on the power play in any given year are limited, and even if we have a hunch someone might fit well in that role, it's costly to try and find out they were never a good fit on the man advantage.

One place we can look for clues is 5-on-5 play. In theory, many of the best offensive players at 5-on-5 should be good options for a team to use on the power play. After all, if a player is able to generate opportunities when they're facing an equal number of opponents, they'll likely still have that same talent when space is opened up on the man advantage. Similarly, we'd also assume that defensive specialists who don't focus on generating offence at even strength likely won't excel on the power play.

The question, then, is which 5-on-5 stats are best to look at if we want to figure out which players may be strong on the power play. While we've got many options, from shot attempts to goals to scoring totals, it turns out that two fairly simple metrics provide the best predictions of power play shot attempt differentials: a player's individual shot attempts per 60 minutes, and their on-ice team shot attempts per 60 minutes (specifically, how many shot attempts per 60 minutes their teammates generate when they're on the ice, basically a rough measure of playmaking skill).

The value of each of these stats differs by position, however. For forwards, we find that individual shot generation is just as important as teammates shot generation, i.e. playmaking ability. But for defencemen, the emphasis is much greater on playmaking than it is on individual offensive ability. This finding makes a lot of sense, as defencemen are often playing the puck distributor role at the top of the power play, and most of their shot attempts are less dependent on their own ability to generate chances.

With these two 5-on-5 stats in hand, we can calculate a player's Expected Power Play Shot Attempt Differential Per 60 (xPPSAD/60). This number represents our best guess of their teams shot attempt differential on the man advantage, if that player were to be given a regular role on the power play. We can then use that data to figure out which teams are effectively deploying their best weapons on the man advantage.

The table below lists each team's "best replacement", the player with the highest xPPSAD/60 among those skaters who didn't play at least 25% of their team's 5-on-4 minutes last year. But it also has each club's "worst regular", the skater with the worst xPPSAD/60 who plays the same position as the best replacement, and who played more than 25% of their team's 5-on-4 minutes over the last three seasons. Lastly, it also lists out the difference in expected differentials between the best possible replacement, and the worst regular.

Table 7: Best Power Play Replacements and Worst Power Play Regulars, 2016–17[155]

Team	Best Replacement	Worst Regular	xPPSAD/60
Los Angeles	Devin Setoguchi	Jarome Iginla	15.0
Edmonton	David Desharnais	Mark Letestu	14.4
Colorado	Matt Nieto	Mikhail Grigorenko	11.2
Dallas	Antoine Roussel	Devin Shore	10.3
Chicago	Michal Kempny	Brian Campbell	9.9
Minnesota	Jason Pominville	Charlie Coyle	9.2
Calgary	Michael Frolik	Troy Brouwer	8.8
Philadelphia	Michael Raffl	Valtteri Filppula	8.4
San Jose	Paul Martin	David Schlemko	8.2
Nashville	Craig Smith	PA Parenteau	7.5
Florida	Colton Sceviour	Thomas Vanek	7.0
Toronto	Zach Hyman	Leo Komarov	6.4
Buffalo	Justin Falk	Rasmus Ristolainen	6.4
Detroit	Darren Helm	Justin Abdelkader	5.4
Pittsburgh	Carl Hagelin	Nick Bonino	4.9
Anaheim	Andrew Cogliano	Antoine Vermette	4.4
Washington	Brett Connolly	Marcus Johansson	3.0
Winnipeg	Paul Postma	Tobias Enstrom	2.9
Vancouver	Christopher Tanev	Ben Hutton	2.6
New Jersey	Ben Lovejoy	Damon Severson	2.5
NY Rangers	Brendan Smith	Brady Skjei	2.3
Arizona	Luke Schenn	Oliver Ekman-Larsson	1.7
Tampa Bay	Jake Dotchin	Anton Stralman	1.6
Montreal	Phillip Danault	Andrew Shaw	1.4
Carolina	Jaccob Slavin	Noah Hanifin	1.4
Ottawa	Marc Methot	Chris Wideman	0.3
St. Louis	Joel Edmundson	Alex Pietrangelo	0.0
Columbus	Lukas Sedlak	Nick Foligno	-0.3
Boston	Brandon Carlo	Torey Krug	-0.5
NY Islanders	Thomas Hickey	Johnny Boychuk	-1.6

The table is sorted by the expected difference between the best replacement and the worst regular on a team, and there are a few interesting things that stand out. First, there were three teams who pretty much played their optimal lineup by this metric: Columbus, Boston, and the New York Islanders. All of their "best replacements" were expected to be a step down from the worst player that played regular minutes on their team, indicating that their coaches' selections were right in line with what our formula would suggest.

155Acknowledgement: Raw data for this calculation from *Puckalytics,* http://www.puckalytics.com.

Second, there are many clubs that could have seen a big change in their expected shot generation rates if they had made the suggested swaps listed above. While Jarome Iginla was only on the Kings for a short period at the end of the year, his presence was clearly not a boon to either Colorado or L.A.'s power plays. Colorado also would have been well advised to end the Mikhail Grigorenko experiment early, although I'm not sure there are any players that could have been plugged in there to save their season.

Obviously, not all of these suggestions are reasonable: no one would dare put Luke Schenn on for a critical 5-on-4 over Oliver Ekman-Larsson, and there are clearly some players who sneak onto the list by playing with the very best players on their team (I'm looking your way, Zach Hyman). There are also zone start and quality of competition issues for some players, but this metric does provide a place to start a conversation and may offer some suggestions for team's whose power plays are struggling.

Chicago finished last season 19th in goals scored per 60 minutes at 5-on-4, and were eighth worst in shot attempt generation[156]. What would be the harm in trying out Michal Kempny on the power play, over Brian Campbell? Campbell was clearly on his last legs this year, so why not give a younger player a chance, particularly when his stats suggest he could be a useful piece?

Although there will always be a good deal of uncertainty with results like these, it's clear that using full-strength data can help you find potential options on the man advantage, and may help identify a diamond in the rough who you otherwise wouldn't have tried on the power play.

Handedness

The last consideration in player selection is balance of handedness on the power play. Players on their off-hand side shot 11.7% on the power play between 2005–06 and 2015–16, 1.4% better than players on strong side[157]. In particular, handedness is critical for shot attempts taken outside of the scoring chance area, as the difference between strong-side and off-hand shooting percentages is greater there.

Table 8: 5-on-4 Shot Attempt Shooting Percentage by Location, 2005–06 to 2016–17[158]

Area	Side	Forward SH%	Defenceman SH%
Scoring chance	Off-Hand	10.2%	4.6%
Scoring chance	Strong-Side	10.0%	4.1%
Perimeter	Off-Hand	6.5%	4.0%
Perimeter	Strong-Side	5.2%	3.4%

156Acknowledgement: Data from *Puckalytics,* http://www.puckalytics.com.
157Arik Parnass, "How Important is Playing the Off-Wing on the Power Play?", *Special Teams Project,* January 19, 2016, Web, http://www.nhlspecialteams.com/blog/2016/1/19/how-important-is-playing-the-off-wing-on-the-power-play.
158Arik Parnass, "How Important is Playing the Off-Wing on the Power Play?", *Special Teams Project,* January 19, 2016, Web, http://www.nhlspecialteams.com/blog/2016/1/19/how-important-is-playing-the-off-wing-on-the-power-play.

Shots from the off-side don't have a significant effect on a team's result, but the more shots that come from players on their off-side, the greater their goal scoring rates tend to be. While handedness is unlikely to turn a bad man advantage into a great one, designing your lineups to maximize the number of shots from the off-hand at least makes sense as a secondary goal of any coach. Even something as simple as swapping one player from the top unit to the second group may provide a slight boost to a team's results when added up over the course of a season.

Step 2: Structure, Structure, Structure

Perhaps the best power play weapon of the salary cap era has been Alex Ovechkin of the Washington Capitals. Since he entered the league in 2005–06, Ovechkin has recorded 212 goals on the man-advantage, 83 more than the second highest skater over that time (Thomas Vanek)[159].

Ovechkin, of course, is famous for putting the puck home from the "Ovi Spot", a broad region roughly centered above the left faceoff dot in the offensive zone. Teams know that Ovi will be there and despite their efforts to key in on him, he still finds the back of the net over and over again from the same place.

The Ovi Spot, however, hasn't always been the Ovi Spot. Before 2012–13, most of Ovechkin's shots came from deeper in the zone and closer to the centre of the ice. What changed? Adam Oates switched up the Caps' power play system, instilling a new discipline and focus on structure that greatly improved their power play results. This change paid immediate dividends: in the two years before he took over, Washington was 19th in the league in 5-on-4 goals scored per 60 minutes; but in his two year tenure behind the bench the Caps were on top of the NHL, finishing 15% higher than the second best team[160].

How You Generate Opportunities Matters

While the Capitals' power play had been full of top-tier talent for years, it's not just the star power that matters when it comes to results. The Caps' power play was still centered on Ovechkin after Oates came in, but how they get the puck into his hands changed. It wasn't just "find a way to get it to Ovi." it was find a way to use all the players to make sure teams can't just key in on Ovechkin. Washington focused on implementing a system that created opportunities for all their skaters consistently, and the effort to ingrain that in the team paid dividends – even after Oates left, the Capitals have remained one of the most dangerous power plays in the league.

The Caps power play doesn't just generate results, it also looks good – it's fluid and dynamic, but you can see that their skaters have a clear objective with every move. They know their

159Acknowledgement: Scoring data from the NHL, http://www.nhl.com.
160Acknowledgement: Data source is *Puckalytics,* http://www.puckalytics.com.

options, and they work through them systematically to create their opportunities. There's creativity, but it is structured creativity, to borrow a phrase from Parnass. He described the Caps power play as having "unpredictability with the advantage of a structure that has been polished over a number of practices[161]". There are roles and plays for each player, but there are enough unknowns in how the puck moves to keep the defense guessing.

A structure like this may be easy to define, but it's not necessarily something that's simple to measure. One way to look at structure from a statistical perspective is to consider how often teams are able to generate opportunities from the same locations. A team that is well structured will be consistently getting shots by the same players in the same location. They'll move the puck well enough to create the space to take the shot, but each player will generally be looking for his teammates in the same area over and over again.

To go back once again to the Caps, this is exactly why the Ovi spot works: he's always in the same place so his teammates know where to look, but they've practiced enough different ways to get it to him there that teams don't know how they're going to do it.

We can use this idea to define a team's Structure Index, a rough measure of how consistent teams are in generating opportunities from the same location. A team's Structure Index is the weighted average of each player's average distance from their central shot location. So if we say that the Ovi Spot is the absolute top of the left faceoff circle, his contribution to the Capitals Structure Index would be the average distance of all his power play shots to that location at the top of the circle.

If we repeat that calculation for all players on the Caps power play, and then take the weighted average of those averages (yes, the word average is overused here, but it's sadly unavoidable), we'll get the Caps Structure Index, which, for the last season was 14.1, best in the league.

Put in plainer terms, a team's Structure Index measures how tight each player's shot distribution is on the man advantage. Teams with well-structured power plays will have set plays to create dangerous opportunities through puck movement, but those opportunities will often come from the same location: the tic-tac-toe pass from the half-boards to the goal-line to the slot is one that teams always go back to, and not just because it almost guarantees a spot on the Sportscentre highlight reel when it works.

Lower Structure Index values are good, because it means that a team is consistently getting their players opportunities from the same location, while a higher Structure Index indicates that teams are having trouble setting up plays, and that their players aren't getting looks from the same spot on each power play.

Unsurprisingly, the kings of structure for several years now have been the Washington Capitals. The Caps have led the league in Structure Index for each of the past five seasons, while also finishing first in 5-on-4 goals per 60 minutes three times.

161Arik Parnass, "Why I Believe in Structured Creativity on the Power Play", *Special Teams Project,* February 7, 2016, Web, http://www.nhlspecialteams.com/blog/2016/2/7/why-i-believe-in-structured-creativity-on-the-power-play.

Table 9: Washington Capitals Power Play Structure Index, 2012–13 to 2016–17[162]

Season	5-on-4 Goals per 60 Minutes	Rank	Structure Index	Rank
2016–17	7.9	5	14.1	1
2015–16	7.8	3	13.2	1
2014–15	9.5	1	13.6	1
2013–14	9.5	1	13.5	1
2012–13	10.1	1	12.0	1

A team's power play structure index is an important indicator of how well it will perform on the power play. Four of the top 10 teams in power play goals scored per 60 minutes finished in the top 10 in Structure Index, while only one team that was in the top third of the league in Structure Index finished in the bottom third. The full structure index data for each team in the past season is given in the table below, along with their shot attempts per 60 minutes and goals scored per 60 minutes.

Table 10: Power Play Structure Index, 2016–17[163]

Team	Structure Index	Shot Attempts per 60 Minutes	Rank	Goals Scored per 60 Minutes	Rank
Washington Capitals	14.1	108.4	3	7.9	5
Columbus Blue Jackets	14.6	85.1	28	6.7	13
Philadelphia Flyers	14.6	108.7	2	6.6	15
Tampa Bay Lightning	14.8	96.4	17	8.0	2
Edmonton Oilers	15.4	106.8	6	7.9	6
Chicago Blackhawks	16.0	90.5	22	6.0	21
Toronto Maple Leafs	16.3	104.1	7	8.0	3
Vancouver Canucks	16.3	85.8	27	4.3	29
New Jersey Devils	16.4	87.4	24	6.3	18
New York Islanders	16.5	94.5	19	5.1	26
Pittsburgh Penguins	16.5	99.7	14	8.0	4
Nashville Predators	16.6	93.7	21	6.1	20
Detroit Red Wings	16.7	87.1	25	5.0	28
New York Rangers	16.8	96.7	16	7.1	10
Minnesota Wild	16.8	98.0	15	7.1	9
Anaheim Ducks	17.0	110.2	1	6.8	12
Calgary Flames	17.0	102.2	10	7.2	8
Dallas Stars	17.3	101.1	12	6.3	17
Colorado Avalanche	17.4	82.4	29	4.1	30
Boston Bruins	17.8	107.6	5	7.4	7
Arizona Coyotes	17.8	85.8	26	5.2	25
Winnipeg Jets	17.9	96.2	18	5.8	24
Buffalo Sabres	18.0	102.6	9	8.7	1

162Acknowledgement: Raw data for this calculation from the *NHL*, http://www.nhl.com.

163Acknowledgement: Raw data for Structure Index calculation from the *NHL*, http://www.nhl.com, other data from *Puckalytics,* http://www.puckalytics.com.

Carolina Hurricanes	18.5		99.9	13	6.2	19
St. Louis Blues	18.7		89.8	23	7.1	11
Montreal Canadiens	18.8		78.3	30	6.6	16
Ottawa Senators	19.1		94.3	20	5.8	23
San Jose Sharks	19.5		102.6	8	5.1	27
Los Angeles Kings	19.6		108.2	4	6.7	14
Florida Panthers	19.9		101.5	11	5.8	22

Astute readers may have noted that for a lot of teams last year, their power play structure numbers were somewhat unrelated to their ability to generate shot attempts on the man advantage. The Kings were second last in structure, fourth in shot attempt generation, and finished middle of the pack in goal scoring.

So while we said earlier that shot attempts were king when it came to the power play, that's only partly true – it's important to generate shot attempts on the power play, but it's clearly not the only thing that matters. Putting a barrage of shots towards the net is clearly one way to succeed, but it's definitely not the only way.

That distinction may help to explain why a team like Columbus has managed to succeed on the power play despite being one of the worst clubs at generating shot attempts over the past three seasons. Columbus is sixth in the league in goals per 60 minutes since 2014–15, despite ranking in the bottom five in shot attempts per 60 minutes. The Blue Jackets, however, have finished the last three seasons second, fourth, and 12th in power play structure, showing that a team doesn't need to be a shot attempt machine to succeed, if they can establish a well-structured setup to generate dangerous opportunities.

The polar opposite of Columbus has been the Boston Bruins. Boston has ranked 20th, 13th, and 26th in power play structure over the last three years, respectively. But the Bruins have generated a league-leading 111.7 shot attempts per 60 minutes at 5-on-4 during that time, which is a major reason why they have the fourth-highest goals per 60 minutes since 2014–15[164].

Given that there are clearly two different ways to succeed, which one should teams focus on? Is it better to try to establish a good system that creates more dangerous opportunities, or is it smarter to focus on getting the puck to the net as often as possible?

The answer is, both. Power play structure is only slightly less important than raw shot generation in predicting power play success. If you look at both factors together, a team's past structure rating and shot attempts per 60 minutes are almost equally important in predicting which clubs will succeed in the future.

While our measure of structure isn't perfect, it can help provide a broad estimate of which power plays are functioning well, and which are having trouble generating dangerous opportunities. Teams who aren't scoring could look at their structure score to help diagnose whether they've been unlucky or have legitimate issues. Similarly, coaches could look at their

---

164Acknowledgement: Team power play data from *Puckalytics,* http://www.puckalytics.com.

opponents structure score to help determine how aggressive or passive they need to be on the penalty kill. Regardless of how you measure it though, finding creative ways to operate within a well-defined system will clearly lead to positive results when you're on the man advantage.

Step 3: Regrouping and Entering the Zone

The final piece to our power play puzzle is the regroup and zone entry. While it would be nice if we could spend the entire man advantage with control of the puck in our opponents end, the reality is that on almost every power play our opponent will get control of the puck and clear it out of their zone. After that, the game changes for a club on the power play, and a focus on structure and puck movement gets replaced by a need to successfully re-enter the zone to re-establish that dangerous formation.

Unfortunately for the analytics world, this is where the amount of data we have tends to drop off significantly. And so because of our drought of data we need to once again rely heavily on the work of Parnass to show us what kind of impact a team's zone entry strategies and ability can have.

The Value of Zone Entries

The importance of zone entries on the power play is simple enough to understand: teams have limited minutes on the power play. Any time that the puck is in the neutral zone or their defensive zone is time that they're not on the attack. Therefore when a team has the puck outside the offensive zone, its primary goal should be getting the puck back in as soon as possible.

Parnass recognized this basic fact, and found a way to quantify a team's ability to do just this. He created a metric to measure how often teams or players were able to turn their entry opportunities into quality offensive chances. He defined his Zone Entry to Formation or dangerous Rush Rate (ZEFR) as the percentage of 5-on-4 zone entry attempts with a certain player on the ice that result in either a scoring chance off the rush or the team getting set up in formation[165].

In his tracked data, he showed that:

1) A player's ZEFR rate is a repeatable skill, indicating that there are players who are consistently better or worse than other players at generating zone entries.

2) A player's ZEFR rate is a significant predictor of future goal scoring, and in fact was a better predictor than past shot attempt or goal rates.

---

[165]Arik Parnass, "ZEFR Rate: A New and Better Way to Evaluate Power Plays", *Hockey Graphs,* April 18, 2016, Web, https://hockey-graphs.com/2016/04/18/zefr-rate-a-new-and-better-way-to-evaluate-power-plays/.

The importance of these findings cannot be overstated. Finding players or schemes that are effective at entering the zone is critical to a team's success, and Parnass showed that there are ways to get better at it.

The problem with knowing the importance of power play zone entries, however, is that we have no way to easily get this data. Manual tracking is a great way for a team with a budget (or a very dedicated individual without one) to collect this data, but it's simply not practical for most amateur analysts to do, and would require a massive effort to fill in the long-term historical data we're missing.

This is where we can get a little creative, and use the NHL's play-by-play and shift data to estimate when teams are entering and exiting the zone on the power play. Our proxy may not be perfect, but as we'll see it'll provide us with a pretty good estimate of how well a team is able to regroup and enter the zone on the man advantage.

Estimating Power Play Zone Entries

How do we go from the raw data in the NHL's real time scoring files to estimating zone entries? The key to estimating power play zone entries relies on the fact that teams tend to change their lines in a somewhat unique way on the penalty kill.

During even-strength play, players know the maximum shift length that they can physically handle (or that their coach will tolerate), and will generally limit their shifts to a fairly standard length. But on the penalty kill, fresh legs are almost always at a premium, and changing skaters when you have the chance is generally preferable to letting your best penalty killers stay on for a few extra seconds.

Despite this, changing lines as often as possible is easier said than done. Since the offensive team frequently maintains possession of the puck for extended periods of time in the offensive zone, teams on the penalty kill usually are only able to change when they get possession of the puck and clear it out of their own end. And so, if we assume that line changes for the defence only occur when they're able to clear the puck out of their zone, we can use the timing of those changes as a proxy for the time when the team on the power play will begin setting up for their zone entry.

That assumption gives us half of the equation. The other half is determining whether the entry was successful or not. To estimate a successful entry, we'll look for whether the offensive team was able to generate a shot attempt following their opponent's shift change or not.

While this is a bit more of a stretch than our first assumption, it does fit nicely with Parnass's original ZEFR definition. We'll capture all scoring chances off the rush because, by definition, a scoring chance requires a shot attempt. And if we assume that players on the power play aren't firing wildly from anywhere, then the first non-rush attempt will be roughly in line with how quickly a team is able to get into formation.

The Method

Now that we have the idea of estimating zone entries, let's look at how we go about doing it in practice. We'll need data from both the NHL's shift files (to identify the line changes) and the play-by-play files (to identify the shots attempts). The method to calculate our Estimated ZEFR Rate is:

1. From the list of all line changes, exclude the changes that occur on a faceoff. This will take care of both the initial line change to start the power play, and any line change that occurs after a goalie freezes the puck.

2. From the list from step 1, exclude all shift changes that occur less than 10 seconds after an earlier shift change. This allows us to identify the first time a player left the ice, which is presumably the closest time to when the defence cleared the zone. We'll call these points the "Clear Times".

3. Calculate the "Entry Attempt Time". This is the time between the Clear Time and when the Entry Attempt ends, or:

   Entry Attempt Time = (Entry Attempt End Time) minus (Clear Time)

   where the Entry Attempt End Time is the soonest of:

   ○ The next clear time from step 2 (i.e. this would indicate the offense either didn't get an entry, or didn't get a shot);
   ○ The first shot for the team on the man advantage (i.e. the rush shot or the shot in formation to end the entry attempt);
   ○ The end of the power play (to cover the cases where the clear occurs late in the power play).

4. Calculate the Estimated ZEFR rate. While Parnass calculated his metric as the percentage of attempted entries that resulted in a dangerous rush attempt or the team getting set up in formation, I'm going to present a slightly different version here due to our data limitations.

   Rather than using the percentage of entry attempts (since we don't know the exact number of entry attempts, particularly on failed attempts), we'll calculate our metric as a rate stat, where the denominator is the total entry attempt time.

   eZEFR/60 = (# of Initial Shot Attempts Following a Change) divided by (Total Entry Attempt Time/60)

   We use only the initial shot attempts, as we're looking to measure the number of times a team was successful at entering the zone, and not their success after they entered.

Limitations of Estimated Zone Entries

The major limitation with our approach is that we probably aren't going to capture any entry attempts where the defence wins the initial faceoff and clears without any players changing. Unfortunately, without a change, there's no easy way to tell whether the defence's "win" resulted in the puck leaving the zone, so we can't just assume there was a clear after a defensive win.

Defences win about 46% of draws on the penalty kill[166], but I think it's safe to assume that not all of those are clear wins that end up with the team clearing the puck out of the zone. This may reduce our estimated ZEFR for teams that have a great first unit and a weaker second unit, but these should make up a small percentage of total entry attempts, and are probably distributed pretty evenly throughout the league. Our metric may be slightly off, but it won't be biased in a significant or systematic way.

Do estimated zone entries match tracked zone entries?

The first thing to check with our estimated stat is whether it agrees with Parnass's data tracking from last year. Ideally, if our estimate is measuring the same skill that he identified, any results that we get from our estimated metric should be broadly in line with his results.

At the team level, our estimated metric seems to agree pretty well with Parnass's estimates – the teams that he identified as having high ZEFR players in his manual tracking are ranked at the top by our estimated metric; similarly the worst teams in Parnass's tracking are also towards the bottom of the league in our proxy.

Table 11: Accuracy of Estimated ZEFR Rates, 2015–16[167]

ZEFR Rank	Team	eZEFR/60	Rank
1	Washington	82.4	1
2	Toronto	79.9	4
3	Philadelphia	69.4	9
4	Tampa Bay	69.4	10
5	NY Islanders	64.6	19
6	Montreal	62.8	23

We can also look at Parnass's top and bottom 10 ZEFR players from his 2015–16 data, and see where they rank using eZEFR/60, to validate whether our metrics are measuring the same thing.

---

166 Acknowledgement: Raw data for that calculation from the *NHL,* http://www.nhl.com.

167 Acknowledgement: ZEFR data from Arik Parnass, http://www.specialteamsproject.com, and data for our estimates from NHL shift carts and play-by-play files, http://www.nhl.com.

Table 12: Accuracy of Estimated ZEFR for Top and Bottom 10 Players, 2015–16[168]

Player	Team	ZEFR Rank	eZEFR/60 Rank
Marcus Johansson	Washington	1	124
TJ Oshie	St. Louis	2	104
Nazem Kadri	Toronto	3	46
Alex Ovechkin	Washington	4	75
Matt Niskanen	Washington	5	25
Nicklas Backstrom	Washington	6	173
Claude Giroux	Philadelphia	7	40
Shayne Gostisbehere	Philadelphia	8	127
Dion Phaneuf	Ottawa	9	196
Evgeny Kuznetsov	Washington	10	14
Sam Gagner	Columbus	10th Last	303
Nathan Beaulieu	Montreal	9th Last	247
Marek Zidlicky	NY Islanders	8th Last	129
Jeff Petry	Montreal	7th Last	33
Josh Bailey	NY Islanders	6th Last	208
Lars Eller	Montreal	5th Last	268
Johnny Boychuk	NY Islanders	4th Last	N/A
Mikhail Grabovski	NY Islanders	3rd Last	N/A
Ryan Strome	NY Islanders	2nd Last	217
Travis Hamonic	NY Islanders	1st Last	N/A

eZEFR/60 rank requires a minimum 50 minutes (324 qualifying players)

Once again, our estimate seems to broadly mirror the manually tracked data. Some players on the Caps seem to rank a bit lower than we'd expect, but that may just be a product of adding in 24 extra teams to our data set. The biggest misses seem to be Jeff Petry, Marek Zidlicky, and Dion Phaneuf, indicating that the method may be a bit less accurate when looking at defencemen versus forwards.

What team has been the best at power play zone entries?

While Parnass's work identified the Caps as one of the strongest clubs at entering the zone within his sample, which clubs have been the best overall? The table below has all 30 teams[169] estimated zone entry rates over the past three seasons, as well as their goals scored per 60 minutes and shot attempts per 60 minutes at 5-on-4.

---

168 Acknowledgement: ZEFR data from Arik Parnass, http://www.specialteamsproject.com, and data for our estimates from NHL shift carts and play-by-play files, http://www.nhl.com.

169 Note: There are now 31 teams in the NHL, but there were only 30 teams in this given time range.

Table 13: Team Strength in Entering the Zone, 2014–15 to 2016–17[170]

Team	eZEFR/60	Goals Scored per 60 Min	Rank	Shot Attempts per 60 Minutes	Rank
Washington Capitals	80.1	8.4	1	109.0	2
Boston Bruins	78.1	6.9	4	111.7	1
Anaheim Ducks	76.0	6.6	12	107.3	3
Los Angeles Kings	72.7	6.7	9	106.7	5
Pittsburgh Penguins	72.4	6.9	5	97.5	12
Toronto Maple Leafs	71.6	6.1	20	101.3	7
San Jose Sharks	70.6	6.7	11	105.3	6
Arizona Coyotes	70.0	5.8	25	95.4	15
Edmonton Oilers	69.9	6.8	8	99.5	9
Dallas Stars	69.3	6.9	7	99.3	10
Philadelphia Flyers	69.2	7.1	3	107.2	4
Florida Panthers	69.0	5.6	28	92.3	21
Calgary Flames	68.9	6.3	16	97.2	14
New York Rangers	67.3	6.4	15	99.6	8
New York Islanders	67.2	5.7	26	93.1	19
Winnipeg Jets	66.4	5.8	23	94.5	17
Carolina Hurricanes	66.1	5.8	24	99.0	11
Ottawa Senators	65.4	5.6	27	95.0	16
Tampa Bay Lightning	64.8	6.3	18	86.4	28
Detroit Red Wings	64.7	6.5	13	93.3	18
Chicago Blackhawks	63.9	6.3	17	91.8	22
Minnesota Wild	63.5	6.2	19	97.2	13
Nashville Predators	62.5	6.0	21	90.1	23
Montreal Canadiens	62.0	5.9	22	90.0	24
Vancouver Canucks	62.0	5.2	29	89.3	26
Buffalo Sabres	61.4	6.7	9	92.5	20
Columbus Blue Jackets	61.2	6.9	5	88.2	27
St. Louis Blues	60.5	7.7	2	90.0	24
Colorado Avalanche	58.4	5.2	30	84.6	29
New Jersey Devils	56.0	6.5	14	81.3	30

Unsurprisingly, the Capitals still sit at the top of the list when we expand our view to all 30 teams. In addition to their ridiculous ability to play in structure, the Caps have been outstanding at re-entering the offensive zone on the power play over the last three years.

The other interesting thing to note is that the estimated ZEFR rate appears to have a pretty strong correlation with both goal scoring and shot attempt generation. This makes sense – it both agrees with what Parnass had found in his tracking data, and is somewhat tied to the fact that we're using shot attempts as our method of defining a successful zone entry. But it's also worth digging into further – have we developed a useful metric that measures something repeatable and valuable?

170Acknowledgement: Data for our estimates from NHL shift carts and play-by-play files, http://www.nhl.com, and data source for the other columns is *Puckalytics,* http://www.puckalytics.com.

Do estimated zone entries represent a talent and is it a useful talent?

The good news is that at both the team and player level, ZEFR and our estimated Zone Entry metric each seem to be measuring a repeatable skill. Neither one is quite as persistent as shot attempts per 60 minutes, but given the limited sample sizes available (after all, we're only looking at the part of the game between a successful clear and the next shot attempt), these metrics show enough internal repeatability to indicate that what we're measuring is probably a product of a player or team's talent.

When it comes to predicting future goals, however, Corsi is still king[171]. While eZEFR/60 does show some predictive power, as Parnass's results indicated, it's not quite as powerful as simply knowing a team or player's shot attempts per 60 minutes on the power play. It is, however, better than knowing their goals scored per 60 minutes, which is promising at least.

In a way, this all makes perfect sense – zone entries only make up a limited portion of each power play, and so to expect them to be better at predicting future results than data taken from the entirety of the power play wouldn't make sense. We know that zone entries are important, and our data confirms that measuring them does have some value, but measuring them can't take the place of a metric that looks at the entirety of the power play.

Beyond just predicting future goals, however, the usefulness of a metric like this comes from the fact that it's able to measure a specific skill-set – knowing which players are best at entering the zone can help you decide who should play on what unit, or who to put out for a draw after you've given up a shorthanded chance. It provides a more nuanced view of a player's skill-set, and allows a coach or GM to better setup their lineup to take advantage of these skills.

What's the best way to enter the zone?

Ever since Eric Tulsky first published his zone entry work in 2012[172], analysts have constantly driven home the importance of carrying the puck into the zone and avoid dump-ins at 5-on-5. On the power play, however, he found something different – dumping the puck in had more utility on the man advantage, as the extra man provided a boost in puck recovery[173]. The question is whether that extra utility is enough to recommend a dump-in over a controlled carry.

Parnass took Tulsky's zone entry work one step further in his Special Teams project, breaking down controlled entries by the type of control that the player had when they entered the zone. His work found that while dump-ins and chips had the highest success rates (as Tulsky's work showed), controlled entries were still preferable.

171Corsi is another term for shot attempts.

172Eric Tulsky, "Zone Entries: Introduction to a Unique Tracking Project", *NHL Numbers,* June 20, 2012, Web, http://nhlnumbers.com/2012/6/20/zone-entries-introduction-to-a-unique-tracking-project.

173Eric Tulsky, "Zone Entries: What Drives Power Play Success?", *Broad Street Hockey,* May 22, 2011, Web, https://www.broadstreethockey.com/2011/5/22/2178537/zone-entries-what-drives-power-play-success.

Neutral zone drop passes prior to the entry and individual carries from one blue line to the next generated the most shot attempts following an entry, a key measure of entry success[174]. On the flip side, the least effective entry types were longer passes in general, with those going into the middle or across the entirety of the ice being the worst. The most obvious takeaway from that data is that teams don't need to force the puck away from the puck carrier if they don't have to, as long passes and dumps/chips tend to result in fewer shot attempts than carries and short drops.

The last way a team can improve their zone entry rate is by using four forwards on the power play[175]. Forwards, in general, are better at generating controlled entries than defencemen are, and so it only stands to reason that adding an extra forward will increase the likelihood of a controlled entry. Looking at the zone entry data tracked by Corey Sznajder in the 2013–14 season confirms this, as four-forward units generated a controlled entry on a significantly higher proportion of their controlled entries than three-forward groups did.

Table 14: Power play zone entry success by lineup, 2013–14[176]

Deployment	Controlled	Dump-In	Failed
Three forwards, two defencemen	52.4%	37.7%	9.4%
Four forwards, one defenceman	60.4%	29.6%	9.3%

Unfortunately, the limited data that we have on zone entries prevents us from knowing too much more about what tactical choices drive zone entry success on the power play. But with the proliferation of video and/or manual tracking projects, our knowledge of which strategies lead to success when entering the zone on the man advantage is certain to grow as we get bigger samples and better data.

Closing Thoughts

The ideas presented above provide a high level overview of what we think we know about the power play within the analytics community. While they can give general guidelines on how a team could improve their systems or structure, or how a skater could improve their play, there are many hidden variables that we don't yet have the ability to measure which have a significant impact on the results we observe.

As we start to get better data, whether it's from manual tracking or automated video systems, our ability to evaluate power play performance will also improve. Knowing the exact route that the puck takes before an opportunity will help us get a better view of the value of pre-shot movement, and knowing player locations will give us a greater ability to identify which

---

174 Arik Parnass, "Which Specific Zone Entry Types are Most Successful?", *Special Teams Project,* March 7, 2016, Web, http://www.nhlspecialteams.com/blog/2016/3/5/which-specific-zone-entry-types-are-most-successful.

175 Matt Cane, "Second Units and Zone Entries: Why teams should go all-in on the 4 forward power play", *Puck++,* March 7, 2017, Web, https://puckplusplus.com/2017/03/07/second-units-and-zone-entries-why-teams-should-go-all-in-on-the-4-forward-power-play/.

176 Acknowledgement: Data provided privately by Corey Sznajder.

formations and structures lead to chances most often.

While we wait for tracking data, however, we can still continue to improve our knowledge of the power play. Finding ways to get more detailed insights out of the data that's already publicly available (for example, by estimating zone entries as we did in this chapter) is one way amateur analysts can continue to drive the field forward. As we start to slice the game into thinner pieces we can find more specific skill-sets that will allow coaches to better design strategies and tactics to take advantage of those abilities.

Ultimately, the power play is a blend of raw ability and tactical decisions or systems that coaches implement. To quote Parnass one last time, "The core tenets of hockey special teams more closely resemble football than they do even strength hockey, and yet the product we observe during man advantages is nowhere near the structured, polished, well-defined package we get when we watch Aaron Rodgers drop back in the pocket.[177]" This balance of structure and creativity provides both challenges and opportunities for the field of analytics. Teams that are able to dig deep into the data to find even marginal edges could see those gains accumulate into significant advantages over the course of multiple years.

[177]Arik Parnass, "ZEFR Rate: A New and Better Way to Evaluate Power Plays", *Hockey Graphs,* April 18, 2016, Web, https://hockey-graphs.com/2016/04/18/zefr-rate-a-new-and-better-way-to-evaluate-power-plays/.

Who is the Best Clutch Scorer?

By Charles Mousseau

The tension, though palpable all game, is now unbearable. Fans sit nervously at the edge of their seats, be those seats in the arena or in their own homes. The action is paused, as athletes adjust and readjust with clockwork precision in the eyes of the storm. Hours have passed, but have been all but forgotten in favour of a moment. This moment.

And make no mistake about it, sports are built on such moments.

No matter what gear you play with, no matter if there's a running clock, no matter how many players are on your team — or if you even have teammates at all! — the balance of the game will almost certain come down to one pivotal moment.

This is true of all sports, and hockey is no exception.

The players fidget nervously, chatting quietly to one another, before they finally line up in formation. Maybe the crowd's cheers kick into second gear, maybe they are replaced by a hushed silence; either way, emotions are high. The game, maybe even the series, maybe even the championship, hangs in the balance.

Everyone that has played hockey — or even *watched* hockey — remembers this feeling all too well. And because we remember the feeling so strongly, we remember the heroes that are generated in such moments. Paul Henderson all alone in front of the Russian net, cementing Canada's reputation as a world hockey power with a flick of the wrist. Marie-Philip Poulin's overtime goal that sparked such a celebration among Canadian media that even they became international sensations. Bill Barilko winning the Stanley Cup for the Toronto Maple Leafs with an overtime goal to end the finals; as did Bobby Orr for the Boston Bruins, Patrick Kane for the Chicago Blackhawks, and fourteen other players in NHL history.

As a result of the emotional impact such moments have, it becomes very easy to over-emphasize those high-stakes, winner-takes-all moments and potentially cloud our view of a player's ability as a clutch performer. After all, those who gave former Montreal Canadians centre Brian Savage the sarcastic nickname of "Mr. October" were undoubtedly thinking of his one goal in 23 playoff games with Montreal, not his 155 goals in 461 regular season games during that span. On the other hand, former Washington Capitals forward John Druce's legendary run in the 1989–90 Stanley Cup playoffs — 14 goals in 15 games! — has cemented his reputation with over two decades of Capitals fans as the name brand of "clutch performance", despite his only scoring three other playoff goals in the span of his 11-year career.

Indeed, even before those big championship moments or the small sample of playoff games that lead up to them, there are still 82 regular season games to be played along the way; plenty of opportunities for players to show that they bring their best when the game is on the line. And while there are plenty of different ways that fans can measure who the best overall performers are throughout the season as a whole, here's an opportunity to ask ourselves just who the best players where when the chips were down.

To answer that, it's time to start exploring ways in which we can measure clutch performances, and there's no better place to start than the work of two legends in the history of hockey analytics: Stan and Shirley Fischler.

Breakaway From The Pack, Out Into The Open

"Breakaway '86: The Hockey Almanac" was a revolutionary and ambitious undertaking, aspiring to be no less that the hockey version of *The Bill James Baseball Abstract*. Before the introduction is over, the authors have already opened fire on the much-maligned plus-minus statistic and suggested a revolutionary new way to keep track of player points; before the first page with any information about the actual 1985–86 season, readers are already treated to an attempt to compare offensive performances across different eras ("scoring equivalents") by factoring in the average number of goals scored.

There are countless other innovations and insights in this work, which rightly belongs on any hockey fan's bookshelf for historical and nostalgic reasons alike, yet throughout this work and the three volumes that came after it, we find the one common theme that should be familiar to any student of hockey analytics: not all events are created equal.

Of course, in standard NHL player scoring, all events are created equal — each goal is worth one point, each assist is worth one point. However, player points in Breakaway were weighted depending on the actual score in the game at the time the goal was scored, with the following criteria:

Weighted Value of Points Based on Game Score[178]

Scoring Type	Value
Go-Ahead Goal (GAG)	2
Game-Typing Goal (GTG)	2
Insurance Goal (IG)	1.5
Proximity Goal (PG)[179]	1.5
All Other Goals (OG)	1
All Assists (A)	0.5

Revisiting this methodology and applying it to the past three regular seasons (2014–15, 2015–16, and 2016–17) gives us the scoring leaders using 'Fischler Points' (FPTS), which gives us the following slightly different list of leading scorers, as follows:

178Stan and Shirley Fischler, "Breakaway '86: The Hockey Almanac", 1986, pgs 9-10.
179A promixity goal is one that brings the score to within one goal.

Top 30 NHL Leading Scorers, Using Fischler Points, 2014–15 to 2016-17[180]

Player	Team	GP	GAG	GTG	IG	PG	OG	A	NHL PTS	NHL Rank	FPTS
Alex Ovechkin	WSH	242	46	31	31	10	18	85	221	8	276.0
Sidney Crosby	PIT	232	41	17	21	8	21	150	258	2	255.5
Vladimir Tarasenko	STL	239	48	21	20	11	16	106	222	5	253.5
Patrick Kane	CHI	225	36	15	22	3	31	152	259	1	246.5
Jamie Benn	DAL	241	31	17	26	6	22	143	245	3	237.5
Joe Pavelski	S.J	245	36	19	25	9	15	112	216	10	232.0
John Tavares	NYI	237	31	17	21	5	25	123	222	6	221.5
Nikita Kucherov	T.B	233	33	12	22	11	21	117	216	11	219.0
Tyler Seguin	DAL	225	28	15	20	14	19	126	222	7	219.0
Brad Marchand	BOS	234	45	18	15	8	14	88	188	26	218.5
Max Pacioretty	MTL	243	38	16	21	6	21	96	198	17	217.5
Evgeni Malkin	PIT	188	29	20	14	11	14	112	200	16	205.5
Blake Wheeler	WPG	243	30	12	14	11	11	135	213	12	200.0
Filip Forsberg	NSH	246	32	19	14	8	17	95	185	27	199.5
Brent Burns	S.J	246	34	14	5	12	8	138	211	13	198.5
Wayne Simmonds	PHI	238	32	19	23	8	9	73	164	43	194.0
Jeff Carter	L.A	241	22	19	18	7	18	106	190	24	190.5
Corey Perry	ANA	231	37	17	9	6	17	84	170	37	189.5
Sean Monahan	CGY	244	30	14	14	7	20	98	183	29	188.5
Jonathan Toews	CHI	233	39	10	16	3	9	105	182	30	188.0
Mark Scheifele	WPG	232	23	15	19	10	9	116	192	21	186.5
Mike Hoffman	OTT	231	28	17	14	11	12	86	168	39	182.5
Johnny Gaudreau	CGY	231	24	9	15	9	15	131	203	15	182.5
Patrice Bergeron	BOS	240	36	10	14	6	10	100	176	34	182.0
Jeff Skinner	CAR	238	29	29	14	4	7	62	145	83	181.0
Nicklas Backstrom	WSH	239	14	10	16	3	18	173	234	4	181.0
Cam Atkinson	CBJ	241	34	15	21	3	11	71	155	61	180.5
Phil Kessel	PIT	246	25	13	16	3	17	116	190	25	179.5
Steven Stamkos	T.B	176	32	12	19	5	20	68	156	56	178.0
Erik Karlsson	OTT	241	19	12	14	5	4	165	219	9	177.0

At first glance, the list provides some very surprising conclusions; Jeff Skinner of the Carolina Hurricanes rises from 83rd in league scoring to 25th overall, and Cam Atkinson of the Columbus Blue Jackets rises from 27th to 61st; conversely, Nicklas Backstrom of the Washington Capitals falls from 4th to 26th overall, while Anaheim Ducks forward Ryan Getzlaf and Ryan Johansen of the Nashville Predators fall out of the top 30 entirely (going from 14th and 22nd to 38th and 54th respectively).

However, a quick review of the NHL scoring stats of these players should bring a glaring issue to light:

180Acknowledgement: Data from the NHL, http://www.nhl.com.

Player	Team	G	A	NHL Rank	FPTS Rank	Change
Jeff Skinner	Carolina	83	62	83	25	58
Cam Atkinson	Columbus	84	71	61	27	34
Nicklas Backstrom	Washington	61	173	4	26	-22
Ryan Getzlaf	Anaheim	53	153	14	38	-24
Ryan Johansen	Nashville	54	138	22	54	-32

Looking at these players that had the most significant change in ranking, we see that the players with the largest upward movement had the majority of their points come from goals, whereas those that had the largest downward movement had the majority of their points coming from assists. This would suggest that this scoring system's ability to measure clutch performance was being outweighed by a more significant bias against assists and for goals of any kind.

To test this hypothesis, let's expand our view to include not just these outliers, but the top 100 NHL scoring forwards for the 2016–17 season. For each of these players, we will measure the percentage of their NHL point totals that was generated by assists, and compare that to the change in their Fischler Point totals.

The following chart shows where each of the top 100 NHL scorers lies with their assist percentage, relative to the increase in their point totals when switching from NHL points to Fischler Points.

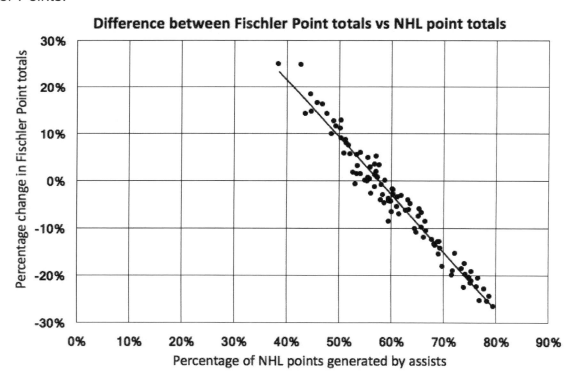

Difference between Fischler Point totals vs NHL point totals

(y-axis: Percentage change in Fischler Point totals; x-axis: Percentage of NHL points generated by assists)

181Acknowledgement: Data from the NHL, http://www.nhl.com.

The R-squared value[182] of over 96% indicates an extremely strong correlation between the two, to the point where the assist percentage appears to completely dominate. This leads us to one of two obvious antidotes: either remove assists from the calculations entirely, or include them in the standard NHL point totals and give them equal value as goals (as per the NHL) but apply our 'clutch' weighting to both of those equally. In the course of refining the process, we will look at both solutions.

The first refinement is an obvious one: take the current Fischler Point model and apply it only to goals scored, and then see who had the largest jumps in goal point totals scored. There is one wrinkle to consider first, however, and that is inflation. After all, with goals now ranging between 1.0 and 2.0 points in value (instead of 1.0 across the board), virtually every player that scored a goal will show an increase in their point totals, even if they were less 'clutch' than the average player. Even if it's just for aesthetics, it would be useful to have a positive value represent an increase and a negative value represent a decrease.

So, we need to total up all of the goals by type, multiply the total goals by their weight, and from here, we can see the average point value of a goal. The figures are as follows:

Total Goals by Fischler Type, 2016–17[183]

Goal Type	Number	Percentage	Weight	Points
Go-ahead Goal	6,977	35.21%	2.0	13,954.0
Tying Goal	3,663	18.48%	2.0	7,326.0
Insurance Goal	3,659	18.46%	1.5	5,488.5
Proximity Goal	1,693	8.54%	1.5	2,539.5
Other Goal	3,826	19.31%	1.0	3,826.0
Totals	*19,818*	*100.00%*		*33,134.0*

Dividing the total new number of points by the number of goals gives us an average point value of 1.6719 points per goal, so we'll divide our new goal point totals by this value to accommodate for inflation, giving us the adjusted Fischler Point goal totals (FPG Adj). This way, anyone with more Fischler Points from goals than standard NHL goal points will have made an above-average 'clutch' contribution, with a negative difference representing a below-average contribution. To measure the latter, we will look at the percent increase between the FPG Adjusted totals and the NHL goal totals.

Goal Totals with Fischler Adjusted Point Values, 2014–15 to 2016-17[184]

Player	Team	GP	GAG	GTG	IG	PG	OG	G	FPG Adj	Change
Alex Ovechkin	Washington	242	46	31	31	10	18	136	139.66	2.69%
Vladimir Tarasenko	St. Louis	239	48	21	20	11	16	116	119.92	3.38%
Sidney Crosby	Pittsburgh	232	41	17	21	8	21	108	107.96	-0.04%
Joe Pavelski	San Jose	245	36	19	25	9	15	104	105.27	1.22%

182R Squared is a statistical method of determining how closely related two sets of numbers are, based on the average distance between points on a chart like this.
183Acknowledgement: Data from the NHL, http://www.nhl.com.
184Acknowledgement: Data from the NHL, http://www.nhl.com.

Brad Marchand	Boston	234	45	18	15	8	14	100	104.37	4.37%
Patrick Kane	Chicago	225	36	15	22	3	31	107	101.98	-4.69%
Max Pacioretty	Montreal	243	38	16	21	6	21	102	101.38	-0.61%
Jamie Benn	Dallas	241	31	17	26	6	22	102	99.29	-2.66%
Nikita Kucherov	Tampa Bay	233	33	12	22	11	21	99	96.00	-3.03%
John Tavares	NY Islanders	237	31	17	21	5	25	99	95.70	-3.33%
Wayne Simmonds	Philadelphia	238	32	19	23	8	9	91	94.20	3.52%
Tyler Seguin	Dallas	225	28	15	20	14	19	96	93.31	-2.81%
Filip Forsberg	Nashville	246	32	19	14	8	17	90	90.91	1.02%
Jeff Skinner	Carolina	238	29	29	14	4	7	83	89.72	8.09%
Evgeni Malkin	Pittsburgh	188	29	20	14	11	14	88	89.42	1.61%
Corey Perry	Anaheim	231	37	17	9	6	17	86	88.22	2.58%
Cam Atkinson	Columbus	241	34	15	21	3	11	84	86.73	3.25%
Steven Stamkos	Tampa Bay	176	32	12	19	5	20	88	86.13	-2.13%
Mike Hoffman	Ottawa	231	28	17	14	11	12	82	83.44	1.75%
Sean Monahan	Calgary	244	30	14	14	7	20	85	83.44	-1.84%
Jeff Carter	Los Angeles	241	22	19	18	7	18	84	82.24	-2.09%
Jonathan Toews	Chicago	233	39	10	16	3	9	77	81.05	5.25%
Brandon Saad	Columbus	242	27	18	16	8	9	78	80.75	3.52%
Blake Wheeler	Winnipeg	243	30	12	14	11	11	78	79.25	1.60%
Rick Nash	NY Rangers	206	35	10	10	6	18	79	78.95	-0.06%
Patrice Bergeron	Boston	240	36	10	14	6	10	76	78.95	3.88%
Tomas Tatar	Detroit	245	25	18	15	8	9	75	77.46	3.28%
Brent Burns	San Jose	246	34	14	5	12	8	73	77.46	6.11%
Anders Lee	NY Islanders	237	30	17	13	3	11	74	77.16	4.27%
Mark Scheifele	Winnipeg	232	23	15	19	10	9	76	76.86	1.13%

Although the new rankings still look fairly close to the original rankings, the percent change categories already reveal a couple of insights that we may have missed earlier. For instance, we might have expected Carolina Hurricanes forward Jeff Skinner to lose ground once we adjusted for his high-goal, low-assist distribution, but he is still well in the pack, and with good reason. He might not have garnered the best reputation as a clutch performer with standard NHL statistics, with only 15 game-winning goals and one overtime goal, but we can see that of his 83 goals, an impressive 58 of them either tied the game or gave his team the lead, tied with Sidney Crosby for third in the league. As a result, his scoring increased 8.09% under the Fischler Point system.

However, the system is still strongly dominated by the raw number of goals scored. After all, over 19% of all goals scored are counted as "other" goals, which we estimate to not have much effect on the game at all. An easy next step would be to simply remove these goals and only look at those which had a close impact on the game, the goals for which we have assigned more than one point to.

At the More Hockey Stats website, the author has taken this idea and gone a step further – only goals that tie or win the game count, with emphasis for those that win the game in overtime; the criteria used are as follows:

More Hockey Stats (MHS) Goal Weighting[185]

Scoring Type	Value
Overtime Goal (OTG)	2.5
Game-Winning Goal (GWG)[186]	1.5
Late Game-Winning Goal (LGWG)[187]	2
Game-Tying Goal (GTG)[188]	1
Late Game-Tying Goal (LGTG)[189]	1.5

Using this new methodology, and adding up the point totals for players between the 2014–15 and 2016–17 seasons, we get a top 30 clutch performer result as follows:

Clutch Performance Results, Using MHS Weightings, 2014–15 to 2016–17[190]

Player	Team	OTG	LGWG	GWG	LGTG	GTG	Rating	FPG Rank
Alex Ovechkin	Washington	4	1	16	1	5	42.5	1
Vladimir Tarasenko	St. Louis	7	0	10	2	5	40.5	2
Jonathan Toews	Chicago	7	3	8	1	2	39	22
Brad Marchand	Boston	6	1	7	2	8	38.5	5
Max Pacioretty	Montreal	4	1	12	2	2	35	7
Jeff Carter	Los Angeles	7	0	7	2	4	35	21
Corey Perry	Anaheim	1	0	14	3	7	35	16
Filip Forsberg	Nashville	3	0	12	2	6	34.5	13
Sidney Crosby	Pittsburgh	4	1	8	2	6	33	3
Sean Monahan	Calgary	6	0	7	0	7	32.5	20
Evgeni Malkin	Pittsburgh	4	0	8	1	9	32.5	15
Brayden Schenn	Philadelphia	3	2	8	3	4	32	43
Marian Hossa	Chicago	4	3	5	3	2	30	83
Johnny Gaudreau	Calgary	4	0	10	1	3	29.5	41
Daniel Sedin	Vancouver	5	0	8	0	5	29.5	59
James Neal	Nashville	3	1	6	3	6	29	32
Nikita Kucherov	Tampa Bay	2	2	8	1	6	28.5	9
Cam Atkinson	Columbus	4	0	7	2	5	28.5	17
Patrick Kane	Chicago	2	0	12	1	3	27.5	6
Wayne Simmonds	Philadelphia	1	0	10	2	7	27.5	11
Kyle Turris	Ottawa	4	1	6	1	5	27.5	47
Rickard Rakell	Anaheim	3	1	6	2	5	26.5	55
Anders Lee	NY Islanders	0	2	10	3	3	26.5	29
Joe Pavelski	San Jose	1	2	10	1	3	26	4
Oliver Ekman-Larsson	Arizona	6	0	4	0	5	26	79
Tyler Johnson	Tampa Bay	4	0	8	0	4	26	71
Claude Giroux	Philadelphia	6	0	2	0	7	25	66

185Acknowledgement: Weightings from More Hockey Stats, http://www.morehockeystats.com/players/clutch.
186Here, a game-winning goal is only counted if it is the last goal to be scored in the game
187A game-winning goal as above, but one scored in the last three minutes of regulation.
188Here, a game-tying goal is only counted if it is the last or second-last goal to be scored in the game.
189A game-tying goal as above, but one scored in the last three minutes of the game.
190Acknowledgement: Data from MoreHockeyStats, http://www.morehockeystats.com/players/clutch.

Brent Burns	San Jose	5	0	6	0	3	24.5	28
Jakub Voracek	Philadelphia	6	1	1	0	6	24.5	112
Mikael Backlund	Calgary	5	1	6	0	1	24.5	99

Now, we're starting to see some significant shake-up in our ranking system. Players such as Marian Hossa of the Chicago Black Hawks, Mikael Backlund of the Calgary Flames, and Philadelphia Flyers forward Jakub Voracek have all risen from rankings outside the top 80 and into the top 30 positions; the latter two in particular on the strength of their overtime goals, which account for almost half of all their 'clutch' moments. And when we think about what our analysis is supposed to represent, it does stand to reason that such goals *should* factor in very heavily – enough so that a player like Voracek (with two more overtime goals yet 84 less goals overall!) should get recognized.

On the other hand, players such as Jeff Skinner have fallen completely off the radar, and that's not entirely fair either. After all, scoring a goal that gets your team the lead (or ties the game) *does* have a significant impact on your winning chances; the whole notion of 'score effects' in analytics is proof positive that you did impact the game at the time, even if other players have scored for both teams in the later minutes.

One might also quibble about the weighting, which takes some very large jumps at discrete boundaries. Right now, a game-winning goal that is scored at 60:01 is worth 2.5 points, yet a game winning goal scored at 56:59 is only worth 60% as much, even though obtaining a one-goal lead at both points has very close to the same impact (more on that later) on your winning chances. Naturally, any such weighting will be arbitrary to a degree, but if we're sticking to the concept that a clutch performance is one that most impacts your probability of victory, we have a simple solution ahead of us that deals with both of the above issues: win probabilities.

What are the odds of that?

Being a mathematician is one of those industries where it's very difficult to discuss what you do in a social setting, if only because people will be quick to ask you how likely something is to happen. It's like how doctors oh-so-often have their "yes, I'm a doctor" met with "yeah? I got this pain right in my side here, what do you suppose it is?"; once they find out you're a "numbers type", *especially* one with an interest in sports, you can count on being asked what the chances are of such-and-such a team making the playoffs, or winning the draft lottery, or especially, what are their chances of winning a game currently in progress.

The development of such "win probability equations" have been one of the most accessible advances in analytics in recent years, and a very practically useful one indeed. Everything from changes in mindsets on when to pull your goaltender for a sixth skater[191] to refining just exactly when to change to a more defensive system, can now be guided much more precisely

---

[191] Though he seemed outrageous at the time, and was often ridiculed by analysts and commentary teams, Patrick Roy will undoubtedly go down as a coaching visionary with regards to pulling the goaltender for a sixth attacker.

with a quick and easy way to convert "time on the clock" and "current score" to a percentage chance to win.

Of course, such an accessible calculation also fuels fan interest, who can now get instantaneous feedback that's fairly reliable to measure just how big a change was made in their team's winning chances after a given event on the ice.

And, as it works out for us here, this is a perfect fit for our definition of a clutch goal. Rather than weighting goals by one of a few, arbitrarily chosen amounts, we can weight them by the actual extent to which they increased a team's chance of winning.

The RinkStats webpage is where Stephen Pettigrew, a research and data consultant with the MIT Election Data and Science Lab, turns his significant actuarial and computational prowess towards the world of sports. Here, he has laid out the groundwork for his NHL Win Probability Metric[192], and while the calculations go extremely in-depth, a preliminary step in his research presents that are a perfect fit for our needs: continuous plots that show the relationship to the current lead and time left on the clock, to the leading team's chances of victory.

After factoring out the home-ice advantage displayed in tied games, we can examine the curves in the Pettigrew's charts to generate some formulas for each goal differential, that give us a probability of victory between zero and one.

In the formulas below, y refers to the probability (from 0 to 1) that the leading team will win, and x refers to the proportion of the clock that has expired; for instance, halfway through the game, x = 0.5; with six minutes left in regulation, x = 0.9, and so forth. Math alert!

- Four or more goals ahead: $y = 1.0$
- Three goals ahead: $y = -0.0370x^3 + 0.0551x^2 + 0.0905x + 0.8947$
- Two goals ahead: $y = 0.0622x^3 + 0.0319x^2 + 0.1031x + 0.8074$
- One goal ahead: $y = 0.5984x^3 - 0.3759x^2 + 0.0921x + 0.6763$
- Tie game: $y = 0.5$

In all cases, we insure that y is never less than 0.0 and never greater than 1.0. For example, here's how the chart looks for a one-goal lead, and the two-goal lead, all based on Pettigrew's formula.

192Stephen Pettigrew, "Win Probabilities Metric, 1.0", *Rink Stats,* March 24, 2014, Web, http://rinkstats.com/2014/03/win-probabilities-metric-10.

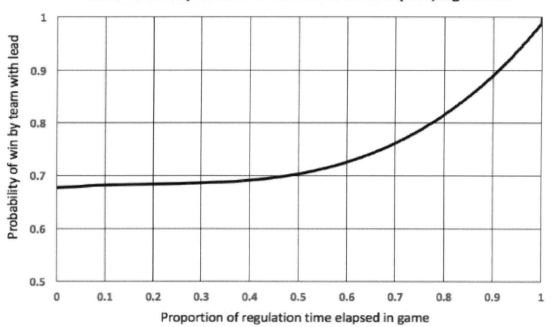

Win Probability relative to fraction of time elapsed, 1 goal lead

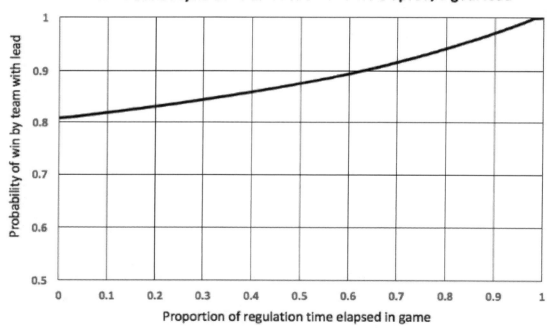

Win Probability relative to fraction of time elapsed, 2 goal lead

Next, as we did with the Fischler Point goals, we will want to determine the average weighting of a goal during our time frame so that we can normalize the results; we'd like a goal with a weighting of 1.0 to be average 'clutch', and once again, have an adjusted goal point total above an NHL goal point total reflect an above-average clutch player.

Summing all the Weighted Goal Points (WGP) over all players for the three given seasons gives us 8507.82; compared to 19,818 goals gives us a factor of 2.3294 to normalize the results. Doing so gives us the following (and final) leading clutch performer table:

Clutch Performance Results, Using Weighted Goal Points, 2014–15 to 2016–17[193]

Player	Team	GP	WG PTS	WGP Adj	G	Change	NHL Rank
Alex Ovechkin	Washington	242	61.10	142.32	136	4.65%	8
Vladimir Tarasenko	St. Louis	239	53.37	124.32	116	7.17%	5
Brad Marchand	Boston	234	48.21	112.30	100	12.30%	26
Sidney Crosby	Pittsburgh	232	45.53	106.05	108	-1.80%	2
Joe Pavelski	San Jose	245	45.26	105.42	104	1.37%	10
Jeff Skinner	Carolina	238	45.03	104.89	83	26.37%	83
Max Pacioretty	Montreal	243	43.30	100.87	102	-1.11%	17
Wayne Simmonds	Philadelphia	238	42.27	98.47	91	8.21%	43
Corey Perry	Anaheim	231	41.93	97.67	86	13.57%	37
Patrick Kane	Chicago	225	41.15	95.85	107	-10.42%	1
Filip Forsberg	Nashville	246	41.00	95.51	90	6.12%	27
Evgeni Malkin	Pittsburgh	188	39.44	91.87	88	4.39%	16
Jamie Benn	Dallas	241	39.05	90.97	102	-10.82%	3
Cam Atkinson	Columbus	241	38.50	89.67	84	6.75%	61
Anders Lee	NY Islanders	237	38.01	88.53	74	19.64%	133
John Tavares	NY Islanders	237	37.78	88.01	99	-11.10%	6
Nikita Kucherov	Tampa Bay	233	37.09	86.40	99	-12.73%	11
Tyler Seguin	Dallas	225	36.89	85.93	96	-10.49%	7
Mike Hoffman	Ottawa	231	36.80	85.72	82	4.54%	39
Jonathan Toews	Chicago	233	36.65	85.37	77	10.87%	30
Brandon Saad	Columbus	242	36.46	84.93	78	8.88%	54
Steven Stamkos	Tampa Bay	176	36.30	84.55	88	-3.93%	56
Brent Burns	San Jose	246	35.90	83.63	73	14.56%	13
Patrice Bergeron	Boston	240	35.77	83.32	76	9.63%	34
Chris Kreider	NY Rangers	234	35.43	82.54	70	17.91%	93
Tomas Tatar	Detroit	245	35.31	82.24	75	9.65%	76
Rick Nash	NY Rangers	206	35.09	81.73	79	3.46%	90
Sean Monahan	Calgary	244	34.49	80.35	85	-5.47%	29
James Neal	Nashville	219	33.92	79.01	76	3.97%	115
Zach Parise	Minnesota	213	33.35	77.68	77	0.88%	55

While Alexander Ovechkin of the Washington Capitals still leads the pack in Weighted Goal points, it's pretty clear given his relatively small change in points, that he's simply had more of these clutch goals simply as a function of having so many more goals. Certainly not a player who wilts when the chips are down, but saying that Ovechkin is the best clutch performer is a little bit like saying your favourite hold'em hand is pocket aces; it might be the correct answer but it seems awfully trivial all the same.

193Acknowledgement: Data from MoreHockeyStats, http://www.morehockeystats.com/players/clutch.

So, based on the tables we've explored here, I'm going to give the nod for "best clutch shooter" to Jeff Skinner of the Carolina Hurricanes. As we saw when examining the Fischler Point totals, a very large proportion of Skinner's goals have come during the most important times on the score clock, and his substantial gains with the Weighted Goal system (second overall among players with 150 or more games played and at least 30 goals, behind only Jay Beagle of the Washington Capitals) suggest that they also came late enough to have a very large impact on his team's win probability.

Honourable mention goes to Anders Lee of the New York Islanders, who showed a very large 19.64% gain and jumped a staggering 118 spots up to 15th place. He, too, had a majority of goals (47 of 74) in either game-tying or go-ahead situations, which was reflected in his 19.64% change in goal point totals.

A second honourable mention, and this one for all of those on the leaderboard: for the three seasons between 2014–15 and 2016–17, all of the top thirty players stayed with the same team. While it may be just coincidental timing related to the fact that all of these players are consistent producers likely to be signed to long term contracts, it also stands to reason that players capable of producing steadily *and* producing during the most important times of the game have an attribute desired by general managers and coaches alike.

Closing Thoughts

Though we have reached the end of our voyage for now, there's definitely lots more room to improve on this model. Micah McCurdy of HockeyViz[194] has taken the win probability curves to the next level, not only factoring in the lead and the time but also the manpower situation and the absolute score, while also measuring by expected value of points (which approaches 1.5 in tied games but 1.0 in lopsided games) rather than just win probability.

One could also find a way to factor in assists, though if we're talking "clutch" we'd absolutely have to find a sufficient way to weight the primary assist, or even better, find a way to determine if the assist mattered at all.

Most intriguing of all would be an idea to weight the goals not just by time on the clock, but by current team standings. Surely a clutch goal to break a tie would matter much more in a game where a playoff spot hangs in the balance?

More research could also be done into the validity and the nature of the statistic itself being measured. While I feel quite confident that our final findings show us exactly the players that *have* been putting up clutch performances, does this statistic have any value in helping us predict what players *will* put up such performances in future seasons? My instinct is that any attempt to measure clutch performance won't have the best predictive value. After all, high-variance events in small sample sizes really give the endeavour sort of a "catching lightning in a bottle" feeling. Players like the 1989–90 John Druce not only come out of the blue, but they

---

194Micah Blake McCurdy, "Leverage", *Hockey Viz*, August 5, 2016, Web, http://hockeyviz.com/txt/leverage.

rarely come back a second time.

Even if there was some predictive value, we would also have to ask ourselves if this is due to anything inherent in the player, or just an effect of playing on strong teams that are almost always in the game and giving such players maximum opportunity to get those big-impact moments. This might be very difficult to measure; as we've seen, these players aren't exactly changing their address on a regular basis.

– NOW HIRING

Maybe you, the reader, have other ideas on how this concept could be improved? I'd love to hear from you, and we could possibly cover those ideas and more in a future edition. Or, maybe you take umbrage with my decision on who the best clutch performer was? I'd love to hear from you about that as well.

But in the meantime, and in-between time, that's it for another chapter of the *Hockey Abstract.* Thanks for reading!

Why Do Rebuilds Fail?

The Failed Rebuild of the Edmonton Oilers and What the Vegas Golden Knights Can Learn From It

By Allan "Lowetide" Mitchell, TSN 1260 Edmonton

The NHL welcomed a brand-new franchise this offseason, the Vegas Golden Knights, who are getting a very good set of expansion rules plus preferable treatment at the entry draft. A team like Vegas has all kinds of options as a startup group, plus they are not bogged down with years of bad signings and poor tradition.

It might be enlightening for an organization like the Golden Knights to search out a team that has made classic mistakes that have cost their organization in order to avoid them. The cost of bad decisions in the hockey department can have massive impact everywhere, including the bottom line.

In my view, the Edmonton Oilers might be the best team to learn from, as the club has made a plethora of errors and then repeated them in order to show a classic pattern. Rebuilds followed by offer sheets followed by managerial change followed by six coaching changes in seven years, Edmonton's decisions post-2006 read like a how-to guide for wastage.

If the Vegas Golden Knights can avoid these issues, chances are that success will come before the excitement and goodwill of expansion fades. I'm going to look at three major areas:
- Role of ownership
- Developing talent
- Procurement and its importance

Role of Ownership

In the early days of 2010, so the story goes, Edmonton Oilers owner Daryl Katz, less than two full years on the job and a rookie owner, suggested a rebuild[195]. Oilers management adopted the owner's plan, and soon went about the business of starting over. If the team had allowed a fan or ticket holder in the room, reaction may have been more vigorous, but that is conjecture.

In my view, the Edmonton Oilers had already been rebuilding, from the moment the club traded Chris Pronger in the summer of 2006. When a pro sports team rebuilds the rebuild, that team is in real trouble. So it was for the Edmonton Oilers, whose first 15 years of business this century may prove to be a cautionary tale for the rest of time.

There are several elements in the story of Edmonton's lost decade, and many lessons that a new team like the Vegas Golden Knights can learn from the Oilers' experience. Over the next few pages, we'll touch on procurement, development, and the high cost of offloading veterans for unproven prospects and draft picks. There's a lot to share over a decade.

The one major factor in all of this is the maturation of Katz. He began his tenure as owner with a great deal of power and an aggressive attitude, and things went predictably. It wasn't until Katz hired Bob Nicholson in June of 2014[196] and appeared to gradually back away from impacting decisions that the organization began to adjust, turning itself from the Glen Sather structure of the 1980's NHL to the massive machine required to run an NHL organization in this century.

Procurement: Mistakes at the Draft Table

Despite winning five Stanley Cups since entering the NHL in 1979, the Edmonton Oilers have had long periods of draft failures. Although the club had an historic run of success from 1979 to 1983, the late 80's and early 90's featured something close to abject failure. A lot of the problems encountered by the Oilers since the fall of 1991 have come from poor drafting.

195Need a citation.
196Jonathan Wilis, "Edmonton Oilers name Bob Nicholson CEO, expand his powers in all areas", *Edmonton Journal,* April 20, 2015, Web, http://edmontonjournal.com/sports/hockey/nhl/cult-of-hockey/edmonton-oilers-name-bob-nicholson-ceo-expand-his-powers-in-all-areas.

An example: In 2002, the Oilers chose Finnish center Jesse Niinimaki at No. 15 overall, despite the fact he had been rated by Central Scouting as the No. 50 European skater[197]. A reasonable estimate for the point in which the 50th rated Euro skater goes off the board? Fifth round.

The Oilers were prone to reach at the draft during the early portion of this century, and it cost them. By around 2000, NHL teams were getting some really good "industry intel" which culminated in Bob McKenzie's final ranking lists for TSN each season. McKenzie, probably the most respected hockey media source on all sides, polled scouts and scouting directors to come up with a consensus list that would number 50 or more.

For the Vegas Golden Knights and the team's management, it showed during their first trip to the entry draft, scouting available players and making those picks count is central to future success. If you look at the draft by general manager George McPhee, and compare the picks to Bob McKenzie's 2017 ranking, it's clear Vegas has already figured out major elements of procurement success.

Vegas Golden Knights Draft Picks, and Bob McKenzie's Rankings[198]

Overall	Pos	Player	McKenzie Rank
6	C	Cody Glass	8
13	C	Nick Suzuki	12
15	D	Erik Brannstrom	29
34	D	Nicolas Hague	25
62	C	Jake Leschyshyn	61
65	RW	Jonas Rondberg	80
96	G	Maksim Zhukov	64
127	RW	Lukas Elvenes	58

Vegas drafted eight of McKenzie's top 93, in what can only be described as a fantastic haul. The Golden Knights' attention to the draft won't pay off this fall, but there is outstanding talent on this list. There is a great deal of position repetition, but centre and defence are vital areas for any hockey team. The Golden Knights delivered a virtuoso performance in the team's first draft, something many other teams have not been able to deliver, despite similar draft boards and opportunities.

Steve Kournianos from The Draft Analyst gave the Vegas draft an "A" in his team-by-team grading, and pointed to the quality and quantity delivered.

"The NHL newbies had 12 picks in their inaugural draft, including three in the first round, so some might say they were almost a lock to get a good grade, especially since the front

197 Acknowledgement: Central Scouting rankins from the Draft Analyst, http://www.thedraftanalyst.com/rankings/year-to-year-central-scouting-rankings/2002-3/2002-csb-final-eur-skaters/.

198 Acknowledgement: Draft results from Hockey Reference, https://www.hockey-reference.com/draft/NHL_2017_entry.html, and Bob McKenzie's draft rankings from TSN, http://www.tsn.ca/kchow-template-100-1.778987.

office is starting with a clean slate. But the smart guys in Vegas clearly did their homework, grabbing in the first round two of the best CHL centers in Cody Glass (Ranked No. 14) and Nick Suzuki (Ranked No. 26) as well as phenomenal puck distributor LHD Erik Brannstrom (Ranked No. 12). They added another potential first-pairing defender in towering LHD Nicolas Hague (Ranked No. 20), and collected a bunch of two-way forwards with top-six upside in C Jake Leschyshyn (Ranked No. 89), Danish RW Jonas Rondbjerg (Ranked No. 66) and Swede C/W Lucas Elvenes (Ranked No. 95). Overage C Jack Dugan (NR) was a kid I didn't think was worthy of a draft nod, but he's got size and playmaking ability. His first year on a deep Chicago squad in the USHL and a commitment to Providence should reveal how he handles legit competition. The Golden Knights in the later rounds added a pair of centers with decent potential – Niagara's Ben Jones (Ranked No. 207) and OJHL top prospect C Nick Campoli (Ranked No. 253), while snatching up two of my top-20 goalies in Maksim Zhukov (Ranked No. 7-G) and Jiri Patera (Ranked No. 19-G) tells me the guys running the show in Vegas were blessed with big brains."
- Steve Kournianos, the Draft Analyst[199]

Vegas has a long way to go, including a designated AHL farm team, but the early results are very good. It's especially interesting to see the Golden Knights add so many picks for the 2018 draft, suggesting we may see a double or triple set of drafts like year one. That would be an excellent way to jump start a new franchise.

College Procurement

The Stanley Cup Final in 2017 saw the Pittsburgh Penguins defeat the Nashville Predators. One of the key elements of success for both teams was quality and depth, gained partly through college procurement. The Penguins deployed college men drafted by the team (Brian Dumoulin, Jake Guentzel, Brian Rust, Tom Kuhnhackl, Scott Wilson and Josh Archibald), but also benefited from a group of college men signed as undrafted free agents. Conor Sheary, Carter Rowney and Chad Ruhwedel all played a role in Pittsburgh's success, basically giving the club an extra pipeline of talent not fully exploited by many other teams.

Bringing the conversation back to the Oilers, since the arrival of Peter Chiarelli, the organization has utilized the college program. Previous to Chiarelli's arrival from Boston, the Oilers did engage in signing college free agents, but not at the top level. The summer of 2016 changed all that, when Matt Benning and Drake Caggiula both signed with Edmonton. Top flight free agents from all quarters have been rare sights in Edmonton since the days of Gretzky and Messier, and certainly in the modern era of free agency. The addition of Caggiula and Benning gave Edmonton instant depth in areas of need and further enabled the team to compete through injuries and slumps.

For Vegas, being a destination for college free agents may take some time. However, it's also true the team can offer graduating free agents quick ascension through a system that will barely exist in the first couple of seasons.

199Steve Kournianos, "Draft Report Cards", *The Draft Analyst,* July 4, 2017, Web, http://www.thedraftanalyst.com/2017-nhl-draft/2017-nhl-draft-report-cards/.

Developing Talent: The First Signs of Trouble

When the EIG (Edmonton Investors Group) stepped in to purchase the Edmonton Oilers in 1998[200], the entire city breathed a giant sigh of relief. The Hail Mary worked, and the Oilers would remain. The EIG brought in a mountain of issues of their own however, and that would have tremendous impact. It was a large and unwieldy group, and there were numerous cash calls in the early days[201]. Despite the best of intentions, and tremendous work by the group, many corners were cut, as I'll try to explain.

One of the main areas the EIG moved away from was the AHL team. Most teams have a dedicated AHL affiliate, but Edmonton "shared" their players for a couple of years during the early part of the decade, and that had a major impact on development. Most of the draft picks from 2002 to 2004 spent time on other team's affiliates, which resulted in playing lesser roles than their age and ability warranted. That kind of negligence impacts the NHL parent team in the years that follow, and the Oilers paid a big price. Among first-round picks from 2002 to 2004, only Devan Dubnyk, a goalie, progressed in what might be described as typical fashion. Jesse Niinimaki, Marc-Antoine Pouliot and Rob Schremp never established themselves as NHL players, and their meandering minor league careers during important development years are part of their stories.

How did that impact the Oilers later in the decade? Well, going back to 1990, in the days after the club won Stanley Cup No. 5, the prevailing issue for the organization has been procurement. The 1990 draft featured no players drafted by the Oilers who played in an NHL game. None. Zero games.

In 2001, the club found a gem in Ales Hemsky, who quickly developed as a substantial offensive player, and had a major role in the team's 2005–06 run to the Stanley Cup Final. In the following years, the club's inability to build on Hemsky's progress (Edmonton drafted Niinimaki in 2002, Pouliot in 2003, and Schremp in 2004, along with Dubnyk[202]) limited the team's ability to continually produce young talent, a vital part of team success. The next first-round pick after Hemsky to enjoy NHL productivity was Andrew Cogliano, who was chosen in 2005, and didn't spend a day in the minor leagues. Whatever the sins of the NHL team, the draft and development side fell down badly in the early portion of this century.

As for their development system, Walt Kyle and Morey Gare were the team's minor league coaches back in the 1999–00 season, and the Hamilton Bulldogs were developing talent at a rapid rate. Among the men on that team who developed into useful NHL players were Daniel Cleary (who finished with 938 NHL games), Jason Chimera (still going, has played in 1,033

---

200 John Zazula, "From the Archives, March 13, 1998: Oilers to stay in Edmonton after deal struck", *CBC News,* March 16, 2017, Web, http://www.cbc.ca/news/canada/edmonton/throwback-thursday-edmonton-oilers-stay-1.4028105.

201 Need a citation.

202 Acknowledgement: Draft information here and throughout this chapter is from Hockey-Reference, https://www.hockey-reference.com/draft/NHL_2004_entry.html.

regular-season games in the league) and Dan Lacouture (337 NHL games[203]); all spent considerable time in the world's best league. If we use that as a line in the sand (three NHL players) for a single minor league season, and make some stops later in the decade, what do we see?

In the final year before the EIG decided against a minor league team of its own, the 2004–05 Edmonton Roadrunners spent the entire season not scoring goals (just 201). However, that club produced an enormous number of actual NHL players: Jarret Stoll (872 NHL games), Kyle Brodziak (766 games and still going), Raffi Torres (635 games), Toby Petersen (398, although many came before 2005–06) and Brad Winchester (390). It should be mentioned that 2004–05 was the lockout season, so names like Stoll and Torres would have been in the NHL if things remained normal. These names formed a big part of the team that would surprise the hockey world the following season by going to Game 7 of the 2006 Stanley Cup Final. After that, the EIG decided to loan players to other AHL teams, all of whom had parent teams they would super serve. The results? Predictable.

So, does a shared team work for the lesser parent club? No. In 2005–06, fans had to search long and hard to find the team's top prospects. Here is a list of the team's top prospects in the spring of 2005, and where they spent the following season[204]:

1. **Marc Antoine Pouliot**. Spent the majority of the season on a shared AHL team in Hamilton. Both Montreal and Edmonton sent their best, Pouliot performed well (finished third in team scoring, behind two Habs prospects) in a second-line role. Also spent his first eight games in the NHL that season. He would stall out at 192 NHL games, despite being a first-round pick. Injuries impacted his career.

2. **Jeff Drouin-Deslauriers**. Played a backup role with the Hamilton team, behind Yann Danis and Jaroslav Halak (Habs prospect). Deslauriers did not have a good season, struggled the following year before finding solid footing. Would eventually play in 62 NHL games.

3. **Matt Greene.** Spent half a season (his first in pro) with the Iowa Stars of the AHL, before getting the call to Edmonton. His minor league experience was minimal.

4. **Kyle Brodziak.** He didn't make the Hamilton Bulldogs squad, instead posting an impressive season with the Iowa Stars on loan. Brodziak would play his first 10 NHL games with the Oilers during the campaign.

5. **JF Jacques.** This might have been the high water mark for Jacques, who scored 24 goals with the Hamilton Bulldogs alongside Pouliot. Jacques would finish with 166 NHL games.

6. **Brad Winchester.** After a season with the Toronto Roadrunners and then the Edmonton Roadrunners, Winchester posted 40 points in 40 games before making it to the NHL. He would finish with 390 NHL games.

203Acknowledgement: NHL games played data is from NHL.com, http://www.nhl.com.
204Acknowledgement: NHL games played data is from NHL.com, http://www.nhl.com.

7. **Zack Stortini.** Split his time between the Iowa Stars and Milwaukee Admirals. Stortini would catch on with Craig MacTavish as a fourth-line role player and dressed for 257 games in the NHL.

8. **Mathieu Roy.** Performed well on the Hamilton Bulldogs defence, got into one game in the NHL that season, 66 games overall.

9. **Jani Rita.** Spent the entire season with the Oilers as a part-time player, before heading to Pittsburgh at the trade deadline.

10. **Danny Syvret.** New pro caught on with the Hamilton Bulldogs and played well in a support role. He would see the NHL for 10 games in 2005–06, 59 games overall.

The big misses from this era were Pouliot (listed) and Schremp, who would come along one year later. The lack of a designated minor-league team likely impacted more than just those men, but injuries and other factors would certainly have to be considered. Dubnyk, Brodziak, and Greene, who arrived in pro hockey basically NHL-ready, were the only success stories.

But the lack of a dedicated affiliate team was not the only problem. Even when the Oilers finally went back to a designated farm team (the Springfield Falcons in 2007–08), the development of players continued to stagnate under coach Kelly Buchberger. Along with Pouliot and Schremp, players who had some promise (but did not develop) included Theo Peckham, Colin McDonald, and Jacques. From the Fall of 2007 through to 2010 (and the team's move to Oklahoma City to become the Barons), Edmonton's prospects either skipped development and arrived in the NHL soon after turning pro (Greene, Cogliano, Sam Gagner) or had a difficult time making progress (Alex Plante, Taylor Chorney).

Once the team arrived in Oklahoma City, the Barons appeared to revert to a more traditional development format. Coach Todd Nelson found a role for Colin McDonald (who scored 42 goals) and Linus Omark (a brilliant skill winger), and new pros like Teemu Hartikainen and Jeff Petry all flourished.

What was the price of cutting corners? Looking back, a case for slow development can certainly be made. Prospects who spent time in Iowa, Pennsylvania, and Ontario playing without affiliation suffered due to lack of time in a feature role. It makes sense on the face of it, these men were never going to be given special treatment by an organization who had other priorities.

The quality of coaching once the team got to Springfield may also have contributed to the stagnation of all this talent. Kelly Buchberger's coaching history began in 2007, and he was dispatched to an NHL's assistant role in the following season. Claude Julien or Todd Nelson may have been a better choice, with years of experience at the AHL level helping the process. Perhaps there are two recommendations for the new Vegas team from the Oilers' minor league experience: Put a dedicated minor league team in place at the earliest possible moment, and make sure you have a coach who is experienced in development of young hockey players 20 to 23 years old.

Stay On Course

Perhaps an even more important area for the Golden Knights to learn from Edmonton's years of misery: Stay on course! The best way for me to describe what happened to Edmonton is through two specific transactions, both famous hockey moments.

After the Oilers lost Game 7 of the Stanley Cup Final in 2006, Chris Pronger's trade request became public[205]. That put the team in a very weak spot and general manager Kevin Lowe made a fateful decision: He would acquire young assets.

In July of 2006, Chris Pronger was dealt to the Anaheim Ducks for youngsters Joffrey Lupul, Ladislav Smid and the draft picks that would turn into Nick Ross, Jordan Eberle and Travis Hamonic[206]. That's the kind of deal that signals rebuild, especially considering the defence it left coach Craig MacTavish to work with that Fall. In reading those names, it's clear there was a lot of talent coming over, but that it wouldn't be useful at the NHL level for some time. For example, Eberle made his NHL debut four years later, in the fall of 2010.

In the summer of 2007, general manager Lowe signed free agent Sheldon Souray[207] and then signed an offer sheet contract with Thomas Vanek of the Buffalo Sabres[208]. Buffalo matched, so Lowe made a different offer sheet, this time to Dustin Penner of the Anaheim Ducks[209]. Brian Burke, general manager of the Ducks, did not match (but he hollered a lot[210]) and so Edmonton gave up a first, second, and third-round selection.

- Tyler Myers, now at 473 regular season NHL games and counting[211]
- Justin Schultz, now at 344 regular season NHL games and counting
- Kirill Petrov, who is a productive player in the KHL

Rebuilding isn't a bad idea in and of itself, but Lowe had signed a bunch of veterans from his successful team and the focus was supposed to be getting back to the Stanley Cup Final. It never happened. Edmonton would not remain patient and undergo a quick rebuild, instead flushing youth in an effort to get back to the postseason as soon as possible.

The Pronger trade juxtaposed against the Penner offer sheet borders on farce. Why would an

205Original sportsnet article unavailable, but reproduced here:
   http://www.leafsforever.ca/index.php?/topic/12823-pronger-demands-trade/.
206CBC Sports, "Pronger traded to Anaheim", *CBC Sports,* July 3, 2006, Web,
   http://www.cbc.ca/sports/hockey/pronger-traded-to-anaheim-1.583044.
207CBC Sports, "Sheldon Souray signs with Oilers", *CBC Sports,* July 12, 2007, Web,
   http://www.cbc.ca/sports/hockey/sheldon-souray-signs-with-oilers-1.653799.
208Associated Press, "Sabres draw the line, match Oilers offer sheet for Vanek", *ESPN,* July 8, 2007, Web,
   http://www.espn.com/nhl/news/story?id=2927805.
209NHL.com, "Ducks decline offer sheet, Dustin Penner signs with Edmonton", *NHL.com,* August 2, 2007, Web,
   https://www.nhl.com/news/ducks-decline-offer-sheet-dustin-penner-signs-with-edmonton/c-335590.
210CBC Sports, "Angry Burke blasts fellow GM Lowe", *CBC Sports,* July 28, 2007, Web,
   http://www.cbc.ca/sports/hockey/angry-burke-blasts-fellow-gm-lowe-1.634868.
211Acknowledgement: NHL games played data is from NHL.com, http://www.nhl.com.

organization trade their best player for futures, and then do such a quick turn the following summer? Start as you mean to go, Vegas!

THE RELOCATING GAME

"SO, COYOTES, WHO'S IT GOING TO BE? BACHELOR NUMBER 1 OR BACHELOR NUMBER 2?"

Closing Thoughts

The Vegas Golden Knights will make their share of mistakes, and can learn good and bad from all organizations. The fact the team doesn't have an AHL team in year one gives them something in common with the Edmonton Oilers of one decade ago. The development results are there for Vegas to interpret and offers an idea about the massive challenge of putting together a feeder team out of nothing.

The Golden Knights can overcome many challenges of an expansion team by learning from Edmonton's mistakes. Here is a to-do list:

1. Make sure ownership appreciates the importance of a minor league system. Things can turn on a dime if the owner gets impatient. George McPhee has a huge job to do with the Vegas Golden Knights. Even if ownership is supportive, expecting a significant playoff run before 2022 might be unrealistic.

2. Hire a minor-league coach with experience. Hiring Kelly Buchberger in and of itself

can't be blamed for specific prospect failure, but Oilers prospects were more successful under Claude Julien and Todd Nelson, and part of that probably had to do with experience in coaching at that level.

3. Make sure the first AHL team (2018–19) is well stocked with actual prospects who are pushing for NHL jobs. The Oilers signed a plethora of "tweener" forwards this summer in free agency. Players like Ty Rattie, Mitch Callahan, and Brad Malone are there to replace the prospects who should have been drafted in 2014 and 2015. Edmonton traded away those picks, and Vegas can learn from that mistake.

4. Procure quality talent for the minor league team via draft and college free agency. Some teams are so good at this (Pittsburgh, San Jose, Anaheim, Dallas), others can't seem to attract college and minor league free agents, or the best Europeans coming over to play the following season. Some of it may have to do with location, but Las Vegas should be very attractive for free agents. A college player graduating next spring (2018) might see a fast-track option in the Golden Knights. The team's weakest positions will be obvious by then, and righty defenders and scoring forwards may flock to the desert.

5. Draft well. Quality drafting is vital to success, and there are no shortcuts. Vegas had a fantastic first draft, and if they can do it two more times, and remain patient in development, then established teams will lose ground in a big way starting in 2020.

6. Stay the course! There are no shortcuts, but there are templates. The 1972–73 New York Islanders were truly awful, winning 12 games in their first season, 19 the second year and then 33 in year three. That third year, the Islanders made the playoffs, making it to round three four of five years, but never farther. During those years, Bill Torrey kept building, brick by brick. When the Islanders broke through, they won four Stanley Cups in a row, a splendid example of building.

As for the Edmonton Oilers, there appears to be real progress in many of these areas. The AHL team is now in Bakersfield, and has produced some talent (Oscar Klefbom, Anton Slepyshev, and Jujhar Khaira are either established at the NHL level or working on it) to fit needs for the NHL team. However, when Peter Chiarelli took over as general manager in 2015[212], he traded away multiple draft picks in order to acquire Griffin Reinhart[213], Cam Talbot[214], Eric Gryba[215] and others for the NHL team. Added to a disastrous 2012 draft, a slow-developing 2013 draft and a curious 2014 edition, and Chiarelli's trades at the 2015 entry draft have Edmonton trying to catch up.

212 Jesse Campigotto, "Oilers hire Peter Chiarelli as president, GM", *CBC Sports,* April 23, 2015, Web, http://www.cbc.ca/sports/hockey/nhl/oilers-hire-peter-chiarelli-as-president-gm-1.3046815.

213 Dan Rosen, "Islanders trade defenseman Reinhart to Oilers", *NHL.com,* June 26, 2016, Web, https://www.nhl.com/news/islanders-trade-defenseman-reinhart-to-oilers/c-772442.

214 Doug Harrison, "Cam Talbot traded to Oilers by Rangers for three picks", *CBC Sports,* June 27, 2015, Web, http://www.cbc.ca/sports/hockey/nhl/cam-talbot-traded-to-oilers-by-rangers-for-3-picks-1.3130365.

215 Luke Fox, "Senators trade defenceman Eric Gryba to Edmonton", *Sportsnet,* June 27, 2015, Web, http://www.sportsnet.ca/hockey/nhl/eric-gryba-trade-edmonton-oilers-ottawa-senators-draft-pick-travis-ewanyk/.

That's a tough thing for the organization to do, as Connor McDavid's impact is going to put the team in contention for the Pacific Division crown for the next decade. The Oilers will be drafting between 21-31 for the foreseeable future, meaning Jesse Puljujarvi needs to turn out in a big way. He'll be the last lottery pick for Edmonton, a fair result considering the 2015 lottery win.

What Does Hockey Analytics and Artificial Intelligence Have In Common?

By Helmut Neher and David A. Clausi, University of Waterloo[216]

The title of this chapter presents a modern take on hockey analytics. If there is one word that describes the application of artificial intelligence (AI) to hockey analytics – from a hockey fan, academic, and pro analyst perspective – is joy. In the context of hockey analytics, capturing stats by hand is tedious. If there was some method to automatically extract data from viewing games and then extracting information to analyze players and their performance, this method would be the Holy Grail working flow of analysts.

Now this may seem like a stretch – some of you may be wondering what is AI and how can AI be in hockey anyway – but this chapter will show you how AI can bring joy to analysts by taking out the monotony of data collection in an analyst's life and explain a recent breakthrough in AI in a hockey application. Let's talk about hockey first.

The Everyday Working Analyst

Before mentioning AI, if there are only a few words that an everyday working analyst finds excitement and happiness in it would be the words results, data, stats and 'Toronto-Maple-Leafs-Winning-The-Stanley-Cup'. Other than the latter word (yes, it is a word, a compound word), the joy comes from the use of molding the statistics and values to form something into a work of art; the process of manipulating data is similar to a potter molding pottery. The process of collecting data on your own accord, however, is tedious and not very pleasant. Getting that data is important regardless if no one likes collecting the data because data is necessary for analysts to implement complicated statistics or methods for evaluating player performance. Player evaluation is important for scouts, coaches, and players alike because player evaluation analyzes talent, aids a coach in determining how a player can best fit in the team's style of play, and can also help the players themselves by identifying areas of improvement.

Currently, there are two methods of extracting data: scraping data from the Internet for leagues where such data exists and live capturing of data as necessity for any other games. We will focus on discussing live capturing as a means of collecting data because it is universal; scouts, analysts, and coaches from every league can analyze a player by simply watching their performance, noting their own statistics, or analyzing a player visually.

216Based on the original paper by Helmut Neher, Mehrnaz Fani, David A. Clausi, Alexander Wong, John Zelek. Fani is at Shiraz University, the other authors are at University of Waterloo.

- IN-GAME ADVANCED STATS -

The process of collecting data through live capturing is similar to a root canal; the process isn't enjoyable, but once it is over, the benefits are numerous. When analyzing players, collecting data necessary to analyze is tedious and painstakingly tough, however manipulating the data is the more enjoyable task. Analysts today need to both find/scrape data while also manipulate and mold the data and stats to get results.

Mike Toth's excellent article in *Hockey Now* entitled "The Modern Age of Hockey Scouting" presents how writing down stats and analyzing players using game video are time consuming[217]. Toth quotes Dennis MacInnis as he discussed stats: "It's tough when you go to a tournament and you've got 16 teams playing on three different ice surfaces." MacInnis is quoted again mentioning visual game viewing analysis describing how meticulous visual game viewing analysis needs to be: "You need multiple viewings of a kid to determine their work ethic, compete level and passion for the game." In other words, to effectively evaluate a

---

217Mike Toth, "The Modern Age of Hockey Scouting", *Hockey Now,* January 28, 2016, Web, http://hockeynow.ca/major-junior/the-modern-age-of-hockey-scouting.

player's performance, a lot of time is needed. Analysts would be able to capture stats and evaluate a single player. The challenge is to capture multiple players over multiple games in a shorter amount of time. Another challenge is being able to evaluate team performance which also involves collecting loads of data i.e., each player on the ice needs their actions inferred and their locations known.

Another inherent problem during data collection is errors. As humans, we are prone to errors, whether we jotted a stat incorrectly or misidentified the performance of a player via visual inspection. How can we circumvent problems such as human error and time to evaluate players? Or rather, how can we make stat collecting more enjoyable? How about to simply not do it? I think it is obvious to say that not doing something that is painful increases happiness. In fact, today's technology is beginning to have the capability to help hockey scouts, coaches, and fans to evaluate player performance by automatically collecting data from game video. Computers would essentially need to act like a scout, which means that new technologies and new developments in the field of artificial intelligence (AI) offer tantalizing approaches for automatic hockey analytics.

Tech Behind the Tech

AI refers to the ability for computers to reason and perform tasks that require some form of intelligence. The field of artificial intelligence is the study of understanding intelligent entities by striving to build those intelligent entities[218]. Now when talking about AI, one might wonder what are the capabilities of artificial intelligence, or rather, what can AI do? The answer is lots.

AI is a rapidly growing field used in many applications (e.g., stock market analysis, self-driving cars, product recommendation, etc.). You may be surprised at how much AI is already in consumer products we use regularly. For example, when you shop online at Amazon, AI is used show you recommended products that you may want to buy. If you watch Netflix, the top picks recommended to you are what an AI thinks matches your preferences[219].

Even in recent new articles, AI is frequently described or noted. One recent news article headlines, 'Google's AlphaGo AI defeats world Go number one Ke Jie', showing that an AI can beat the best competitor in the one of the most, if not the most, complicated board game ever developed[220]. Another headline asks the question if AI will be used as service to sell to companies in need of AI[221]. If you would like to know more about trends in artificial intelligence, Stanford University invited leading innovators in the field to be part of a study called the One Hundred Year Study on Artificial Intelligence to study and anticipate the effects of AI in every aspect of life. A recent report entitled Artificial Intelligence and Life in 2030 was

218Russell and Peter Norvig, "Artificial Intelligence: A Modern Approach", ISBN 0-13-103805-2
219Kyle Russell, "Netflix is Training its Recommendation System by Using Amazon's Cloude to Mimic the Human Brain", *Business Insider,* February 11, 2014, Web, http://www.businessinsider.com/netflix-using-ai-to-suggest-better-films-2014-2.
220Sam Byford, "Google's AlphaGo AI defeats world Go number one Ke Jie", *The Verge,* May 23, 2017, Web, https://www.theverge.com/2017/5/23/15679110/go-alphago-ke-jie-match-google-deepmind-ai-2017.
221Danny Vena, "Will AI-as-a-Service be the Next Evolution of AI?", *Motley Fool,* June 21, 2017, Web, https://www.fool.com/investing/2017/06/21/will-ai-as-a-service-be-the-next-evolution-of-ai.aspx.

recently published and it highlights important trends of AI[222].

Artificial intelligence refers to how a computer learns patterns based on information the computer receives. Inspired by the human brain, artificial intelligence mimics the decision process of a human brain. Within a brain, there are over a billion neurons, the basic building block. Neurons in the brain are each connected to other neurons forming a complex network of neurons known as a neural network. The interactions and connections between each neuron are how people interpret their surroundings. As a person learns new concepts, neurons are strengthening themselves. Neurons receive input signals from sensory organs and combines this information to recognize patterns. This signal is finally used by our brain to make a decision. As mentioned before, in the brain, based on the strength of a neuron (its weight), and the inter-connections between neurons, a person can learn.

Therefore, to mimic the brain's learning mechanism, artificial neural networks (ANN), algorithms programmed in computer software, have been developed to mimic the capabilities of the human brain. Artificial neurons, as the name implies, are not biological cells within a brain, but rather a mathematical model describing how a biological neuron works. Artificial neurons are connected together and receive inputs and interact with other mathematical neurons.

A machine can be taught to learn in a manner similar to a human if the ANN is designed properly. It's taken decades of effort, but the ANNs today are more effective at mimicking the learning ability of a human.

For example, suppose we are explaining hockey to someone who has no prior knowledge of the sport. How would that person learn the game of hockey? The expert (which is you!) may first describe to a person the overall structure of a game. There would be references to goalies, nets, players with hockey sticks, and ice. However, how can someone with no knowledge even understand hockey with no experience? Through repetition and repeated examples of hockey a person will learn. The more examples, the more a person can infer how to play hockey. The learner will initially make mistakes of how hockey works, but eventually, a learner will adjust his/her way of thinking to correctly identify how to play hockey. Eventually, after some experience of watching game video, reading, and getting help from an avid hockey fan, a person can learn; in other words, a person learns by experience through repeated examples.

Much like the example with a person with no prior knowledge of hockey, ANN principles are the same way. A neural network learns through experience and repetition in order to identify a certain aspect in hockey. By using many data samples, a neural network will begin to learn.

The more data used, the better. The ANN first receives data that is already defined and the computer learns the patterns, or, in other words, is "training". Following training, computer scientists test the algorithm to see how it performs by using test data that is similar to the training data, except that the computer has not seen it previously.

222Peter Stone, et al. "Artificial Intelligence and Life in 2030." One Hundred Year Study on Artificial Intelligence: Report of the 2015-2016 Study Panel, Stanford University, Stanford, CA, September 2016, Web, http://ai100.stanford.edu/2016-report.

The Hockey Tech

In the context of hockey, how can AI help evaluate player performance? Although AI has been applied to many fields in the academic world, AI applied to hockey is in its infancy. Here at the University of Waterloo in the Vision and Image Processing (VIP) Research Lab, we have created a system to identify a hockey player's pose using AI[223].

Pose is defined as a person's posture; how a person sits, stands, and skates are poses. The computer learns pose by identifying joints (e.g., wrist, pelvis, knee, etc.). So, by learning the joints of a hockey player, the machine can infer associated limbs (arm, hand, foot, etc.) and interpret a person's pose.

We can use an ANN to interpret a hockey player's pose in a digital image. The ANN will first be trained by using images with poses already determined. After the ANN is trained, we will test the ANN using images that the ANN did not use for training.

The researchers trained an ANN and tested that network using 20 images. The 20 images are from players within the NHL. The researchers trained the artificial neural network to identify 16 body joints (limbs are inferred) as shown in Table 1.

Table 1: Body joints identified in the artificial neural network

Number	Body Joint
1	Right ankle
2	Right knee
3	Right hip
4	Left hip
5	Left knee
6	Left ankle
7	Pelvis
8	Thorax
9	Upper neck
10	Head top
11	Right wrist
12	Right elbow
13	Right shoulder
14	Left shoulder
15	Left elbow
16	Left wrist

For this research we used as a basis an existing algorithm known as the "stacked hourglass network[224]". This stacked hourglass network was trained using ordinary poses from a large set

223Note: The author's full paper can be found online here http://statsportsconsulting.com/main/wp-content/uploads/Neher_OTTHAC17_Final_Submission-1.pdf.
224Alejandro Newell, Kaiyu Yang, and Jia Deng, "Stacked Hourglass Networks for Human Pose estimation",

of images and then tested using hockey images that the AI has never seen before. Below are some images evaluated. The white lines on the image indicate where the ANN determined where the joints and limbs are located.

Figure 1. Left images shows how effective the ANN effectively determined a player's joints, while the right image shows an image of the ANN misidentifying joint location such as elbows and wrists[225].

Through visual inspection you can see that overall the AI can infer the pose of a hockey player fairly well, however, the AI does predict joints in wrong places. Generally, the ANN is able to identify big joints such as hips, shoulder, and pelvis, however, the ANN is not as effective locating smaller joints such as elbows and wrists.

Using a total of 20 still images of hockey players similar to the images above, we calculated the percentage of correctly identified joints in the following table (Table 2):

Table 2: Body joints identified in the artificial neural network

Joint	Accuracy of Detection
Head	90%
Shoulder	87.5%
Elbow	70%
Wrist	65%
Hip	80%
Knee	82.5%
Ankle	90%

European Conference for Computer Vision (ECCV), March 22, 2016, Web, https://arxiv.org/abs/1603.06937.
225Original images underneath the white overlay is Copyright 2006, USA Hockey Inc., and included in this form, and in this publication with their written consent.

Total	81.56%

The joints can be localized by their (x,y) coordinates in the image. The accuracy of joint locations is determined by comparing the actual joint locations we identified manually to the ANN determined joint locations and taking the average for each joint over the 20 images. Table 2 shows the accuracy for each joint obtained by the ANN.

The values from Table 2 shows how accurate the artificial neural network correctly identified each joint. If you compare the images shown previously with Table 2 you will see that the quantitative analysis explains the visual analysis (looking at the pictures). The ANN was more successful identifying heads, shoulders, and ankles than wrists and elbows. One reason why the elbow and wrist are more difficult to recognize is that these joints are difficult to isolate when they are close to and blend in with the body. Another possible reason is that the joints were hidden from view because of the viewpoint of the image. For example, the wrist may be difficult to identify because the actual wrist joint is hiding inside a glove.

Now obviously, we want to correctly identify each joint 100% of the time, however, these results are preliminary, and, to the best of our knowledge, they offer the first published pose detection for hockey players. An overall accuracy of 82% is exceptional given that we have yet to train on a full set of dedicated hockey images. This proof-of-concept offers a tantalizing start to full game tracking of player pose in hockey. A total percentage of 82% is really good in artificial neural network terms. The goal of this research was to determine how accurately we can identify pose. The goal is to improve accuracy as much as possible. Identifying the pose of a hockey player is the first step to evaluating player performance.

The above images are taken by a camera pointing at ice level. The next set of images demonstrates that this ANN can also learn from images taken from a broadcast video without any algorithm changes. This is not necessarily expected because the 2D image representation of the pose does change when the camera is at ice level or further up in the stands.

Figure 2. A few images showing how effective the ANN can identify joint locations using

broadcast video[226]

In this figure, the ANN is able to determine the pose of the hockey player using exactly the same algorithm applied to images from a broadcast video. Joints such as the wrist are still more difficult to identify. Notice that even when the ANN cannot 'see' the shoulders, it still is able to make a prediction on the limbs that are occluded.

The ANN was not modified in any way and we expect that we can improve the results of this testing by accommodating aspects of hockey. For example, by training the network using hockey images rather than normal pose images, the accuracy would be expected to improve. For those interested in understanding more of the technical details, our full paper is available online[227].

Where do we go from here?

Why did we choose pose as the approach to analyze player performance? There is an abundance of visual information in a hockey game video and having a means to automatically determine the pose of a player is far more efficient than manual and tedious data collection. At any point in a hockey game, we can easily get pose information from anywhere a fan can take a picture without an analyst lifting a finger.

Pose estimation itself is necessary, but not too exciting if you are an analyst because information still needs to be derived from the poses. By knowing a player's pose, we can then infer player actions such as skating, shooting, and passing. For example, we could determine whether a player is skating forwards or backwards, assess their speed, and also assess their speed transitioning from forwards to backwards (and backwards to forwards) and this can be done for all players on the ice. Knowing when and from where a shot has been taken will relieve the analyst from having to capture this manually. Completed passes can be captured automatically, something that is extremely tedious for a human to capture. Automated data capture will provide far more information than basic stats provided online via scraping.

By extracting images from broadcast video, one should be able to identify the pose of a player. In fact, to evaluate one pose of a hockey player from a single image, the AI identifies the pose within 1/3 of a second. Evaluating a hockey player that fast can provide a lot of data for analysts; we can capture vital information at every important play of the game.

An analyst can spend less time writing notes and evaluating one person by letting AI collect information about the players. Doing so will free up an analyst's time and will decrease the amount of time to evaluate multiple players significantly. By knowing the pose, we can extend pose information to get even more data that is beneficial to evaluating player performance such as the speed of a player, the technique, or the actions of a player. Pose estimation is a

---

226 Original images underneath the white overlay is Copyright 2006, USA Hockey Inc., and included in this form, and in this publication with their written consent.

227 Note: The author's full paper can be found online here http://statsportsconsulting.com/main/wp-content/uploads/Neher_OTTHAC17_Final_Submission-1.pdf.

gateway to extracting more data. To summarize, pose estimation extracts meaningful data from camera images for player evaluation. This makes analysts' lives easier by eliminating live game data capture, by allowing many games to be processed without a human viewing the game, and by allowing them to spend more time analyzing instead of collecting.

Closing Thoughts

To recap, we introduced a state-of-the-art AI method using an ANN to demonstrate a method to determine pose of a hockey player which can then be used to determine their actions. Overall, the system used for estimating the pose of a hockey player evaluated hockey images fairly accurately.

By obtaining a hockey player's pose, that information can then be used to obtain actions and subsequent performance of a player which analysts, coaches, and scouts can utilize to evaluate a hockey players based on their on-ice performance during games and practices. For example, we can see if their technique is repeatable and if their performance is quantitative. Intra- and inter- comparisons between players of the same team and different teams can be achieved. Ultimately, by adding an automated procedure to produce data for scouts and others, more information at a faster rate can be extracted for player evaluation.

Analyzing a player's actions will help scouts and coaches alike to understand player performance. Automatic data capturing from video through the use of AI will help the analysis to understand reaction and action patterns of a player, key indications about a player arises.

In future iterations of the project, we hope to use video rather than images to understand pose. We hope to be able to extract pose from video more accurately than still images given the temporal information in the video. As such, pose estimation can be captured as the broadcast game is progressing bringing exciting opportunities for between period assessments of players, teams, and strategies.

Look for AI to be incorporated into more sports. AI is starting to become popular for analyzing statistics, and extracting information just as we saw in this chapter. The idea behind AI in hockey is to get the AI to perform mundane, time consuming tasks so that analysts can skip the data collection part of analyzing data. By incorporating AI in an analysts' life, more time can be enjoyed analyzing hockey data.

Can We Predict Injuries?

Modeling The Probability and Severity of Man Games Lost Due to Injury in an NHL Season
By Jeremy Sylvain and Michael E. Schuckers, St. Lawrence University

The goal of this project is to estimate the probability of an injury to an NHL player, and with that information predict the severity of the injury. To do this we model the probability that players will be injured by their ice time and position and we use on-ice events as part of these models. This allows us to assess the distribution of injuries across a typical NHL team. Further, we model the expected amount of games lost when a player is injured. Our data covers multiple years of injury and time on ice data from *Man Games Lost*[228] and *Hockey Reference*[229]. Using predictions from our model, we can predict the impact of staying healthy on a typical NHL team.

For our analysis, we collected several variables potentially useful in predicting injuries for regular season games. These variables included; games played during the regular season, time on ice per game, games lost due to injury, hits a player recorded during the season, and the number of shots blocked in the season. The data was collected for several seasons to gather information about injury rates through the season.

To analyze injury likelihood, we built several regression models using the above variables. Separate models were built for forwards and for defencemen. Our approach is a two-stage one, we first modeled the probability that a given player would be injured in a given season. Next, we model the length of injury given that an injury occurred. From these models, we can gain an understanding of the impact of these factors on injuries in the NHL.

The main outcomes from this project are that we built models of injury risk in the NHL and from those we can identify factors that impact the probability and longevity of an injury.

Background

Among the many decisions that NHL coaches and general managers face, lineup adjustments due to injury is one of the most common. Injuries can not only plague an individual player; they can affect the outcome of a whole team's season. Traditionally the teams who have the most man games lost due to injury (MGL) are also the same teams that struggle to make or fail to make the playoffs each year. The correlation between injuries and a team's success throughout the season comes as no surprise as teams who lose players will continually call up players from their farm teams. For example, for the 2016–17 NHL season the correlation between the percent cap hit of injured players per game and team points per game was -0.31[230]. Thus, it is clear that injuries have an impact on team performance.

228Man Games Lost website is http://mangameslost.com.
229Hockey Reference website is http://hockey-reference.com.
230Thomas Crawshaw, "2016–17 NHL Injury Breakdown", *NHL Injury Viz,* October 25, 2016, Web,
http://nhlinjuryviz.blogspot.ca/2016/10/201617-team-injury-breakdowns.html.

Seeing the correlation between injuries and success of a team, it is important to understand and to model the probability of injury based on key factors of the game. The factors we will use include hits, blocked shots, and time on ice. The key is to use such variables to create a model that will indicate the importance of these factors and how they increase or decrease a player's probability of injury. Below we fit such a model to data from recent NHL seasons using data from *Hockey Reference* and *Man Games Lost*. This is done by position for both forwards and defencemen.

Having built a model for injury probability, we create a model based on the same key factors to predict the duration of the injury. The goal is that the model will be able to approximate the length of an injury given the level of hits, blocked shots, and time on ice an individual player faces. Here we can also estimate the value to the team the player has based on their contribution to the team.

By using this two-step process we can hope to calculate the expected man games lost by multiplying the predicted probability of injury to the predicted length of injury. We find that the primary driving factor for the chance a player is injured is the amount of time per game that a player is on the ice, while injury severity is driven by multiple factors, such as hits per game. These results are same for forwards and defencemen.

Data

In order to fit prediction models to injury data, we first obtained data on injuries in the NHL as well as some possible metrics that might impact potential for injury such as the number of hits a player carries out. To allow us to create stable estimates and validate our results, we used data from the seven NHL seasons between 2009–10 and 2015–16. Below we list the metrics that we focused on as being possible factors in the likelihood of a player being injured.

Table 1: List of variables and their abbreviations

Variable	Definition
INJ	Games a player lost due to injury
GP	Games played by a player
TOI.GM	Average time on ice played per game in all situations
HPG	Hits a player gives divided by games played
BPG	Shots a player blocks divided by games played
AGE	Age of player as if January 1st, of each season in years
AGE^2	Age of a player squared in years

We divided our data by position into forwards and defencemen (goalies are excluded from study) since we felt that forwards and defencemen were affected differently by the predictors in the models.

The data include regular season games, as well as all situations during a game. That is, we did not distinguish between time on ice during even strength or shorthanded and power play time on ice. Further, we removed any player whose games lost due to injury was 82, as we felt that they did not play in game during the season, therefore the injury did not occur in the current season. We also did the same thing in the 2012–13 season with games lost due to injury that were 48 as this was the length of the shortened season. We did not remove the 2012-13 season because we were looking at time on ice and not games played; we saw the minutes played during a game as a valuable addition to our analysis regardless of how many games were played in the season.

In total, we had 5,664 observations. Table 2 has the breakdown of players per season.

Table 2: Numerical Summaries of Injury Data by Season[231]

	2009–10	2010–11	2011–12	2012–13	2013–14	2014–15	2015–16
Number of Players	862	982	985	902	957	979	963
Percent of Players with INJ ≥ 1 GP	43.2%	49.1%	52.9%	40.2%	52.9%	51.5%	51.0%
Percent of Players with INJ ≥ 5 GP	31.6%	33.7%	38.0%	24.7%	38.1%	34.7%	34.5%
Percent of Players with INJ > 10 GP	18.7%	21.9%	21.5%	13.6%	22.2%	22.1%	21.4%
Average Games Missed for Injured Players	5.86	7.05	7.25	4.01	6.83	6.67	6.65
Median Games Missed for Injured Players	0	0	1	0	1	1	1

From the summaries in Table 2, we can see that approximately 20% of NHL players are injured for more than 10 games in a season. Similarly, the average games missed for each player was in the neighbourhood of six or seven games missed, and the median games missed was between zero and one. The larger magnitude of the mean number of games missed relative to the median number of games missed suggests that there is a long right tail on the distribution of games missed per player. We see exactly that in Figure 1, the histogram of games missed per player per season. Noteworthy among these results by season is the results for the 2012–13 shortened lockout season. During that campaign, the percent of significant injuries, those lasting more than 10 games, was fewer than the average games missed and was substantially lower.

231Acknowledgement: Raw injury and player data for these calculations came from *Man Games Lost* http://www.mangameslost.com and *Hockey Reference* http://www.hockey-reference.com.

Figure 1: Histogram of INJ, 2009–10 to 2015–16[232]

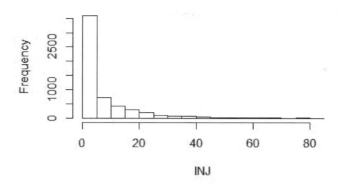

Analysis

In this section, we introduce our approaches for modeling NHL injury data. This will be done in two parts. For the probability of an injury, we use a logistic regression, and for length of the injury we use a log-linear regression model. We include hits per game (HPG) and blocks per game (BPG) in each model, as these involve collisions that may cause injury. Additionally, we include time on ice per game (TOI.GM) in our models to account for increased opportunities for injury. To account for increased injury susceptibility due to aging, we include both age in years (AGE) and a quadratic term age in years squared (AGE^2).

Injury Probability Model

The first model in our two-model process is the injury probability model. It predicts the probability of an injury based on the variables from the data.

To do this, we created an indicator variable (INJPROB=1 if injured, 0 otherwise). Using the indicator as a response, we created a logistic regression model predicting the probability of injury based on HPG, BPG, TOI.GM, AGE, and GP.

Equation 1
Logit(INJPROB)~HPG+BPG+TOI.GM+AGE+AGE^2

The model given in equation 1 was run for both forwards and defencemen for each season in the study, and then again run by position for all seasons combined. The model is set up in such a way that each variable should have a deleterious effect on the probability of injury.

232Acknowledgement: Raw injury and player data for these calculations came from *Man Games Lost* http://www.mangameslost.com and *Hockey Reference* http://www.hockey-reference.com.

That is, we anticipate each predictor to have a positive coefficient so as the variable increases, so does the likelihood of being injured throughout a regular season.

When a team starts to get into a comfortable spot towards the end of the season, coaches might make the decision to rest the players who might see a lot of ice time and who might be of verge of a long-term injury, or players who are sick and cannot play at their full potential. Such incidents get rolled into a game lost due to injury. Therefore, a player who might not have actually been injured during the course of an actual game played might record a game lost due to injury. To try to capture this possibility, we increased the response variable to the probability of missing at least five games (INJ≥5). We call this INJPROB5. We used the same factors that are found in Equation 1 for the model for this additional response. The results for this model can be viewed in Table 5.

Injury Severity Model

The second of the two models is used to model the severity of an injury, given that a player was injured based on the same variables from the injury probability model.

The model is based on a Poisson distribution, where the response variable (INJ) is modeled using a logarithmic link function. We do this so that we can model the severity of the injury, assuming that the player was injured during the season. The logarithmic link function used as the function is designed to handle count data, and the variable of interest here is the number of games missed due to injury (INJ). The Poisson model works for modeling the length of injuries.

Equation 2
Log(INJ)~HPG+BPG+TOI.GM+AGE+AGE^2

Like the injury probability model, we fit the model for each season of the data set separately, for forwards and for defencemen. Once again, we fit the model with all seasons still differentiated by position.

The two models are used together in such a way that gives us the probability of an injury predicted by certain levels for the data, then based on the same levels as the probability equation we can predict the severity of the injury given that the player was injured.

Results

We fit the Injury Probability and Injury Severity models given above for each season and for forwards and defencemen separately. The coefficients for our Injury Probability and Injury Severity Models by year can be found in Tables 3 to 8.

Starting with the Injury Probability model for forwards, we find that the most significant variable is TOI.GM, which was significant for all seasons. The remaining variables HPG, BPG, AGE, and AGE^2 were not consistently significant for forwards in this model. BPG was not significant for any of these seasons while HPG and AGE were significant in two seasons and one season, respectively.

A similar picture emerges for defencemen. The coefficient for TOI.GM is significant in all but one season (2012–13) while BPG is not significant in any of these models, and HPG and AGE are significant in at most two of the models. Thus, for both forwards and defencemen, the number of blocked shots per game and the number of hits per game are not significant predictors of a player missing more than one game.

Table 3: Coefficients and their Significance for the Injury Probability Model, Forwards[233]

Season	TOI.GM	HPG	BPG	AGE	AGE²
2009–10	0.1632	0.3137	-0.0113	0.3002	-0.0037
2010–11	0.1300	-0.1498	-0.4418	-0.0124	0.0017
2011–12	0.1255	-0.0333	-0.0980	0.2574	0.0034
2012–13	0.0919	0.0980	-0.0040	0.4798	-0.0070
2013–14	0.1783	0.1737	0.2649	0.2678	-0.0031
2014–15	0.2137	0.2580	0.3381	0.1840	-0.0014
2015–16	0.1826	-0.0584	0.0308	0.2026	-0.0026
All Seasons	0.1489	0.0767	0.0477	0.2358	-0.0028

Table 4: Coefficients and their Significance for the Injury Probability Model, Defencemen[234]

Season	TOI.GM	HPG	BPG	AGE	AGE²
2009–10	0.1129	0.3753	0.1259	0.4488	-0.0069
2010–11	0.1411	0.1660	-0.1334	0.1034	-0.0006
2011–12	0.1503	0.4184	0.1622	0.2756	-0.0029
2012–13	0.0455	-0.0513	0.4614	0.3657	-0.0051
2013–14	0.1355	0.4488	0.3376	-0.2547	0.0067
2014–15	0.1988	0.0543	0.1357	0.0002	0.0008
2015–16	0.1803	0.2656	-0.3823	0.7199	-0.0109
All Seasons	0.1363	0.2094	0.0647	0.2627	-0.0030

Turning to the Injury Severity Model, the estimates can be found in Table 4 and Table 5. The most significant factor in predicting the duration of an injury is split between AGE and AGE². Both variables are significant in all models. The AGE variable has a positive coefficient, meaning that the older a player gets, the larger the severity of their injury (in terms of games lost). AGE² is a very interesting variable. Not only is it statistically significant across all models, it also consistently has a negative coefficient. The negative coefficient implies that the more severe injuries happen to players that are in in the middle of their careers.

HPG is more frequently significant in the Injury Severity model, however some of the coefficients are negative (and significant), implying that more hits lead to a *smaller* severity of injury. A similar occurrence happens with BPG as well, where the variable is more frequently significant, but also some models have negative coefficients. As was the case in the Injury

233Acknowledgement: Raw injury and player data for these calculations came from *Man Games Lost* http://www.mangameslost.com and *Hockey Reference* http://www.hockey-reference.com.
234Acknowledgement: Raw injury and player data for these calculations came from *Man Games Lost* http://www.mangameslost.com and *Hockey Reference* http://www.hockey-reference.com.

Probability Model, average time on ice per game is a consistently significant predictor of injury severity.

Table 5: Coefficients and Their Significance for the Injury Severity Model, Forwards[235]

Season	TOI.GM	HPG	BPG	AGE	AGE²
2009–10	0.0733	0.1292	0.3738	0.3398	-0.0050
2010–11	0.0505	-0.1830	-0.5150	0.1950	-0.0022
2011–12	0.0599	0.0049	-0.6280	0.4974	-0.0079
2012–13	0.0361	0.0939	-0.6027	0.5072	-0.0073
2013–14	0.0438	0.0242	0.5464	0.2845	-0.0036
2014–15	0.0671	0.2467	-0.0513	0.2611	-0.0034
2015–16	-0.0048	-0.0750	0.0084	0.1722	-0.0016
All Seasons	0.0466	0.0325	-0.1300	0.2894	-0.0039

Table 6: Coefficients and Their Significance for the Injury Severity Model, Defencemen[236]

Season	TOI.GM	HPG	BPG	AGE	AGE²
2009–10	0.0872	0.0955	-0.3462	0.7850	-0.0124
2010–11	0.0436	-0.0188	-0.0255	0.3341	-0.0044
2011–12	0.0303	-0.2320	0.1862	0.4876	-0.0073
2012–13	-0.0005	0.1403	-0.1102	0.4976	-0.0082
2013–14	-0.0033	0.0906	0.2256	0.2533	-0.0028
2014–15	0.0155	0.0518	0.1205	-0.0930	0.0026
2015–16	-0.0487	0.2779	0.0237	0.2630	-0.0027
All Seasons	0.0190	0.0613	0.0071	0.3180	-0.0042

Moving on to the estimates in the probability model for predicting missing more than five games, Table 7 and Table 8, we see that TOI.GM became insignificant in all of the seasons across both models when you are predicting the probability of missing more than 5 games.

HPG became insignificant for the forwards in the model, and the defencemen only had one season where HPG were significant at predicting the probability of missing more than 5 games during a regular season.

Like the probability of missing at least one game, BPG was not significant at predicting the probability of an injury during any season, making it ineffective at predicting the probability of missing five or more games due to injury, as well.

AGE was only significant in one season at predicting the probability of missing five or more games due to injury for forwards, and one season for defence. AGE² was significant for the same season for defence, and not significant for the forwards. That is slightly worse than the probability model for predicting at least one game lost due to injury, where AGE and AGE² were significant in two seasons each.

235Acknowledgement: Raw injury and player data for these calculations came from *Man Games Lost* http://www.mangameslost.com and *Hockey Reference* http://www.hockey-reference.com.

236Acknowledgement: Raw injury and player data for these calculations came from *Man Games Lost* http://www.mangameslost.com and *Hockey Reference* http://www.hockey-reference.com.

Table 7: Coefficients and Their Significance for the Injury Probability Model, Forwards[237]

Season	TOI.GM	HPG	BPG	AGE	AGE²
2009–10	0.0072	0.1971	-0.1118	0.3500	-0.0048
2010–11	0.0360	-0.1138	-0.0839	-0.1762	0.0043
2011–12	0.0300	0.0283	-0.1277	0.1770	-0.0023
2012–13	-0.0014	0.1101	-0.6281	0.4710	-0.0074
2013–14	-0.0135	0.0575	1.1111	0.0634	0.0037
2014–15	0.0059	0.2130	0.1628	0.1576	-0.0017
2015–16	0.0226	-0.1486	0.2023	0.1458	-0.0019
All Seasons	0.0125	0.0379	0.0506	0.1550	-0.0017

Table 8: Coefficients and Their Significance for the Injury Probability Model, Defencemen[238]

Season	TOI.GM	HPG	BPG	AGE	AGE²
2009–10	0.0834	0.1649	0.1854	0.1878	-0.0033
2010–11	-0.0077	0.2573	0.0655	0.2035	-0.0021
2011–12	-0.0508	-0.1201	0.1780	0.0950	-0.0057
2012–13	-0.0323	0.2078	-0.5272	0.2944	-0.0049
2013–14	-0.0256	0.3325	0.3141	-0.3673	0.0081
2014–15	0.0459	0.1954	0.0860	0.0650	0.0004
2015–16	0.0289	0.1605	0.2090	0.8314	-0.0130
All Seasons	-0.0028	0.1783	0.0453	0.1480	-0.0015

Application

To apply the models to a real-life situation, we decided to use a 23-man roster from the Ottawa Senators during the most recent season (2016-2017). To create a predicted man games lost for the Senators, we fit each model to the players in the roster, then added all of the predicted man games lost in the season to create a predicted man games lost for the team. We then compared this to the actual numbers number of games lost due to injury for the 2016-17 regular season.

We took the probability models encompassing both forwards and defencemen and fit these models to the Senators data. To gain an understanding of the variation in our models, we simulated the injury impact of 1000 2016–17 seasons for the Senators. This allows us to create a stable distribution of predicted man games lost due to injury. The results are shown below in Figure 3, the probability of missing at least one game, and Figure 4, the probability of missing at least five games.

The actual man games lost due to injury was 133, which is represented by the vertical line. Ottawa's actual man games lost during the 2016-2017 regular season was 211, but 78 of the

237Acknowledgement: Raw injury and player data for these calculations came from *Man Games Lost* http://www.mangameslost.com and *Hockey Reference* http://www.hockey-reference.com.
238Acknowledgement: Raw injury and player data for these calculations came from *Man Games Lost* http://www.mangameslost.com and *Hockey Reference* http://www.hockey-reference.com.

211 came from Clarke MacArthur, who was not injured during the regular season, and therefore was not considered for this simulation.

For our model, we used two different simulation:, one for the probability of missing at least one game, and another for the probability of missing five or more games. For the probability of missing at least one game of the regular season, 133 fell within a 95% confidence interval between 70 and 156 games lost due to injury.

When you increase the probability model so that it is predicting the probability of missing five or more games, the model loses some its predictive power. The 95% confidence interval for the simulation was between 44 and 126 and where the Ottawa Senators only lost 133 games due to injury our model predicted lower than the actual.

Figure 2: Distribution of Predicted Man Games Lost for the Ottawa Senators 2016–17 Season (INJ≥1)

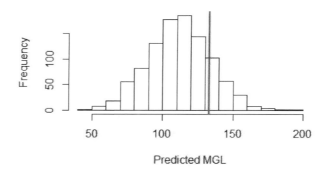

Figure 3: Distribution of Predicted Man Games Lost for the Ottawa Senators 2016–17 Season (INJ≥5)

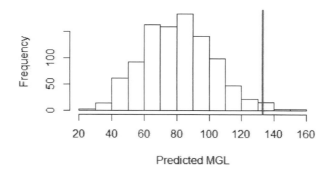

You can see in Figure 3, the probability of missing one game, that the actual number of

233

missing games is much closer to the center of the distribution, where the probability of missing at least five games, in Figure 4, was much farther right, and at the end of the distribution. This can imply that the factors in our model are better at predicting probability of lower end injuries (fewer than five games missed), and a model for predicting lengthier injuries could be much better explained by factors other than those studied here.

Closing Thoughts

In this chapter, we have built statistical prediction models for injuries during a single NHL season.

We fit logistic regression models for the probability of missing at least one game, and logistic models for the probability of missing five or more games. To consider injury severity, we fit log-linear regression models to the number of games lost due to injury by a player in a given season. We created separate models for forwards and defencemen.

For all of these models, the most consistently significant variable is ice time per game, TOI.GM. It was almost always a statistically significant variable when predicting the probability of a forward or defenceman being injured by year, and it is always significant when we modeled the data in all seasons. This may be due to players being exposed to more risk more as their time on ice increases, which could create a potential problem for coaches and general managers as team's push for the playoffs. They need their star players on the ice, but as they increase their time on ice they are also increasing their player's probability of injury.

A surprising variable that was always insignificant was blocks per game, BPG. Between both position types, BPG was never statistically significant in predicting whether or not a player would be injured. There are many possible explanations for this, including the possibility that those who often block shots are proficient at that task and thus, less susceptible to injury from blocking shots.

A similar problem arises with HPG as well; a hit is recorded when one player initiates contact with their opponent. When a player is making contact with an opponent, he is ready for the hit and is bracing for the hit.The ability to prepare for the hit allows for a player to better protect him from injury. It is rare in hockey to see a person throwing a hit to be injured. It is much more likely for a player that gets hit to get injured, therefore the number of hits received might be a better predictor of injury probability. Another useful metric for modeling injuries might be penalty minutes, which could be a proxy for reckless or borderline behavior by players.

If you compare the significance of the coefficients between positions in both models, then you can see that the forwards have more consistently significant p-values in their models, especially when looking that the Injury Severity Models (Table 5 and 6). One possible reason is the sample size, the forwards subset sample size is 3,703 players whereas the defencemen subset is only 1,961 players. The sample size difference could be the reason for the difference in the p-value's significance. However, the problem of the different sample sizes arises naturally in the NHL (on a 20-man roster only about seven players are defencemen) and the rest are forwards. Therefore there are disproportionately larger number of forwards to collect data from than there are defencemen.

— NHL DISCIPLINARY PROCESS —

STEP 1
DETERMINE IF THERE SHOULD BE A SUSPENSION:

STEP 2
CALCULATE THE NUMBER OF GAMES:

The goal of this was to create a framework for predicting the probability of an injury occurring, and also the severity of that injury. We introduced a two-part approach that modeled the probability of injury and severity of the injury in terms of man games lost. While the results are not quite as robust as one would like, we have laid the ground work for modeling injuries in the NHL.

The framework here allows for future models with additional predictors. Among these additional predictors that we would like to investigate in the future are time on ice at difference strengths (even strength, power play, shorthanded), as well as penalty minutes per game and hits received per game. The current models only use all strengths, and the addition of more granular strength data could be vital to improving the how we model the probability of injury and the severity of injury. We conjecture that additional penalty kill time leads to increased probability of injury because of the exposure to shots and the increased shot-blocking responsibilities of penalty killers.

Other metrics about the player being considered such as height and weight might prove beneficial as well. We might expect smaller players to be more susceptible to injuries, but a full investigation of that would be necessary. Addressing how these variables differentially impact our responses at different ages is another avenue we hope to pursue.

Along those lines, we would like to examine the impact of previous injury on a player's susceptibility to future injuries. This and the other extensions above would allow us to gain a better insight into the frequency and severity of injuries during the NHL regular season.

Updates to Previous Edition's Questions

By Rob Vollman

Every edition of *Hockey Abstract* includes 100% all-new content, and is meant to be a timeless reference that anyone can pull off their shelves decades from now, just as we often consult a copy of *The Klein and Reif Hockey Compendium* from 1986[239], or the 1,878-page, spider-killing *Total Hockey* tome from 1999 by Dan Diamond, et al[240].

That being written, it's also important that each edition of *Hockey Abstract* feels like a part of the greater whole that the entire series represents. That's why we included this last chapter, which re-visits some of our past explorations, and provides some key updates into what new insights have been learned over the past few years.

For those who are opening the pages of *Hockey Abstract* for the first time, we will explain everything that you need to know to follow along. If something is of particular interest to you, then check the footnotes to find out which edition has more detailed explanations of the concept in question.

For the long-time readers, our goal is to avoid being repetitive, and to cover only the new ground that has been freshly discovered since you last read each topic. With any luck, it will help you find new and greater value in the books in which we're so glad you have previously invested.

Since there have been about 50 chapters in the combined *Hockey Abstract* series, we have been somewhat selective in which topics offer the greatest value in re-visiting. Emphasis was placed on topics of the greatest popular demand, where there have been interesting new insights, that vary significantly from what we've already covered in earlier chapters, and/or where coverage is hard to find anywhere else.

In the end, we decided to re-visit the team cap management model from the opening chapter of *Stat Shot*, the league's best passers, and best do-it-all players, how to use the NHL's real-time stats (RTSS), and which players can draw penalties. We'll start with that last one.

Who is the Best at Drawing Penalties?

Statistically, one of last season's greatest puzzles was Nazem Kadri of the Toronto Maple Leafs. The well-established master of drawing penalties actually took more penalties than he drew. Quite frankly, it's almost unbelievable. It would be like Patrice Bergeron losing the majority of his faceoffs, Matt Martin throwing a below-average number of hits, or Alex Ovechkin failing to lead the league in shots. Err ... scratch that last one[241].

239Jeff Z Klein and Karl-Eric Reif, "The Klein and Reif Hockey Compendium", 1986.
240Dan Diamond et al, "Total Hockey", 1999.
241For only the second time in his 12 seasons, someone actually outshot Alex Ovechkin. San Jose's Brent

People often ask us to find underrated players using stats, and drawing penalties is definitely one of those little things in a game that can add up to enough extra goals, wins, and points in the standings to turn some otherwise average players into incredible values. Based on the extra 21.5 power plays that Kadri was giving the Leafs over an 82-game season, he was generating about an extra 4.0 goals per season. But then last year he actually *cost* Toronto 3.8 power plays, relative to a league-average forward assigned the same minutes.

So, what happened to Kadri, and who is the new leader? Well, let's take a step back, and quickly remind ourselves of everything that we learned when first exploring this topic in the 2014 edition of *Hockey Abstract*[242].

First of all, we figured out what factors can influence a player's ability to draw penalties. For example, forwards and defencemen draw penalties at different rates, and in different manpower situations. The impact of the score, the period, home ice advantage, and even the impact of the so-called compassionate referee[243] were all measured.

Once we identified these factors, the second step was to figure out a way to adjust for them,

Burns edged him 320 to 313.

242 Rob Vollman, "Who is the best at drawing penalties?", *Hockey Abstract 2014,* 2014, pgs 204-215.

243 The compassionate referee refers to the statistically established tendency for officials to be less likely to assess a penalty to the team who was most recently penalized, especially if the call resulted in a goal.

which we did using a statistic called Net Penalty Differential (NPD), which was originally introduced in *Hockey Prospectus 2013–14*[244]. The two main factors it adjusts for is a player's position, and the basic manpower situation. For those of you continuing to use this metric at home (or in your mom's basement), here is an updated table of adjustments. Be aware that the small sample sizes inherent to 5-on-4 and 4-on-5 situations can cause the numbers to swing quite a bit from season to season.

Penalty Drawing/Taking Rate by Manpower and Position, 2014–15 to 2016–17[245]

Player	Drawn/60	Taken/60	Diff/60
Forwards 4v5	0.388	0.285	0.103
Defencemen 4v5	0.441	0.360	0.081
Forwards 5v5	0.667	0.594	0.071
Defencemen 5v5	0.297	0.573	-0.276
Defencemen 5v4	0.145	0.659	-0.514
Forwards 5v4	0.285	0.800	-0.615

A table full of numbers isn't for everybody, so let me sum it up. Basically, the various situations are ranked by how easy it is to get a positive penalty differential for every 60 minutes played. For example, the easiest situation is a forward killing a penalty, who will draw 0.103 more penalties than are taken, per 60 minutes of play. On the flip side, a forward on the power play will take 0.615 more penalties than are drawn, per 60 minutes of play. All else being equal, that means that defencemen who work the power play but who don't kill penalties will probably have a truly awful penalty differential.

And no, the numbers will not add up to zero, because not every penalty that is taken was drawn by somebody else. For example, flipping the puck over the glass in the defensive zone will count as a penalty taken, but not as one that was drawn.

So, given Kadri's unexpected results last season, and using these updated adjustments, who is the league's new penalty-drawing leader? Well, now you know why I was dragging my heels answering that question, because the it's exactly who you expected, Connor McDavid.

Top 50 Penalty Drawers 2014–15 to 2016–17[246]

Player	Team(s)	GP	Taken	Drawn	Diff	NPD	NPD/82
Connor McDavid	Edmonton	127	17	57	40	37.1	23.9
Johnny Gaudreau	Calgary	231	14	64	50	46.0	16.3
Ryan Ellis	Nashville	208	26	46	20	37.6	14.8
Tim Gleason	Car/Wsh	72	9	17	8	13.0	14.8
Jeff Skinner	Carolina	238	30	74	44	39.4	13.6
Nikolaj Ehlers	Winnipeg	154	25	52	27	24.2	12.9
Nathan MacKinnon	Colorado	218	23	61	38	33.3	12.5
Nazem Kadri	Toronto	231	65	103	38	33.5	11.9

244Rob Vollman, "Los Angeles Kings", *Hockey Prospectus 2013–14*, August 2014, pg 167–169.
245Acknowledgement: Raw data on penalty information from *Behind the Net* http://www.behindthenet.ca, and the latest season for *Corsica Hockey* http://www.corsica.hockey.
246Acknowledgement: All raw penalty data for my calculations came from *Behind the Net*: http://www.behindthenet.ca and *Corsica Hockey,* http://www.corsica.hockey.

T.J. Brodie	Calgary	233	27	38	11	33.0	11.6
Andreas Athanasiou	Detroit	101	7	23	16	14.1	11.5
David Pastrnak	Boston	172	26	53	27	23.7	11.3
Darren Helm	Detroit	202	25	58	33	27.7	11.2
Vladimir Tarasenko	St. Louis	239	23	60	37	32.5	11.1
Marcus Johansson	Washington	238	10	46	36	32.3	11.1
Tobias Rieder	Arizona	234	12	50	38	31.8	11.1
Dustin Brown	Los Angeles	244	31	70	39	32.8	11.0
Seth Jones	Nsh/CBJ	238	28	39	11	31.0	10.7
Alex Pietrangelo	St. Louis	234	26	34	8	30.5	10.7
Chris Tanev	Vancouver	192	13	22	9	24.8	10.6
Scott Wilson	Pittsburgh	103	9	24	15	13.2	10.5
Torey Krug	Boston	240	28	38	10	30.1	10.3
Mark Scheifele	Winnipeg	232	32	66	34	29.0	10.2
Zemgus Girgensons	Buffalo	207	24	55	31	25.5	10.1
Jason Zucker	Minnesota	201	30	60	30	24.7	10.1
Michal Jordan	Carolina	74	8	12	4	9.1	10.1
Kris Russell	Cgy/Dal/Edm	209	20	26	6	25.2	9.9
Jack Eichel	Buffalo	142	21	41	20	17.0	9.8
Pavel Datsyuk	Detroit	129	9	27	18	15.4	9.8
Matt Duchene	Colorado	235	21	53	32	27.1	9.4
Nathan Gerbe	Carolina	125	12	29	17	14.1	9.3
Charlie Coyle	Minnesota	246	24	57	33	27.8	9.3
Alexander Wennberg	Columbus	217	19	48	29	24.4	9.2
Rob Klinkhammer	Ari/Pit/Edm	83	11	22	11	9.3	9.2
Bryan Rust	Pittsburgh	112	9	24	15	12.4	9.1
Tyler Johnson	Tampa Bay	212	24	52	28	23.3	9.0
Jaccob Slavin	Carolina	145	8	11	3	15.9	9.0
Jared Spurgeon	Minnesota	219	16	20	4	23.9	9.0
Chris Tierney	San Jose	202	13	40	27	21.7	8.8
Brandon Sutter	Pit/Van	181	13	37	24	19.3	8.7
Roman Josi	Nashville	234	32	34	2	24.7	8.7
Anze Kopitar	Los Angeles	236	23	54	31	24.9	8.6
Mika Zibanejad	Ott/NYR	217	20	47	27	22.8	8.6
Brett Pesce	Carolina	151	13	16	3	15.6	8.5
Oliver Ekman-Larsson	Arizona	236	62	64	2	24.0	8.3
Brandon Saad	Chi/CBJ	242	14	44	30	24.5	8.3
John-Michael Liles	Car/Bos	174	16	20	4	17.5	8.3
Curtis Lazar	Ott/Cgy	180	10	32	22	17.9	8.2
Tommy Wingels	SJ/Ott	216	36	62	26	21.0	8.0
Dennis Wideman	Calgary	188	26	28	2	18.3	8.0
Troy Stecher	Vancouver	71	10	11	1	6.9	8.0

Minimum 70 Games

Over the course of an entire season, McDavid is worth an extra 23.9 power plays, relative to a forward assigned the exact same minutes. That's twice as many as Kadri, and all but six players on the list, one of whom is retired.

So what happened to Kadri last year? After being repeatedly penalized and fined for diving, there is the possibility that the rest of the league and its officials started to catch on to some of his tactics, and it stopped working. A blogger at Leafs Nation compared Kadri's situation to Dustin Brown, who had a similar reputation for drawing penalties (and diving), but he wasn't completely convinced by that theory[247].

Given the massive influx of young scoring talent on Toronto's roster, we know that Kadri's role changed significantly. So, another theory is that he was no longer in an offensive-minded position to draw as many penalties, and his more defensive role meant having to take a few more of his own.

Judging from this list, there are also a number of varying styles of players who are successful at drawing penalties. As briefly explored a little more in *Hockey Abstract 2014*[248], the different qualities include youth, speed, throwing hits, small size, and (in some cases) the willingness to embellish. It's possible that the effectiveness of some of these qualities are more consistent and/or lasting than others.

Finally, there is also the possibility that this is just random variation. A single season is a small sample size, and it wouldn't take a swing of very many penalties to have a significant impact on a player's end results. After all, Kadri still ranks eighth on this list, which is pretty darn good.

247Draglikepull, "What Happened to Nazem Kadri's Penalty-Drawing Ability", *Leafs Nation,* December 31, 2016,
     Web, https://theleafsnation.com/2016/12/31/what-happened-to-nazem-kadri-s-penalty-drawing-ability/.
248Rob Vollman, "Who is the best at drawing penalties?", *Hockey Abstract 2014,* 2014, pgs 204-215.

But, to answer the original question, McDavid is the best at drawing penalties. And at everything else hockey-related, for that matter. I'm glad he's not into writing about hockey analytics.

Who is the Best Passer?

McDavid. Next question, please.

But seriously, we can't statistically determine the league's best passer, because that data isn't in the NHL game files. There's a complete account of every hit, blocked shot, takeaway, giveaway, and faceoff, but there's no passing data whatsoever. It's really the most glaring oversight in those files.

A player's passing results have to be sussed out indirectly from the information we do have in the NHL game files. Yes, we know when and where every single shot attempt was made, and who was on the ice at the time, but we have no idea if it was preceded by a pass and, if so, by whom. Even if the shooter scores, we can't be certain if the first assist that was awarded was the result of a direct pass, or whether it was a deflected shot or something.

So, let's go back to our knee-jerk answer. Why did we so quickly assume that McDavid is the best passer? It's because he has so many dang assists. If he has that many assists, then it stands to reason that he has been making a lot of effective passes, right?

Well, that's the exact reasoning behind the setup passes estimates that were first introduced on Hockey Prospectus[249] back in 2012, and explained in far more detail when we first explored this question in the original edition of *Hockey Abstract*[250] back in 2013. Basically, the premise of our setup passes metric is that the percentage of all on-ice scoring for which a player earned a primary assist is probably closely related to the percentage of all on-ice shot attempts that were preceded by one of his setup passes. We know the former, and so we can use that to estimate the latter.

For example, McDavid had 29 primary assists at even-strength last season. Given that the Oilers scored on 10.7% of their shots when he was on the ice, that means that McDavid must have had to set up 271 shots in order to produce 29 goals, and therefore earn those 29 primary assists. Add that up for all three manpower situations, and over his entire career, and it can be estimated that McDavid has set up 456 shots in 127 games, or 3.56 shots per game.

Is that a reasonable design that will produce accurate estimates? Well, that's where Ryan Stimson comes in. Given the lack of information in the NHL game files, he began manually counting them himself a few months later, and published his results in his Hockey Prospectus

249Rob Vollman, "Howe and Why: Passes", *Hockey Prospectus,* December 31, 2012, Web,
    http://www.hockeyprospectus.com/puck/article.php?articleid=1417.
250Rob Vollman, "Hockey Abstract", August 2013, pgs 210-217.

debut at the end of that season[251].

Although his work was partly motivated by his dissatisfaction with our estimates[252], Stimson's research found that they fell within roughly 5% of his actual counts, once the appropriate adjustments were made[253], and once it involved a sufficient volume of data[254]. While encouraging, that's not a statistically valid measure of the stat's accuracy, given that it was based only on a single season, and on a single team of players. Rather than trying to figure out how accurate the estimates might be, we agreed that our time would be better spent manually collecting the actual data.

Despite a growing collection of volunteers watching every game to manually count the passes, Stimson is still short of having a public dataset that encompasses the entire league, even for just a single single season. Until his work is complete, we will have to continue to rely on our estimates, as accurate as they may or may not be. And, as it turns out, McDavid is *not* the leader[255].

Forwards Top 50 Setup Passes per Game (SP/GP), 2014–15 to 2016–17[256]

Forward	Team(s)	GP	A	SP	SP/GP
Ryan Getzlaf	Anaheim	228	153	883	3.87
Alexander Wennberg	Columbus	217	94	527	3.77
Taylor Hall	Edm/NJ	207	96	748	3.61
Connor McDavid	Edmonton	127	102	456	3.59
Jakub Voracek	Philadelphia	237	144	826	3.49
Blake Wheeler	Winnipeg	243	135	845	3.48
Sidney Crosby	Pittsburgh	232	150	799	3.44
Nicklas Backstrom	Washington	239	173	787	3.29
Mikael Granlund	Minnesota	231	105	744	3.22
Patrick Kane	Chicago	225	152	718	3.19
Henrik Zetterberg	Detroit	241	137	765	3.17
Johnny Gaudreau	Calgary	231	131	729	3.16
Daniel Sedin	Vancouver	246	118	775	3.15
John Tavares	NY Islanders	237	123	738	3.11
Anze Kopitar	Los Angeles	236	137	722	3.06
Matthew Tkachuk	Calgary	76	35	232	3.05
Evgeni Malkin	Pittsburgh	188	112	571	3.04

251 Ryan Stimson, "Passing stats: What are they and why should we care?", *Hockey Prospectus,* January 29, 2014, http://www.hockeyprospectus.com/passing-stats-what-are-they-and-why-should-we-care-part-one/ and http://www.hockeyprospectus.com/hockey-passing-statistics-what-are-they-and-why-should-we-care-part-two/.

252 Stimson isn't alone in his grouchiness towards estimates. Many of our colleagues prefer to view this stat as a re-packaging of primary assists, on-ice shooting percentage, and on-ice shots, rather than an actual measurement of a player's passing volumes. And there's nothing wrong with that perspective.

253 For example, Stimson found that passes preceded only about four in five shots.

254 Ryan Stimson, "Why Setup Passes and PSR are Unreliable", *All About the Jersey,* May 7, 2014, Web, https://www.allaboutthejersey.com/2014/5/7/5677850/why-estimating-passes-is-unreliable.

255 Why do I feel like Maury Povich?

256 Acknowledgement: Assist and shooting percentage data on which the estimate is based from *Behind the Net*, http://www.behindthenet.ca and *Corsica Hockey* for the last season, http://www.corsica.hockey.

Alexander Steen	St. Louis	141	75	424	3.01
Tyler Seguin	Dallas	225	126	670	2.98
David Krejci	Boston	201	101	597	2.97
Joe Thornton	San Jose	239	155	703	2.94
Evgeny Kuznetsov	Washington	244	123	711	2.91
Henrik Sedin	Vancouver	238	134	688	2.89
Jack Eichel	Buffalo	142	65	408	2.87
Alex Radulov	Montreal	76	36	218	2.87
Ryan Johansen	CBJ/Nsh	244	138	696	2.85
Jonathan Toews	Chicago	233	105	654	2.81
Pavel Datsyuk	Detroit	129	72	361	2.80
Thomas Vanek	Min/Det/Fla	222	85	620	2.79
Jonathan Huberdeau	Florida	186	94	519	2.79
Max Domi	Arizona	140	63	389	2.78
Elias Lindholm	Carolina	235	84	647	2.75
Logan Couture	San Jose	207	88	568	2.74
Jamie Benn	Dallas	241	143	661	2.74
Ryan O'Reilly	Col/Buf	225	112	612	2.72
Ryan Spooner	Boston	187	74	507	2.71
Jaden Schwartz	St. Louis	186	85	504	2.71
William Nylander	Toronto	103	46	278	2.70
Derek Stepan	NY Rangers	221	108	596	2.70
Mats Zuccarello	NY Rangers	239	113	644	2.69
Kyle Okposo	NYI/Buf	204	101	549	2.69
Claude Giroux	Philadelphia	241	137	646	2.68
Jeff Carter	Los Angeles	241	106	644	2.67
Leon Draisaitl	Edmonton	191	87	504	2.64
Mike Ribeiro	Nashville	209	111	548	2.62
Brandon Dubinsky	Columbus	202	83	524	2.59
Nathan MacKinnon	Colorado	218	92	559	2.56
Jaromir Jagr	NJ/Fla	238	99	602	2.53
Mitch Marner	Toronto	77	42	193	2.51
Kyle Turris	Ottawa	217	85	542	2.50

Minimum 70 games and 25 assists

While this is just a very high-level estimate, I was expecting McDavid to dominate this list. In fact, I was expecting him to be so far ahead, that even an error rate much higher than 5% still would be required to dislodge him. So, this was a real eye-opener for me.

Plus, if you had told me that someone other than McDavid would sit atop the list, I would have assumed it would be Sidney Crosby, right? After all, he had a massive lead when we first explored this topic in *Hockey Abstract*, with an average of 4.34 setup passes per game, well ahead of Joe Thornton in second, with 3.88, and Henrik Sedin, with 3.85. While I half-expected to see Sedin slide down the list, Crosby's drop from 4.34 in 2013 to 3.44 today, and Thornton from 3.88 to 2.94, were quite the eye-openers as well.

Instead, Ryan Getzlaf is in first. Suffice it to say that my eyes couldn't possibly be opened any wider than they are right now. Getzlaf barely scraped into the top-10 back in 2013, with an average of 3.43 setup passes per game, and here he is in first, with 3.87. And Alexander Wennberg is in second? Oops, my eyeball just popped out.

At least there are no major surprises on defence. Just as he was in 2013, Erik Karlsson tops the list, and by a reasonably comfortable margin over the expected runner-up, Brent Burns.

Defencemen Top 50 Setup Passes per Game (SP/GP), 2014–15 to 2016–17[257]

Defenceman	Team(s)	GP	A	SP	SP/GP
Erik Karlsson	Ottawa	241	165	751	3.12
Brent Burns	San Jose	246	138	703	2.86
Roman Josi	Nashville	234	124	668	2.85
Andrei Markov	Montreal	225	109	632	2.81
Torey Krug	Boston	240	110	634	2.64
John Carlson	Washington	210	102	540	2.57
John Klingberg	Dallas	221	113	542	2.45
Tyson Barrie	Colorado	232	108	566	2.44
Victor Hedman	Tampa Bay	216	121	521	2.41
Keith Yandle	NYR/Fla	248	124	580	2.34
Kris Letang	Pittsburgh	181	123	414	2.29
Drew Doughty	Los Angeles	246	108	551	2.24
Noah Hanifin	Carolina	160	43	358	2.24
P.K. Subban	Mtl/Nsh	216	120	481	2.23
Kevin Shattenkirk	StL/Wsh	208	109	434	2.09
Duncan Keith	Chicago	227	116	470	2.07
Alex Pietrangelo	St. Louis	234	103	478	2.04
Colton Parayko	St. Louis	160	55	324	2.03
Mike Green	Wsh/Det	218	85	413	1.89
Jake Muzzin	Los Angeles	240	82	448	1.87
Ryan McDonagh	NY Rangers	221	86	411	1.86
Nick Leddy	NY Islanders	240	97	440	1.83
Dion Phaneuf	Tor/Ott	222	75	403	1.82
Dustin Byfuglien	Winnipeg	230	100	416	1.81
James Wisniewski	CBJ/Ana/Car	70	26	125	1.79
Justin Faulk	Carolina	221	75	393	1.78
Matt Niskanen	Washington	242	88	430	1.78
Mark Giordano	Calgary	224	99	391	1.75
Ryan Ellis	Nashville	208	62	363	1.75
Alex Goligoski	Dal/Ari	245	94	425	1.73
Zach Werenski	Columbus	78	36	132	1.69
Morgan Rielly	Toronto	239	69	397	1.66
Dougie Hamilton	Bos/Cgy	235	100	389	1.66
Seth Jones	Nsh/CBJ	238	77	393	1.65
Travis Hamonic	NY Islanders	192	55	315	1.64
Johnny Boychuk	NY Islanders	208	59	339	1.63

257 Acknowledgement: Assist and shooting percentage data on which the estimate is based from *Behind the Net*, http://www.behindthenet.ca.

T.J. Brodie	Calgary	233	99	380	1.63
Shea Weber	Nsh/Mtl	234	86	380	1.62
Michael Stone	Ari/Cgy	220	57	355	1.61
Shayne Gostisbehere	Philadelphia	142	61	229	1.61
Ben Hutton	Vancouver	146	38	233	1.60
Rasmus Ristolainen	Buffalo	239	83	381	1.59
Dmitry Orlov	Washington	164	48	257	1.57
Andrew MacDonald	Philadelphia	159	33	249	1.57
Nikita Zaitsev	Toronto	82	32	126	1.54
Jason Demers	Dal/Fla	224	55	344	1.54
Ryan Suter	Nashville	241	110	369	1.53
Zdeno Chara	Boston	218	59	332	1.52
Jake Gardiner	Toronto	240	78	363	1.51
Oscar Klefbom	Edmonton	172	52	260	1.51

Minimum 70 Games and 25 Assists

As interesting as these results might be, there's no doubt that future developments will some day make these estimates obsolete, either because the NHL begins tracking it, or because of new player-tracking technology, or because some other brand new metric comes along. Already, I have seen some of the Stimson's results, and some confidential results from various private tracking companies, and their findings are absolutely fascinating.

As one of the greatest untapped areas in hockey analysis, passing metrics are too important an advantage for front offices to ignore for much longer. Understanding how passes contribute to scoring, knowing how to measure an individual player's passing abilities, designing effective strategies, and placing everyone with linemates and in situations where their talents have the greatest value, are all clear examples of how this type of work can translate into results that can be seen in today's scoresheets.

Who is the Best Hitter?

McDavid. Oops, sorry. Force of habit.

In this case, the obvious answer is Matt Martin, right? He has thrown 1,047 hits over the past three seasons combined, which is a lot more than Ottawa's Mark Borowiecki, who is in second place with 868.

However, now that he's with Toronto, Martin did fail to lead the league in hits for the first time since his rookie season in 2010–11, finishing second to Borowiecki, 364 to 300. So, maybe we should re-visit the numbers.

Iain Fyffe was the one to tackle this topic, in *Stat Shot*[258]. He identified that the main factors that can influence a player's hits include ice time, manpower situation, and where he plays. Wait a minute, where he plays? I know that the Maple Leafs isn't exactly a fear-invoking team

---

[258]Iain Fyffe, "Who is the Best Hitter?", *Stat Shot,* September 2016, pgs 158-168.

name, but how could the team he plays for affect Martin's hit totals (or anyone else's)?

As it turns out, there's no formal definition for a hit, so different scorekeepers tend to count them differently. And, since the same crew of scorekeepers work all of team's home games, their subjective opinions can skew the hit counts for the local team, in one direction or another. This bias can even change from one season to the next, if the scorekeeping team changes.

This is known as scorekeeper bias, or recording bias, and it's one of the banes of our existence in the hockey analytics community. It affects any statistic that has a degree of subjective judgment or opinion involved, like hits, blocked shots, faceoff wins, and even saves.

Fortunately, this bias can be measured and adjusted for, by comparing each team's average at home with their own scorekeepers, and on the road, where there will be a league-average mix of different scorekeepers.

When it comes to the statistic in question, here's a look at the number of hits thrown at home and on the road by the various teams for each of the past three seasons, along with the resulting scorekeeper bias, and a three-year weighted average. The last column is what is used to adjust a player's scoring totals on an entire season, which is simply half that weighted average, since most players play only half of their games under the bias of their local scorekeepers.

Recording Bias for Hits, 2014–15 to 2016–17[259]

Team	2017 Hits (Hm-Rd)	2016 Hits (Hm-Rd)	2015 Hits (Hm-Rd)	2017 Bias	2016 Bias	2015 Bias	Wt Avg Bias	Bias Factor
Chicago	697-481	869-520	737-620	1.415	1.602	1.262	1.460	1.230
Pittsburgh	1236-824	1115-832	1371-1124	1.465	1.285	1.295	1.359	1.180
San Jose	875-664	941-745	1108-822	1.287	1.211	1.431	1.286	1.143
Philadelphia	1160-903	1242-954	1409-1102	1.255	1.248	1.358	1.273	1.136
Carolina	875-736	874-676	1139-814	1.161	1.240	1.486	1.258	1.129
Arizona	1131-967	989-826	1459-1030	1.142	1.148	1.504	1.217	1.109
Toronto	1062-874	1143-976	1423-1122	1.187	1.123	1.347	1.193	1.097
Montreal	1017-847	1085-848	877-819	1.173	1.227	1.137	1.187	1.094
Florida	807-858	1064-846	1299-969	0.919	1.206	1.423	1.134	1.067
Ottawa	1100-1014	1222-1040	1217-1062	1.060	1.127	1.217	1.118	1.059
Detroit	863-781	885-766	776-793	1.079	1.108	1.039	1.083	1.041
Dallas	777-775	829-727	897-760	0.979	1.093	1.253	1.080	1.040
Edmonton	1073-1000	946-872	1023-957	1.048	1.040	1.135	1.062	1.031
Anaheim	1093-1050	1158-1076	1204-1097	1.017	1.032	1.165	1.053	1.026
Los Angeles	1216-1107	1233-1262	1368-1262	1.073	0.937	1.151	1.034	1.017
Tampa Bay	909-933	877-805	877-882	0.952	1.045	1.056	1.010	1.005
Boston	951-825	1055-1109	1008-1104	1.126	0.912	0.970	1.009	1.005
St. Louis	878-810	953-984	866-981	1.059	0.929	0.937	0.982	0.991

259Acknowledgement: Uses data from NHL's official website, http://www.nhl.com.

Washington	865-862	989-1005	1160-1175	0.980	0.944	1.048	0.979	0.990
NY Islanders	981-1145	1181-1130	1437-1248	0.837	1.002	1.223	0.980	0.990
NY Rangers	859-856	1062-1102	939-974	0.980	0.924	1.024	0.967	0.983
Winnipeg	829-1077	1031-1072	1223-1186	0.752	0.922	1.095	0.889	0.944
Columbus	724-930	1001-1144	1328-1182	0.760	0.839	1.193	0.878	0.939
Vancouver	728-743	705-828	691-891	0.957	0.816	0.824	0.874	0.937
Colorado	752-935	879-969	979-1039	0.786	0.870	1.001	0.862	0.931
New Jersey	775-886	859-981	733-913	0.854	0.840	0.853	0.848	0.924
Buffalo	893-979	863-1053	994-1210	0.891	0.786	0.872	0.845	0.923
Minnesota	591-693	628-778	552-771	0.833	0.774	0.760	0.795	0.897
Nashville	713-947	813-1073	752-939	0.735	0.727	0.850	0.755	0.877
Calgary	625-925	707-993	817-965	0.660	0.683	0.899	0.717	0.858

In this case, it doesn't seem like there's a huge bias for either the Islanders or the Maple Leafs. If anything, Martin's hit totals were slightly under-counted with the Islanders, and over-counted in Toronto. Maybe having a leaf on his chest really did mellow him out.

On the other hand, watch out for Lance Bouma, who went from the Flames to the Blackhawks this summer. In Calgary, you pretty much have to send someone to the hospital in order to get credit for a hit, while in Chicago it may be sufficient to merely think about sneering at someone.

Beyond adjusting for scorekeeper bias, opportunity can be taken into account by only considering even-strength situations, and calculating a player's hits on a per-60 minutes basis. Even with the slight decline in Toronto, Martin is still well in front of his old Islanders teammate Cal Clutterbuck, Borowiecki himself, and everybody else. Including McDavid.

Top 50 Hitters, 2014–15 to 2016–17[260]

Player	Team	Pos	GP	ESHt	ESTOI	AESHt	Per 60
Matt Martin	NYI/Tor	LW	240	1037	2385.2	1014.9	25.53
Cal Clutterbuck	NY Islanders	RW	219	813	2334.2	827.5	21.27
Ryan Reaves	St. Louis	RW	225	720	1896.4	645.2	20.41
Cody McLeod	Col/Nsh	LW	223	637	1950.9	625.5	19.24
Mark Borowiecki	Ottawa	D	196	807	2532.2	685.3	16.24
Zach Sill	Pit/Tor/Wsh	C	73	183	568.6	150.0	15.83
Tom Wilson	Washington	RW	231	674	2488.8	644.5	15.54
Matt Hendricks	Edmonton	LW/C	181	460	1857.3	477.7	15.43
Zac Rinaldo	Phi/Bos	C/LW	110	367	926.6	235.6	15.26
Nick Ritchie	Anaheim	LW	110	338	1287.7	326.0	15.19
Rob Klinkhammer	Ari/Pit/Edm	LW/C	83	283	895.2	226.3	15.17
Nicolas Deslauriers	Buffalo	LW	194	567	1932.0	485.2	15.07
Micheal Ferland	Calgary	LW/RW	173	410	1882.6	472.5	15.06
Marcus Foligno	Buffalo	LW	212	643	2819.4	701.0	14.92
Leo Komarov	Toronto	C	211	679	2628.6	631.8	14.42
Tanner Glass	NY Rangers	LW	134	466	1280.1	306.1	14.35

260Acknowledgement: Raw data obtained from *War on Ice*, http://www.waronice.com and *Corsica Hockey*, http://www.corsica.hockey.

Derek MacKenzie	Florida	C	228	589	2244.5	532.6	14.24
Adam Lowry	Winnipeg	LW	236	620	2792.2	648.8	13.94
Lance Bouma	Calgary	C/LW	183	494	1961.0	449.4	13.75
Jim Slater	Winnipeg	C	82	126	563.1	128.9	13.74
Craig Adams	Pittsburgh	RW	70	169	501.0	113.7	13.61
Mike Brown	SJ/Mtl	RW	70	217	552.8	124.5	13.52
Brandon Bollig	Calgary	LW	116	252	1019.1	227.4	13.39
Anthony Peluso	Winnipeg	RW	84	181	512.0	113.7	13.33
Ryan White	Phi/Ari/Min	C/RW	172	469	1783.6	392.2	13.19
Tuomo Ruutu	New Jersey	LW/RW	110	234	1177.5	255.0	12.99
Brandon Dubinsky	Columbus	C	202	603	2730.9	591.3	12.99
Chris Neil	Ottawa	RW	171	458	1502.8	319.7	12.77
Dustin Brown	Los Angeles	RW/LW	244	600	3223.0	671.8	12.51
Chris Porter	StL/Min	LW	85	209	745.6	153.6	12.36
Radko Gudas	TB/Phi	D	174	621	2855.9	583.1	12.25
Matt Greene	Los Angeles	D	111	244	1462.0	296.6	12.17
Steve Ott	StL/Det/Mtl	C	152	347	1425.7	281.9	11.86
Gabriel Bourque	Nsh/Col	LW	97	207	994.6	196.3	11.84
Brad Malone	Carolina	C	122	277	1108.7	217.0	11.74
Andreas Martinsen	Col/Mtl	LW/C	119	320	1153.5	222.9	11.60
Tommy Wingels	SJ/Ott	C/RW	216	558	2491.5	479.4	11.55
Boone Jenner	Columbus	C	195	516	2683.0	513.4	11.48
Nic Dowd	Los Angeles	C	75	149	778.4	145.1	11.19
Matt Beleskey	Ana/Bos	LW	194	487	2464.2	458.6	11.17
David Backes	StL/Bos	C/RW	233	607	3262.4	604.3	11.11
Troy Brouwer	Wsh/Cgy	RW	238	519	2955.1	545.5	11.08
Trevor Lewis	Los Angeles	C	230	507	2814.4	517.6	11.03
Chris Thorburn	Winnipeg	RW	227	347	1790.5	329.1	11.03
Casey Cizikas	NY Islanders	C	209	430	2241.5	411.8	11.02
Alex Ovechkin	Washington	LW	242	660	3660.4	669.9	10.98
Luke Schenn	Phi/LA/Ari	D	208	641	3189.5	578.9	10.89
Milan Lucic	Bos/Edm	LW	244	647	3473.5	630.3	10.89
Austin Watson	Nashville	LW	134	210	1281.8	232.2	10.87
Cedric Paquette	Tampa Bay	C	178	400	1894.5	340.9	10.79

Minimum 70 Games Played

Two years ago, Iain also ranked Martin number one, so I believe it's reasonably fair to stick with that assessment, given these latest results. Next question, please.

Who is the Best Shot-Blocker?

Obviously, blocking shots matters a great deal to NHL front offices. The three players with the most blocked shots over the past three seasons combined all signed hefty contracts this summer that couldn't otherwise be justified by their other stats. Kris Russell, who leads the NHL with 706 blocked shots, signed a four-year, $16 million contract with the Oilers, Dan

Girardi, who ranks second with 545 hits, signed a two-year, $6 million contract with Tampa Bay, and Karl Alzner, who ranked third with 534 hits, signed a five-year, $23.125 million contract with Montreal.

Continuing to skim down the list of the league's other top shot-blockers, it's amazing how many of these players signed far heftier contracts than expected recently. Blocking shots appears to be a skill that is highly prized by the NHL front offices, or at the very least it is seen to be indicative of a great and otherwise intangible talent. If that is the case, then it is particularly important to study this statistic as accurately as possible.

In the past, blocking shots has been compared to bailing water out of a boat – it's only possible on a leaky boat. Russell may be the best at bailing water, or he may simply have been on some awfully leaky boats[261]. That is, Russell may be blocking a lot more shots because there are a lot more shots to block whenever he's out there.

With any statistic, it's important to take opportunity into account before you start comparing players. Normally that is done by dividing a statistic by games played, or by minutes played. In the case of blocked shots, it should be done by dividing that by the number of shots attempts. And that's exactly what Derek Zona did, when he introduced the Even-Strength Blocked Shot Percentage (ESBS%), back in 2011[262].

Starting from that same basic idea, Iain's spin in *Stat Shot*[263] was to add a regression component for those who didn't block enough shots. Specifically, any player who faced fewer than 1,000 shot attempts would have their stats padded to that point, at a league-average shot-blocking rate for their position. This is a very simple and common way to deal with the random variation that can creep into smaller sample sizes, and it's highly recommended for any stat.

Again, there's no big surprise in the updated results. Russell finished on top in Iain's study, and he's still in first today. He blocks 15.9% of all shot attempts when he's on the ice at even-strength, which is really quite remarkable when you stop and think about it. I mean, it's not $16-million-over-four-years-remarkable given that the player in second place was paid the league minimum last year, but it is remarkable.

Top 50 Shot-Blockers, 2014–15 to 2016–17[264]

Player	Team	GP	ESBk	USATA	EBS%	REBS%
Kris Russell	Cgy/Dal/Edm	209	560	3520	15.91	15.91
Nate Prosser	Minnesota	156	195	1367	14.26	14.26
Calvin de Haan	NY Islanders	219	395	2956	13.36	13.36
Stephen Johns	Dallas	75	126	915	13.77	13.36
Brooks Orpik	Washington	198	341	2570	13.27	13.27

261He may even be *causing* some of those leaks.
262Derek Zona, "Which Oilers Really Block the Most Shots?", *Copper n Blue,* December 14, 2011, Web, https://www.coppernblue.com/2011/12/14/2636304/oilers-block-the-most-shots.
263Iain Fyffe, "Who is the best shot-blocker?", *Stat Shot,* September 2016, pgs 148-157.
264Acknowledgement: Raw data obtained from the NHL http://www.nhl.com, *War on Ice,* http://www.waronice.com, and *Corsica Hockey,* http://www.corsica.hockey.

Tom Gilbert	Mtl/LA	135	215	1652	13.01	13.01
Alec Martinez	Los Angeles	216	349	2725	12.81	12.81
David Schlemko	5 Teams	173	234	1837	12.74	12.74
Mike Weber	Buf/Wsh	109	179	1407	12.72	12.72
Christopher Tanev	Vancouver	192	303	2400	12.63	12.63
Nick Schultz	Philadelphia	189	295	2337	12.62	12.62
Ryan Stanton	Van/Wsh	55	95	653	14.55	12.61
Nate Guenin	Colorado	105	159	1291	12.32	12.32
Dan Girardi	NY Rangers	219	425	3464	12.27	12.27
Carl Gunnarsson	St. Louis	189	248	2044	12.13	12.13
Ian Cole	StL/Pit	225	325	2708	12.00	12.00
Karl Alzner	Washington	246	393	3275	12.00	12.00
Robert Bortuzzo	Pit/StL	129	136	1135	11.98	11.98
Kevin Klein	NY Rangers	194	315	2642	11.92	11.92
Radko Gudas	TB/Phi	174	270	2272	11.88	11.88
Mark Giordano	Calgary	224	368	3113	11.82	11.82
Josh Morrissey	Winnipeg	82	121	1024	11.82	11.82
Ladislav Smid	Calgary	53	80	578	13.84	11.78
Derek Forbort	Los Angeles	96	132	1121	11.78	11.78
Brandon Davidson	Edm/Mtl	101	142	1206	11.77	11.77
Matt Greene	Los Angeles	111	119	1018	11.69	11.69
Simon Despres	Pit/Ana	108	145	1242	11.67	11.67
Johnny Boychuk	NY Islanders	208	336	2879	11.67	11.67
Andrew MacDonald	Philadelphia	159	240	2057	11.67	11.67
Raphael Diaz	Calgary	56	65	431	15.08	11.60
Barret Jackman	StL/Nsh	153	169	1457	11.60	11.60
Matt Irwin	SJ/Bos/Nsh	129	168	1452	11.57	11.57
Johnny Oduya	Chi/Dal	210	325	2834	11.47	11.47
Mark Stuart	Winnipeg	176	220	1924	11.43	11.43
Deryk Engelland	Calgary	226	313	2746	11.40	11.40
Trevor van Riemsdyk	Chicago	158	241	2115	11.39	11.39
Kevin Gravel	Los Angeles	54	64	452	14.16	11.31
Jordie Benn	Dal/Mtl	208	274	2442	11.22	11.22
Greg Pateryn	Mtl/Dal	91	115	1025	11.22	11.22
Tyson Strachan	Buf/Min	48	81	676	11.98	11.01
Niklas Hjalmarsson	Chicago	236	357	3249	10.99	10.99
Tim Gleason	Car/Wsh	72	89	769	11.57	10.97
Victor Bartley	Nsh/Mtl	47	66	514	12.84	10.96
Michael Stone	Ari/Cgy	220	361	3306	10.92	10.92
Andrej Sekera	Car/LA/Edm	234	348	3200	10.88	10.88
Justin Braun	San Jose	231	327	3007	10.87	10.87
Zbynek Michalek	Ari/StL	141	197	1815	10.85	10.85
Ivan Provorov	Philadelphia	82	106	977	10.85	10.81
Michal Jordan	Carolina	74	90	805	11.18	10.75
Erik Johnson	Colorado	166	282	2626	10.74	10.74

If teams really value the shot-blocking skill, or believe that it is indicative of certain intangible qualities, then there are some far more affordable options in the NHL than the high-priced free agents this summer. Like Nate Prosser, quite a few of these players are available right now for practically nothing, and several more will probably be placed on waivers at some point this season.

Naturally, there are no forwards among the league leaders in blocked shots, so we have built a special table just for them. Iain previously identified Nick Bonino, Ryan Getzlaf, and Boyd Gordon among the best shot-blocking forwards. In the updated figures, Bonino ranks second behind his new Nashville teammate, Austin Watson, Gordon ranks third, and Getzlaf is fifth, with Matt Hendricks of the Oilers in-between them. It certainly looks like Iain was abslutely bang on.

Top 50 Shot-Blocking Forwards, 2014–15 to 2016–17[265]

Player	Team	GP	ESBk	USATA	EBS%	REBS%
Austin Watson	Nashville	134	90	1006	8.95	8.95
Nick Bonino	Van/Pit	218	183	2062	8.87	8.87
Boyd Gordon	Edm/Ari/Phi	146	96	1092	8.79	8.79
Matt Hendricks	Edmonton	181	126	1519	8.29	8.29
Ryan Getzlaf	Anaheim	228	201	2465	8.15	8.15
Drew Miller	Detroit	165	101	1241	8.14	8.14
Ben Smith	Chi/SJ/Tor/Col	142	86	1102	7.80	7.80
Devin Shore	Dallas	85	69	781	8.83	7.77
Frans Nielsen	NYI/Det	238	169	2207	7.66	7.66
Lance Bouma	Calgary	183	116	1547	7.50	7.50
Marcus Kruger	Chicago	192	111	1497	7.41	7.41
Mike Fisher	Nashville	201	139	1920	7.24	7.24
Tom Pyatt	Ottawa	82	64	800	8.00	7.19
Joe Pavelski	San Jose	245	182	2580	7.05	7.05
Jarret Stoll	LA/NYR/Min	153	100	1440	6.94	6.94
Casey Cizikas	NY Islanders	209	117	1691	6.92	6.92
Manny Malhotra	Montreal	58	45	396	11.36	6.90
Tom Kuhnhackl	Pittsburgh	99	59	755	7.81	6.87
Cedric Paquette	Tampa Bay	178	93	1359	6.84	6.84
Tim Schaller	Buf/Bos	94	57	718	7.94	6.82
Dennis Rasmussen	Chicago	112	60	808	7.43	6.76
Pierre-Edouard Bellemare	Philadelphia	237	129	1916	6.73	6.73
Patric Hornqvist	Pittsburgh	216	138	2092	6.60	6.60
Boone Jenner	Columbus	195	154	2336	6.59	6.59
Gabriel Bourque	Nsh/Col	97	54	709	7.62	6.56
Torrey Mitchell	Buf/Mtl	214	118	1803	6.54	6.54
Colton Sceviour	Dal/Fla	222	122	1875	6.51	6.51
Tanner Kero	Chicago	64	48	596	8.05	6.41
Kyle Brodziak	Min/StL	218	97	1518	6.39	6.39
John Mitchell	Colorado	204	135	2133	6.33	6.33
David Backes	StL/Bos	233	151	2390	6.32	6.32

[265]Acknowledgement: Raw data obtained from the NHL http://www.nhl.com and *War on Ice*, http://www.waronice.com and *Corsica Hockey*, http://www.corsica.hockey.

Eric Fehr	Wsh/Pit/Tor	183	90	1433	6.28	6.28
Steve Bernier	NJ/NYI	91	54	784	6.89	6.26
Chris VandeVelde	Philadelphia	232	116	1867	6.21	6.21
Joe Vitale	Arizona	71	44	547	8.04	6.20
Curtis Glencross	Cgy/Wsh	71	49	673	7.28	6.20
Richard Panik	Tor/Chi	188	99	1597	6.20	6.20
Melker Karlsson	San Jose	185	98	1626	6.03	6.03
Charlie Coyle	Minnesota	246	154	2556	6.03	6.03
Dennis Everberg	Colorado	70	44	599	7.35	5.99
Auston Matthews	Toronto	82	57	928	6.14	5.99
Antoine Roussel	Dallas	220	127	2134	5.95	5.95
Tommy Wingels	SJ/Ott	216	115	1939	5.93	5.93
Logan Couture	San Jose	207	124	2099	5.91	5.91
Alex Wennberg	Columbus	80	50	776	6.44	5.89
Chris Kelly	Bos/Ott	173	79	1361	5.80	5.80
Marcus Foligno	Buffalo	212	136	2343	5.80	5.80
Tomas Hertl	San Jose	212	119	2054	5.79	5.79
Ryan Callahan	Tampa Bay	168	97	1682	5.77	5.77
Brian Flynn	Buf/Mtl	170	81	1411	5.74	5.74

By the way, even though recording bias can impact shot-blocking totals, these figures are not adjusted like the best hitters were, so keep that in mind if you plan to take a deeper dive of your own.

Who is the Best at Faceoffs?

Nobody is better than Patrice Bergeron in the faceoff circle, and there's very little argument about that.

So, the interesting aspect of this discussion isn't the end result, but in how we get there. You see, we have a very different way of measuring faceoff success than the traditional method of wins and losses.

You've doubtlessly seen a lot of faceoffs, many of them being big, giant messes where everybody gets tied up and the puck just winds up getting dumped somewhere. So, did you ever wonder about how those wins and losses are determined? Well, it's actually based on a scorekeeper's subjective opinion about which centre's team touched the puck first, after the draw. To us, that seems like an awfully arbitrary and rather pointless way of measuring faceoff success.

The point of a faceoff is to gain useful possession of the puck, or to deny that to your opponents. In our view, if the attacking team wins the faceoff and gets a shot attempt within 10 seconds, then we call that a win. If they fail to do so, then the defending team won the faceoff, right? For faceoffs in the neutral zone, the winner is whichever team got the next shot attempt, assuming it also occurred within 10 seconds, and before the next stoppage in play.

And the 10 seconds isn't being chosen completely arbitrarily, by the way. When we carefully studied faceoffs in *Stat Shot*[266], we counted the number of shot attempts that occurred within a certain number of seconds of an offensive zone faceoff. As you can see from the following chart, 10 seconds is the most generous estimate of how long the value of winning a faceoff is likely to last.

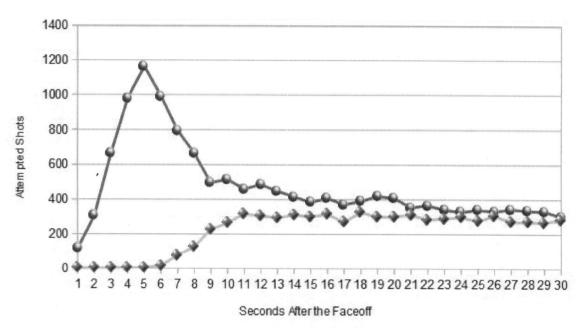

Shots Attempted After Offensive Zone Faceoffs, 2014-15

That's why we measure faceoff success not by a subjective opinion about which team touched the puck first, but based on the number of shot attempts the team generates after a given player takes a draw.

This perspective is called Net Shots Post Faceoff (NSPF), and it is the brainchild of Craig Tabita of *Puck Base*, whose work was featured heavily in that chapter. Yes, there is a goal-based version, but there are far too few goals that occur within 10 seconds of a faceoff, so we generally stick to shot attempts instead. And, from this perspective, Bergeron is still the master of the draw.

Obviously, this approach gives a huge advantage to centres who frequently take faceoffs in the offensive zone. That's why our modest contribution to Tabita's metric was to calculate it relative to how a league-average centre would have performed if he took the same number of faceoffs in each zone.

The following table shows you exactly what we mean. Over the past three seasons, Bergeron took 1,146 faceoffs in the offensive zone, and 1,311 in the defensive zone. And, despite taking more faceoffs in the defensive zone, the Bruins bested their opponents 449 shot attempts to

266Rob Vollman, "Who is the best faceoff specialist", *Stat Shot,* September 2016, pgs 121-147.

312 after Bergeron took the draw. The resulting NSPF of 137 is simply incredible, but it's actually 175.3 shot attempts better than how a league-average centre would have performed in the same number of draws (-38.3). That gives Bergeron a simply massive lead over everybody else.

Top 50 Faceoff Specialists, 2014–15 to 2016–17[267]

Player	Teams	Off Zone	Def Zone	SAF	SAA	NSPF	Exp	Adj NSPF
Patrice Bergeron	Boston	1146	1311	449	312	137	-38.3	175.3
Ryan Johansen	CBJ/Nsh	1026	1045	428	317	111	-4.1	115.1
Claude Giroux	Philadelphia	1298	1185	491	350	141	27.2	113.8
Mike Fisher	Nashville	817	891	337	251	86	-18.2	104.2
Ryan Kesler	Anaheim	890	1296	336	335	1	-97.9	98.9
Jordan Staal	Carolina	725	817	302	229	73	-22.4	95.4
Tyler Bozak	Toronto	1071	1002	418	313	105	17.2	87.9
Sidney Crosby	Pittsburgh	1389	989	510	327	183	95.2	87.8
Anze Kopitar	Los Angeles	1106	1035	420	328	92	16.9	75.1
Jeff Carter	Los Angeles	1090	834	393	259	134	61.2	72.8
Tomas Plekanec	Montreal	981	1063	402	352	50	-20.2	70.2
Vernon Fiddler	Dal/NJ/Nsh	475	747	193	190	3	-65.4	68.4
Joe Pavelski	San Jose	762	638	283	186	97	29.7	67.3
Vincent Trocheck	Florida	830	845	269	211	58	-4.0	62.0
Martin Hanzal	Ari/Min	661	755	265	229	36	-22.8	58.8
Jason Spezza	Dallas	820	611	303	206	97	49.3	47.7
Tyler Seguin	Dallas	544	548	242	196	46	-1.1	47.1
Nicklas Backstrom	Washington	1058	974	392	326	66	19.2	46.8
Paul Gaustad	Nashville	93	884	68	208	-140	-186.1	46.1
Brandon Sutter	Pit/Van	625	773	230	220	10	-35.4	45.4
Joe Thornton	San Jose	540	575	211	174	37	-8.0	45.0
Anton Lander	Edmonton	263	389	118	105	13	-30.4	43.4
Boyd Gordon	Edm/Ari/Phi	259	840	116	209	-93	-136.2	43.2
Paul Stastny	St. Louis	911	963	315	285	30	-12.4	42.4
Mikko Koivu	Minnesota	1071	1137	379	354	25	-17.1	42.1
Calle Jarnkrok	Nashville	576	523	199	145	54	12.4	41.6
Jean-Gabriel Pageau	Ottawa	536	804	223	246	-23	-64.3	41.3
Jay McClement	Carolina	422	609	173	178	-5	-44.2	39.2
Casey Cizikas	NY Islanders	519	780	176	200	-24	-62.9	38.9
Derek MacKenzie	Florida	536	656	178	171	7	-29.1	36.1
Antoine Vermette	Ari/Chi/Ana	984	970	329	292	37	2.8	34.2
Jamie Benn	Dallas	378	316	143	97	46	14.5	31.6
Dominic Moore	NYR/Bos	369	878	159	250	-91	-120.5	29.5
Matt Cullen	Nsh/Pit	439	739	157	202	-45	-72.8	27.8
David Krejci	Boston	882	782	299	249	50	23.6	26.4
Nick Shore	Los Angeles	541	442	179	130	49	23.7	25.4
Jay Beagle	Washington	359	625	127	166	-39	-64.3	25.3

267Acknowledgement: Faceoff data from Craig Tabita, http://www.puckbase.com.

John Tavares	NY Islanders	1375	746	427	252	175	149.7	25.3
Darren Helm	Detroit	267	199	90	50	40	16.0	24.0
Derek Stepan	NY Rangers	919	895	309	281	28	5.8	22.2
Steven Stamkos	Tampa Bay	607	489	193	144	49	27.6	21.4
Jason Pominville	Minnesota	166	10	61	3	58	37.3	20.7
Mike Richards	LA/Wsh	283	275	110	88	22	1.7	20.3
Matt Hendricks	Edmonton	184	251	85	81	4	-16.2	20.2
Joel Ward	Wsh/SJ	260	327	95	91	4	-16.1	20.1
Nick Bonino	Van/Pit	717	859	229	243	-14	-34.0	20.0
Bryan Little	Winnipeg	911	784	298	248	50	30.0	20.0
Pavel Datsyuk	Detroit	638	396	193	116	77	57.4	19.6
Victor Rask	Carolina	875	652	307	235	72	53.1	18.9
Ryan Strome	NY Islanders	227	216	79	58	21	2.5	18.5

Since these are based on each player's absolute numbers, the sheer volume of faceoffs Bergeron takes gives him an even greater edge. However, even on a per-faceoff basis, Bergeron is still way ahead of everybody else.

Well, that makes three easy questions in a row. What's next?

Who is the Most Versatile Player?

At last, we're going to bring a lot of this information together, and try to find a player who can score, pass, draw penalties, throw hits, block shots, kill penalties, work the power play, and score in the shootout, all while scoring at a decent rate, and posting above-average shot-based metrics.

Did anybody pop into your mind while you read that list? The first time I attacked this problem back in 2011 for Hockey Prospectus[268], Pavel Datsyuk was the specific player that I had in mind. Then, when I flushed out the idea in greater detail in the original *Hockey Abstract*[269], I mostly focused on players like Patrice Bergeron.

To provide some objective clarity to the topic, I constructed an index. In this case, it is a simple checklist of 10 measurable aspects of a player's usage and/or performance. Specifically, the do-it-all index awards a player a single point for having each of the following:

1. Above-average even-strength playing time of 12.4 minutes/game (+33% for defencemen)
2. Above-average power play ice time of 1.7 minutes/game
3. Above-average penalty killing ice time of 1.7 minutes/game
4. Top-six even-strength scoring rate of 1.7 points/60 minutes (half for defencemen)
5. Above-average shot blocking of 1.7 blocks/60 minutes (times three for defencemen)

268Rob Vollman, "Do-it-all players", *Hockey Prospectus*, May 19, 2011, Web, http://www.hockeyprospectus.com/puck/article.php?articleid=949.
269Rob Vollman, "The do-it-all index", *Hockey Abstract,* 2013, pgs 218-226.

6. Above-average hitting of 5.1 hits/60 minutes
7. A positive penalty-drawing differential
8. At least three shootout attempts
9. A relative quality of competition within the team's top-7 (forwards) or top-4 (defencemen)
10. Defensive zone starts within the team's top-7 (forwards) or top-4 (defencemen)

Given that the categories were arbitrarily chosen, that they weren't adjusted for outside factors, and haven't been shown to have any correlation with goals or wins, it's easy to admit that an index like this doesn't hold the same statistical significance as most of the other developments in these pages. However, not everything has to be an academic paper reviewed by Michael Schuckers. Sometimes, the value is in providing a fun and interesting perspective.

An index like this is a crude but effective way to remove some of our subjective evaluations for cold, hard, objective facts. For example, I have worked with a few coaches who use an index to evaluate their team's performance on a game-by-game basis. Rather than arbitrarily determining if the team played well or not, or if a specific aspect of the team's performance was satisfactory, the coach would build an index of the 10 goals. For example, a coach would award a point if the team didn't take any undisciplined penalties, if they didn't allow a goal in the opening or final minute of a period, if they allowed no more than a certain number of odd-man rushes, and so on. After every game, the coach writes down the team's score out of 10, and then whether the game was a win or a loss. Yes, there is the occasional cheap win or tough loss, but, over time, the team begins to understand that there's a direct relationship between their game index, and the bottom line in the standings. And, over time, the coach begins to learn the most effective way to build that index.

Getting back to the matter at hand, the do-it-all index can help us answer the question before us, and craft an updated do-it-all team. Up front, there's a four-way tie for first, between frequent Selke finalists Ryan Kesler and Anze Kopitar, along with Ryan O'Reilly and T.J. Oshie.

Top Do-it-all Forwards, 2014–15 to 2016–17[270]

Forward	Teams	Average
Ryan Kesler	Anaheim	8.3
Anze Kopitar	Los Angeles	8.3
Ryan O'Reilly	Col/Buf	8.3
T.J. Oshie	StL/Wsh	8.3
Jakob Silfverberg	Anaheim	8.0
David Backes	StL/Bos	8.0
Charlie Coyle	Minnesota	7.7
Patrice Bergeron	Boston	7.7
Brandon Dubinsky	Columbus	7.7
Joe Pavelski	San Jose	7.3

270Acknowledgement: The raw data for do-it-all calculations came from *Behind the Net* http://www.behindthenet.ca, the NHL's website http://www.nhl.com, and *Corsica Hockey,* http://www.corsica.hockey.

Frans Nielsen	NYI/Det	7.3
Vincent Trocheck	Florida	7.3
Ryan Callahan	Tampa Bay	7.3
Blake Wheeler	Winnipeg	7.0
Jamie Benn	Dallas	7.0
Mats Zuccarello	NY Rangers	7.0
Wayne Simmonds	Philadelphia	7.0
Nazem Kadri	Toronto	7.0
Gabriel Landeskog	Colorado	7.0
Nathan MacKinnon	Colorado	7.0
Ondrej Palat	Tampa Bay	7.0
Jordan Staal	Carolina	7.0
Mike Fisher	Nashville	7.0
Aleksander Barkov	Florida	7.0
Nicklas Backstrom	Washington	6.7
Andrew Ladd	Wpg/NYI	6.7
Matt Duchene	Colorado	6.7
Derek Stepan	NY Rangers	6.7
Nick Bonino	Van/Pit	6.7
Mika Zibanejad	Ott/NYR	6.7
Patric Hornqvist	Pittsburgh	6.7
Jean-Gabriel Pageau	Ottawa	6.7
Zach Parise	Minnesota	6.7
Sean Couturier	Philadelphia	6.7
Brandon Sutter	Pit/Van	6.7
Patrick Eaves	Dal/Ana	6.7

Minimum 100 Games Played

As for defencemen, with only six of them in the lineup on any given night, it's far more difficult to specialize their deployment the way coaches can with forwards.

It may be perfectly normal for a team to have one sheltered, puck-moving option like Keith Yandle or Shayne Gostisbehere, or one physical, stay-at-home penalty killer-like Josh Gorges or Niklas Hjalmarsson, but the majority of defencemen need to be effective in all game situations.

Yes, this problem could be addressed by dressing 11 forwards and seven defencemen instead – or even 10 and eight, if one of the defencemen could also play forward early in the game, like Dustin Byfuglien or Brent Burns. But, that's a topic for another day (and for Eric Cantor[271]).

According to the updated numbers, Roman Josi, T.J. Brodie, and John Carlson are the most versatile defencemen, and I can't argue too forcefully against that.

---

[271] Eric Cantor, of Johns Hopkins University, has studied the optimum quantity of defencemen in a hockey lineup, and has documented the benefits of having more than six defencemen in the lineup.

Table: Do-it-all Defencemen, 2014–15 to 2016–17[272]

Defenceman	Teams	Average
Roman Josi	Nashville	7.3
T.J. Brodie	Calgary	7.3
John Carlson	Washington	7.3
Alex Pietrangelo	St. Louis	7.0
Johnny Boychuk	NY Islanders	7.0
Shea Weber	Nsh/Mtl	6.7
Mark Giordano	Calgary	6.7
Erik Johnson	Colorado	6.7
Jake Muzzin	Los Angeles	6.3
Duncan Keith	Chicago	6.3
Justin Faulk	Carolina	6.3
Alec Martinez	Los Angeles	6.3
Kris Letang	Pittsburgh	6.3
Michael Del Zotto	Philadelphia	6.3
Christopher Tanev	Vancouver	6.0
Cam Fowler	Anaheim	6.0
Ryan McDonagh	NY Rangers	6.0
David Savard	Columbus	6.0
Calvin de Haan	NY Islanders	6.0
Dan Girardi	NY Rangers	6.0
Jared Spurgeon	Minnesota	6.0
P.K. Subban	Mtl/Nsh	6.0
Marc-Edouard Vlasic	San Jose	6.0
Ryan Ellis	Nashville	6.0
Travis Hamonic	NY Islanders	6.0
Jaccob Slavin	Carolina	6.0
Drew Doughty	Los Angeles	5.7
Alex Goligoski	Dal/Ari	5.7
Erik Karlsson	Ottawa	5.7
Rasmus Ristolainen	Buffalo	5.7
Oliver Ekman-Larsson	Arizona	5.7
Andrej Sekera	Car/LA/Edm	5.7
Justin Braun	San Jose	5.7
Dion Phaneuf	Tor/Ott	5.7

Minimum 100 Games Played

While the do-it-all index sheds some light on the question of who the game's most versatile player may be, it's still largely a matter of personal taste.

In 2013, the original do-it-all team was composed of Jamie Benn, Patrice Bergeron, and Ryan Callahan up front, with Dan Girardi and Brent Seabrook on defence.

272Acknowledgement: The raw data for do-it-all calculations came from *Behind the Net* http://www.behindthenet.ca, the NHL's website http://www.nhl.com, and *Corsica Hockey,* http://www.corsica.hockey.

In 2014, I placed Oliver Ekman-Larsson and Shea Weber on the blue line instead, with a new forward trio of Gabriel Landeskog, Ryan Kesler, and David Backes – although Benn and Bergeron were only really removed for the sake of variety.

Last year, I replaced Weber with his former partner Roman Josi, and placed T.J. Brodie at his side. Up front, I switched from Kesler to Anze Kopitar at centre, because he did win the Selke that year. Oshie was placed on the right wing, and Landeskog will stay put on the left wing.

This year, we'll stick with Josi and Brodie on defence, and with Oshie on the right wing. We'll let Ryan O'Reilly have a turn at centre, and place the highly underrated Jakob Silfverberg on left wing.

As for the single most versatile forward, I'll go with Oshie. Granted, it's very much a matter of opinion, so I wouldn't challenge someone who picked someone like Bergeron to a monkey knife fight. So, feel free to have your own, differing opinion.

Who Has the Highest-Value Contract?

McDavid, of course!

Yes, that joke may be getting a little bit old, but seriously, he *does* have the highest-value contract. I know that sounds bizarre, given that he has the highest annual cap hit in the NHL, and that he is going to be paid $100 million in the eight seasons following this one.

I formed this opinion based on the results of the long-term team cap management model constructed in the opening chapter of *Stat Shot*[273]. For those of you without a copy, it was my most ambitious project yet – and that's saying a lot. It described how to use stats to build a team, including how to establish a player's performance in a single number measured relative to his cap charge, how to identify and remove the impact of random variation in that measurement, and how to project the player's future performance as he ages. It was really quite nifty, if I do say so myself.

After McDavid signed that historic extension on July 5, I updated all the contracts in my model, and re-ran the numbers. I also replaced Tom's GVT and Delta statistics as the primary player measurements with Goals Above Replacement (GAR), which is the latest new catch-all statistic, coming courtesy of Dawson Sprigings of Don't Tell Me About Heart[274]. And no, I didn't make that change to annoy Tom, but to test how easy it is to swap out one component for another, and to help highlight the excellent work done by others in our community. Annoying Tom was just a bonus.

I'm sure that Tom would agree how exciting and rewarding it is to see the rebirth of the catch-all statistic. They were all the rage around the time we met, back in 2003 – Tom, Iain, and

273Rob Vollman, "What's the Best Way to Build a Team?", September 2016, Stat Shot, pgs 12-74.
274Dawson Sprigings, "Testing and Final Remarks", *Hockey Graphs,* October 28, 2016, Web, https://hockey-graphs.com/2016/10/28/testing-and-final-remarks/.

Alan Ryder were among the first to create one. Everybody loved them, and they were used by everyone, everywhere.

Then, in around 2010, they were suddenly perceived to be the foulest and most horrendous creatures in the world of hockey analytics. Michael Schuckers was instantly vilified for creating his own (Total Hockey Rating, or THoR), and any use of such metrics was looked down upon, and would even result in boycotts of any websites that used them, and its writers. Suffice it to say, catch-all stats were quite unpopular for a few years.

At last, it's great to see them back in vogue, and I was particularly eager to experiment with the cap management model using the various new options, as well as testing a few different multi-year weighting on those metrics, different age curves, different regression calculations, and different other components of various kinds. But no matter which ones I used, McDavid always wound up on top.

According to my GAR-based calculations, McDavid will be worth an extra 96.3 goals over the life of his entire contract, or 10.7 goals per season. That may not sound like a game-breaker, but every three-goal improvement in a team's goal differential is worth an extra point in the standings.

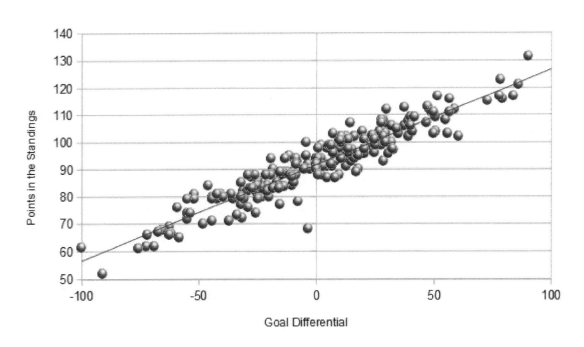

Team Goal Differential vs Points, 2007-08 to 2013-14

That means that McDavid's contract is worth an extra three or four points in the standings per season, on average. That can easily be the difference between making the playoffs and missing them, or getting a valuable home seed, or having to open the playoffs on the road against a division champion.

Despite his tremendous value, it is admittedly quite difficult to fit $12.5 million on to a team with a total cap hit of $75 million. I discovered this when building this year's All-Cap Team, which is normally a simple variation of the knapsack problem. If you've never heard of that problem, just imagine you have a knapsack that can hold 75 pounds work of items. Items are of different weights, and different long-term values, and you want to maximize the value of the items you stuff into your knapsack. The problem gets quite a bit trickier when the first item you place into your back weighs 12.5 pounds.

To make my solution to the McDavid Knapsack problem that much more challenging, I disallowed the inclusion of any players on entry-level deals, which tend to be highly affordable. In other words, if I wanted to include some low-priced players to make room for McDavid, then I'd have to find a value-priced veteran. Here are my selections.

The Hockey Abstract All-Cap Team, as of August 1, 2017[275]

Player	Team	Age	Cap Hit	Expires	GAR	Value
John Gibson	Anaheim	24	$2,300,000	2019	8.1	9.6
Ryan Miller	Anaheim	37	$2,000,000	2019	7.2	7.5
Oscar Klefbom	Edmonton	24	$4,166,167	2023	17.4	62.5
Ryan Ellis	Nashville	27	$2,500,000	2019	16.3	25.1
Mattias Ekholm	Nashville	27	$3,750,000	2022	12.1	29.1
Jaccob Slavin	Carolina	23	$5,300,000	2025	10.1	24.5
Josh Manson	Anaheim	26	$825,000	2018	8.8	8.5
Trevor van Riemsdyk	Carolina	26	$825,000	2017	6.9	6.6
Connor McDavid	Edmonton	21	$12,500,000	2026	28.5	96.3
Johnny Gaudreau	Calgary	24	$6,750,000	2022	18.4	33.5
Brendan Gallagher	Montreal	25	$3,750,000	2021	16.8	42.2
Filip Forsberg	Nashville	27	$3,750,000	2022	15.4	28.2
Mark Schiefele	Winnipeg	24	$6,125,000	2022	15.0	32.6
Nazem Kadri	Toronto	27	$4,500,000	2022	13.1	27.1
Sean Couturier	Philadelphia	25	$4,333,333	2022	11.5	22.3
Charlie Coyle	Minnesota	25	$3,200,000	2020	10.4	16.2
Jonathan Marchessault	Vegas	27	$750,000	2018	8.5	8.3
Radek Faksa	Dallas	24	$2,200,000	2020	8.0	14.7
Jussi Jokinen	Edmonton	34	$1,100,000	2018	7.4	6.5
Paul Byron	Montreal	28	$1,166,667	2019	6.2	10.3

Adding up the second-to-last column, this team would have a combined GAR of 246.1 this season, which would make it the best team in NHL history. Furthermore, it has a nice blend of players who can play different roles, and whose contracts expire gradually, a few per season. Without question, this is my best All-Cap Team ever.

While most of these columns are self-explanatory, it's probably a good time to remind *Stat Shot* readers of where that last column comes from. The total contractual value (Value) is the sum of the player's projected season-by-season value over the duration of his contract. For

275Acknowledgement: Salary data from Cap Friendly, http://www.capfriendly.com, GAR data from Dawson Sprigings, http://dtmaboutheart.blogspot.com.

the first season, that value is the three-year weighted average of each player's GAR, regressed back to the mean to remove the effect that random variation can have on observed results, and calculated relative to the value that's expected for the same cap space. Then, in the following years, it is adjusted by the player's age, and the value is re-calculated using the conservative assumption of a 4.7% year-over-year increase in the league's cap ceiling.

Of course, this All-Cap Team is just a fantasy hockey exercise, and not something that has any practical value in and of itself. However, it nicely illustrates the basic construction of a more-or-less ideal team, highlights the types of players (and specific individuals) who are currently undervalued, and identifies a few teams that are managing their cap particularly well.

For example, being able to add a low-priced veteran like Jussi Jokinen was a handy way to make room for players like McDavid, both for me and the real life Oilers. This summer, Jokinen was one of many free agent forwards in their early 30s who signed ridiculously affordable one-year contracts. Benoit Pouliot of the Sabres, Mike Cammalleri of the Kings, Ales Hemsky of the Canadiens, Scott Hartnell of the Predators, David Desharnais of the Rangers, and Patrick Sharp of the Blackhawks all signed in that same $1.0 million neighbourhood. It was a particularly great summer to find experienced secondary scorers.

On the flip side, mediocre veteran No. 4 defencemen went for a premium this summer. Karl Alzner of the Canadiens, Dmitry Kulikov of the Jets, Kris Russell of the Oilers, Michael Stone of the Flames, and Trevor Daley of the Red Wings all signed deals that were in the four-year, $4.0 million per season neighbourhood. These overall trends are far more fascinating than any individual players or situations.

While putting together the All-Cap team, it also became clear which teams appeared to be managing their long-term cap space more effectively than others, like the Oilers, Hurricanes, Predators, and Ducks. Summing up all active contracts as of August 1, for each team, and for all seasons through 2024–25, here are the teams that are poised to receive the greatest bang for their buck. Also, I've provided some indication as to which direction each team is trending, based on their prior results over the past two seasons.

Contract Value by NHL Team, 2017–18 to 2024–25

Team	Value	Trending
Edmonton	117.5	Way Up
Carolina	74.8	Way Up
Nashville	71.7	Up
Winnipeg	68.9	Up
Florida	51.4	Way Up
Columbus	37.4	Way Up
Anaheim	32.7	Up
Toronto	29.6	Way Up
Philadelphia	28.6	Way Up
Tampa Bay	28.0	Down
Arizona	8.8	Up
Pittsburgh	8.1	Way Up

San Jose	6.5	Way Down
Calgary	5.1	Up
Colorado	-2.8	Up
New Jersey	-3.7	Even
Buffalo	-7.6	Way Up
Los Angeles	-8.8	Up
St. Louis	-15.0	Down
NY Islanders	-25.4	Way Down
NY Rangers	-28.5	Even
Dallas	-31.8	Way Down
Minnesota	-35.6	Down
Washington	-36.5	Way Down
Boston	-39.7	Even
Vegas	-42.0	N/A
Vancouver	-44.5	Even
Montreal	-51.7	Way Down
Ottawa	-57.7	Down
Detroit	-98.0	Way Down
Chicago	-102.5	Down

Statistically, the top 10 seems pretty clear, and the common thread appears to be a stockpile of great organizational strength. With the exception of Anaheim and Tampa Bay, whose front offices deserve a lot of credit for managing their cap while still remaining competitive, these teams are those whose struggles have led to an accumulation of value-priced young players.

On the flip side, many of the teams at the bottom of the list are those who deliberately took on some hefty contracts in recent years, in order to compete for the Stanley Cup while their windows were still open. Boston, Chicago, Detroit, and Washington are the most obvious examples of that, but perhaps the Canadiens, Rangers, and Islanders qualify as well, to an extent.

As for Vegas, they deliberately took on some bad contracts in order to pick up a lot of picks and prospects. In my view, they might have overdone it.

So who exactly did Chicago and Detroit sign that was so bad? First of all, truly bad contracts are quite rare. To me, a bad contract is one in which the player has absolutely no chance of delivering full value, no matter how healthy he remains or how well he plays. These are the contracts that the team can't even give away, without taking on another bad contract in exchange, or including a pick or a prospect as a sweetener. For example, think about the deal Brad Richards signed with the Rangers in the summer of 2011, or David Clarkson's infamous contract with Toronto in 2013.

Most contracts are more correctly classified as merely being risky. With few exceptions, you never really know which contracts are bad until after the fact. Even though the following table has a big fat negative sign next to a player's value, these players don't actually hurt their teams. They provide value, but simply at greater cost. This is the sort of data that people love to take out of context, so please read the entire first chapter in *Stat Shot*, before passing judgment on any of these players, or their contracts.

Top 30 Riskiest Individual Player Contracts, as of August 1, 2017[276]

Player	Team	Age	Cap Hit	Expires	Value
Carey Price	Montreal	30	$10,500,000	2026	-78.8
Brent Seabrook	Chicago	32	$6,875,000	2024	-55.7
Marc Staal	NY Rangers	31	$5,700,000	2021	-44.3
Erik Johnson	Colorado	29	$6,000,000	2023	-39.6
Ryan Suter	Minnesota	33	$7,538,462	2025	-38.2
Alex Radulov	Dallas	31	$6,250,000	2022	-38.1
Jonathan Toews	Chicago	29	$10,500,000	2023	-34.7
Zach Parise	Minnesota	33	$7,538,462	2025	-34.4
Alexander Steen	St. Louis	33	$5,750,000	2021	-33.9
Brent Burns	San Jose	32	$8,000,000	2025	-33.6
Henrik Lundqvist	NY Rangers	35	$8,500,000	2021	-33.3
Dion Phaneuf	Ottawa	32	$7,000,000	2021	-32.8
Andrew Ladd	NY Islanders	32	$5,500,000	2023	-32.5
Dustin Byfuglien	Winnipeg	32	$7,600,000	2021	-29.6
Ryan Johansen	Nashville	25	$8,000,000	2025	-29.5
Jamie Benn	Dallas	28	$9,500,000	2025	-29.4
Jonathan Quick	Los Angeles	31	$5,800,000	2023	-29.3
Patrick Kane	Chicago	29	$10,500,000	2023	-29.1
Karl Alzner	Montreal	29	$4,625,000	2022	-28.9
P.K. Subban	Nashville	28	$9,000,000	2022	-28.6
David Clarkson	Vegas	33	$5,250,000	2020	-26.6
David Krejci	Boston	31	$7,250,000	2021	-26.1
Justin Abdelkader	Detroit	30	$4,250,000	2023	-25.7
Jonathan Ericsson	Detroit	33	$4,250,000	2020	-25.0
Bobby Ryan	Ottawa	30	$7,250,000	2022	-23.9
Kris Letang	Pittsburgh	30	$7,250,000	2022	-23.8
Rasmus Ristolainen	Buffalo	23	$5,400,000	2022	-23.4
Luke Glendening	Detroit	28	$1,800,000	2021	-21.8
Zach Bogosian	Buffalo	27	$5,142,857	2020	-21.7
Johnny Boychuk	NY Islanders	34	$6,000,000	2022	-21.6

Yes, the list of the 30 riskiest contracts usually looks deceptively like an all-star team. Here, we have Carey Price in nets, Ryan Suter and Brent Burns on the blue line, and Jamie Benn, Patrick Kane, and Jonathan Toews up front. Quite frankly, these results are surprising enough to cast doubt on the entire idea of using analytics to help manage a team's long-term cap.

In fairness, the all-star moniker doesn't exactly fit everybody on this list. Many of these players are actually mediocre, middle-of-the-lineup players that got overpaid.

As for the truly great players, remember that this was intended to be a list of the riskiest contracts, not the worst. Whether or not you believe that Carey Price is the best goalie in the

[276]Acknowledgement: Salary data from Cap Friendly, http://www.capfriendly.com, GAR data from Dawson Sprigings, http://dtmaboutheart.blogspot.com.

world right now (which we do), there's a lot of risk in signing a 30-year-old goalie to an eight-year deal with a $10.5 million cap hit. What if he gets hurt? What if his play starts to regress in his 30s, like most goalies? What if he reverts to his previous form, in which he spent the first six seasons of his career? Sure, he may become the next ageless wonder like Patrick Roy or Martin Brodeur, but what if he's like all those other goalies who had really high but unsustained peaks? That's risk.

Why doesn't the same risk apply to McDavid? Well, it does. But, McDavid is almost 10 years younger than Price, and so the odds are that he's going to get better, not worse. Plus, there's less volatility in skaters, relative to goalies. That is, we can predict with greater confidence that McDavid's performance will continue at, or near, this current level.

And, compared to the other skaters on this list, McDavid's current level of performance far, far exceeds what would be required to earn his cap hit. He could actually suffer a pretty steep decline and still earn his contract. However, players like Suter, Burns, Benn, Kane, and Toews, as great as they may be right now, have to continue to play at or near their current level, or their contracts lose value quickly.

So, the answer to this question remains McDavid. When in doubt, the answer is always McDavid.

Closing Thoughts

Initially, I wasn't even planning on writing this chapter, but when two of the contributing authors dropped out in the final weeks, and a third came up well short of his target, I felt that we needed more material to give our readers maximum value for their time and money.

In the end, I hope this helped long-time readers get more value not just out of this book, but out of previous editions. For new readers, I hope this sampler of some of the questions that we have explored in the past triggered your interest in exploring some of these topics in greater detail.

Question and Answers

Traditionally, we close every edition with some quick answers to questions that we have received from readers throughout the season, whether it's about home-ice advantage, zone exits, or why we so clearly hate your favourite team.

Now that I have a blog on my website[277], have helped kick off all these hockey analytics conferences[278], and have conducted an Ask-Me-Anything (AMA) on Reddit[279] [280], there are ways to publicly answer questions as they arise – even those that require more than 140 characters.

That's why this year's closing chapter will summarize some of the most frequent and/or topical questions that we have received over the past year, the first two answered by Tom, who starts with one of the greatest puzzles of them all.

Why Does Washington Always Lose in the Playoffs?

By Tom Awad

As long as there have been playoffs, there have been playoff chokers. There are always some teams that are elite during the regular season but just can't seem to close when push comes to shove; in recent years in the NHL, the Ottawa Senators, San Jose Sharks, and St. Louis Blues have all had this reputation at one time or another. But there is little doubt that the team that fans would point to most in 2017 as recent playoff chokers are the Washington Capitals.

The Capitals have been one of the league's elite teams over the last decade; in fact, since first putting Nicklas Backstrom on a line with Alexander Ovechkin in the 2007–08 season, the Capitals have piled on the regular season achievements: a 458-236-92 record over the decade from 2007 to 2017, best in the NHL, and three Presidents' Trophies for finishing first overall in the league, including both 2015–16 and 2016–17.

Yet despite this persistent regular season success, the Capitals have never even gotten out of the second round. Worse than that, they have been eliminated three times by their arch-rivals, the Pittsburgh Penguins, who have gone on to win the Stanley Cup all three years that they have defeated Washington! This has fed into an inescapable narrative: the Penguins are champions, while the Capitals are chokers. Is it true?

---

277 Rob's blog: http://www.hockeyabstract.com/thoughts.
278 List of hockey analytics conferences:
    http://www.hockeyabstract.com/thoughts/abriefhistoryofhockeyanalyticsconferences.
279 Rob Vollman, "I am Rob Vollman of Hockey Abstract – AMA!", *Reddit*, November 24, 2015, Web,
    https://www.reddit.com/r/hockey/comments/3u3j5c/i_am_rob_vollman_of_hockey_abstract_ama/.
280 Rob Vollman, Iain Fyffe, and Tom Awad, "We are Tom Awad, Iain Fyffe, and Rob Vollman, authors of Stat
    Shot – AMA! (Or AUA ...)", *Reddit,* September 13, 2016, Web,
    https://www.reddit.com/r/hockey/comments/52h5a3/ama_with_hockey_abstracts_rob_vollman_iain_fyffe/.

NHL RULEBOOK

REGULAR SEASON   PLAYOFFS   OVERTIME

To determine whether the Capitals, or any other NHL team, are truly chokers, I built a simple model of playoff success based on regular season record. I assigned a simple points system for playoff success: one point for losing in the first round, two points for losing in the second round, three in the third, four points for losing the final, and five points for winning the Cup. I then predicted, based on goal differential and shot differential, how many rounds a team would be expected to win. I then summed up these results for each NHL team over the entire decade, from 2007–08 to 2016–17. Here are the results:

Playoff Performance, 2007–08 to 2016–17[281]

Team	Won	Predicted	Difference
Pittsburgh Penguins	29	21.1	7.9
Los Angeles Kings	16	12.2	3.8
Nashville Predators	13	9.6	3.4
Philadelphia Flyers	14	10.7	3.3
Chicago Blackhawks	25	21.8	3.2
Detroit Red Wings	19	16.3	2.7
New York Rangers	19	16.6	2.4
Tampa Bay Lightning	11	8.6	2.4

281Acknowledgment: Playoff results from *NHL.com*, http://www.nhl.com.

Montreal Canadiens	14	12.4	1.6
Ottawa Senators	9	7.5	1.5
Anaheim Ducks	14	12.9	1.1
Arizona Coyotes	5	5.1	-0.1
New Jersey Devils	7	7.1	-0.1
Carolina Hurricanes	3	3.5	-0.5
Toronto Maple Leafs	2	2.7	-0.7
New York Islanders	4	4.8	-0.8
San Jose Sharks	18	18.9	-0.9
Edmonton Oilers	2	3.2	-1.2
Colorado Avalanche	4	5.5	-1.5
Boston Bruins	18	19.6	-1.6
Minnesota Wild	8	9.6	-1.6
Calgary Flames	5	6.7	-1.7
Dallas Stars	6	7.7	-1.7
Florida Panthers	2	4.0	-2.0
Vancouver Canucks	11	13.1	-2.1
Winnipeg Jets	1	3.5	-2.5
Columbus Blue Jackets	3	6.0	-3.0
St. Louis Blues	11	14.5	-3.5
Washington Capitals	15	19.2	-4.2
Buffalo Sabres	2	6.4	-4.4

And, here is the same information, but in chart form.

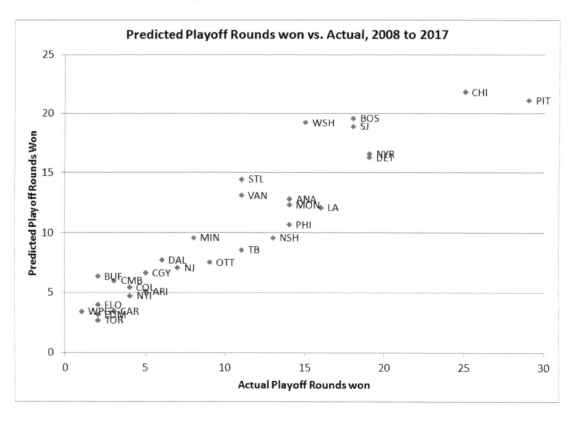

For once, conventional wisdom and statistics agree completely! The Penguins are, unsurprisingly, the biggest playoff overachievers of the decade, with their three Stanley Cups: while they have always been a good team, only twice, in 2012–13 and 2016–17, did they finish as high as second in the regular season standings. The Los Angeles Kings, also multiple Cup champions who were never dominant in the regular season, also rank highly in this assessment.

At the other end, there are three teams that truly stand out: the Blues, the Capitals, and the Sabres. The Sabres are a special case: while they have underachieved, expectations were never particularly high for them in the first place, and they've been out of the playoff picture since 2011. Two years ago, the Blues would have been, by far, the biggest chokers in the NHL: despite a string of very impressive teams and regular seasons from 2009 to 2015, they won only one playoff series in seven years! But they have made up for it over the past two seasons, making it all the way to the Conference finals in 2016 and to the second round in 2017. They still can't be tagged as playoff masters, but they have gotten the worst of their reputation off their back, just like the Sharks did by reaching the Final in 2016.

And then we have the Capitals. What's interesting is that, despite being the best regular season team of the decade, they are not the one for whom the model had the highest expectations: Pittsburgh, Chicago, and even Boston were all expected to win more playoff rounds than the Capitals. This gives us the first element of an answer.

The Capitals are a percentage team. They have succeeded in the regular season by maintaining the league's highest shooting percentage, an incredible 9.91% over the decade while the league average has been 9.08%. While this may not seem like much, this 0.83% has to be multiplied by the 24,025 shots the Capitals have taken over the decade, leading to an extra 199 goals! Even on the goaltending side, the Capitals have averaged a .913 save percentage, slightly better than the league average of .909, which has saved them an additional 87 goals against. The Capitals have benefited from an extra goal differential of +29 just thanks to their percentages. While percentages in the short term are mostly due to luck, percentages in the long term have a large portion of skill, so this is true talent that has manifested itself.

Meanwhile, they have only outshot their opposition by 70 shots per season. This is not bad, but it is much less than more dominant teams such as San Jose (+316), Detroit (+268), Chicago (+248) or Los Angeles (+208)… or even the arch-rival Penguins, at +143. Over the last decade, as during the regular season, shot differential has been about as important as goal differential at predicting playoff success. Despite their regular season success, the Capitals only provide two of the ten teams for whom we would have predicted the greatest playoff success over the last decade:

Teams With the Best Expected Playoff Result, 2007–08 to 2016–17[282]

Team	Year	Expected	Result
Detroit Red Wings	2008	4.3	Won Stanley Cup
Chicago Blackhawks	2013	3.7	Won Stanley Cup

282Acknowledgment: Playoff results from *NHL.com*, http://www.nhl.com.

Chicago Blackhawks	2010	3.6	Won Stanley Cup
Washington Capitals	2010	3.4	Lost in First Round
Boston Bruins	2014	3.4	Lost in Second Round
Washington Capitals	2017	3.3	Lost in Second Round
Pittsburgh Penguins	2013	3.2	Lost in Conference Final
Boston Bruins	2009	3.2	Lost in Second Round
Vancouver Canucks	2011	3.2	Lost in Stanley Cup Final
Detroit Red Wings	2009	3.2	Lost in Stanley Cup Final

Despite all this, there is no doubt that the Capitals have underperformed in the playoffs. Is this because they have gotten unlucky, their superstars don't know how to "raise their game" when the stakes are high, or because the Penguins simply have their number and know how to play against them? We may never know the true answer to that question.

Who Won the Subban-Weber Trade?

By Tom Awad

Short version: Nashville.

Long version: The Subban-Weber trade is one of those deals that you rarely see in the NHL, a straight player-for-player trade involving two elite players still in their primes. Both P.K.

Subban and Shea Weber are more than first-pairing defencemen: they are both arguably among the top ten defencemen in the entire NHL. This is not just my opinion: Subban won the Norris Trophy as the NHL's best overall defenceman in 2013, was a finalist again in 2015, and made the first end-year all-star team both seasons. Weber, meanwhile, has been named to the All-Star teams four times and was sixth in Norris voting during the most recent season. Both have routinely been among the top ten in ice time among all NHL players for the last five seasons. Subban and Weber are the best of the best.

To understand, then, who may have won this trade, we have to dig deeper than just stating that "Weber got more points than Subban" or "Nashville got to the Stanley Cup Final with Subban", although that second one is fairly significant. There are many factors at play here that cannot be summarized with a single line.

First of all, let's get the big one out of the way: Subban is four years younger than Weber. This doesn't matter much right now, when Subban is 28 and Weber is 32, but it will matter much more in three to five year's time, when Weber will be in the second half of his 30s. So far, Weber's ice time numbers and offensive totals have not really declined; he is statistically very similar to the player he was five years ago. The good news is that NHL defencemen age much better than forwards do: because their game relies more on smarts and positioning than forwards, they can continue to be effective longer. I'm not ready to anoint Weber as the next Nicklas Lidstrom, but he may continue to be elite for the next five seasons. Subban, on the other hand, is still just 28. He certainly has another seven years of elite play ahead of him, and he could stretch it out to almost a decade.

Second: the contracts. In the modern NHL, cap hit and term are kings. On this, Subban's contract is a clear winner over Weber's. More specifically, in order to get Weber's contract to its reasonable annual cap hit of $7.9 million, the Predators signed him all the way through 2024–25, at which point he will be close to 40. There's little question that the last years of Weber's contract are a bad deal from a salary cap perspective, so the Canadiens will either have to trade Weber to a cap-rich, cash-poor team to take on the final years, or suffer from being hamstrung by that $7.9 million cap hit for a 39-year-old defenseman. This is a problem that is only a few years away, but it is a problem nevertheless.

By contrast, Subban's cap hit is even higher, at $9 million per season, but has the benefit of finishing in 2022, by when Subban will be 33 years old. In other words, Subban's contract offers elite money for elite performance, without saddling the team with an albatross in the future. This will allow the Predators, or another team, to fairly assess the value of a 33-year-old Subban and pay him accordingly. To be clear, given the market for free agents and Subban's talent level, should he actually hit the market in 2022 it's likely he would command a salary not far from what he currently earns.

Both players have been fairly durable: while Subban has missed 30 games the last two seasons, he only missed seven in the four years before that, for a total of 37 games missed over six years. Weber has been even more of a rock and has missed a grand total of 19 games over the last six years. These are good numbers to hear when you are committing a chunk of your franchise's future on one player.

Many would think that Subban is the better offensive player and Weber is the better two-way player. While this is certainly how their reputations go, the reality is much muddier. First of all, Weber is just as good an offensive player as Subban. Over the last six years, Subban has maintained a slightly better points-per-game average than Weber, 0.66 to 0.62. However, almost all of this is due to a differential in opportunity: Subban has averaged 3:14 of PPTOI per game over those years, while Weber has averaged 2:48, about 13% less. I took each player's even-strength ice time and their power-play ice time, multiplied by the average number of goals and assists scored by NHL defencemen during those situations (0.168 goals and 0.543 assists per 60 min at even-strength, 0.708 goals and 2.803 assists on the power-play) to obtain their "expected goals", and then calculated by how much they exceeded the average.

Shea Weber's Points Above Expectations (PAX), 2011–12 to 2016–17[283]

Season	Team	GP	G	A	PTS	GAX	AAX	PAX
2011–12	Nashville	78	19	30	49	11.3	2.8	14.1
2012–13	Nashville	49	9	19	28	4.2	1.9	6.1
2013–14	Nashville	79	23	33	56	15.4	6.4	21.8
2014–15	Nashville	78	15	30	45	7.6	4.1	11.7
2015–16	Nashville	78	20	31	51	12.9	6.1	19.1
2016–17	Montreal	78	17	25	42	9.9	-0.1	9.8
	Total	439	103	168	271	61.4	21.1	82.5

P.K. Subban's Points Above Expectations (PAX), 2011–12 to 2016–17[284]

Season	Team	GP	G	A	PTS	GAX	AAX	PAX
2011–12	Montreal	81	7	29	36	-0.5	2.5	2.0
2012–13	Montreal	42	11	27	38	6.7	11.3	17.9
2013–14	Montreal	82	10	43	53	1.1	10.9	11.9
2014–15	Montreal	82	15	45	60	6.8	15.8	22.5
2015–16	Montreal	68	6	45	51	-1.4	18.4	17.1
2016–17	Montreal	66	10	30	40	4.3	10.2	14.5
	Total	421	59	219	278	17.0	69.0	86.0

Amazingly, over six seasons Subban has a whole three and a half points more than Weber. Weber is a much better goal-scorer, while Subban is a superior playmaker. I'm not teaching you anything you didn't already know.

But surely Weber is a superior defensive defenceman? Even here the evidence is more mixed than we would think. Weber gets more short-handed ice time, but that may be because Subban is more valuable with the man advantage. Both the Canadiens and, last year, the Predators, had no hesitation about deploying Subban on the penalty-kill for more than 2 minutes per night, averaging 2:14 with the Canadiens from 2014–16 and 2:05 with the Predators last year. Let's not forget that the Predators have Roman Josi, Mattias Ekholm, and Ryan Ellis as an incredible top-four core with Subban, reducing the workload for each defenceman, while the Canadiens leaned heavily on Subban and an aging Andrei Markov for the big minutes.

283Acknowledgment: Scoring results from *NHL.com*, http://www.nhl.com.
284Acknowledgment: Scoring results from *NHL.com*, http://www.nhl.com.

What about puck possession? Here both players are fairly good, although Subban's numbers are better and they have very different profiles. Weber has often been disparaged by the analytics community for his puck possession numbers, which are worse than his team's average, until one considers that he faces the difficult combination of very defensive zone starts and strong opposition. His numbers over the past three years have been perfectly average, while Subban's have been slightly above-average:

Shea Weber's Unblocked Shot Attempt Percentage (USAT%), 2014–15 to 2016–17[285]

Season	Team	Raw USAT%	Team-Adj USAT%	Team & Zone Adj USAT%
2014–15	Nashville	51.8%	48.5%	49.5%
2015–16	Nashville	51.9%	49.0%	49.3%
2016–17	Montreal	52.1%	50.2%	50.7%
	Total	51.5%	49.2%	49.8%

P.K. Subban's Unblocked Shot Attempt Percentage (USAT%), 2014–15 to 2016–17[286]

Season	Team	Raw USAT%	Team-Adj USAT%	Team & Zone Adj USAT%
2014–15	Montreal	51.5%	52.7%	52.0%
2015–16	Montreal	51.2%	50.0%	49.4%
2016–17	Nashville	55.2%	53.8%	54.1%
	Total	52.6%	52.2%	51.8%

However, simply adjusting for team and zone-starts is fairly coarse[287]. To put this in perspective, by this metric, the four best players in the NHL last season all played for the Calgary Flames, where Michael Frolik, Matthew Tkachuk, Mikael Backlund, Dougie Hamilton and Mark Giordano put together a great five-man unit while the rest of the team languished, making their numbers look spectacular compared to their team.

When using more advanced puck-possession metrics, such as Delta, which corrects for linemates as well as shot quality, we see that both Weber and Subban have excellent numbers, and that Weber's are actually even better than Subban's, although both of them had excellent seasons last year:

Shea Weber's Delta, 2014–15 to 2016–17[288]

Season	Team	Raw Delta	Delta QS	Delta QO	Delta QT	Delta SOT
2014–15	Nashville	10.4	2.4	2.1	-10.0	5.0
2015–16	Nashville	10.6	0.6	0.9	-5.5	6.6
2016–17	Montreal	7.8	0.6	0.9	-2.9	6.3

285Acknowledgment: Raw data from *NHL.com*, http://www.nhl.com.
286Acknowledgment: Raw data from *NHL.com*, http://www.nhl.com.
287USAT% is the team's share of all unblocked on-ice shot attempts while that player is on the ice. Team-adjusted USAT% is player's USAT% subtracting the team's average. Team and Zone-Start Adjusted USAT% subtracts the team average and also takes into account Zone Starts and Faceoff Wins/Losses.
288Acknowledgment: Raw data from *NHL.com*, http://www.nhl.com.

| | Total | 28.8 | 3.6 | 3.9 | -18.4 | 17.9 |

P.K Subban's Delta, 2014–15 to 2016–17[289]

Season	Team	Raw Delta	Delta QS	Delta QO	Delta QT	Delta SOT
2014–15	Montreal	-1.0	-2.0	0.8	3.2	1.4
2015–16	Montreal	1.0	-1.2	0.5	-0.4	-0.2
2016–17	Nashville	12.8	0.4	-0.1	-3.4	9.7
	Total	12.8	-2.8	1.2	-0.3	10.9

For new readers, Delta is an Expected Goals measure that calculates the difference between Expected Goals For and Expected Goals Against while a player is on the ice. Raw Delta is simply EGF minus EGA, and is equivalent to USAT incorporating shot quality. QS compensates for the Quality of Zone Starts, QO for the Quality of Opposition and QT for the Quality of Teammates. DeltaSOT is a fully adjusted measure of a player's impact on Expected Goals while he is on the ice[290].

It's also possible that Subban was being poorly utilized in Montreal, given how management and coaching seemed to dislike his flashy style. If that is the case, his numbers last season in Nashville, which were very good, could be a good omen of things to come.

The bottom line is that Weber and Subban are very comparable in terms of performance and talent, even if they bring different things to the table, so the difference in this trade will end up being age, cap hit, and contract length. In these respects, the Predators are clear winners. Nashville has already won the first round, proving that they can get to the Stanley Cup Final riding Subban, as he, Roman Josi, and Mattias Ekholm all averaged more than 25 minutes of ice time per game in the playoffs. I suspect that once the entire story is written, years from now, the Predators will be the overall winners as well.

How Much Cap Space Would a Team Like the 1984–85 Oilers Need Today?

By Matt Cane

Over $100 million.

How did we arrive that that estimate? We built a model to predict a player's cap hit using a player's data from the last three seasons. The stats used were games played, goals, assists, points, penalty minutes, plus minus, position, and age. We used contracts signed over the past 10 seasons[291], and then applied our model to era-adjusted data for the 1984–85 Oilers.

The predicted cap hit for each player who finished the 1984–85 season with the Oilers is given in the table below.

289Acknowledgment: Raw data from *NHL.com*, http://www.nhl.com.
290Tom Awad, "Numbers on Ice, Plus/minus and Corsi have a Baby", *Hockey Prospectus*, January 21, 2010, Web, http://www.hockeyprospectus.com/puck/article.php?articleid=436.
291Acknowledgement: Salary cap information from *Cap Friendly*, http://www.capfriendly.com.

Estimated Cap Hit for the 1984–85 Edmonton Oilers, Today

Player	Cap Hit
Wayne Gretzky	9.1
Jari Kurri	8.7
Paul Coffey	8.4
Glenn Anderson	6.9
Mark Messier	6.0
Charlie Huddy	5.4
Mike Krushelnyski	5.4
Kevin Lowe	4.7
Lee Fogolin	3.9
Randy Gregg	3.8
Don Jackson	3.4
Dave Hunter	2.5
Willy Lindstrom	2.3
Pat Hughes	2.2
Raimo Summanen	2.0
Dave Semenko	1.8
Jaroslav Pouzar	1.6
Steve Smith	1.5
Larry Melnyk	1.3
Kevin McClelland	1.2
Billy Carroll	1.0
Marc Habscheid	1.0
Ray Cote	0.8

Cap Hit in Millions of Dollars

While many of the cap hits look reasonably accurate, there are some who are clearly over or undervalued by the model, most notably The Great One, Wayne Gretzky. This isn't altogether unexpected – players like Gretzky come along once in a generation and expecting the model to be able to value these players correctly with such a small sample to work off of is unrealistic.

Nonetheless, the model still views these Oilers as a remarkably valuable team. Wayne Gretzky, Jari Kurri, and Paul Coffey would all be amongst the 10 highest paid skaters today, a staggering collection of talent for one team to accrue. And that's not even counting a clearly undervalued Mark Messier, whose predicted cap hit was driven down by the fact that he played only 55 games in 1984–85.

What would their total cap hit be? We need to make a slight adjustment to each player's cap hit in order to account for the differences in games played between players and the fact that some players would have been healthy scratches or injured, but still on a team's roster during the season. If we adjust the cap numbers to ensure that the Oilers have 1600 total skater-games over the year (20 skaters times 80 games), we predict the Oilers cap hit for their skaters only would be $91.5 million – and that's including Wayne Gretzky on an obviously undervalued deal. If you bump Gretzky up near the league maximum and add goalies to the mix, this team could easily have a cap hit of over $100 million, which is more than $25 million above the cap today.

With that being said, you'd rarely ever try to sign the entire Oilers roster in a single season. Many of the deals would be staggered and would have been signed in earlier years for less money. That likely doesn't save you enough to make up more than $25 million in overages, but it could get you a little bit of the way there.

Is there any way they could get under the cap? Potentially, but it would be really, really hard. If we assume they need to cut $25 million to get below the cap, you could start by getting rid of one of the goalies, Andy Moog or Grant Fuhr. Let's assume that saves us about $4 million, a reasonable amount for a 1A goalie. Jari Kurri would probably have to go too, just because of the size of his deal, which would save $8.7 million.

That leaves us with roughly $13.3 million to cut elsewhere. Getting rid of older defencemen is usually a safe bet, so let's axe Lee Fogolin and Don Jackson to save $7.4 million. Where does the last $5.9 million come from? Cutting Dave Semenko and Dave Hunter loses nearly 300 penalty minutes and only 54 points, but it saves us $4.3 million. And to push us over the top, let's lose Willy Lindstrom to get $2.3 million back.

So we've got the team below the cap but created another problem: we've lost seven players, including one of the key pillars of the team. All of which is to say, it would be very, very difficult to put together a team like the 1984–85 Oilers in today's salary cap era.

How Have Hockey Analytics Impacted My Life?

By Sydney Stype

I don't think my parents knew what they were getting into when they became season ticket holders for the new NHL team in Columbus, Ohio in 2000. My mom worked at Nationwide, the arena's namesake, and decided to see what the hype was all about. I was only seven at my first game, so I don't have really any memories from those first few seasons, however I remember the feeling of awe as I watched hockey. How did they see the puck? How could they move so fast? How did they know when to come on and off the ice? As we went to more and more games, I learned more and more. I read the sports section of the Columbus Dispatch every day, soaking in Aaron Portzline's stories about the teams that the Jackets were playing. As each season passed, I became more and more passionate about hockey.

Hockey analytics came into my life when I stumbled across the 2014 version *Hockey Abstract*. I had seen the book on Amazon and asked for it for Christmas. I wasn't sure what it was, but I love adding to my collection of hockey books (which is currently at 283 at the time of this book's publication) and figured that this is something I should have. When I got it, I flipped through it, and found myself a little lost. This was a side of hockey I hadn't seen. I wasn't familiar with phrases such as Corsi, player usage, and relief goaltending. I was scared off a little. I put *Hockey Abstract* on my bookshelf and stuck to biographies and memoirs for a while. That all changed when I got a manual tracking internship with an NHL team in 2015.

This opened my eyes to a new side of hockey that I could understand. Watching the game in a different way made me appreciate the sport I love even more. Unfortunately, I wasn't given much of an opportunity to see how the data I was collecting was being used. This led me to do more research into manual tracking and hockey analytics, which led me to stumble upon Rob's website. I contacted him about helping me find jobs and other opportunities in the hockey analytics world.

Now let's be clear: I am not a mathematician or statistician. I took one math class and one stats class at university. I was not a math major nor is it my strongest subject by far. What has been great about working with Rob is that you don't have to be any of that. I have learned so much from him and the community. I participated in a mock expansion draft for the 2017 Ottawa Hockey Analytics Conference with Rob and several others who welcomed me despite my lack of knowledge and experience. Being the editor of this book has taught me so much too. There is still plenty of the information that has gone over my head, but I found myself understanding more and more. Because of Rob, the world of hockey analytics isn't as scary as it might seem. When you speak to Rob, you don't feel stupid; you feel enlightened. Hopefully everyone who reads this book feels the same way.

I'm sorry my contribution does not bring the knowledge that the other chapters of this book bring. Mine is more of a testimonial of the fact that anyone who is even the slightest bit interested in hockey analytics can dive in headfirst and not drown. The community is so incredibly supportive and kind. If you get a chance to go to a conference or just sit down for a beer with someone in the community, take it. You won't regret it.

Do You Even Watch the Games?

By Rob Vollman

We always have to finish with a joke question. For some people, the opposite of watching a hockey game is checking the scoresheet, and it's somehow physically impossible to do both.

It doesn't make a whole lot of sense to me. I mean, when you go for your annual physical and the doctor wants to gather some data using blood tests or something, do you call him a nerd and tell him to go back to his mom's basement? If he finds something wrong with your cholesterol or blood pressure numbers, do you dismiss that with the argument that the fact that your heart is beating is all that matters?

I'm not trying to win an argument with people who are very unlikely to be reading these pages, but simply trying to make an important point. The statistical analysis of hockey is a direct consequence of watching a game. After all, the very act of recording a statistic comes through observation.

In my experience, some of the people I know who have watched the *most* hockey games in their lives are statisticians. So many of our field's top analysts got their start by watching hundreds of hours of hockey games, and recording events, such as scoring chances, shot attempts, zone exits and entries, power play formations, and passes. Partly it was to collect the data, but it was also to understand the context behind all of these types of events.

Sometimes people are turned off statistical analysis by the way that numbers are used. One prominent pundit said that he has ignored the numbers ever since they said that Shea Weber was a bad defenceman. But, the numbers didn't say that. In fact, numbers don't say anything at all, they just sit there. Someone had to look at the numbers, and make that interpretation.

That's a big reason why I always run my conclusions by the experts before I publish them in a book, or online. I'm fortunate to have access to a lot of great hockey minds, including many who have direct, day-to-day access to the players, scouts, and coaches, so it's important to ask if my interpretations make sense, or if there's something I'm missing. In fact, I've often been quoted saying that watching the game without checking the numbers is like covering one eye, but making assessments without actually watching someone play is just like covering the other. We need to use both eyes.

In a similar vein, I'm also asked how I respond to those who say that hockey is just too dynamic and complex for statistical analysis to have any value.

I actually have no response to that, and I don't need one. In statistical terms, I'm defending the null hypothesis, which is that there is *not* something inherently different about hockey that negates the usefulness that statistical analysis has when applied to any other sport, or any other field outside of sports. In my view, the onus is on those challenging that null hypothesis to prove how and why hockey is different, not on us to prove that it isn't.

But, we'll save that argument for another time, because we are done with another edition of *Hockey Abstract*.

Conclusion

As is tradition in *Hockey Abstract*, this is the only conclusion that you will find in this book. There are plenty of interpretations, informed opinions, and confident judgments throughout these pages, but statistical analysis is at its best when it helps shed new insight into an interesting discussion, and not when it claims to have definitively ended it.

If these books have any lasting legacy, then it's hopefully to inspire more objective analysis of hockey by showing how fun, useful, and easy it can be. We strongly urge you to dive in, and try it for yourself.

Like last year's edition of *Hockey Abstract*, which was entitled *Stat Shot*, we're pleased to announce that next year's edition will once again be published by ECW Press, and will therefore be in book stores everywhere. It will head out in new directions, devoting almost half the book to studying hockey outside the NHL, which includes a look at the European leagues and U.S. College hockey, and a quest for the world's best women's hockey player.

This 2018 edition will open with a chapter about the absolute basics of statistical hockey analysis that will be perfect for those brand new to this field, and closes with a comprehensive glossary of the purpose, formula, and origins of every single hockey stat known to us.

To keep everybody up to date with the latest stats, team analysis, and player usage charts, there will be an electronic update, just as we had in 2015 and 2016, and it will be available in both languages.

We would also like to acknowledge our good friend Michael Schuckers, who organized and coordinated the student paper competition from which the contributors to this book were selected, Jeremy Sylvain as the undergrad winner, and Helmut Neher for the graduate students.

In addition, Jeremy and Michael would also like to acknowledge that without the contributions of the excellent data sources used in his study, Hockey Reference and Man Games Lost, they would have been unable to complete their study. Nathan Currier of Man Games Lost, in particular, was especially generous with his comments and data for this project.

As for Helmut, he would like to acknowledge his supervisor David A. Clausi, and their co-authors of the original paper on which his chapter is based, Mehrnaz Fani, Alexander Wong, and John Kelek. They would like to thank SPORTLOGiQ for their guidance in using AI for hockey analytics.

CZECH MATE

DESPITE A LACK OF INTEREST FROM THE LEAGUE'S 31 TEAMS, JAROMIR JAGR FINDS A WAY TO STAY IN THE NHL...

In closing, I can't possibly tell you how much of a pleasure it is to prepare this book for you, and you probably wouldn't even believe me if I tried. It is a lot of work, but it is incredibly rewarding.

On behalf of me, Tom, my friends and contributors, our copy editor, our illustrator, and our french-language translators, please accept our sincere thanks for all of your support over the years. There's no way that we could (or would) do any of this without you.

As always, remember that all the raw data for the charts and tables in every edition can be found on the *Hockey Abstract* website, and our Twitter handles and emails can be found in the author biographies. Please don't be shy about reaching out to us, and let the discussions continue!

"We shall not cease from exploration. And the end of all our exploring will be to arrive where we started and know the place for the first time." - T.S. Eliot.

Glossary of Terms

This is only a quick and dirty reference of analytic terms used in this book. Use the alphabetical index to find more complete explanations.

3-1-1 Rule
Three goals gets a team about one point in the standings and costs about one million dollars.

Above-Average Appearances (AAA)
The number of games in which a goalie saved more shots than league-average, given the quality of shots faced.

Adjusted Even Strength Hits (AESHt)
The number of hits thrown at even-strength, once adjusted for home scorekeeper bias.

Adjusted Save Percentage, or Quality-Adjusted Save Percentage
A goalie's save percentage adjusted to reflect a league-average number of low, medium, and high danger shots.

Advanced Statistics
All statistics beyond those recorded in newspaper box scores. Also, non-traditional statistics.

Artificial Intelligence (AI)
A computer simulation of intelligent thought.

Artificial Neural Network (ANN)
A computer algorithm meant to simulate the brain's learning mechanism.

Blocks per Game (BPG)
The number of shots a player blocked, divided by games played.

Cap Hit of Injured Players (CHIP)
The cap hit of all of a team's injured players, weighted by games missed.

Correlation
A statistical term calculating the extent to which two variables are related.

Corsi, or SAT, or Shot Attempts
A differential based on all attempted shots, including those blocked or that missed the net.

Delta, DeltaSOT
The first shot-based, all-in-one metric.

Do-it-All Index
Out of 10 statistical areas, the number in which a player is above average for his position.

Even-Strength Blocked Shot Percentage (EBS%)
The percentage of all opposing even-strength shot attempts blocked by the given player.

Expected Goals (xG), or Weighted Shots
Shots weighted by the probability of it going in, based on its location and possibly other quality-related factors.

Fenwick or USAT
A differential based on all attempted shots, including those that missed the net but (unlike Corsi) not including blocked shots.

Fischler Points (FPTS)
Goals and assists that are weighted by the score when they were recorded.

Goals Above Replacement (GAR)
Same purpose as GVT, but calculated much differently.

Goal Differential
Goals scored by a team minus those allowed.

Goal Support
Average number of goals a team scores in games that a given goalie started.

Goals Saved Above Average (GSAA)
Number of saves that a goalie made over and above that season's league average, per 60 minutes.

Goals Versus Threshold (GVT)
The value of a player's contributions in terms of goals relative to a replacement-level player.

Hits per Game (HPG)
The number of hits a player has thrown divided by games played.

Hockey Abstract Checklist
A high-level checklist to establish a team's approximate level of competitiveness.

Home Plate Save Percentage (HP SV%)
A goalie's save percentage in shots taken in a dangerous zone in front of the net.

Man Games Lost (MGL), or Player Games Lost (PGL)
The number of games a team's players lost due to injury.

Manpower-Adjusted Save Percentage (MASP%)
A goalie's save percentage if a league-average number of shots were faced in each manpower situation.

Mercad
A form of GSAA that is adjusted for the quality of shots faced.

Net Penalty Differential (NPD)
Penalties drawn minus those taken, adjusted for manpower situation and position.

Net Shots Post Faceoffs (NSPF)
The number of shot attempts that occurred within 10 seconds of taking a faceoff.

NHL Equivalency (NHLe), or NHL Translation
An estimate of what a player's non-NHL scoring totals would be in the NHL.

Parity
Equality of teams in a league, in terms of talent and/or performance.

PDO or SPSV%
Shooting percentage plus save percentage.

Penalty Killing Percentage (PK%)
The number of penalties a team killed divided by the number of times shorthanded.

Persistence
A statistical term that measures the extent to which a variable is consistent over time.

Player Usage Chart (PUC)
A graphical portrayal of how a player is being used.

Point Shares (PS)
The calculated share of a team's points for which a given player was responsible.

Points Above Expectations (PAX)
The number of points a team or player earned over and above what was expected.

Points per 60 minutes (P/60)
The number of points a player scored per 60 minutes of play, normally in a specific manpower situation.

Possession-based
A hockey system aimed at keeping possession of the puck and denying such possession to the opponents.

Power Play Percentage (PP%)
A team's power play goals divided by power play opportunities.

The Projectinator
A system to predict a player's NHL scoring totals form his scoring totals in the juniors.

Prospect Cohort Success (PCS)
An estimate of a player's odds of NHL success based on the performance of those with similar, adjusted stats from the past.

Quality of Competition (QoC)
A high-level and Corsi-based measure of the average level of competition a player faces.

Quality Start (QS)
A measurement of whether a goalie played well enough for his team to win.

Recording Bias
The bias introduced by the different way scorekeepers judge game events, most notably shots. Also, scorekeeper bias.

Relative
Expressing a statistic relative to a player's team and their results without the given player.

Replacement Level
A general term for a player whose contributions are similar to that of an AHL call-up.

Sample Size
A statistical term referring to the amount of data on which an analysis is based.

Save Percentage (SV%)
A goalie's saves divided by all shots faced. Or, 1 minus goals divided by shots faced.

Score Effects
The skewing effect teams either sitting on or chasing leads can have on statistics, most notably shots.

Score-Adjusted Stats
Statistics adjusted for the calculated impact of score effects.

Selection Bias
The bias introduced when the manner in which players are selected for an analysis affect the outcome.

Setup Passes
The estimated number of shots generated from passes made by this player.

Shooting Percentage (SH%)
Goals divided by shots.

Shot Attempt Percentage
The percentage of all shot attempts taken by a given team in the games they played (rather than their opponents).

Shot Quality
The combined impact of the timing, type, circumstances, and location of a shot, sometimes together with the shooter's skill.

Shot Quality Neutral Save Percentage (SQNSV%)
An estimate of a goalie's save percentage against a league-average distribution of shots.

Structure Index
An indication of how repeatedly teams set up and shoot from similar locations on the power play.

Top-Four Defenceman
A defenceman who is in one of the top four positions of his team's depth chart.

Top-Six Forward
A forward who is in one of the top six positions (or top two lines) of his team's depth chart.

Tough Minutes
A player usage assignment that usually begins in the defensive zone and against top-line competition.

Two-Way Player
A player whose focus is both on defensive play and on scoring.

Zone Entry into Formation Rate (ZEFR)
The rate at which teams enter the zone and set up into formation on the power play.

Zone Starts (ZS)
The percentage of all non-neutral shifts a player started in the offensive zone (not counting on-the-fly line changes).

About the Authors and Contributors

Tom Awad, Co-Author

Email: tom.awad@gmail.com

There is likely no single person on Earth who likes numbers more than Tom Awad. He started tabulating hockey statistics by hand at age 11 while watching the Montreal Canadiens games in his parents' basement. Even back then, he found the numbers to be as fascinating as the games. His Eureka moment came when he came across a friend's copy of *Total Baseball* and discovered Pete Palmer's Linear Weights. He immediately designed something similar for hockey and tested it by transcribing the full statistics of the 1995–96 season by hand. Goals Versus Threshold (GVT) was born.

Tom may be best known for GVT but, over the years, he has performed statistical analysis of the draft, shot quality, player usage, goaltending, and much more. He developed the projection system known as VUKOTA which was found by David Staples of the Edmonton Journal to be the most accurate of seven systems for two consecutive seasons. He is a founding member of *Hockey Prospectus* and his analysis has also been published in *ESPN Insider*, *Arctic Ice Hockey*, and Montreal's *Journal Metro*.

When not analyzing hockey numbers, Tom can often be found analyzing other numbers in his job as an Electrical Engineer in Montreal, or discussing mathematics, physics or the relative merits of Sauron and Unicron with his children David, 11, and Karina, 9. His wife Marisa (age redacted) sadly does not share his love of numbers, but nobody's perfect.

Matt Cane, Contributor

Twitter: @Cane_Matt
Email: puckplusplus@gmail.com
Website: http://www.puckplusplus.com
Photo with permission from Rohit Saxena.

As a Sens fan living in Toronto, Matt Cane has come to rely on statistics as a defence against the constant insistence of friends, coworkers, and random strangers that this year will really be different for the Maple Leafs.

He has been researching and writing about hockey analytics since 2013 at Hockey Graphs, Hockey Prospectus, and on his own website, Puck++. His work to date has focused on player salary prediction, evaluating strategies for success on special teams, developing new metrics to evaluate defensive play, and looking at other pressing questions such as whether an AHL team could have beaten the 2014–15 Buffalo Sabres. Together with Ryan Stimson he presented a poster on evaluating defensive play using passing data at the 2017 Sloan Sports Analytics Conference in Boston.

Matt holds a Bachelor's degree in Engineering and Management from McMaster University, and a Master of Science in Applied Math from Ryerson University. When he's not splitting his laptop screen between a Gamecentre window and a spreadsheet, Matt can be found flailing helplessly in net for his ball hockey team or willing the Blue Jays to finally end their World Series drought.

Allan "Lowetide" Mitchell, Contributor

Twitter: @Lowetide

Allan Mitchell - Lowetide online - is the weekday 10-Noon host on TSN 1260 Edmonton. The highly-rated show focuses on hockey and advanced statistics, and guests include some of the most respected names in hockey analytics.

Allan's blog Lowetide came to prominence during the Oilers 2006 Stanley Cup run and is considered one of the best Oilers' blogs on the internet. He also writes for Oilers Nation and Puckrant.

Charles Mousseau, Contributor

Email: charles@tgscience.com
Website: http://www.tgscience.com

Charles Mousseau has been working with mathematics and computer programming from a young age, with a keen interest in applying these skill sets to games of all sorts. From poring over 50/50 equations in Monopoly, to begging his parents and family friends to bring back the score sheets from their card games, no amusement was too trivial for a little good-old fashioned number-crunching. This naturally led to the world of casino games and slot machines, the industry where he presently works doing researching analysis for developers of new games and slot machines, and mathematical integrity tests for online casinos under the Certified Fair Gambling label.

Charles has also been an avid hockey fan all his life, always loyal to his hometown of Winnipeg and to the Winnipeg Jets, even during a minor 26-year blip where he lived in Calgary and a 15-year blip where the Jets remained statutorily undefeated. He constantly refers to witnessing the "Welcome Back, Jets" announcement at The Forks as the greatest moment in his life, a fact of small consternation to his wife and two children. In close second, the four hours of phone calls to friends and family who spent fifteen years telling him he was delusional for thinking the NHL was returning to Winnipeg, which explains why his list of hobbies also includes "holding grudges".

Charles's ultimate hockey dream is to be an NHL play-by-play commentator, where he would employ a style that he describes as "a subtle mixture of Mike Lange, Harnarayan Singh, and Brian Blessed". Upon hearing of this dream, *Hockey Abstract* management was happy to give Charles an opportunity to apply his number-crunching skills to his passion of hockey in a medium that employs the written word with no working microphones to be found anywhere.

It is Charles' hope that this work will be the start down a road bringing him deeper and sounder insight into the game of hockey; whether or not you should parse that as "help him with his sports bets" depends on what jurisdiction you are reading this page in.

Helmut Neher, Contributor

Twitter: @HelmutNeher
Email: helmutneher@gmail.com

Helmut, raised in an avid hockey town, thrives on the thrill of hockey. He has played, watched and due to his affinity with technology, he often wonders how modern technology can be applied to hockey analytics. In fact, Helmut is currently a master's student at the University of Waterloo, studying how the use of technology can aid in the game of hockey such as evaluating player performance.

Helmut has contributed, along with his colleagues at the University of Waterloo, to hockey by creating and developing novel methods to extract useful information. Such information includes estimating how a hockey player stands or skates (the pose of a player) and a player's actions (i.e., shooting, cross-over, straight skating) from images using artificial intelligence. Helmut's goal is to develop useful tools to automate the mundane tasks of hockey analytics.

In his free time, Helmut enjoys hiking, playing board games and attends local technology venues.

Josh Smith, Illustrator

Twitter: @joshsmith29

Josh is a freelance illustrator, photographer, writer, musician, former radio host, and one-time -- literally, just once -- stand-up comedian from Long Beach Island, New Jersey.

He also runs Scouting the Refs (scoutingtherefs.com), the leading resource for hockey officiating news, rule clarifications, and statistics.

Sydney Stype, Contributor, Copy Editor

Sydney Stype hails from Columbus, Ohio. She attended the Ohio State University and received her degree in Sport Industry. Hockey dominates Sydney's life. She was a goalie on the OSU Field Hockey team for five seasons and has loved hockey from the moment the NHL came to Columbus. She is a voracious reader has a collection of over 250 hockey books (and counting). She is an extremely passionate Blue Jackets fan and is known to scare people off due to her love of the team. Starting in September 2017, Sydney will be pursuing a Master of Information and a Master of Museum Studies at the University of Toronto. She wants to thank her friends, family, and boyfriend that have listened to her constant prattling on about hockey and its history and for supporting her unconventional dream to live and study in Canada.

Jeremy Sylvain, Contributor

Twitter: @ImaSlyGuy
Email: j.sylvain01@gmail.com

Jeremy Sylvain has been playing hockey since before he can remember. Following in his older brother's footsteps he first strapped on the skates at age 3. He did not become interested in hockey statistics until high school, when he wanted to find better ways to quantify player contributions both offensively and defensively. Playing goalie throughout his career, Jeremy was also fascinated with the geometry of goaltending and how angles and proper positioning eliminated an opposing player's ability to score. Jeremy was inspired to write about injury statistics partly because of a hip surgery that led him to end his competitive hockey career.

Jeremy is a die-hard Boston Bruins fan, however he maintains that his favourite player of all time is Martin Brodeur, and says he was the reason he wanted to become a goalie. Outside of hockey, Jeremy is an avid golfer and spends most summer nights on the course and most weekends looking at golfing statistics as well as watching the Red Sox and analyzing baseball statistics surrounding pitchers.

Jeremy is entering into his final semester of college at St. Lawrence University where he will graduate with a degree in economics and statistics. He hopes to be able to work with sports statistics in the future.

Rob Vollman, Author

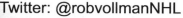

Twitter: @robvollmanNHL
Email: vollman@hockeyabstract.com
Website: http://www.hockeyabstract.com

Rob Vollman is an author, speaker, consultant, and long-time pioneer in the field of hockey analytics. His popular innovations have helped win Stanley Cups and Gold medals, and have shaped the way that teams are built, and the way the game is covered.

A former member of the Professional Hockey Writers Association, Rob was first published in the Fall 2001 issue of the *Hockey Research Journal*. He has since co-authored all six *Hockey Prospectus* books, two *McKeen's* magazines, and has authored four books in his own Bill James-inspired *Hockey Abstract* series, including the highly popular 2016 book, *Stat Shot*.

While modern advanced statistical hockey analysis stands on a mountain of complexity, Rob's work is best known for being expressed in clear, focused, and applicable terms.

Rob's most popular innovations include player usage charts, quality starts, and home-plate save percentage for goaltenders, goals versus salary (GVS) to measure a player's cap value, the team luck index, a history-based projection system, coaching metrics, the setup passes statistic, and advances in the field of NHL translations and league equivalencies (NHLe) to understand how well prospects and veterans coming from other leagues will perform.

In 2014, Rob organized a grassroots hockey analytics conference in Calgary as a platform for the field's latest innovations, starting a movement that has since spread to eight other cities, including annual events in Ottawa, Rochester, and Vancouver.

Rob's work can be found every week on *NHL.com* and *ESPN Insider,* where he has been featured since the 2008-09 season. In all, Rob has written 800 columns for a variety of hockey websites, and has been featured in the *Hockey News, the Globe and Mail*, the *Washington Post, Forbes*, and *Rolling Stone*.

Since his first guest appearances on Nashville Predators radio in the summer of 2011 and throughout the subsequent season, Rob has become the field's most passionate voice, having made over 300 appearances on 60 different radio programs, TV shows and podcasts in 20 NHL cities, including most notably *NHL Game Day, Hockey Night in Canada* radio, Sportsnet's *Hockey Central* and 2015 Trade Deadline coverage, Boston Bruins NESN television, TSN's *That's Hockey*, ESPN's *Sportscenter* and *Hockey Today*, CBC Radio, and Wharton Business Radio.

Based in Calgary, Rob is one of the field's most trusted and entertaining voices, and has helped bring what was once a niche hobby into the mainstream.

Alphabetical Index

Made in the USA
Lexington, KY
11 August 2018